PRAISE FOR
On the Front Lines of the Cold War

"All old Asia hands have their stories. Seymour Topping's were gathered at the most important crossroads of two epochal civil wars into which our country blundered. He tells them with authority and, as if they happened yesterday, an eyewitness's sense of immediacy. We can all be grateful."

—JOSEPH LELYVELD, former executive editor of the *New York Times*

"Seymour Topping was a preeminent foreign correspondent of his time, often filing exclusive stories that chronicled pivotal events at the onset of the Cold War and during the decades following as they shaped the history of the major powers following World War II. Top was everywhere in Asia, from the Chinese Civil War through the Korean Conflict to the fall of Vietnam and Mao's Cultural Revolution. *On the Front Lines of the Cold War* engages us with precise detail, eloquent writing, and authoritative insights."

—BOB GILES, curator of The Nieman Foundation

"For half a century, Seymour Topping chronicled the rise of Communism as it swept across Asia from China down through the Indochinese peninsula, ensnared capitals from Berlin to Havana, enslaving much of Eastern and Central Europe. Now, in this magisterial book, Top, as he's known to friends and colleagues alike, has brought it all together—weaving a compelling and intricate tale of global events, where he had a ringside seat, with personal stories of heroism and humor. The sweeping photo gallery alone is worth the price of admission. Of all the books on Communism and the Cold War, journalistic careers, and daring-do, this is the one worth reading."

—DAVID A. ANDELMAN, editor, *World Policy Journal*

"For the romance, for the history, for the political lessons learned (or not), this is a book to savor. To witness so many world-changing events, to know so many world-changing people, and to have such an impact on them all—I think no journalist is likely ever again to have quite such an adventure as Seymour Topping has had. What a life! Topping fell in love with journalism (by reading Edgar Snow). He fell in love with Audrey (the beautiful and brilliant daughter of an ambassador). He stacked up 'firsts'—first American correspondent stationed in Saigon, his kids the first Americans in Moscow to attend a Russian school—with every career move. And now he shares it all with us."

—GENEVA OVERHOLSER, director of the School of Journalism
at the University of Southern California's Annenberg
School for Communication

ON THE FRONT LINES OF THE COLD WAR

From Our Own Correspondent

John Maxwell Hamilton, *Series Editor*

Illuminating the development of foreign news gathering at a time
when it has never been more important, "From Our Own Correspondent"
is a series of books that features forgotten works and unpublished
memoirs by pioneering foreign correspondents. Series editor
John Maxwell Hamilton, once a foreign correspondent himself,
is dean of the Manship School of Mass Communication at
Louisiana State University.

———————

Previous books in the series:

Evelyn Waugh, *Waugh in Abyssinia*

Edward Price Bell, *Journalism of the Highest Realm: The Memoir
of Edward Price Bell, Pioneering Foreign Correspondent for the Chicago
Daily News,* edited by Jaci Cole and John Maxwell Hamilton

William Howard Russell and Others, *The Crimean War: As Seen
by Those Who Reported It,* edited by Angela Michelli Fleming
and John Maxwell Hamilton

ALSO BY SEYMOUR TOPPING

The New York Times Report from Red China. With Tillman Durdin
and James Reston. Photographs and additional articles
by Audrey Ronning Topping (1971).

Journey Between Two Chinas (1972)

The Peking Letter: A Novel of the Chinese Civil War (1999)

Fatal Crossroads: A Novel of Vietnam 1945 (2004)

SEYMOUR TOPPING

ON THE FRONT LINES OF THE COLD WAR

AN AMERICAN CORRESPONDENT'S JOURNAL
from the CHINESE CIVIL WAR to the
CUBAN MISSILE CRISIS and VIETNAM

LOUISIANA STATE UNIVERSITY PRESS

BATON ROUGE

Published with the assistance of the V. Ray Cardozier Fund

Published by Louisiana State University Press
Copyright © 2010 by Louisiana State University Press
All rights reserved
Manufactured in the United States of America
First printing

Designer: Laura Roubique Gleason
Typefaces: Minion Pro text with Franklin Gothic display
Printer and binder: Thomson-Shore, Inc.

The frontispiece photo of Seymour Topping was taken in Berlin in 1958.
Photographer unknown.

The maps in this book were drawn by Robert Paulsell.

LIBRARY OF CONGRESS CATALOGING-IN-PUBLICATION DATA

Topping, Seymour, 1921–
  On the front lines of the Cold War : an American correspondent's journal
from the Chinese Civil War to the Cuban Missile Crisis and Vietnam /
Seymour Topping.
    p. cm. — (From our own correspondent)
  Includes bibliographical references and index.
  ISBN 978-0-8071-3556-3 (cloth : alk. paper) 1. Military history—20th
century—Anecdotes. 2. Cold War—Anecdotes. 3. Topping, Seymour, 1921–
—Travel. 4. Topping, Seymour, 1921– —Diaries. 5. War correspondents—
United States—Diaries. I. Title.
  D431.T67 2010
  909.82'5—dc22

                                                                2009028555

FOR AUDREY

And for our daughters: Susan, Karen, Lesley, Robin, and Joanna,
who shared in our adventures

CONTENTS

ILLUSTRATIONS

MAPS

PHOTOGRAPHS

following page 110

Author in Nanking shortly before the city fell to Mao Zedong's forces in
April 1949

Nationalist cavalry company retreating from Pengpu on the Huai River,
November 1948

A suicide attack squad of the People's Liberation Army during the Battle of
the Huai-Hai

Defeated Nationalist commanding general, Tu Yu-ming, captured during the
Battle of the Huai-Hai

General Chiang Wei-kuo, who commanded the Nationalist Armored Corps
during the Battle of the Huai-Hai

Lin Biao, Liu Bocheng, and Chen Yi, field commanders of the People's
Liberation Army in the Chinese Civil War

Generalissimo Chiang Kai-shek on Chinese New Year's Day, 1949, shortly
before his resignation and retreat to Taiwan

Execution of captured Communist agents in Shanghai's Chapei Park, November 1948

American Ambassador J. Leighton Stuart chatting with Generalissimo Chiang Kai-shek in Nanking, 1947

Mao Zedong reviewing his troops in Peking's Tiananmen Square

Liu Shaoqi, head of state of China, eventually purged from the Communist Party and placed under house arrest

Jiang Qing, wife of Mao Zedong and driving force in the Cultural Revolution

Edgar Snow, author of the epic *Red Star over China,* with interpreter Huang Hua, 1970

Author traveling with a Foreign Legion convoy to the Vietnam-China frontier, 1950

Jean de Lattre de Tassigny, commander of the French forces in the French Indochina War, 1951

Graham Greene in the author's Saigon apartment, 1951

Tiger hunt in Vietnam's Central Highlands, 1950

Ho Chi Minh, president of the Democratic Republic of Vietnam

Major General Charles Willoughby accepting the surrender of Japanese troops in the Philippines in 1945

Douglas MacArthur being briefed on the advance of American troops in the Korean War, September 1950

Chinese Communist troops crossing the Yalu River border into North Korea, October 1950

following page 224

Correspondents at Berlin's Checkpoint Charlie, 1957

Author meeting with captive American servicemen in Dresden, Communist East Germany, 1958

U.S. Ambassador Lewellyn Thompson with Soviet leader Nikita Khrushchev, Jane Thompson, and Nina Khrushchev, 1960

AUTHOR'S NOTE

I am indebted to numerous wise and generous individuals who contributed to the creation of this book. Foremost, Audrey, my wife and journalistic partner, for her recollections of our life experience and for sharing her field reporting as a photojournalist and writer on behalf of such publications as the *New York Times* and *National Geographic* magazine. I am also grateful to her for making available the extensive private papers of her father, Chester Ronning, ambassador-at-large for Canada, a central figure in the diplomacy which reordered Asia. My profound thanks to my editor, John Maxwell Hamilton, for his vision and devoted editing of my book in form and content. I am also indebted to Professor Lawrence Sullivan of Adelphi University for his painstaking reading and many useful suggestions, particularly in the China sections of the book, and to Grace Carino for her meticulous, thoughtful line editing of my manuscript. I extend my gratitude also to Henry Graff, professor emeritus of history at Columbia University and editor of *The Presidents: A Reference History,* for lending his unique historical perspective. My appreciation also to Donald Shanor for his encouraging early read. I am very much indebted to Professor Li Xiguang, executive dean of Tsinghua University's School of Journalism, and his staff for facilitating my research during my tours of China. I feel most fortunate in that the distinguished Louisiana State University Press, directed by MaryKatherine Callaway, elected to publish my book and provide the valued services of Catherine Kadair, senior editor, and the designer, assistant director Laura Gleason. Patiently, during the years of composition, my friend and computer wizard Sonal Vaidya faithfully transcribed sections of my manuscript, and I offer her my thanks once again. The reader will find in my Notes and Bibliography lists of others who were most helpful together with citations of books and documents which I consulted.

ON THE FRONT LINES OF THE COLD WAR

PROLOGUE
CHINA BOUND

The artillery thundered through the night but now at dawn fell silent. It was January 7, 1949. I lay awake beneath the cotton blanket atop the sacks of grain in the Chinese peasant hut listening, wondering what the silence portended. Then, I groped in the darkness toward the doorway but retreated when I came face to face with a soldier, his carbine leveled. I was a prisoner of the People's Liberation Army (PLA), held in a hut near the battlefield where 130,000 of Chiang Kai-shek's troops were encircled by 300,000 of Mao Zedong's forces. I would soon learn that the abrupt halt in the gunfire meant that the trapped Nationalists had surrendered. It was the end of the Battle of the Huai-Hai. In running engagements across the frozen Huaipei Plain of Central China, Chiang Kai-shek had in sixty-five days lost more than a half million of his troops. Mao Zedong's triumph in the decades-long Civil War had thus become a certainty.

A correspondent for the Associated Press, I had ventured across the Nationalist front lines into the no-man's-land of the Huaipei Plain bent on reaching Mao's headquarters, to seek an interview and cover the advance of his armies on Nanking, Chiang Kai-shek's capital. Intercepted by Communist guerrillas, I was led on foot and horseback to the hut on the edge of the battlefield, put under guard, my typewriter and camera confiscated. On that morning when the gunfire ceased, the Communist political commissar who had interrogated me upon my arrival two days earlier reentered the hut. "We ask you to return," he said. "The horses are outside the door." When I protested, demanding to know the outcome of my request for an interview with Mao Zedong, the commissar shook his head impatiently and stalked out. I paced the hut and in frustration beat my fist against a stack of grain stalks. So, Mao would not receive me. The victor was no longer talking to Americans.

That was the defining moment for me in the tumultuous years of 1946–80 when I covered the East-West struggle in Asia and Eastern Europe. Mao's victory in the Battle of the Huai-Hai marked the onset of an era in which East Asia would be engulfed in war, revolution, and genocide. Tens of millions

1

would die in China, Korea, Indochina, and Indonesia in wars, political purges, and sectarian violence. The United States would suffer in the region its worst military and political defeats. And at the end of the era, with the collapse of the Cultural Revolution in 1976, China would reconstitute itself and be launched on the path toward becoming the leading power in East Asia. In the Epilogue of this journal I advance my thesis that the White House can derive lessons from the American reverses in China and the Indochina wars which would be of significant value in coping with other foreign conflicts such as those current in Iraq and Afghanistan.

During those decades of turmoil I worked as a correspondent in turn for the International News Service, the Associated Press, and the *New York Times*. I covered the turning points in the Chinese Civil War, the events leading to the Chinese intervention in the Korean conflict, Mao's Cultural Revolution and monumental ideological split with Nikita Khrushchev, the French Indochina War, America's Vietnam War, and the genocides in Cambodia and Indonesia.

The first American correspondent to be stationed in French Indochina after World War II, I traveled with the Foreign Legion along the embattled China frontier and briefed John F. Kennedy in Saigon when he visited Vietnam as a young congressman in 1951. At the 1954 Geneva Conference, which divided Vietnam into the North and the South, I was thrust into the role of a participant, more than a reporter, in the negotiations between the major powers. Decades later, as a senior editor of the *Times*, I delved into the Pentagon Papers, the Defense Department's history of the Vietnam War, extracts of which the paper published, and found revealed there the top-secret political decision making which led to events that I had witnessed earlier on the ground.

From posts in Eastern Europe I reported on America's Cold War with the Soviet Union. Working for the Associated Press I covered the Soviet threats to divided, isolated West Berlin from 1956 to 1959. Based in Moscow for the *Times* from 1960 to 1963, I was in the Kremlin reception hall on the night when Nikita Khrushchev, vodka glass in hand, told those of us gathered about him that thermonuclear war in the 1962 Cuban missile crisis had been averted. I would spend an evening with Fidel Castro in November 1983 and talk with him about his ties to the Russians.

Transferred from Moscow to Hong Kong as chief Southeast Asia correspondent, I traveled to Indonesia, where I covered the dethroning of Indonesian president Sukarno after the 1965 leftist putsch that brought on the retaliatory purge coup by army generals in which an estimated 750,000 people died. Bill Moyers, press secretary to President Lyndon Johnson, tells of the summer of 1966 when Johnson kept copies of my Indonesia dispatches about the army coup and the genocide that followed "in his pocket and on his desk so that he could show them to reporters and visiting firemen." Johnson was contending then that his stand in Vietnam had emboldened the Indonesian generals to crush the Communist bid for domination of the archipelago.

———————

I mark August 6, 1945, that day when the atom bomb was dropped on Hiroshima, as the date of my entry into Asia. I was then an army infantry lieutenant aboard the troop transport *Lydia Lykes,* bound for Leyte in the Philippines, tagged to lead a platoon in the invasion of Japan. There were wild rousing cheers that day aboard the ship packed with infantrymen who hailed the atomic bombing as their escape from predictable deadly fire on the beaches of Japan. I was among the celebrants giving no thought to what devastation might have been wrought on the people of Hiroshima.

Forty-two years later, standing amid the ruins of Hiroshima, I recalled that celebration aboard the *Lydia Lykes.* The mayor of Hiroshima had invited chief editors of the leading newspapers of the nuclear powers—China's *People's Daily,* the *Times* of London, *Le Monde* of Paris, *Pravda* of Moscow, and the *New York Times*—to a memorial service for victims of the bomb. I was summoned from among the five thousand mourners in the Peace Memorial Park to walk side by side with Victor Afanasyev, the editor of *Pravda,* the Soviet Communist Party newspaper, bearing bouquets of white chrysanthemums, to the Memorial Cenotaph, on which was chiseled the names of the dead and the inscription "Let all the souls here rest in peace; For we shall not repeat the evil." Upwards of 200,000 had died from the bomb blast and its aftereffects. We bowed and deposited the flowers before a flickering flame. We were guided then to the Peace Memorial Museum, where we were shown images of the destruction wrought by the bomb and the mutilated dead. Asked by Japanese reporters of my impressions, I spoke of my shock and profound sympathy. I inquired then why there were no photographs of the carnage at Pearl Harbor or what was perpetrated by the Japanese military in China. As consequence of the Japanese invasion begun in 1931, some 15 million Chinese had died. There was only silence. Viewing the horrific photographs of the Hiroshima dead, I was impelled to ponder President Harry Truman's decision to drop the bomb. It is said that the bomb spared the lives of hundreds of thousands of American soldiers, likely me among them, who would have died in an invasion of Japan. But yet I wondered then, and have never ceased wondering, whether such an invasion was inevitable and whether there was sufficient justification for dropping the bomb on Hiroshima and later Nagasaki. What if, rather than dropping the bombs, there had been a delay while other attacks were pressed on Japan? The Japanese navy had been effectively destroyed by the American fleet in the engagement in the Gulf of Leyte. Would not the Japanese have surrendered soon enough as they continued to suffer firebombing and starvation by blockade? As humanity confronts the threat of nuclear proliferation among rogue nations and theft of bomb components by terrorists, questions persist for me about the wisdom of the decision to introduce nuclear weapons and wage atomic warfare.

These questions are implied in recent policy statements by some world leaders. Shortly after he assumed office in January 2009, President Barack Obama joined with Russian president Dmitry Medvedev and British prime minister Gordon Brown in calling for the reinforcement of curbs on nuclear proliferation and reduction of arms in existing arsenals as steps toward the realization of a world free of nuclear weaponry. The American president said: "The goal will not be reached quickly—perhaps not in my lifetime. It will take patience and persistence." His pronouncement was the first step toward reversing the policies that led to Hiroshima and the terrors of nuclear proliferation.

I had volunteered for duty in the Pacific, rather than Europe, for reasons frankly somewhat peripheral to devotion to patriotic duty. From high school days in New York when I read Edgar Snow's epic *Red Star over China,* I had dreamed of becoming a correspondent in China. I chose, therefore, to study at the School of Journalism at the University of Missouri because the school had long-standing contacts with universities in China. It was my crash course at Missouri in the Japanese language and other Asian studies that persuaded the army assignment officer to ship me to the Pacific rather than the European battleground. I was pleased, since I had planned, if I survived the war, to make my way to a news reporting job in China. My duffel aboard the *Lydia Lykes* was stuffed with books about China.

On landing in Leyte's steamy jungle-encased port of Tacloban, I joined an infantry battalion engaged in rounding up Japanese stragglers in the jungle. In the grand strategy, Leyte had been the stepping-stone to Luzon, the larger island of the Philippines, and ultimately Japan. The Joint Chiefs of Staff targeted the Philippines rather than Japanese-held Taiwan, the other possible choice, in deference to General Douglas MacArthur's plea that we were indebted to the ever loyal Filipino people who had endured Japanese occupation. At 10:00 hours on October 20, 1944, Sixth Army forces landed on the east coast of Leyte, and at 13:30 General MacArthur waded ashore to broadcast his message: "People of the Philippines, I have returned. By the Grace of Almighty God our forces stand again on Philippine soil." But MacArthur's intelligence staff, headed by Colonel Charles Willoughby, had underestimated Japanese capabilities. The struggle lasted longer than he projected, and MacArthur was not able to declare the island won until December 31. In fact, the ferocious battle was not completely over until May 8, when the last major Japanese holdouts were crushed. I cite these miscalculations because in retrospect I found them prescient of subsequent intelligence failures by Willoughby in the Korean War when he underestimated the capabilities of the Chinese Communist troops much as he did the Japanese on Leyte.

On the island, my battalion guarded thousands of Japanese prisoners. During my inspections of the stockade in which generals were confined, I gained my first direct insight into the Japanese mind. When, I, a first lieutenant, entered their stockade, the generals would leap to attention and salute. Authority was paramount to them, as it was when they obeyed their blundering emperor.

After six months on Leyte, while on leave in Manila, I encountered Captain Ernie Ernst, a polo teammate at Missouri, at an American officers' club. Inevitably, the reunion began with the recollection of a hilarious tale from the annals of Missouri's polo teams. When I entered the university in 1939, I was required to enroll in the Reserve Officers' Training Corps. The ROTC unit at Missouri specialized in horse-drawn field artillery. My first day in the stables I attempted to mount a horse from the wrong side, evoking guffaws from the other students, many of them farm-born youths, at the spectacle of this New Yorker thrown by a startled steed. With that humiliation, I became obsessed with horses and spent countless hours training on the riding paths. In my junior year I made the polo squad to the astonishment of Ernst, who was the captain of the team. When I met him in Manila, Ernie was stationed at Camp John Hay near Baguio, the summer capital of the Philippines, as a public relations officer and liaison to the city government. He was homeward bound and proposed that I replace him. There followed transfer from the jungles of Leyte to the mountaintop camp near lovely Baguio.

Fortuitously, the new posting brought me in contact with Preston Gro-

ver, the Associated Press bureau chief in Manila, who listened sympathetically to my journalistic aspirations. He introduced me to Frank Robertson,
an Australian correspondent who was the Asian bureau chief of the International News Service, a subsidiary of the Hearst Newspapers. At a bar, I told
Robertson that I was due for terminal leave, that I had declined a regular
army commission, and that I had enrolled in the College of Chinese Studies
in Peking. (The city was customarily referred to by old China hands as "Peking," the Western rendering of its historical imperial title. Nor did China
hands bow to the decision of Chiang Kai-shek to bestow the name "Peip'ing,"
meaning Northern Peace, in the 1930s when he moved the capital south to
Nanking. It would later become in Pinyin romanization "Beijing," meaning
Northern Capital, under Mao Zedong.) Robertson grinned when I told him
of my plan to study the Chinese language at the college while I freelanced as
a journalist. After a short cease-fire, fighting between the forces of Chiang
Kai-shek and Mao Zedong had reignited, and Robertson was looking for a
stringer in Peking to cover the Civil War. He ordered another scotch and
offered me the job. The title that would adorn my name card in English and
Chinese would be "Chief Correspondent for North China and Manchuria."
The imposing title would compensate, I rationalized, for the meagerness of
salary: fifty dollars a month plus payments for what was published. On a
September morning in 1946 I boarded a U.S. Army transport plane bound
for China. It was beyond my imagination that in a matter of weeks I would
be flying from Peking to report from Mao Zedong's headquarters in Yenan
and that I would be covering the Chinese Civil War for the next three years.
And during those years in China, I would meet and fall wildly in love with
the beautiful Audrey Ronning, who would become my wife, the mother of
our five daughters born in Saigon, London, Berlin, and New York, and my
journalist partner in reporting assignments around the world.

1
PEKING

COVERING THE CIVIL WAR

The Chinese Communist official in the black tunic scrutinized me skeptically as I stood before his desk in the uniform of a recently promoted U.S. Army captain. I had just identified myself as a correspondent for the International News Service. An amused expression replaced the frown as I explained that I was newly arrived in Peking from Manila, still on terminal military leave, and I had not yet found time to buy civilian clothes. The Communist official was Huang Hua, and this meeting in September 1946 was the first of many encounters with him, some at historical junctures when he was a key figure in shaping relations between the United States and China.

I had stopped at Huang Hua's desk while making the rounds of Executive Headquarters, the truce organization established by President Truman's envoy, General George C. Marshall, who arrived in China on December 20, 1945, with the mission of bringing about an end to the Civil War between the forces of Chiang Kai-shek and Mao Zedong. Before approaching Huang Hua, who was the spokesman for the Communist branch of Executive Headquarters, I had introduced myself to the American commissioner, Walter Robertson, and to the American military officers, who were so numerous that Peking residents jokingly spoke of the headquarters, which was housed in the former Peking Union Medical College, as the "Temple of One Thousand Sleeping Colonels." Marshall at this moment was in Chungking attempting to bring the two warring factions into a coalition government. From Executive Headquarters, American, Nationalist, and Communist commissioners were sending out joint truce teams to battlefields to resolve violations of the cease-fire agreement negotiated by Marshall on January 13, 1945. Huang Hua was the personal aide to as well as spokesman for the Communist commissioner, General Ye Jianying, chief of the general staff of the People's Liberation Army.

I hastened from my meeting with Huang Hua to Morrison Street, a thoroughfare lined with shops hawking everything from forbidden opium to precious antiques. There I found a Chinese tailor who promised to outfit me overnight in civilian garb. While being measured, peering through the

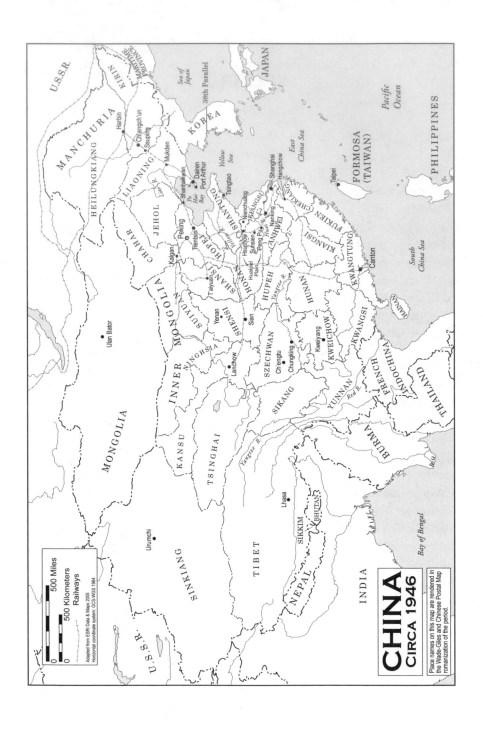

U.S.S.R.

MARITIME PROVINCE

KIRIN

MANCHURIA

HEILUNGKIANG

LIAONING

Harbin
Changch'un
Suping
Mukden

Liao R.

JEHOL

CHAHAR

Shanhaikwan

Dairen
Port Arthur

Pa Hai Bay

KOREA

38th Parallel

Sea of Japan

JAPAN

Pacific Ocean

PHILIPPINES

FORMOSA (TAIWAN)

Taipei

East China Sea

Yellow Sea

Tsingtao

SHANTUNG

Shanghai
Hangchow

KIANGSU

Hopei
Peking
Tientsin

Kalgan

HOPEH

Pienchuang

Nanking
ANHWEI

Hsuchow
Suhsien
Peng Pu

HONAN

Huaipei Plain

Grand Canal

HUPEH

Yangtze R.

KIANGSI

CHEKIANG

FUKIEN

KWANGTUNG

Canton

South China Sea

HAINAN

SHANSI

Taiyuan

SHENSI

Yenan

Sian

SZECHWAN

Ch'engtu

Chungking

HUNAN

Kweiyang

KWEICHOW

KWANGSI

FRENCH INDOCHINA

THAILAND

BURMA

YUNNAN

Red R.

Mekong R.

SUIYUAN

INNER MONGOLIA

NINGHSIA

Lanchow

KANSU

TSINGHAI

SIKANG

Yangtze R.

TIBET

Lhasa

NEPAL

SIKKIM

BHUTAN

INDIA

Bay of Bengal

MONGOLIA

Ulan Bator

SINKIANG

Urumchi

U.S.S.R.

500 Miles
500 Kilometers
Railways

Adapted from ESRI Data & Maps 2005
Horizontal coordinate system: GCS-WGS 1984

CHINA
CIRCA 1946

Place names on this map are rendered in the Wade-Giles and Chinese Postal Map romanization of the period.

tailor shop window, I watched the traffic on Morrison Street, which ran north–south linking the massive ancient gates of the walled city. Rickshaws and bicycles went by in large number, along with vintage foreign-made cars, and an occasional dust-laden camel or donkey caravan trekking in from the edges of the Gobi Desert. It was impossible to foretell that in August 2008 this same thoroughfare, renamed Wangfujing, would be lined with glistening office skyscrapers, high-rise apartment houses, and fashionable department stores and thronged with thousands of tourists attending the Olympic Games.

Within days of my arrival, decked out in the ill-fitting pinstriped suit with massive shoulder pads made by the Chinese tailor, I was swapping gossip with other correspondents at the bar of the elegant Peking Club and lunching there with sources in the diplomatic community. I chatted with Andrei M. Ledovsky, the Russian consul general, who would later rank as the leading Soviet specialist and historian on East Asian affairs. I lived at first in the dormitory of the College of Chinese Studies, a Christian missionary-supported institution. When not out reporting, I took language lessons there from a bespectacled Mandarin-like professor who insisted that I apply myself rigorously and had me practicing Chinese tones endlessly. For generations the college had provided language training to foreign missionaries, military men, and businessmen. Among the people I met at the school was a former Louisiana schoolteacher who was simply boarding there. She was one of a number of unattached foreign women sashaying those days about China, slipping from one job to another, some becoming consorts of wealthy Chinese. She told me tales of her affair with a Chinese general. She would become Joan Taylor, a character in my first novel, *The Peking Letter*, published in 1999. In the warlord days of 1922, Chester Ronning, my future father-in-law, and his wife, Inga, then Lutheran missionaries, were students at the school in the company of General Joseph W. Stillwell and his wife, Win. Stillwell made extensive use of his Chinese during the war against Japan. Chinese divisions were deployed under his command in the operations against the Japanese which opened the vital Burma Road, the main overland route for delivery of supplies to Generalissimo Chiang Kai-shek's forces. Quarrels with Chiang, stemming from what Stillwell considered the Generalissimo's inept leadership in the war against Japan, led to the general's recall by President Franklin D. Roosevelt.

After several months, I left the school dormitory to share a house with Captain David Galula, a brilliant young French assistant military attaché, who confided in me details of the briefings he was getting from his excellent

Chinese and diplomatic sources. Galula went from Peking in the next years to observing insurgencies in Greece and Southeast Asia. In 1963 at Harvard University he wrote the book *Counterinsurgency Warfare: Theory and Practice,* which was still being quoted in 2005 by Americans searching for stratagems to cope with the insurgency in Iraq. The College of Chinese Studies was located in Peking's Inner City, known as the old Manchu or Tartar city, which embraced the Forbidden City and the Legation Quarter. When Chiang Kai-shek moved the capital south to Nanking (later rendered in Pinyin as Nanjing), the foreign embassies followed; only their consulates remained open in the Legation Quarter. On some evenings Galula and I would go by rickshaw down the narrow, cobbled *toutiao hutung* (alleyways) along Hatamen Street, past the crimson walls of the Forbidden City, pausing at times to gaze at the purple and golden tile roofs of its palaces and temples before being wheeled through the Front Gate of the Outer City into the old Chinese quarter. There we would loll in the boisterous wine shops exchanging gossip and quips with Chinese acquaintances, at times visiting the company houses where slim joy girls with tinkling voices in silken cheongsams slit to the thigh offered jasmine tea and other delights.

Persuaded that I was a correspondent and not some kind of a spy, Huang Hua dined with me in the fabulous duck and Mongolian restaurants where conversation was enhanced with cups of *hsiao hsin,* the hot yellow wine. A trim man of thirty-eight, with a quick smile, he spoke good English and enjoyed chatting and tilting ideologically with American correspondents. One of his closest friends was the American journalist Edgar Snow. In 1936, when Huang Hua was a militant leader of the underground student movement at Yenching University (later Peking University) and being hunted by the Nationalist secret police, Snow provided him with refuge in his Peking apartment. Later that year, Huang Hua joined the Communist Party and slipped out of Peking to meet Snow in the cave city of Yenan. Two years earlier, facing annihilation by Chiang Kai-shek's Nationalist forces in the Civil War, the Red Army had made the 8,000-mile Long March to the Yen River valley. In Yenan, Huang Hua served as translator and recorder for the American journalist when he interviewed Mao and other Communist leaders for his book.

Huang Hua was intensely curious about the United States. He would bring books about America to my room in the college's monastic stone dormitory, and we would spend many hours discussing their contents. It was a harbinger of his future extensive involvements with the United States. In 1949, after the Communist occupation of Nanking, he became Premier Zhou

Enlai's envoy in negotiations with J. Leighton Stuart, the American ambassador in Nanking, when Mao was seeking Washington's recognition. He was the chief delegate confronting the Americans at the Panmunjom peace negotiations during the Korean War. Later, he would become the first ambassador of the People's Republic of China to the United Nations and then foreign minister. He would be at the airfield in July 1971 to welcome Henry Kissinger when the national security adviser arrived secretly to prepare for President Nixon's historic visit to China.

When the Civil War reignited in 1946 in full fury, I seized every opportunity to fly to the remote battlefields of North China and Manchuria to report on the collision of hundreds of thousands of troops in some of the largest battles in history. Little or no news was reaching the outside world about these battles during which many tens of thousands of combatants and civilians were killed. My first trip in September was to Communist-besieged Tat'ung, a coal-mining and industrial city which lay in a basin surrounded by mountains in northern Shansi Province, between the Inner and Outer Great Wall. I traveled aboard an Executive Headquarters plane with a truce team made up of American, Nationalist, and Communist delegates. We landed on a rough airstrip outside the city encased by massive walls. Passing through the Communist lines under a flag of truce, we crossed a wide moat, went through a strangely incongruous electrified barbed-wire fence, and entered Tat'ung through its towering ancient gate. Inside the isolated city, garrisoned by 10,000 Nationalist troops, more than 100,000 inhabitants were carrying on their daily lives stoically awaiting the impending Communist assault. The truce team made no progress in its talks with either the garrison commander or his Communist besiegers, commanded by General He Long. The January 13 cease-fire which General Marshall had arranged in Chungking with Chiang Kai-shek and Zhou Enlai, the Communist negotiator, was no longer being complied with by either side. Several days after our departure, General He Long's Communist forces stormed Tat'ung and seized the Northern Gate. But he was compelled to break off the attack, having suffered some 10,000 casualties, as a Nationalist column, including mounted cavalry, commanded by General Fu Tso-yi, approached the city. Exploiting the Communist retreat, Fu continued his advance and on October 10 took Kalgan, the capital of Chahar Province (named after a Mongolian clan and in 1952 incorporated into Inner Mongolia), which was the principal Communist stronghold in North China.

Shortly after his victory, I flew to Kalgan to interview Fu Tso-yi, one of the most remarkable of the Nationalist generals. A stout, good-humored man, the general had held sway for years as a warlord in Suiyuan Province (now part of Inner Mongolia), with a regional army of nearly a half million men loyal solely to him. Through efficient and relatively enlightened rule he had earned the devotion of the peasantry and was widely respected as a just ruler by the Communists as well as the Nationalists. His seizure of Kalgan, a city of some 200,000 near the Great Wall, was a severe blow to the Communists. After accepting the surrender of the city by Japanese occupiers in 1945, the Communists had transformed Kalgan into a major communications center, where it also established the North China Associated University. In taking the city, Fu partially blocked the Communists' vital corridor extending from Central and North China to Communist-held areas in northern Manchuria. General Nie Rongzhen, the Communist regional commander, withstood three days of bombing by Nationalist planes as Fu Tso-yi's cavalry approached, before abandoning the city. Foreseeing accurately a time when he would recapture the city, Nie did not destroy the railroad yards, the six key river bridges, or the large tobacco factory before he retreated.

In Kalgan I stayed at a hostelry that no longer bore the Communist-given name of "Liberation Hotel." Fu welcomed me warmly, briefed me on his Tat'ung and Kalgan campaigns, and then put on a show with a ride past one of his famed cavalry units mounted on the small rugged Mongolian ponies which the Mongol hordes of Genghis Khan rode in their conquests of Asia and eastern Europe. The use of these horsemen in the drive on Kalgan may have been the last time in history that mounted cavalry was employed in a major military operation. The general also provided me with an escort for a visit to the Belgian Catholic mission at the Inner Mongolian village of Siwantse, thirty miles north of Kalgan. I toured the mission's twin-towered cathedral, erected in the eighteenth century, which loomed over an adjacent seminary and convent. I stayed that night in one of the outlying parish compounds whose priest had the job of sending supplies farther into the interior to other clergy in isolated areas who worked as farmers and teachers while propagating their faith. Awake near midnight, I saw a lantern shining in the courtyard and going there found the priest in the freezing weather hauling water from the well. I offered to help and then asked how he endured his arduous daily labor. "Oh, I have good news," he said. "The Vatican is sending another priest to help me." "Good," I said. "When do you expect him?" "He will come, perhaps in two years," the priest replied. He was typical of other Catholic missionaries I met in remote areas living in the most spartan conditions.

Several weeks after my visit to Siwantse, I learned from the Nationalist-censored press that there had been a guerrilla raid on the mountain village. The defending local militia had been massacred, and before going off on the following day the guerrillas had burned the church and other buildings of the mission, including the library with its priceless collection of ancient Tibetan and Mongolian manuscripts. Several of the Belgian priests were said to have been kidnapped. While Nationalist officials described the raiding guerrillas as Communists, the manner in which Siwantse had been savaged and then abandoned, as I noted in my dispatch, suggested that they might not have been Communists but bandits, many of whom operated in the no-man's-land between the contending armies.

Traveling with the truce teams to battlegrounds throughout North China and Manchuria, I found the members courageous and willing but ineffective. General Alvin Gillem, the senior American officer, complained that neither of the two Chinese sides fulfilled commitments they made to disengage the combatants. They signed agreements which they knew they were not going to keep, he said. So the American side could do nothing but get signatures, knowing that those agreements and the accompanying documents had no practical value. In January 1947, when the Marshall mediating mission finally collapsed, Executive Headquarters was closed down.

In early November, Huang Hua arranged for me to visit Mao's headquarters in Yenan, whose approaches were being blockaded by Chiang Kai-shek's armies. The blockade had been imposed during the war against Japan. One of Stillwell's complaints about the Generalissimo's behavior during that war was his practice of diverting troops from operations against the Japanese to blockade his Communist foes in the internal struggle for power. I had no forewarning that I would be in Yenan at a crucial turning point in Chinese Communist relations with the United States.

2

YENAN

AT MAO ZEDONG'S HEADQUARTERS

I flew to Yenan aboard a rattling old U.S. Air Force C-47 transport, one of the Executive Headquarters' planes, in a two-and-a-half-hour flight that took us over the Shensi Mountains to the edge of the Gobi Desert. Maneuvering through twisting mountain passes, we bypassed a Tang dynasty pagoda atop a hill and bumped to a hard landing on an airstrip in a narrow valley. Members of the U.S. Army Observer Group, famed as the Dixie Mission, and Chinese officials were on the airstrip to meet this monthly supply aircraft. In a jeep we forded the murky Yen River, a tributary of the Yellow River, and driving into Yenan entered the compound of the U.S. Army Group, where I was to be quartered. The compound had been hollowed out of the adjacent loess hill and was enclosed in an earthen wall. It encompassed a row of cavelike living quarters with a mess hall and a recreation center named after Captain Henry C. Whittlesey, a former member of the Dixie Mission. Whittlesey, a talented writer, had been captured and executed by the Japanese in February 1945 after he and a Chinese photographer entered a town thought to be secure. A Chinese Communist battalion was destroyed in great part when it was deployed against the Japanese in a failed effort to rescue the pair. The remains of the photographer were found in a cave many years later, but not those of Whittlesey. The members of the Dixie Mission, originally eighteen military officers and diplomats, had their living quarters and offices in the cave structures, which were actually tunnels with whitewashed clay walls about eighteen feet long lined with stone blocks and a wooden frame window at the entrance. Light bulbs powered by the compound's generator dangled from the arched ceiling. Charcoal braziers provided meager heat. The size of the Dixie Mission had been recently cut back to a small number of army liaison officers, and the Chinese were using some of the empty cave dwellings as guest rooms. I was assigned to one of them and slept on a straw mattress resting on wooden planks supported by sawhorses.

The compound fronted on a city in which thousands of people dwelled in small houses on the valley floor while others occupied some ten thousand caves dug out of the hillsides. Once a thriving ancient walled city, Yenan had been almost entirely destroyed in 1938 by Japanese bombing. The Communists brought it back to vibrant life by making it their headquarters, expanding the community with hospitals, a university, a radio station, and a large open wooden amphitheater in which traditional Peking Opera and other performances were staged. Apart from the peasants bringing their produce into the city, everyone on the streets and in the government buildings wore similar padded blue cotton tunics and trousers, and leather-soled sandals or cloth shoes. Unlike in Peking, there were no beggars on the streets. Pausing at the little shops along the streets, I encountered students from every part of China. As many as 100,000 cadres had been trained in the Central Communist Party School in the valley and sent out to organize party cells in the countryside. Evenings I watched the cave dwellers, some twenty thousand of them, mainly workers in the Chinese Communist Party (CCP) apparatus, bearing flickering kerosene lanterns—there was no electricity except for that supplied by generators at the American compound or in the hospitals—wend down the hillsides to the wood and stone buildings on the valley floor to attend political meetings and performances by theatrical groups. There was a Saturday night dance at which Mao himself and a mix of officials and ordinary folk would prance to American tunes played by a small string orchestra. Mao, said to be ill, was not at the dance I attended. When the weather was mild, the dances would take place in a grove of trees called the Peach Orchard.

Soon after I arrived in Yenan, I was at a dinner attended by the top leaders, one of whom was Liu Shaoqi, general secretary of the Communist Party, second in power to Mao and Zhu De, commander in chief of the newly organized People's Liberation Army (PLA), a force then of about a million troops comprising the legendary Eighth Route Army, the New Fourth Army, and the Democratic Forces of Manchuria. Mao Zedong was not there, and my promised interview with him never materialized. I was told that he was ill and under the care of two Russian doctors, Orlov and Melnikov. Members of the Dixie Mission surmised correctly that the doctors were also being used by Mao for liaison to Moscow. Mao also had the medical attention of an American doctor, George Hatem, known to the Chinese as Dr. Ma Haide, with whom I had very useful conversations. Hatem, a personable, dark-eyed man of Lebanese origin who wore the usual cotton clothes except for a black beret, arrived in China during the war against Japan at the age of twenty-three after receiving some medical training in his native Lebanon and Europe and attending pre-med school in the United States. He traveled to Yenan with Edgar Snow, stayed on to work in public health, married a Chinese girl, Zhou Sufei, became a Chinese citizen, and joined the Communist Party. When I met him, he was a senior staff member of the Norman Bethune Memorial Hospital, named after a much celebrated Canadian who journeyed to China in 1938 during the war against Japan and provided medical assistance with meager equipment and supplies to Communist troops at camps in remote areas.

Mao was absent from all the events which I attended. While I was told simply that he was ill, I speculated that he had retreated into isolation, possibly suffering one of his bouts of depression to which he had been subject over many years. It was said that he was most prone to these depressions when his political and military fortunes ebbed. He was living in a small wood and mud-plastered house with his third wife, Jiang Qing, and their eight-year-old daughter, Li Na. I saw Jiang Qing only once. One night there was a performance in the Peking Opera House of *yang-ko* peasant dances. In the *yang-ko*—literally the "seedling song dances"—the performers did chain-step folk dances while singing ideological-themed songs. Jiang Qing was there seated in the front row beside Liu Shaoqi, Zhu De, and other members of the Central Committee. I sat in the row behind them. I had seen photographs of Jiang Qing before her marriage to Mao when she was a glamorous, bejeweled movie actress: her hair long, eyebrows penciled thin, and lips heavily rouged. The woman seated beside Liu wore glasses, no makeup, her hair cut in a bob, and she was dressed like the others in a cotton tunic padded against the November chill, baggy trousers, and a black cap. She was chatting gaily and applauding the performance. Although seated with the notables, she was not at the time in the inner circle of political leadership. She was active in Yenan's cultural life but in the main simply Mao's attentive housewife. She was restricted to that role by the party leaders, who never quite approved of Mao's marriage to this woman with a risqué Shanghai past replete with prior marriages and affairs. Recalling that scene in later years, I thought there was far more theater in the front row than on stage. Two decades later, Jiang Qing would become the driving force in the Cultural Revolution and locked in a power struggle with Liu Shaoqi, who was seated at her side on that theatrical evening in Yenan. Their struggle ended for both in turn in imprisonment and ghastly deaths.

Three months prior to my arrival in Yenan, I was told that Mao had granted an interview to the sixty-year-old leftist American writer Anna Louise Strong, one of his most fervent admirers. He received her on the earthen terrace in front of the cave he used as an office. The cave had been enlarged into a three-room apartment with white plastered walls and a brick floor. The interview, published eventually in Strong's monthly *Letter from China* and in the *Selected Works of Mao Zedong,* became probably the most quoted interview ever given by Mao to a journalist. When Strong asked Mao about the possibility of the United States employing an atom bomb in a war with the Soviet Union, he replied: "The atom bomb is a paper tiger which the U.S. reactionaries use to scare people. It looks terrible, but in fact it isn't. Of course, the atom bomb is a weapon of mass slaughter, but the outcome of a war is decided by the people, not by one or two new types of weapons." When I toured China in 1971 I recalled that interview with ironic amusement. The "paper tiger" had become more real to Mao following his furious ideological split in the early 1960s with Nikita Khrushchev. The Chinese were feverishly building air raid shelters, which I was shown in China proper and Manchuria, against the possibility of nuclear war with the Soviet Union. They were also girding for the possibility of a Russian strike at Lop Nor in Xinjiang Province, where they were testing their own atom bomb.

My dinner with the Communist leadership in Yenan, despite an abundance of toasts with *mou-t'ai,* a clear 120-proof liquor distilled from fermented sorghum, was a very gloomy affair. It was punctuated with denunciations of the deceitful Chiang Kai-shek and to my discomfort expressions of disillusionment with the United States. They saw the United States moving toward greater intervention on behalf of the Nationalists. Zhou Enlai, who ranked with General Zhu De behind Mao and Liu Shaoqi in the party hierarchy, was returning shortly to Yenan from Chungking, Chiang Kai-shek's wartime capital, bearing details of yet another American aid program for the Nationalist government. Zhou had been recalled to Yenan by Mao after talks with Chiang on the formation of a coalition government, conducted in Chungking by General Marshall, had ended in total failure. Chiang's Kuomintang (KMT) Party had reneged on an agreement reached earlier for a constitutional framework which would have provided for a degree of autonomy for the provinces, thus assuring the Communists continued political dominance in the areas which they currently held. Chiang had also refused to pull Nationalist troops back to the positions of January 13, 1946, specified under the terms of the cease-fire negotiated by Marshall. The breaking point had been the Nationalist seizure on October 11 of Kalgan, which I had just visited. Prior to Fu Tso-yi's seizure of Kalgan, Zhou had asked Marshall to warn the Nationalists: "If the Kuomintang government does not instantly cease its military operations against Kalgan, the Chinese Communist Party feels itself forced to presume that the Government is thereby giving public announcement of a total national spilt, and that it has ultimately abandoned its pronounced policy of peaceful settlement."

Marshall, frustrated and impatient with the deadlock in the negotiations, would leave China in January complaining that both Chiang and Mao had sought to exploit his mediation efforts for political and military advantage. As recorded in the so-called White Paper on China, reviewing events from 1944 to 1949, published by the U.S. State Department in August 1949, President Truman had sent a message to the Generalissimo before Marshall's departure deploring the lack of progress in the negotiations. In denouncing extremists of both the Kuomintang and Communist parties, Truman said:

> The firm desire of the people of the United States and of the American government is still to help China achieve lasting peace and a stable economy under a truly democratic government. There is an increasing awareness, however, that the hopes of the people of China are being thwarted by militarists and a small group of political reactionaries who are obstructing the advancement of the general good of the nation by failing to understand the liberal trend of the times. The people of the United States view with violent repugnance this state of affairs. It cannot be expected that American opinion will continue in its generous attitude toward your nation unless convincing proof is shortly forthcoming that genuine progress is being made toward a peaceful settlement of China's internal problems.

The criticism in the Truman message was directed in the main at the Generalissimo's government. However, except for a brief freeze on arms deliveries to facilitate the Marshall negotiations on a coalition government, there had been no interruption in the American military and economic aid program for the Nationalist government. Truman was bowing to the pressure being exerted on him for continued aid to Chiang Kai-shek by the Republican Party and the China Lobby, an American citizens' group committed to support of the Nationalists. While Zhou Enlai was still in Chungking negotiating on the creation of a coalition government, the Truman administration concluded an agreement for the sale of war surplus equipment and supplies to the Nationalist government at a fraction of their procurement value of $900 million. Marshall was unable to persuade Zhou Enlai that the surplus was essentially of a "civilian type," an obvious misrepresentation of the nature of most of the matériel. In the bitterest and most denunciatory terms, I was told by the Communist leadership at my dinner with them that this latest aid program was final proof that the United States was committed to unilateral support of Chiang Kai-shek. It was a breaking point in relations with the United States that would not be mended until the visit of President Richard Nixon to China in 1972.

From V-J Day to the time that I arrived in Yenan, apart from the latest transfer of surplus war matériel, the United States had provided the Nationalist government with more than $800 million in military aid under the 1941 Lend-Lease Act. This included funds for the transport in September 1945 by the U.S. Air Force of three Nationalist armies to cities in East and North China to take the surrender of the Japanese forces. At that time, the Nationalists possessed an estimated five-to-one superiority over the Communists in combat troops, a practical monopoly of modern heavy equipment and transport, as well as an unopposed air force. The bulk of Japanese military equipment, enough to arm forty divisions, had fallen to the Nationalists in the regions below the Great Wall. By the end of December 1945, under Lend-Lease, the United States was completing delivery of equipment for thirty-nine army divisions and twenty-five air force squadrons. Although the war against the Japanese had been fought based on the concept of a United Front of the Nationalists and Communists, Chiang had vetoed American plans to provide aid to Mao Zedong's forces. The Communists were scheduled to receive equipment for the training of ten divisions as part of the creation of a new national army of sixty divisions, but the Generalissimo refused to allow the delivery of any of this equipment prior to the integration of the Communist troops into his own forces. As a consequence, the Communists never received any aid from the United States. As noted in the State Department's White Paper on China: "With respect to the United States military aid programs, General Marshall was placed in the untenable position of mediating on the one hand between the two Chinese groups while on the other hand the United States government was continuing to supply arms and ammunition to one of the groups, namely the Nationalist Government."

Prior to the November collapse of the Marshall negotiations in Chungking, the Communists had high hopes for some kind of understanding and material aid from the United States. Mao saw the Marshall mission as the insurer of his party's interests in any coalition arrangement with Chiang Kai-shek. In February, in an interview in Yenan granted John Roderick of the Associated Press, Mao had praised President Truman, saying that he had made a major contribution to Sino-American friendship. In his book *Covering China,* Roderick quoted Mao as having said that he stood ready to form a coalition government with Chiang Kai-shek and to demonstrate goodwill he would hold his own socialist program in abeyance. He said that China must have a long period of peace in which to rebuild its war-torn economy and during that time there could be controlled capitalism and socialist democracy in order to create the economic and financial base for socialism. By professing this moderate approach, Mao obviously was reaching out to Truman in much the same way that he had sought an accommodation with President Franklin D. Roosevelt. It was Roosevelt who had put an end to the isolation of the Yenan government. Acting on a recommendation of John Paton Davies, a Foreign Service officer at General Stillwell's headquarters, Roosevelt in February 1944 messaged the Generalissimo stating that he wished to send an observer group to the Communist areas to facilitate the flow of intelligence information about Japanese operations in North China and Manchuria. The Generalissimo reluctantly gave his qualified assent, and on July 22, 1944, the U.S. Army Observer Group, commanded by Colonel David D. Barrett, and comprising both military personnel and State Department officers, landed in Yenan. Arrival of the Observer Group was a historic event in that it opened Mao's blockaded headquarters to international contacts, a succession of journalists, and any other visitors he saw fit to invite. The only prior official American contact had been that of Captain Evans Carlson, the famed U.S. Marine leader in Burma of Carlson's Raiders, who in 1938 had dodged Japanese troops to make an arduous overland trip to Yenan. The Observer Group collected and transmitted intelligence on Japanese operations and reported on Communist military and political activities. Relations were close with Mao and other Communist leaders who occasionally visited the Observer quarters to be entertained by American movies. Films starring Charlie Chaplin and the Laurel and Hardy comic twosome were favorites. Huang Hua served initially as Mao's liaison to the group.

In January 1945, Mao used the Observer Group to make his first direct approach to Washington. He had resisted suggestions by Stalin that he oust the Americans from Yenan. In early January, Colonel Barrett was reassigned to the China Combat Command in Kunming, and his subordinate, Major Ray Cromley, an air force intelligence officer, became the acting chief of the Observer Group. On January 10, at the request of Zhou Enlai, Cromley sent a message to General Albert C. Wedemeyer, commander of the China Theater Headquarters in Chungking, for relay to Washington. It proposed a visit to Washington by a Communist mission. Cromley's message stated: "Mao and Zhou will be immediately available either singly or together for exploratory conference at Washington should President Roosevelt express desire to receive them at the White House as leaders of a primary Chinese party." If no invitation was forthcoming, Mao asked that the proposal remain secret. In proposing the visit to Washington, Mao intended to put forward the Communist position as regards his negotiations with Chiang Kai-shek. He was also seeking military and economic aid in the war against the Japanese.

In talks with John Service of the State Department and other members of the Observer Group, Mao had not hidden his political agenda. He was willing to enter into a coalition government with Chiang's Kuomintang, as long as he retained a measure of military and economic autonomy in the provinces he presently controlled. It was his undisguised conviction that eventually his party would become the sovereign power based on "the will of the people." Mao may have thought that he had an opening to the president. When Roosevelt was reelected in November 1944, Mao sent him a congratulatory message. Roosevelt replied that he looked forward to "vigorous cooperation with all the Chinese forces" against the common enemy, Japan. Mao was fascinated by American technological achievements and economic power, and Cromley had the impression he was thinking of the possibility of negotiating a long-term trade and technical assistance arrangement for the regions under his control. Mao, like Liu Shaoqi and later Zhou Enlai, the latter two in conversations with me, dwelled on the theme that China and the United States were natural economic partners, indicating that the Chinese had no desire to be solely dependent on aid from the Soviet Union. A Washington visit would have been Mao's first trip abroad.

In April 1946, the Observer Group was reduced in size, and Cromley departed puzzled by the lack of a reply to Mao's message. There was still no reply when I arrived in Yenan and was told about Mao's overture. Cromley, who eventually returned to his prewar job as a Pentagon reporter for the *Wall Street Journal,* did not get an explanation until 1972. Barbara Tuchman, the distinguished American historian, after learning from members of the Observer Group about the secret Mao message to Roosevelt, located the pertinent memoranda in official American files, had the papers declassified, and wrote an article about the exchanges in *Foreign Affairs,* the magazine of the Council on Foreign Relations. She found that in the absence of General Wedemeyer, who was on a visit to Burma, the Mao message had gone directly to the American ambassador in Chungking, Patrick J. Hurley, an Oklahoma businessman appointed by Roosevelt. The ambassador was new to Chinese politics and had quarreled with Mao in a fumbled attempt to negotiate with the Communist leader on a coalition government. The ambassador also by chance saw a message on the following day from Zhou Enlai asking Wedemeyer not to reveal Mao's message to Hurley, since he did not "trust his discretion." Hurley, an ardent support of Chiang Kai-shek, had held up the Mao message. He accused the members of the Observer Group, particularly Colonel Barrett and John Service, of plotting on behalf of the Communists behind his back to the detriment of the Nationalist government. Apart from the secretive transmission of Mao's message, the ambassador cited in particular a contact with the Communists made by Colonel Barrett. On instructions of Wedemeyer's chief of staff, General Robert B. McClure, Barrett had approached the Communists to ask their cooperation in a projected American military operation. After the defeat of Nazi Germany, a paratroop division was to be sent to China to take part in an attack on the Japanese islands. The operation involved the establishment by the parachute division of a northeastern beachhead on the China coast in Shantung Province which was under the control of the Communist general Chen Yi. The Communists were asked to provide the initial logistic support when the paratroopers landed. Barrett was assured by the Communists that they would cooperate, although the colonel came away from the exploratory talks not sure that the Communists had the logistical capability to fully support such an operation involving twenty-eight thousand American troops. The Barrett approach to the Communists had not been cleared with Hurley, although the colonel had been assured by McClure this had been done. When I met Barrett years later, he was still bitter about Hurley's complaint, which had also led to quashing his projected promotion to brigadier general.

Roosevelt became aware on January 14, 1944, of the Mao proposal but only vaguely in the context of a message from Hurley in which the ambassador strongly advised the president against military cooperation with the Communists, which he said would be destructive of the Nationalist government and American policy in China. Seeking a solution to the China deadlock and acting on Hurley's advice, rather than inviting Mao, Roosevelt decided to attempt to persuade Stalin to lend his support to the Nationalist government, believing this would pressure the Communists to enter a coalition government with Chiang. At the Yalta Conference, which opened on February 4, Roosevelt and Prime Minister Winston Churchill entered into a secret agreement with Stalin under which he would sign a Treaty of Alliance with Chiang Kai-shek's government. Stalin received in return concessions in Manchuria and, in disregard of traditional Chinese territorial claims, recognition of the so-called independence of the Mongolian People's Republic (Outer Mongolia, formerly a part of the Chinese empire, whose government, established in 1924, was subservient to the Kremlin). It was the first move by the Soviet dictator in a double game for expansion of Soviet power in Asia which dismayed not only Chiang Kai-shek but also Mao. In March, Mao and Zhou were still expressing to members of the Observer Group their desire for cooperation with the United States, but the channel closed with Roosevelt's death the next month. Truman made no effort to follow up, despite Mao's fulsome praise of him as a friend of China. At Hurley's instigation, the China specialists of the embassy staff and those attached to Wedemeyer's military command, who had differed with the ambassador on policy, were sent home. At a critical juncture in the formulation of China policy, the U.S. government was thus deprived of the advice of its most experienced State Department officers, experts such as John Service and John Paton Davies. Hurley effectively closed the sole channel of communication between Mao and Washington.

Barbara Tuchman contended that, if the channel had not been closed and had Roosevelt extended an invitation to Mao and reached an understanding with him, the Chinese Civil War might have been ended at once. She also concluded:

> If, in the absence of ill feeling, we had established relations on some level with the People's Republic, permitting communication in a crisis, and if the Chinese had not been moved by hate and suspicion of us to make common cause with the Soviet Union, it is conceivable that there might have been no Korean War. From that war rose the twin specters of an expansionist Chinese Communism and an indivisible Sino-Soviet partnership. Without those two concepts to addle statesmen and nourish demagogues, our history, and our present and our future, would have been different. We might have never come to Vietnam.

I concur with Tuchman in her thesis that a Korean War might have been averted, or at least that Mao might not have undertaken the massive Chinese military intervention so destructive to General Douglas MacArthur's forces. The approach to Roosevelt presented one of several opportunities to open a channel between the Communists and Washington, which, if materialized, could have resulted in an exchange that would have had a bearing on the course and duration of the Indochina wars, given the influence that Mao was able to exert as the principal foreign supporter and donor of military aid to the Indochinese Communists. In 1949, I reported from Communist-occupied Nanking on the last such opportunity, which was never exploited, prior to the Nixon visit to China in 1972. At the time of the visit, the United States was still locked with China in the costly decades-long military stalemate in Korea and the Nixon administration had decided to begin the withdrawal of American troops from Vietnam in keeping with the policy of "Vietnamization," the turning over of all combat ground operations to the South Vietnamese army.

———————

Several days after my dinner with the Communist leadership, Liu Shaoqi granted me a lengthy interview at the Wangchiap'ing military compound on the floor of the valley, which housed party and army offices. We met at a rough, long table on wooden saws about which were seated other members of the Central Committee. They were lean men dressed in black caps and loosely fitted cotton tunics, deeply bronzed by years in the field resisting the Japanese and battling the Nationalists. Liu, a gaunt gray-haired man, about forty-seven years old—his precise age was never made public—smoked his Great Wall cigarettes continually during my interview, and his frequent cough was indicative of his tubercular condition. Regarded as the most likely successor to Mao, Liu was second only to Mao as the leading theoretician of the party. He was the author of the core text *How to Be a Good Communist,* based on a series of lectures he had given in Yenan in 1939. He had studied earlier in Moscow at the University of the Toilers of the East.

Speaking through a translator, Liu told me that China must pass through a stage of "New Democracy" on the road to socialism and Communism. He said socialism was still something for the "rather far future." Perhaps it was for the American ear, but he professed to be an admirer of the revolutionary changes carried out by Thomas Jefferson and Abraham Lincoln, adding that China was learning from their experience. To build an economic and social foundation for the attainment of socialism, he said, the Communist Party was reaching out to all sectors of Chinese society and democratic groups. He said the aim was to "unite China under correct leadership into an independent, democratic, peaceful, and prosperous nation." In the new China envisioned by Liu, obviously the "correct leadership" would be that of the Communist Party.

In his comments Liu was borrowing from Mao's essays in *On New Democracy,* published in 1940, and *On Coalition Government,* a further elaboration of the concept of New Democracy, which was published in 1945. I was presented with a copy of the latter, issued in coarse grass paper, in which Mao said the "New Democracy" he envisioned would be valid for "several dozens of years." In fact, twenty years later, reporting from Hong Kong on the Cultural Revolution, I detailed how Mao had abandoned the concept of embracing diverse sectors of Chinese society including democratic groups and turned to the rigid Stalinist strategy of eliminating any potential opposition through class struggle.

When in Yenan I was told that the "New Democracy" was already being practiced in the principal Communist base territory, the Shensi-Kansu-Ninghsia Border Region, of which Yenan was the capital. In the land reform program, landlords with small landholdings who were deemed enlightened and cooperative were tolerated as well as so-called middle peasants, the comparatively well-off farmers who tilled their own land. However, I learned later that with the intensification of the Civil War, the Central Committee had embarked on a more radical agrarian policy. To secure its hold on contested rural regions, the Central Committee had in May 1944 issued a decree that sanctioned more extensive redistribution of landlord holdings to gain the more active support of poorer peasants, who made up the majority of the rural population. In subsequent travel in regions occupied by the Communists, I came upon cases where local Communist cadres had gone beyond the license of the May mandate and were violently disenfranchising landlords of their land and other possessions. The poor peasants, in gratitude for the gifts of the confiscated land, repaid the PLA with army recruits, provision of supplies often delivered on their backs, and other support in military operations.

At the interview in the Wangchiap'ing compound, I asked Liu Shaoqi if he would be looking to the Soviet Union for large-scale aid and diplomatic backing. Around the table there were quick exchanges of glances and secretive smiles and only ambiguous replies. Manifest was their discomfort about the extraordinary double game that Stalin was playing out in Manchuria. This ambiguity in relations would escalate in the next years to violent confrontation.

Stalin's power play began on August 9, 1945, in the last days of World War II, when he declared war on Japan. His troops invaded Manchuria and accepted the surrender of the Kwangtung Army, consisting of 400,000 Japanese troops and 275,000 Chinese puppet troops of the satellite Manchukuo state established by the Japanese in 1932. On August 14, in keeping with the secret agreement at Yalta, Stalin concluded a Treaty of Alliance with Chiang Kai-shek recognizing his regime as the sole legitimate government of China.

Truman had strongly urged the Nationalists to sign such a treaty, as the president recounted in his memoirs, because he felt it essential to bring the Soviet Union into the war against Japan, a move he thought, by shortening the war, would spare the lives of thousands of American soldiers. In return for signing the treaty with the Chiang Kai-shek government and entry into the war against Japan, Stalin gained control in Manchuria of the commercial port of Dairen; use of Port Arthur, known in Chinese as Lüshun, as a naval base; and joint control of the key Eastern and South Manchurian railways. Alarmed by the Soviet treaty with the Nationalist government, a Communist delegation headed by Liu Shaoqi traveled to Moscow to plead for renewal of Stalin's support. The Soviet Union was seen as the only possible source of support to balance what Washington was providing Chiang Kai-shek. The Soviet dictator, fulfilling his trade-off with Chiang Kai-shek, advised Liu to pursue a political strategy akin to that of the European Communist parties. He urged Liu to enter into a coalition government with Chiang Kai-shek but also suggested that compromise would give the Communists time to consolidate their forces for any future contention with the Nationalists. Pressured by Stalin, Mao reluctantly went to Chungking on August 28, 1945, to negotiate with Chiang. He returned ailing and exhausted to Yenan on October 11 after the negotiations with Chiang deadlocked.

During Mao's absence in Chungking, the Soviets flew Zeng Gelin, commander of a small Chinese Communist task force in Manchuria, with their Russian advisers from Mukden to Yenan, where they met with Liu Shaoqi, who was in control of the party and military during Mao's absence. The Russians told Liu that they intended to allow the Nationalists to take over the major cities of Manchuria, including Harbin, Ch'angch'un, and Mukden, now known as Shenyang, in keeping with the treaty that Stalin had signed with Chiang, but the Communists could operate freely elsewhere in the northeast, implying they would receive Soviet assistance. Based on this report, the Central Committee decided that Manchuria could fall into its grasp if its troops were free to maneuver in the countryside against the Nationalist-held cities. The committee saw conquest of Manchuria as key to victory in the Civil War. With Mao's approval, Liu immediately diverted eighty thousand troops of the New Fourth Army and the Eighth Route Army, with a large number of political cadres, northward.

To lead the Manchurian campaign, Liu turned to General Lin Biao, one of the PLA's most accomplished field commanders and writers on military doctrine. It put Lin Biao on a ladder to eminence that would eventually culminate in the 1960s when Lin would be promoted as Mao's official successor, only to come later to a violent end. Lin's rise to eminence and his mysterious downfall have a storybook quality. Lin graduated in 1925 from Whampoa Military Academy during the first KMT-CCP United Front. But unlike many of the newly minted officers, Lin became a protégé of Zhou Enlai, the political tutor at the academy, rather than of Chiang Kai-shek, the commandant. At the age of twenty, Lin became a colonel in the Nationalist Army, but in the aftermath of the KMT-CCP split in 1927, he defected to the Communists. Mao gave him command of the First Red Corps of the Red Army, and in 1924 he led the vanguard troops on the 8,000-mile Long March to Yenan. There, at the age of twenty-eight, Lin became president of the Red Army Military Academy and gave a series of lectures published as *Struggle and War and Revolution* that became Communist military doctrine much like Mao's essay *On Protracted War*. He also became a devastating guerrilla fighter, jolting the Nationalists into putting a price of $100,000 on his head. In 1937, at the Battle of the Ping-hsing Pass, where his division defeated Japanese troops, the young commander suffered a severe chest wound. To convalesce he was sent to the Soviet Union, where he studied military science.

To carry out the mission, given to him by Liu Shaoqi, of preparing a Manchurian offensive, Lin Biao led a vanguard of 30,000 troops to join the guerrillas already operating in Manchuria. The Communist reinforcements moved into Manchuria through the northwestern corridor of Chahar and Jehol provinces and also from Shantung to ports on the coast of Manchuria's Kwangtung Peninsula.

Stalin's exchanges with Mao and Chiang did not divert the Soviet dictator from pursuing his reach for the spoils of Manchuria. While withdrawing his main occupation force, which consisted of some 300,000 troops, in May 1946, he asserted Soviet rights to "trophies of war of the Red Army," and his forces stripped the region's Japanese-built factories, transporting their machinery by rail to Siberia. Touring the region, the American Pauley Mission estimated in its November 1946 report to President Truman the value of the Russian take at about $900 million. Typically, as I found when traveling in Manchuria in 1971, at the huge Kirin hydroelectric project the Russians had hauled away six of the eight turbines.

While the Russians took with them much of the heavy Japanese military ordnance, they abandoned arsenals containing substantial quantities of light arms and munitions. To assure Communist advance access to these depots, the Russians delayed the debarkation of Nationalist troops into Manchuria through the ports of Dairen, Hulutao, and Yingkou. In the opposing race for the surrendered Japanese spoils, the U.S. Air Force in September flew 26,000

Nationalist troops aboard two hundred Douglas C-54 Skymaster transports into Nanking and Shanghai and then a further 5,000 troops into Peking. As Truman noted in his memoirs, the operation was accelerated to forestall a move by the Communists to take the surrender of the Japanese at all towns and cities within their reach. But before the airlifted Nationalist divisions could drive north to take possession of the Manchurian cities, the Communists pounced on Japanese arms depots at Harbin, Mukden, and other sites before retreating to the countryside. However, Stalin delayed until 1947 the turnover to the Communists of the largest cache of Japanese weapons, including tanks and heavy artillery, stored at the Russian base at Manchouli in Manchuria. The Russians had appropriated these weapons at a Japanese depot south of Mukden with the apparent intention of eventually transporting them to the Soviet Union. In yielding these arms Stalin seemed to put aside earlier doubts about whether the Communists were capable of defeating the Nationalists in the Civil War and decided to render more substantial aid to Mao. He also may have become concerned about continued American military aid to Chiang's forces and the possibility that a total Nationalist victory might provide the Americans with bases in proximity to his eastern borders. The acquisition of the Japanese weaponry was of critical help to the Communists in their conquest of Manchuria. The troops, commanded by Lin Biao, had been equipped prior to acquisition of the Japanese arms mainly with crude Chinese manufactured weapons along with a motley collection of old European arms. Apart from supplying Lin Biao with the Japanese arms, the principal assistance given the Communists by the Russians was in the transport of PLA troops on the Manchurian railways which the Russians had retained under their control. While Lin Biao prized the military help given to him by the Russians, he stood by helplessly while they were looting the Manchurian industrial complex.

As I was leaving Yenan in late November, it became increasingly evident that the Communist leadership was bracing for a long struggle with Chiang Kai-shek. Three Nationalist army groups, comprising 250,000 men, had advanced within striking distance of Yenan. Bolstered by American military aid, Chiang was enjoying an overwhelming superiority in troops and equipment, including his unopposed air force. His troops numbered about 2.6 million men, while Communist forces totaled about 1.1 million. Four months after my departure from Yenan, the Maoist leaders and their followers, heavily outnumbered by advancing National divisions, abandoned their long-held stronghold.

Before leaving Chungking, Zhou Enlai obtained a promise from Marshall that American transports would evacuate all Communist political representatives from Nationalist-held territory if peace negotiations were not resumed. On February 27–28, in an operation dubbed "Catfish," the U.S. Air Force returned Communist officials and their families to Yenan from Peking, Chungking, Nanking, and Shanghai. As the last evacuation aircraft departed Yenan, American pilots observed Communist troops blowing up the airstrip to deny use of it to advancing Nationalist columns. As Huang Hua recalls in his *Memoirs,* published in 2008, the party's Central Committee met and decided to disperse leaders, central organizations, and schools to the various bases held by the Communists. Mao, Zhou Enlai, and General Peng Dehuai, the deputy commander in chief of the army, would go to a remote county in northern Shensi to "carry on the war of liberation in the whole country." On the morning of March 19, the Nationalist First Division descended from the heights above undefended Yenan and took possession of the city that was by then empty of Maoist adherents. Mao, who had been sheltering with other leaders out of fear of Nationalist air raids in a gully behind the Peach Orchard, left Yenan in a jeep with Jiang Qing and their daughter escorted by a small contingent of bodyguards for the northern Shensi mountains, where he set up a new headquarters in the small village of Chengyangcha to plan his counteroffensive in the intensifying Civil War.

3
BATTLE FOR MANCHURIA

One month after my return in late November to Peking from Yenan, I traveled to Manchuria as fighting flared along the lower Sungari River front. The battles were being fought on grasslands crisscrossed by rivers and along the railway lines linking the principal cities and towns. The front extended from Communist-held northern Manchuria south to the Liao River valley, controlled by the Nationalists. From Peking I flew in an Executive Headquarters plane to Ch'angch'un, the Nationalist-occupied former capital of the Japanese puppet state of Manchukuo, situated not far from the southern banks of the broad Sungari. The city, which the Japanese had built in imitation of some features of Washington, D.C., was in ruins. Its pretentious white government buildings and outlying factories had been looted, first by the withdrawing Russians and then by Chinese mobs before the arrival of Nationalist troops.

Under heavy armed escort, I visited Nationalist units dug in along the Sungari front. The soldiers in their thick padded uniforms were hunkered down in cold so bitter that they could not with bare hands touch the metal of their weapons without losing skin. At his headquarters, I interviewed the Nationalist commander, Lieutenant General Sun Li-jen, a slim handsome forty-seven-year-old graduate of the Virginia Military Academy and Purdue University who was regarded by General Stillwell as one of the ablest Nationalist field commanders. In the Burma campaign against the Japanese he had earned the sobriquet of "Rommel of the East." In the spring of 1946, Sun's American-trained and -equipped New First Army, which had a component of 70,000 Burma veterans, spearheaded the Nationalist drive into Manchuria. Ferried into North China aboard U.S. Air Force transports, Sun's forces had pushed north as Russian occupation troops withdrew and took control of Mukden, the great metropolis of southern Manchuria. Sun's troops then struck farther north against the principal Chinese Communist stronghold position at Ssuping city on the critical rail line linking Mukden with Ch'angch'un. Sun's tanks overran Ssuping on May 19 in a hard-fought forty-day struggle against 110,000 entrenched Communists, both sides suf-

fering extremely heavy casualties. Four days later, although his divisions had
suffered 25,000 casualties in the Ssuping street fighting, Sun's armored columns backed by the Nationalist Fifth Army went on to take Ch'angch'un
on May 23. The battered Communist forces defending Ch'angch'un, which
had expended virtually all their munitions, were sent reeling back across
the Sungari River. Sun then established a bridgehead over the Sungari for a
further advance on Harbin, the principal city of northern Manchuria and
headquarters of Lin Biao, the Communist commander. His troops exhausted
after their retreat from the south and having suffered 20,000 casualties, Lin
Biao drafted an order on June 6 for withdrawal from Harbin. However, under
pressure from General Marshall, Chiang Kai-shek agreed to a fifteen-day
truce on June 7, and the Generalissimo called a halt to the Nationalist drive
north. Marshall had warned Chiang, with President Truman's sanction, that
the United States would not support an advance into northern Manchuria,
which Stalin held to be a sphere of special Russian interests under the terms
of the Yalta Agreement and the Treaty of Alliance between the Nationalists
and the Soviets of 1945. Marshall was unwilling to risk Stalin taking retaliatory military action.

Marshall was strongly criticized by some American observers for halting
the Nationalist advance and depriving Sun Li-jen of the opportunity of seizing Harbin and thus dealing a crippling blow to the Chinese Communists.
But the Soviet diplomat and historian Andrei Ledovsky, whom I had come
to know in Peking, retorted in a retrospective essay that Marshall made the
right decision, that a Nationalist advance into northern Manchuria "could
have had unpredictable and dangerous consequences—not only for the Kuomintang, but also for the United States and the entire international situation
in the Far East." He said that Stalin might have sent his army back into Manchuria, justifying his action as a response to atrocities committed against
Russian citizens by Nationalist troops. The abuse of the Russians, which I
had reported in my own dispatches, had led to the withdrawal of Soviet specialists operating the Chinese South Manchurian Railway under the 1945
treaty arrangements.

Following the cease-fire, Sun told me, the Communists had regrouped
and were preparing for a counteroffensive. He was not underestimating his
Communist adversary Lin Biao, the hero of the Battle of the Ping-hsing Pass
in the war against the Japanese. After his humiliating retreat from Ssuping,
Lin Biao had reorganized the Northeast Democratic United Army, a ragtag
force made up of Northern Chinese, Manchurians, Mongol cavalrymen,
and North Korean units, into his New Fourth Army. About ten days after

my departure from Ch'angch'un, Lin Biao sent 300,000 of his troops, many equipped with the newly acquired Japanese weaponry, across the frozen Sungari River in three successive thrusts on a broad front and for a short time enveloped Ch'angch'un, cutting off the power station supplying electricity and water to the city. However, Lin fell back in disarray across the river when Sun counterattacked. The armies then dug in, confronting each other across the Sungari.

On Christmas Eve I left Ch'angch'un by train for Mukden, the Manchurian metropolis in the south. It was one of the last trains to leave the city. I was accompanied by Jules Joelson, a sober, rather nervous correspondent for the Agence France-Presse, and Vladimir Drozdov, a pint-sized Russian correspondent who wore a big square fur hat with a red star on it. Drozdov worked for the *Russian Daily News,* which served the twenty thousand Russian émigrés living in Shanghai. Not long out of Ch'angch'un on the 200-mile journey, the train jolted to a stop, and we were told that Lin Biao's guerrillas had ripped up the rails. The guerrillas employing what they called their "sparrow" tactics were raiding the rail and highway links between the various Manchurian cities garrisoned by the Nationalists. Guarded by the Nationalist Railway Police aboard the train, we sat in a crowded, unheated coach in subzero temperatures as the rails were repaired. Drozdov huddled close to me as Chinese passengers snarled "*tapitze*" (big nose) at him. The Chinese, angered by maltreatment during the Russian occupation, were harassing the White Russian communities in the Manchurian cities.

Without food and growing hungrier as the hours passed, I became curious and inquired about a paper bag which Joelson kept close at his side. He confessed he had been to Harbin and was returning to Peking, and as ordered by his French wife, he was bearing a jar of the finest caviar obtained in a White Russian shop. Yielding to our piteous whimpers for food, Joelson reluctantly opened the jar and placed it between us. We dipped into the jar, eating it by the handful. (I had no taste for caviar for years thereafter.) After fourteen hours on the tracks, the rails were repaired, and the train clanked on to Mukden. I spent Christmas in the Shenyang Railway Hotel, venturing out to dine with Drozdov at the superb White Russian restaurants, whose proprietors seemed impervious to the Civil War, and returned after New Year's to Peking.

In early March 1947, with the conflict in Manchuria shaping up as one of the most decisive battles of the Civil War, I flew to Ch'angch'un once again, this time in the company of six other correspondents: Walter Bosshard of the Swiss *Neue Zürcher Zeitung,* who was the dean of the press corps in Peking;

Benjamin Welles, of the *New York Times;* Don Starr, of the *Chicago Tribune;* Jules Joelson; and my two news agency competitors, who had become legendary figures on the China scene, John Roderick of the Associated Press and Reynolds Packard of the United Press. In all they made up a coterie who were professionally and in lifestyle typical of the array of journalists covering the Civil War. Bosshard, the Swiss, a tall dignified man with a shock of gray hair, a correspondent in the old tradition of the adventurer and explorer, lived, of course, in the best Peking style. He rented a house in Wangfuchien, one of sixteen owned by Prince Pu Lun, a cousin of Pu Yi, the last monarch of the Qing dynasty, who in 1934 had become the puppet emperor of Manchukuo under the Japanese. Invited to dine, I would recline in the main room under polished hardwood beams of his Chinese house beside the blazing hearth fire to listen enthralled to his tales of mandarins, revolutionaries, warlords, and famous concubines. At dinner there would be French wine and liqueurs made in a Catholic monastery near Peking, which would be served by two long-gowned servants, who moved wraithlike anticipating every wish. Beyond the red-painted front door there was a courtyard with moon gates and flower beds. His antiques came from a shop just down the road owned by Walter Plaut, a German aristocrat, who sold his treasured wares only to those appreciative clients he personally held in esteem.

Much of the social life in Peking whirled about Ben Welles, son of Sumner Welles, then U.S. Undersecretary of State, and his beautiful English wife, Cynthia. He married Cynthia while stationed in London covering World War II after she had divorced the son of Lord Beaverbrook, the British press baron. John Roderick was the very able Associated Press man who had lived for several months in Yenan before my visit there, transmitting his dispatches via the Yenan Radio to the AP listening station in San Francisco. Then there was Reynolds Packard of the United Press, celebrated for less flattering reasons. A fleshy, lusty man, Packard felt he had to write the kind of copy that would be read by the "Kansas City Milkman," which became the title of a book he later wrote exposing the foibles of his news agency. He was fired upon our return from Manchuria after filing a story that he picked up from the imaginative Chinese press about a "human-headed spider," which caused a sensation around the world. A jokester on my International News Service cable desk, in keeping with the agency's concern about cable transmission costs, sent me a message instructing me not to file unless I located a spider with two human heads.

Our flight to Ch'angch'un aboard a very worn C-47 of the U.S. Air Force was occasioned because the battle for Manchuria had intensified and also by a diplomatic uproar over the Communist capture and jailing of two American assistant military attachés, Major Robert Riggs and Captain John Collins. The incident had become a major source of tension between Washington and the Communists. At Ch'angch'un we were met beside the snow-packed runway by the seventeen-year-old son of O. Edmund Clubb, the U.S. consul general, driving an army ambulance. At the consulate, as we thawed out from the subzero cold before a roaring fire, the consul general told us about the rather freakish circumstances of the attachés' misfortune which had landed them in a Harbin prison. They were touring the Sungari front and had dismounted from their jeep to survey with binoculars distant troop movements when the Chinese driver of their jeep and their interpreter suddenly panicked and drove off, leaving them stranded. The isolated officers were soon nabbed by Communist soldiers. The attachés were freed after fifty-five days in captivity. Clubb, a cool, resourceful diplomat, managed to negotiate their release by radio. Holding a white flag, Clubb went to a crossing on the tense Sungari front, where he accepted their handover. Clubb was later to become the last American diplomat to be stationed in Peking after the Communist takeover. It fell to him, as consul general, to haul down the American flag there in April 1950.*

From Clubb's residence, we proceeded to the Chinese telegraph office, where we wrote our dispatches. Packard produced a pair of dice, which we tossed to determine the order in which we would file, a procedure of some importance given the vagaries of the Chinese telegraph. Packard came in first and Roderick fifth. Bosshard casually agreed to file last, since he said his newspaper was in no hurry. We spent the night on cots in the desolate Manchukuo parliament building on the outskirts of the city. In the morning we rendezvoused at the consulate, where I encountered Packard and Roderick in heated argument. Packard had gone alone to the telegraph and found that Roderick had cunningly marked his dispatch "urgent" so that it would go out first. Roderick was unapologetic and chagrined only when he learned that his alleged trickery had been to no avail. In Chinese fashion, the telegraph clerk had put the last dispatch handed him atop the pile, and

---

*Clubb was one of the ablest and most distinguished China specialists, but his career in the Foreign Service was shattered after his return from China when he, among other China specialists in the State Department, was denounced during the McCarthy witch-hunting campaign as having in his critical reporting of Chiang Kai-shek's policies contributed to "the loss of China." Suspended by a Loyalty Board but later cleared, Clubb resigned from the State Department and started a new career as an eminent writer and professor at the East Asia Institute of Columbia University.

as a consequence Bosshard's cable had gone out first with no consideration given Roderick's urgent stamp. The Swiss fox had triumphed again.

A telephone call from the consulate interrupted, summoning us to a meeting with General Tu Yu-ming, the commander in chief of Nationalist forces in Manchuria. We traveled to the Northeast General Headquarters huddling against the intense cold in an open weapons carrier. I had expected to see Sun Li-jen, the conqueror of Ssuping, who had also successfully defended Ch'angch'un against Lin Biao's initial assaults, but he was not among those greeting us. He had been removed from his Ch'angch'un command, evidently having clashed with General Tu by opposing his policy of relying too much on a network of pillbox defenses and barbed wire systems around the Manchurian cities rather than engaging the Communists in offensive operations. Sun shared the view of Major General David Barr, chief of the Joint U.S. Military Advisory Group (JUSMAG) in Nanking: "In modern warfare the most disastrous of all things to do is to retreat into a city behind walls and take a defensive position."*

At the headquarters we were ushered into a map room, where we were greeted by General Tu, a forty-two-year-old officer, well turned out, his close-cropped hair carefully coiffed. He was wearing a well-tailored uniform with three rows of decorations including the U.S. Army parachutist badge awarded him at the school run during World War II at Kunming by the Office of Strategic Services (OSS). He had distinguished himself during the 1942 Burma campaign as the commander of the first Chinese motorized corps. The general shook hands with each of us, taking our calling cards in his left hand while his aide offered cigarettes. From his Ch'angch'un headquarters, Tu commanded seven divisions covering the city with its bridgehead over the Sungari and twelve divisions based at Mukden, guarding the approaches from North Korea and Inner Mongolia. Most of his 225,000

---

*I did not see Sun Li-jen again. On Taiwan, soon after Chiang Kai-shek fled the China mainland in 1949, Sun was appointed commander of the army divisions which the Generalissimo had transferred to the island before the fall of Nanking and Shanghai. In August 1955, Sun was accused of plotting a coup against Chiang. He was placed under house arrest. More than three decades later, in March 1988, the Nationalist government Control Yuan declared him exonerated and released him. The timing was significant in that the amnesty was granted after the death that year of the Generalissimo's son, President Chiang Ching-kuo, who evidently had viewed Sun as a contender for power. Sun died two years after his release at the age of ninety-one. In 2001, the convictions of members of Sun's staff who were accused with him in 1955 and jailed were reviewed by the government. Their trials were declared to have been conducted improperly on a basis of forged evidence. The officers were released and awarded financial compensation.

troops were American equipped, and he benefited from the cover of the un-opposed Nationalist Air Force.

Tu told us Lin Biao was readying another assault across the Sungari but he was optimistic that he could hold his positions on the river. He would not say whether he intended to resume the Nationalist drive north to Harbin from his Sungari bridgehead or a sweep farther South down the Liaotung Peninsula, which would bring his troops close to the Russian-held port of Dairen. The previous October he had mounted an offensive with seven di-visions down the peninsula to Tantung, on the Yalu River bordering North Korea, routing the Communists and inflicting heavy casualties on them. However, when two of his divisions pursued the Communists farther south, one of them was ambushed and only 1,000 of its troops escaped. Bolstered by replacement divisions, Tu renewed his offensive and secured control of the southern Manchurian railway network, but at a cost of 11,000 casualties. Tu told us his forces were ready to resume the advance on Harbin from his Sungari bridgehead but the timing turned on the outcome of diplomatic ex-changes between the Nationalist government and Moscow. If the continuing threat of Russian intervention was removed, he was ready to take the offen-sive. Tu's optimism about his prospects was short lived. When I returned to Manchuria in the spring of 1947, I found that the balance of forces in Man-churia had changed fundamentally from the glory days of Sun Li-jen's march to the Sungari.

4
FALL OF MANCHURIA

Six months after his retreat from Yenan, Mao issued, on September 7, 1947, a new directive to the PLA from his Shensi mountain headquarters. He began by summarizing military operations from July 1946 to June 1947. He said his forces had "wiped out" 1,120,000 Nationalist troops and militia supporters. But then he conceded that the Communists had been forced to yield considerable territory of the "Liberated Areas" and had suffered 300,000 casualties. After stressing the fundamental need of forging ahead with land reform to gain the support of the peasantry, he then laid down the strategic and tactical guidelines for the next phase of military operations.

The Maoist strategy called for maneuver in the countryside followed by step-by-step encirclement of Nationalist-held towns and cities. He had first employed this strategy in the 1920s and 1930s against Chiang Kai-shek's vastly superior forces. In 1938 Mao elaborated on this strategy in his classic work *On Protracted War,* drawn from lectures he made in Yenan in 1938, which became the basic text for war against the Japanese and used subsequently in the Civil War. The book laid out tactics by which the morale and combat effectiveness of an enemy army superior in numbers and equipment could be broken down. "To achieve success," he said, "Chinese troops must conduct their warfare with a high degree of mobility on extensive battlefields, making swift advances and withdrawals, swift concentrations and dispersals. This means large scale mobile warfare, not positional warfare . . . It does not mean the abandonment of all the vital strategic positions, which should be defended by positional warfare as long as profitable. Besides employing trained armies to carry on mobile warfare, we must organize great numbers of guerrilla units among the peasants."

As recorded by Lionel Max Chassin in his book *The Communist Conquest of China,* these were the specific tactics which Mao elaborated in his September 7 directive to his widely dispersed troops:

> Attack dispersed isolated enemy forces first . . . attack concentrated strong enemy forces later; take medium and small cities and extensive rural areas first; take big cities later.

> Make wiping out the enemy's effective strength our main objective; do not make holding or seizing a place our main objective . . .
>
> In every battle concentrate an absolutely superior force, encircle the enemy forces completely . . . do not let any escape from the net.
>
> Fight no battle unprepared. Fight no battle you are not sure of winning.
>
> Strive to draw the enemy into mobile warfare . . .
>
> Resolutely attack and seize all fortified points and cities which are weakly defended. For the time being leave alone all fortified points and cities which are strongly defended
>
> Replenish our strength with all the arms and most of the soldiers captured from the enemy (80 to 90 per cent of the men and a small number of the junior officers).

This Maoist protracted war strategy was adapted in the 1950s, with the help of Chinese Communist advisers, by Vo Nguyen Giap, Ho Chi Minh's top military commander, and effectively employed in the wars against the French and then against the United States and its South Vietnamese allies.

In the spring of 1948, the PLA launched a general counteroffensive retrieving lost territory including Yenan. The offensive was in progress in March when I returned to Mukden, wangling a ride on a U.S. Air Force transport carrying supplies to the American consular mission, headed by Angus Ward. I found that the strategic situation had changed radically in all of Manchuria since my interview with Tu Yu-ming in Ch'angch'un a year earlier. Mounting a strike force of 600,000 troops, Lin Biao had succeeded in isolating Mukden and Chinchow, the vital communications and supply center south of the metropolis, as well as Ch'angch'un in the north. Lin Biao massed antiaircraft artillery around the encircled cities, which were being supplied by air, compelling the Nationalist transport planes to make their drops from high altitudes. Many, if not most, of the parachuted packets floated into the hands of the PLA.

Alarmed, Chiang flew from Nanking to Peking to take personal command of Manchurian field operations. As General Ho Ying-chin, the defense minister, groused privately to American advisers, Chiang began issuing orders without consulting with the general staff. When his New Fifth Corps was wiped out in a Communist ambush as it ventured beyond the Mukden defense perimeter, Chiang in a fury flew on to the metropolis, where he reshuffled the Manchurian High Command. He appointed General Wei Li-huang as commander in chief, demoting Tu Yu-ming to deputy. In the 1930s,

Chiang had bestowed the title "Ever Victorious General" on Wei as a reward for having wiped out a Maoist guerrilla base area.

Mukden was a city in panic when I landed there. The Nationalist garrison of 200,000 troops, although better armed than the Communists, had sat too long behind the pillbox defenses, erected on the orders of Tu Yu-ming. When I toured the defense perimeter, interviewing field commanders, I found that Lin Biao's columns had drawn a noose about the entire city and its environs. To guard against a Communist incursion into the city, other garrison troops in their yellow padded uniforms were manning pillboxes at intersections with machine guns sited down the thoroughfares. The streets were almost entirely empty except for refugees and beggars. Shops were boarded up. The big redbrick factories built by the Japanese, bombed by American troops during the war and then looted by the withdrawing Russians, were crumpled, abandoned shells. Three China-based commercial airlines, including General Claire L. Chennault's Civil Air Transport (CAT), were bringing in food and other supplies for the military garrison and selected civilians. Huge salaries were being paid to the American pilots making the risky low-level flights over the Communist lines.

There were 4 million people employed in farming areas within the Mukden perimeter, about sixty miles in diameter, but their produce was insufficient to feed the city's population of 1.2 million and the great influx of refugees. More than 300,000 people were subsisting on bark and leaves and pressed soybean cakes, ordinarily used as fertilizer or animal fodder. Thousands were dying, many of them children, wasted by malnutrition and such diseases as pellagra and scurvy. Many were going blind because of diet deficiencies. I walked along the desolate streets past skeletal dead sprawled in the gutters. I was pursued by unbearably pitiful child beggars and women crying out for help, and soon my pockets were empty of coins and Chinese yuan bills. At elegant restaurants you could still get any kind of drink or food—if you had lots of money. Prices had soared to one million times the prewar index. A large stack of the local Manchurian dollars was needed to pay for a meal. Beggars squatted outside the restaurants, holding out their hands to well-fed Chinese officials emerging after rich dinners.

At the airfields people were offering bribes and scuffling for places aboard the airlift shuttle planes, which were taking out about fifteen hundred passengers each day. I glimpsed air force planes departing loaded with personal possessions of officials, including valuable antiques which could be purchased for virtually nothing from desperate families in the dying city.

I was staying at the Shenyang Railway Hotel, where drinks, food, and women were readily available for dollars. At the long hardwood bar, an improbable assortment of Americans, Russians, and Chinese sat gossiping about how to survive or profit from the mayhem. American civilian pilots speculated about how long they could go on with their flights for the Nationalists, for which they were being paid weekly salaries in the many thousands of dollars. Russians of the jointly operated Chinese-Soviet South Manchurian Railroad grumbled because they were at loose ends since the railways were cut, both the one leading north to Communist-held Harbin and the line southeast to Russian-occupied Port Arthur and Dairen. American military officers of JUSMAG joked cynically and despairingly about corrupt, cowardly Nationalist generals who would not heed their advice. Officials of the U.S. economic aid office spoke bitterly about the hopelessness of trying to feed the starving population and accused the Communists of driving refugees into the Mukden perimeter to aggravate the famine. Well-to-do Chinese talked about the money to be made in the manipulation of the currency, and several told me that since the Communists, after all, were Chinese, they were sure they could do business with them. The despairing talk and the drinking went on into the morning hours, many of the barflies fixed in place by fear of going out into the dangerous city. When I left Mukden, the crack of artillery fire reverberated ever more loudly on the empty streets.

The Nationalist reverses in Manchuria did not surprise American military advisers. They had warned the Generalissimo as early as 1945 about the dangers of attempting to reoccupy all of Manchuria while the struggle with the Communists for control of China proper was still in progress. They cited the danger of positioning Nationalist forces in cities along a 1,000-mile defense corridor which would be difficult, if not impossible, to supply and sustain against Communist interdiction. Nevertheless, the Generalissimo, eager to retake control of the Manchurian industrial complex, decided to risk overextension of his forces and committed many of his best divisions to the struggle.

Returning from Mukden to Nanking, where I was newly based after being posted in Peking for six months, I was told that General David Barr, the commander of JUSMAG, was urging the Generalissimo to make a progressive withdrawal from Manchuria. Barr had warned Chiang that the Nationalist garrisons could not be indefinitely supplied by air and were becoming increasingly vulnerable to destruction piecemeal by the gathering Communist forces. The Communist guerrillas, pressing their "sparrow" warfare, were raiding Nationalist lines of communication between North China and Manchuria. To consolidate their hold on the countryside the Communists had instituted an even more radical land redistribution program. It brought them the widespread support of the poorer peasants and served to eliminate local opposition through the disenfranchising of thousands of landlords and middle peasants who fled into the Nationalist-held cities. Barr's withdrawal plan, which would have begun with the transfer of the exposed Ch'angch'un garrison south to Mukden, was rejected by Chiang. Barr then advised the Generalissimo to reopen the Communist-severed 120-mile rail corridor extending south from Mukden to Chinchow, the principal supply base for the some 300,000 troops of the Manchurian garrisons. The strategic aim was to assure a continuous flow of supplies northward from Chinchow to the Nationalist garrisons and to provide, if necessary, an escape corridor for them south into North China. The clearing of the corridor was to be effected by a convergence of strike forces from the Mukden and Chinchow garrisons with the help of troops from Taiwan landed at the port of Hulutao.

The Generalissimo concurred on the plan on March 8, but he did not actually order Wei Li-huang to launch the operation until September 25. Thereafter, despite repeated prodding by Chiang and the general staff, apparently because he feared that a reduction in the strength of the Mukden garrison would invite a Communist attack, the Manchurian commander did not attempt his breakout until October 9. Wei committed only eleven divisions of the Mukden garrison to a Western Strike Force to open the corridor to Chinchow rather than the fifteen divisions as ordered.

As the strike force advanced toward Chinchow, Lin Biao, who had anticipated the Nationalist maneuver, attacked the Chinchow complex. The city was defended by some 120,000 troops under General Fan Han-chieh, the second in command in Manchuria. Lin Biao encircled the city with twenty divisions. As the siege progressed, 5,400 Nationalist troops were flown into Chinchow from Mukden to bolster the garrison just before the Communists shelled and shut down the airport. Buckling under a succession of assaults, the Nationalist Ninety-third Army, holding a section of the Chinchow perimeter, defected. Eight divisions of Communist troops then broke through gaps in the city walls which they had blasted open with artillery fire and in a bloody battle decimated 34,000 of the defenders. The rest of the garrison surrendered on October 20. The Communists took 88,000 prisoners including General Fan Han-chieh. The reinforcement of nine divisions sent from Taiwan, which had landed at the port of Hulutao, was blocked from reaching the Chinchow battle area and reembarked. The Communist victory effectively destroyed the Nationalist communications system in Manchuria. Enormous stores of military supplies and equipment stockpiled at

Chinchow were garnered by the Communists. Lin Biao then wheeled north and pounced with eleven columns of 200,000 troops on the strike force, which had been moving southwest from Mukden toward Chinchow. The strike force attempted to retreat to Mukden but was blocked. In three days of heavy fighting, during which the commanding general, General Liao Yao-hsiang, a respected veteran of the Burma campaign, was killed early in the battle, the entire strike force was decimated or surrendered by October 28. At Ch'angch'un, the Sixtieth Army, composed of Yunnanese troops brought in from the Indochina border, defied orders to attempt a breakout from the encircled city to the aid of Mukden. They turned on the garrison commander, General Cheng Tung-kuo, and defected to the Communists. Cheng was taken prisoner while trying to hold out in the city's Central Bank building with two of his trusted battalions. The rest of his garrison of 80,000 troops then surrendered on October 20. Mukden's turn came on November 2. The garrison, depleted by the departure of the troops of the Western Strike Force, surrendered after the garrison commander, General Chou Fu-cheng, defected with his Fifty-third Army.

Abandoning their beleaguered field commands, Generals Wei Li-huang and Tu Yu-ming escaped from Mukden by air to the port of Hulutao. Wei continued on to Canton in South China, arriving there on November 6. Three days later, on Chiang's orders he was placed under house arrest. He was charged with disobedience and responsibility for the fatal delay in carrying out orders to open the Mukden-Chinchow corridor, but the following April he was allowed by Vice President Li Tsung-jen to go into exile in Hong Kong. In a report to the U.S. Defense Department, in which he cited Wei's delay in undertaking the breakout operation as critical, Barr said: "That General Wei Li-huang was able to get away with such complete disobedience of orders without punishment or even censure, as far as I know, points to one reason why the Nationalists are losing the present war." As for Tu Yu-ming, Barr described him as an officer of "little worth."

In 1955, Wei returned to the mainland from Hong Kong and was warmly welcomed by the Communists. In 1959, Mao appointed him a vice chairman of the National Defense Council. When he died in Peking in 1960, Wei was given a grandiose funeral, which gave rise to speculation that he had been a tool of the Communists all along. However, attributing the loss of Manchuria largely to complicity by Wei with the Communists as portrayed in some accounts is flat wrong. When Wei took command in Manchuria in January 1948, the Nationalist city garrisons were already isolated and encircled by the Communists and had suffered heavy losses. The Generalissimo was as much at fault as Wei in delaying the Mukden-Chinchow operation. When General Barr told Ho Ying-chin, the Nationalist defense minister, that the corridor could have been kept open if Wei had moved promptly as ordered, thus allowing the Nationalist garrisons to escape into North China, the defense minister replied: "You are correct, but my hands were tied because the Generalissimo directed the entire operation alone from Peking without any reference to me or the General Staff."

Apart from the delays, I felt there was reason to doubt that the Mukden-Chinchow operation could have succeeded. The railroad tracks between the two cities had been torn up by the Communists, and it would have taken months to make the line fit for military transport. Certainly, Lin Biao would not have camped idly by on the flanks of the corridor allowing the Nationalist garrisons to escape into North China.

When the Generalissimo returned to Nanking from Peking after directing the abortive Manchurian operations, he said in a message to the Chinese people: "The loss of Manchuria is discouraging but it relieves the government of a formidable burden, so far as military defenses are concerned, and allows it to concentrate its war effort to the south of the Great Wall." In Manchuria Chiang had lost seven armies, comprising thirty divisions plus other brigades, many of them American equipped and trained, a total of more than 400,000 troops, of which about 245,000 were taken prisoner or defected. Many of the Nationalist units, finding themselves isolated, operating on territory far from home, and lacking confidence in the strategy of the top leadership, had deserted to the Communists simply to escape annihilation. As I reported in my dispatches, I found no evidence that Nationalist troops defected for ideological reasons. Those who surrendered were treated extremely well by the Communists inducing them to join the ranks. During the Civil War more than 800,000 former Nationalist soldiers eventually served with the Communists.

Summing up the Nationalist disaster, General Barr said in his report to the Department of the Army: "The Nationalist troops in Manchuria were the finest soldiers the government had. The large majority of the units were United States equipped and included many soldiers and junior officers who had received United States training during the war with Japan. I am convinced that if these troops had proper leadership from the top, the Communists would have suffered a major defeat."

Lin Biao's forces suffered an estimated 75,000 casualties in the Manchurian campaign. The losses were more than made up by Nationalist defections to his forces. His war booty included a vast supply of American weapons and equipment, more significant in determining the eventual outcome of the Civil War than what had been obtained from Japanese arsenals in Manchuria. At the conclusion of the Manchurian campaign, Lin Biao had a well-equipped force of 360,000 troops available for a decisive thrust into North China.

The Nationalist defeat in Manchuria was one of the two military reverses which sealed the loss of the China mainland to Mao. The other was the Battle of the Huai-Hai, during which the Nationalist Army was finally shattered. Before all else, the debacle suffered by the Nationalists in Manchuria stemmed from Chiang Kai-shek's bungling strategy. But no doubt, a major factor was Lin Biao's brilliant exploitation of the fumbles of the Generalissimo and his generals.

Lin Biao would eventually become a nonperson in official Chinese archives as a consequence of his falling-out with Mao during the Cultural Revolution. Yet he must rank as the most effective of the Communist field commanders. The proof lies in his accomplishments in the war against Japan, the conquest of Manchuria, and his subsequent campaigns through North and Central China south to the Indochina border. His ranking as such is not diminished by Mao's assertions in two articles of his *Selected Works* that the main instructions for both the Manchurian and North China campaigns were drawn up by him rather than by Lin Biao. Mao was a brilliant overall strategist, like Zhu De, the commander in chief of the armies, and no doubt Lin Biao and the other field commanders made use of the strategic, tactical, and political guidelines laid down by him in his directive of September 7, 1947, from the Shensi headquarters. But Mao is not to be ranked with Lin Biao, Chen Yi, Liu Bocheng, and Peng Dehuai, who certainly were the most effective field commanders of the Civil War.

5

NANKING

On the morning of November 23, 1948, three weeks after the fall of Mukden, standing on the bleak Nanking airfield, chilled by the biting wind off the turbulent Yangtze River, I watched disconsolately as the Australian Air Force plane lifted over the city wall and headed east toward Tokyo. With Communist armies advancing toward the Nationalist capital, the dependents of foreign diplomats were being evacuated. Audrey, to whom I was newly engaged, the daughter of Chester Ronning, minister-counselor of the Canadian Embassy, was aboard the plane with her mother, two siblings, and other women and children of the Canadian and Australian embassies. As the plane disappeared into the clouds, I wondered when I might see Audrey again. We'd had so little time together.

I climbed back into my jeep. Glancing at the rows of Nationalist B-24 and B-25 bombers and P-38 fighters on the tarmac, I thought of how impressive they looked, and yet they had been so ineffectual in operations against the Communists. Washington had provided Chiang Kai-shek with a sizable air force, much of it delivered since the end of the war against Japan. It comprised 939 aircraft in 15 squadrons. More than 5,000 personnel had been trained by American instructors. But the performance of the air crews was ranked as being of the lowest order by frustrated officers of the Air Advisory Division of JUSMAG. The bomber and fighter pilots habitually clung to such high altitudes in combat operations so as to render the Nationalist Air Force virtually useless. Fighter strafing runs were usually carried out ineffectively at altitudes of 1,500 to 2,000 feet. Parachute drops to beleaguered garrisons and units were often made from such high altitudes that the supplies frequently drifted into the hands of besieging Communist forces. Some American advisers believed that the poor performance by the pilots was deliberate, reflecting their lack of belief in the cause for which they supposedly were fighting. General Barr bluntly said he thought that the Chinese pilots simply did not want to kill any of their compatriots, irrespective of whether they were "enemy" Communists.

For weeks prior to the fall of the Manchurian cities, there had been frequent frenzied scenes at the Nanking airport. Nationalist transports were swooping in from the north, harbingers of the imminent fall of some city to the Communists, bearing the families and concubines of generals and senior officials, together with large cases of personal belongings. Observing the traffic, I thought of what better use might have been made of those transports—rescuing troops from Communist encirclements on the Manchurian plain.

I drove from the airport into Hsinchiehkow, the central district of Nanking, where most of the government offices and the best shops were located. The approaches to the city were guarded by well-armed Nationalist army divisions under the cover of the air force, but the capital nevertheless was gripped with a pervasive sense of impending doom. The war was going badly for the Nationalists on all fronts. Whereas the Nationalists had begun the year with almost a three-to-one numerical superiority in military manpower, the Communists now held the advantage in terms of combat effectives. They had taken the initiative in all sectors. The Communists admitted to suffering at least 300,000 casualties in two years of aggressive offensives, but the losses had been more than made up by Nationalist defections and recruiting. To the northwest of the capital, beyond the Huai River, which flowed east to west about one hundred miles north of Nanking, one million troops of the opposing camps were moving into confrontation on the approaches to both Nanking and Shanghai for what would become one of the largest military engagements in history. I drove past hundreds of Nationalist soldiers in disheveled yellow uniforms, stragglers and deserters from the defeated armies in the north, wandering aimlessly through the streets. Thousands of refugees from the carnage of the war zone, among them elites fleeing Communist purges in the countryside, were camped with their families on the sidewalks, huddled against buildings for shelter. The city was under martial law. Police stood with fixed bayonets at street intersections. Gendarmes had been deployed to beat back mobs clamoring to loot shops in which speculators were selling hoarded stocks of rice at ever soaring prices. There were pitiful sights of refugee families squatting before restaurants hoping scraps would be thrown to them. Each morning sanitation trucks patrolling the streets picked up the bodies of those who had died of hunger or cold during the night.

A week before Audrey's departure I had looked on stunned as the eight hundred American officers and enlisted men of JUSMAG were evacuated overnight in a pell-mell rush. In Washington, the Joint Chiefs of Staff had decided to withdraw the advisers hastily, believing that JUSMAG could no longer serve a useful purpose and that Nanking would soon be in the hands of the Communists. In the JUSMAG compounds, tons of warehoused supplies were abandoned as well as personal possessions in family apartments of officers, everything from record players to fancy draperies. The leavings disappeared within hours as former Chinese employees and scavengers ravaged the premises. I walked through the empty American Officers' Club, where I months earlier met Audrey at a dinner hosted by the American military attaché. The leader of the club's White Russian band would strike up our favorite song, "Golden Earrings," as we entered the club. The swank club, a palatial residence with stately gardens, once occupied by Wang Ching-wei, president of the Japanese puppet regime during World War II, now stood stripped, empty, discarded sheets of music littering the bandstand.

General Barr, frustrated and bitter after the withdrawal of his advisory group in unseemly haste, fired off a report on November 18 to the Department of Defense on his relations with Chiang Kai-shek and his generals, in which he said: "No battle has been lost since my arrival due to the lack of ammunition or equipment. Their military debacles in my opinion can all be attributed to the world's worst leadership and many other morale destroying factors that led to a complete loss of the will to fight. The complete ineptness of high military leaders and the widespread corruption and dishonesty throughout the Armed Forces could in some measure have been controlled and directed had the above authority and facilities been available. Chinese leaders completely lack the moral courage to issue and enforce an unpopular decision." Barr, who shared the contents of his report with me, also told the department that the military situation had deteriorated to the point where only the active participation of U.S. troops and a secure American supply pipeline could provide a remedy. But the general recommended against any such commitment, which he said would require thousands of American troops.

The general had been frank and forthcoming when Chiang Kai-shek solicited his advice, but his guidance was rarely heeded. As he departed, Barr had reason to recall Marshall's caution at the time he was appointed chief of JUSMAG a year earlier:

> I am willing that General Barr should make his advice available to the Generalissimo on an informal and confidential basis and that the Army Advisory Group should supply advice with respect to reorganization of Chinese Army Services of Supply should that be desired. I am, however, not willing that we should accept responsibility for Chinese strategic

plans and operations. I think you will agree that the implications of accepting that responsibility would be very far-reaching and grave and that such responsibility is in logic inseparable from the authority to make it effective. Whatever the Generalissimo may feel moved to say with respect to his willingness to delegate necessary powers to Americans, I know from my own experience that advice is always listened to very politely but frequently ignored when deemed unpalatable.

Amid the chaos in the capital, in a modern Nanking office building erected in an inner courtyard of the old "Heavenly" Palace built by leaders of the Tai'ping Rebellion who with a distorted view of Western Christianity had risen up against the Qing dynasty in the mid-nineteenth century, the Generalissimo sat behind a massive desk defiantly warding off entreaties by panicky ministers. The vice president, Li Tsung-jen, and other leaders of the ruling KMT Party and government were eager for peace talks with the Communists, but the Generalissimo thwarted them at every turn. A lean, erect indomitable man, the sixty-one-year-old Chiang was unshaken in his conviction that ultimately he would defeat his Communist foes. This was the essence of what I heard him declare at one of his rare press conferences in the palace. Presumably it was also the import of the message he asked Madame Chiang Kai-shek, his Wellesley-educated wife, to convey to Washington in personal appeals to President Truman and Secretary of State Marshall for a new infusion of massive assistance.

I was appalled by the evident ineptitude and corruption of Chiang's regime, but I was not totally without sympathy for the struggling Generalissimo. After establishing Nanking as his capital in 1928, the Generalissimo had found little time to unify China and transform the "Southern Capital" of the Ming emperors into the proud Nationalist capital he envisioned. In 1931, four years after he had marched to Peking from Canton, the southern metropolis where Sun Yat-sen founded the Chinese Republic, and succeeded in compelling the northern warlords to bow to him, the Japanese attacked in Manchuria and then, in 1932, at Shanghai. Renewing their advance in 1937, the Japanese seized Nanking, where their troops slaughtered as many as 200,000 people and raped, according to reliable foreign accounts, some 20,000 women. Chiang fled to Chungking, which became his temporary wartime capital. When he returned to Nanking in 1946, he was still at war with Mao Zedong in a divided China, but he began rebuilding his capital. He also settled a score, as best he could, with the Japanese. Soon after I

arrived in 1947, I went outside the city to a large dusty field and watched as
three Japanese generals among those who had been in command in Nanking in 1937 were hauled roughly from the back of a truck, their hands tied
behind their backs. Forced to their knees, they were executed, each with a
single pistol shot to the back of their shaven heads, while Chinese spectators
jostled and jeered behind a cordon of Nationalist soldiers.

After driving through the littered streets of Hsinchiehkow, scribbling notes
on the pitiful scenes and trying to put Audrey's departure out of my mind,
I drove to the Associated Press compound in the northern district to meet
Harold Milks, the bureau chief. I had just left the International News Service and joined the AP as his deputy. The unexpected move to the AP came
after a falling out with INS. I had been transferred from Peking to Nanking
as a staff correspondent, but without the reward of pay sufficient to live comfortably in a city in which a hefty sack of the inflated local currency was necessary to buy a restaurant meal. The breaking point came when I received
a circular letter addressed to the INS foreign staff stating that living allow-
ances would no longer be paid. Young reporters, eager to get a start as foreign
correspondents, were typically being paid shoestring salaries by INS and the
United Press. In my case, the timing was incomprehensible. The Civil War
was at its height, and my copy was receiving wide play around the world.
Also, unbeknownst to my INS bosses, I had just received tentative job offers
from the *New York Times* and the Associated Press. I was sharing a house
with Henry R. Lieberman, the *Times* bureau chief, Christopher Rand of the
Herald Tribune, and other correspondents. Lieberman had offered me a job
which gained the approval of Ted Bernstein, then the foreign news editor,
and I had already begun filing stories to the *Times* without a byline during
Hank's absence in the field. Fred Hampson, the AP bureau chief in Shanghai, had also offered me a job. I messaged good-bye with some satisfaction
to Barry Farris, the editor of INS, and awaited a final word from the *Times.*
One morning, it came in the form of a cable: "Negative on Topping," signed
by Cyrus Sulzberger, the chief correspondent for the *Times,* a nephew of
Arthur Hays Sulzberger, the publisher. I had never met Cyrus Sulzberger,
who was based in Paris and had the final say on hiring for the foreign staff.
Within the hour, I telephoned Hampson and took the job with the AP. It
was a move I never regretted. I worked for the AP for the next eleven years

in China, Vietnam, London, and Berlin before joining the *Times* in 1959. I came to regard the AP as the most essential and finest news organization in the world.

On that November morning in 1948 just after Audrey left Nanking, I sat pensively for a time in my jeep in the courtyard of the AP compound looking eastward to the pine-covered slopes of Purple Mountain. Audrey and I had often picnicked there. Sitting beside the old observatory on the peak, sipping cold wine from a thermos jug, we would gaze down on the city that was encased in the twenty-two-mile-long brick wall built by Ming emperors. Chiang had sought hastily to dress up his capital soon after his return from Chungking. But the city lacked the grace of Peking and the dynamism of industrial Shanghai or commercial Canton. With scant planning, broad pretentious boulevards, swept every morning by Japanese prisoners of war dressed in green overalls, had been slashed across the city. They were lined with government office buildings whose blue and green tiled roofs were failed imitations of the classical Ming style. Side streets remained as they had been for hundreds of years, the only additions being two-story slapdash buildings and refugee shacks. The rich dwelled behind compound walls shutting out the misery of the impoverished living in the narrow, crooked cobbled alleys. Patches of rice fields were plowed by water buffalo. Mercifully, the stagnant ponds dotting the city came alive with color in the spring with the bloom of the giant lotus. Perched on the southern bend of the Yangtze, 150 miles from Shanghai, Nanking was accursed with a foul climate, four months of unbearably humid heat in the summer, and a dank winter of penetrating cold. Only when the spring came, when the fruit trees blossomed and the hillsides adorned with temples and shrines turned vivid green, did the successors of the emperors who resided here seem to inherit the Mandate of Heaven bestowed on the former imperial rulers.

Atop Purple Mountain looming on the outskirts of the city, on an evening in the spring of 1948, I asked Audrey, then nineteen, a slender, beautiful blonde, to marry me. She was a student at Nanking University and taught English at Ginling Women's College. The university had disintegrated into shambles just after Audrey left, with police agents swarming over the campus beating up and arresting militant students. They had joined with students at other universities in demonstrations demanding an end to the Civil War and termination of the American intervention in support of Chiang Kai-shek's regime. Audrey's most disturbing memory of her last days in Nanking was an exchange with a Chinese government official. As she was being driven in the company of the official to the Canadian Embassy residence from a diplomatic reception, looking out on beggars and refugees on the streets, she exclaimed: "Seeing the suffering of these people must be very painful to you." The official shrugged and said: "We don't think of these as people." It was a remark that went to the heart of the Nationalist government's inability to rally the masses to its support in the Civil War. Apart from teaching at Ginling, Audrey worked as an assistant to Captain Wong, the dentist of the American Military Advisory Group. One of her tasks was to chat with Madame Chiang Kai-shek in a reception room while the Generalissimo was being fitted for a new pair of false teeth. In fun she once asked the dental technician to carve her initials on one of the Generalissimo's molars. Rebuffed by Audrey when he asked for a date, the technician put aside the plot.

Dutifully, after that evening on Purple Mountain when Audrey gave her assent to marriage, I waited for an opportunity to ask Audrey's father to bless our engagement. Although friendly with Chester Ronning, I was still somewhat hesitant about seeking his consent—a Jewish boy born in Harlem of eastern European immigrants asking the hand in marriage of a young woman whose Lutheran family traced its ancestry to Norwegian aristocracy. Like other correspondents, I had often sought out Ronning as a source for news and political analysis. Born in China of missionary parents, Ronning spoke fluent Mandarin, his first language, and was widely regarded as Canada's foremost expert on Asia. Serving in Chungking during General Marshall's mediation mission, he had become very friendly with Mao's deputy, Zhou Enlai, who, like Ronning, was first educated in a missionary elementary school. It was a friendship that through the next thirty years would have a significant influence on Western relations with China.

As minister of the Canadian Embassy, Ronning was also on good terms with President Chiang Kai-shek. When Chiang learned that Ronning in his youth had been a cowboy broncobuster in Alberta, Canada, the Generalissimo invited him to ride and exercise his spirited Arabian horse. It was one of several steeds captured from the Japanese. The stable boys were Japanese prisoners of war. In the summer of 1946 Ronning was a guest of the Chiangs in their Kuling residence, a vacation retreat on Mount Lushan in Kiangsu Province. He was especially close to Madame Chiang Kai-shek, who often confided in him. She once told him of her distress about being pictured in the American press as something of a snob. It had been reported that while staying at the White House she had brought her own purple silk bed sheets. She explained to Ronning that it was not hauteur but a matter of being allergic to the detergents used in the United States to wash bed linen. During the

Kuling visit Ronning was startled on one occasion when Madame Chiang came to him weeping. In a burst of temper during a quarrel the Generalissimo had whipped out a pistol and shot her pet German shepherd dog. It was a rare insight into what disharmony there might have been in this celebrated marriage. The Generalissimo relied on his wife to enlist American support in the Civil War and to present a sophisticated, cultured face to the Western world that would cloak his own stiff warlord image. In 1931, on her insistence and prior to their marriage, although very much the Confucian authoritarian, he joined the Methodist Church. Madame Chiang told foreigners in later years that the Generalissimo had become a devout Methodist who read the Bible every day, neither smoked nor drank except for ceremonial toasts, the latter a dubious accolade, since her husband's propensity for scotch whiskey was well known. The Generalissimo's professed Christian piety and anti-Communist stand were factors in winning him support in the United States from such notables as Henry Luce, publisher of *Time* and *Life* magazines, himself a son of a China missionary. Perhaps the most influential member of the "China Lobby," a group of American supporters of Chiang Kai-shek, Luce was unremitting in his support of Chiang during World War II and throughout the Civil War.

Pursuing Audrey, in the summer of 1948 I made my own visit to Kuling, where the Ronnings were vacationing. From Hankow on the Yangtze, where I had gone to cover the catastrophe of a great flood, I traveled by riverboat to a landing at the foot of Mount Lushan. The only means of reaching Kuling was to be carried by sedan chair up a narrow path cut into the mountainside. I felt guilty about riding a swaying sedan chair on the backs of four bearers but then persuaded myself this was work needed by them to feed their families. In Kuling, I stayed in the Ronning bungalow and strolled with Audrey among the mountain pines. One day, her father and I hiked up the mountainside, and I told him that Audrey and I wished to marry. We walked on in silence for a time, and then after posing only one question— "Do you love her?"—he gave his assent. When Audrey left Nanking for Canada, she wore my ring. She next heard of me under the most extraordinary circumstances.

6

BATTLE OF THE HUAI-HAI

In the last days of November 1948, I made ready to cover what was to become one of the largest battles in history. It would affect the balance of power in world politics for generations to come. Strangely, perhaps because it was fought on distant hidden fronts, cloaked by Nationalist censorship and obscured by propaganda of the opposing sides, the Battle of the Huai-Hai would attract little notice abroad. During the climactic phase, I was the lone Western reporter with the Communist forces on a remote battlefield of the vast engagement and for a time their prisoner.

The Battle of the Huai-Hai, upon which the fate of Nanking and Shanghai would turn, pivoted on Hsuchow, a city of 300,000 in population, 175 miles north of Nanking, on the vast Huaipei Plain. The battle, involving more than a million troops, historically took its name from the Huai River, which flowed some 100 miles north of Nanking. Chinese historians would later compare the battle with Gettysburg, the decisive campaign of the American Civil War.

On October 11, Mao Zedong issued to his generals the field order which heralded the start of an offensive on the Nationalist-held Hsuchow salient. "You are to complete the campaign in two months, November and December. Rest and consolidate your forces in January . . . by autumn your main force will probably be fighting to cross the Yangtze to liberate Nanking and Shanghai." To coordinate the vast operations Mao created a General Front Committee headed by Deng Xiaoping, later to become the paramount leader of China, then serving as trusted political commissar whose role was to ensure the loyalty of the troops. Mao's field order contained detailed instructions to his commanders for the array of their divisions. To the battle Mao committed his Eastern China Field Army of some 420,000 troops commanded by Chen Yi, who was based in nearby Shantung Province. Chen Yi's forces had been freed for the Huai-Hai campaign the previous month with his seizure of Tsinan, the capital of Shantung Province. Tsinan fell on September 24 after eight days of continuous fighting when the Nationalist Eighty-fourth Division, under General Wu Hua-wen, guarding the western

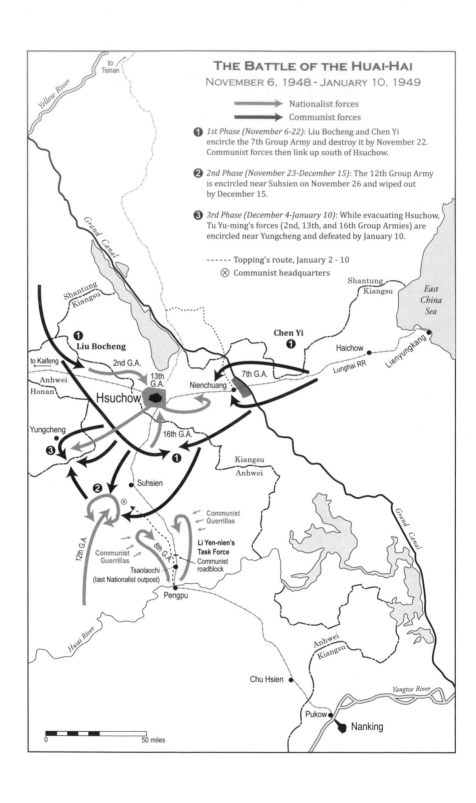

THE BATTLE OF THE HUAI-HAI
NOVEMBER 6, 1948 - JANUARY 10, 1949

→ Nationalist forces
→ Communist forces

1 *1st Phase (November 6-22):* Liu Bocheng and Chen Yi encircle the 7th Group Army and destroy it by November 22. Communist forces then link up south of Hsuchow.

2 *2nd Phase (November 23-December 15):* The 12th Group Army is encircled near Suhsien on November 26 and wiped out by December 15.

3 *3rd Phase (December 4-January 10):* While evacuating Hsuchow, Tu Yu-ming's forces (2nd, 13th, and 16th Group Armies) are encircled near Yungcheng and defeated by January 10.

------ Topping's route, January 2 - 10
⊗ Communist headquarters

to Tsinan

Yellow River

Grand Canal

Shantung
Kiangsu

1 Liu Bocheng

to Kaifeng

Anhwei
Honan

2nd G.A.

13th G.A.

Hsuchow

Nienchuang

Yungcheng

3

16th G.A.

1

Suhsien

2

⊗

12th G.A.

Communist
Guerrillas

8th G.A.

Tsaolaochi
(last Nationalist outpost)

Pengpu

Hwai River

Shantung
Kiangsu

Chen Yi
1

Haichow

Lunghai RR

Lienyungkang

East
China
Sea

7th G.A.

Kiangsu
Anhwei

← Communist
← Guerrillas

**Li Yen-nien's
Task Force**

Communist
roadblock

Grand Canal

Anhwei
Kiangsu

Chu Hsien

Yangtze River

Pukow

Nanking

0   50 miles

sector, defected, opening a gap that allowed a tank-led Communist column to penetrate the city walls and overwhelm the 110,000 troops of the defending garrison. Prior to the Communist attack, determining that Tsinan was indefensible, General Barr had advised Chiang Kai-shek without success to withdraw its garrison into Hsuchow.

The other major prong of the Communist offensive was to be the Central Plains Field Army of 130,000 troops, commanded by Liu Bocheng, the famous "One-Eyed Dragon." For the Battle of the Huai-Hai, the armies of Chen Yi and Liu Bocheng were better armed than in past campaigns, having received Japanese arms made available by the Russians in Manchuria as well as American equipment captured from the Nationalist armies there by Lin Biao. For the first time the Communists deployed a special tank column, which included American-made Sherman tanks captured from the Nationalists and Japanese light tanks turned over to them by the Russians. Initially, while learning to operate the tanks, the Communists pressed captured Japanese and Nationalist tank crews into service.

As the Communist armies trained and grouped for the attack, Chiang Kai-shek met with his generals on November 4 to 6 to plan the defense strategy. His senior military commanders pressed for the withdrawal of troops from the Hsuchow salient to a defense line south of the Huai River. American advisers were of the same view. Chiang initially offered command of his troops for the impending battle to General Pai Chung-hsi, the Central China commander, widely regarded as the ablest of the Nationalist generals. When Pai insisted with other generals on a defense line along the Huai River, Chiang decided that he would direct overall operations himself from the Ministry of National Defense in Nanking. He gave field command to Liu Chih, regarded by many military observers as a very weak general pliant to Chiang's every wish, and as deputy appointed Tu Yu-ming, one of the generals held responsible for the Nationalist debacle in Manchuria. On November 25, as General Barr received intelligence on the concentrations of the Communist armies, he became alarmed. He urged the Generalissimo to withdraw the Nationalist divisions holding the exposed Hsuchow salient to a new defense line farther south. Chiang demurred and made the fateful decision to confront the Communists armies on the Huaipei Plain. With his unopposed air force and American-equipped and -trained divisions, he gambled that his forces could trap and destroy the advancing Communists columns. To engage the Communist armies, Chiang arrayed more than half a million of his troops in six army groups north of the Huai River, hinging their defense line on the Hsuchow salient.

On November 25, I flew with other foreign correspondents on a Nationalist Air Force C-47 transport to Hsuchow. Our pilot was Lieutenant Joseph Chen, who was to become a Nationalist hero on Taiwan in 1958 when, leading a squadron of U.S.-supplied F-86 Sabres, he would shoot down a Communist MIG with a Sidewinder missile in a dogfight over the Taiwan Straits. Our transport circled over the Huaipei battlefield just after the Communists, employing their classic encirclement tactics, reaped their initial success. Attacking on a broad front, the armies of Chen Yi and Liu Bocheng pinned down the Nationalist divisions, commanded by General Liu Chih, which were strung out in fixed positions to the east and west of Hsuchow. One of Chen Yi's fast-moving columns then snapped a pincer around the town of Nienchuang, thirty miles east of Hsuchow, which was garrisoned by ten Nationalist divisions of the Seventh Army Group under the command of General Huang Pai-tao. A Nationalist armored column commanded by the Generalissimo's son, Colonel Chiang Wei-kuo, dispatched from Hsuchow to the relief of besieged Nienchuang, was blocked and immobilized by Chen Yi's troops twelve miles west of the town. The Communists broke into Nienchuang after two of Huang Pai-tao's generals defected to the Communists with three divisions. Huang committed suicide, and only about 3,000 of his 90,000 troops managed to break through the Communist encirclement to the protection of the Nationalist armored relief column. From our transport, circling before landing on an airfield within the Hsuchow perimeter, I looked down on the smoking ruins of Nienchuang. Corpses and abandoned equipment lay throughout a network of trenches radiating from the edge of an outer moat. The Communist tank-led assault had penetrated two brick and mud concentric walls and moats in overrunning the town. Sorties flown in support of the defenders by Nationalist bombers and fighters failed to beat back the attackers.

We circled over Hsuchow to learn whether the airfield was secure before landing there. The city was laid out in a hilly region on the shores of the large Dragon Cloud Lake. Strategically located, it had been the site of many great battles fought during its 2,500-year history. It was a city revered for its rich cultural heritage dating from the Han dynasty (202 B.C.–A.D. 220). But savoring its culture by visiting the nearby imperial Han tombs was not our interest when we landed in the Communist-besieged city whose defense perimeter was being raked with artillery fire. The city was totally disheveled, its rows of dilapidated two-story buildings jammed with refugees, the hospitals filled with untended wounded, the airfield crowded with panicky civilians mobbing and bribing pilots to be given seats on outgoing transports.

At the Nationalist headquarters, our party of correspondents was loaded into a truck and driven over the rutted roads to the perimeter as artillery shells fired by Nationalist batteries whined overhead, targeted on the Communist forces in the outskirts. We were taken to a perimeter village where a Communist thrust had been repulsed nearby during the night. The bodies of some twenty Communist soldiers lay in a field. The bodies, lashed behind ponies and the bumpers of trucks, had been dragged in from the outlying Nationalist entrenchments. In their yellow padded tunics and leg wrappings, the dead men, their features gray and frozen, looked no different from the Nationalist soldiers gathered about us. Some of them had been shot in the back of their heads. When Henry Lieberman, the correspondent for the *Times,* asked about these executions, a Nationalist officer only shrugged. There were no adequate medical facilities for the Nationalist wounded, certainly not for Communists found on the battlefield.

The next day, we left Hsuchow bound for Shanghai on one of General Claire Chennault's Civil Air Transport planes that was loaded with wounded Nationalist soldiers.* As we were leaving Hsuchow, as I would be told subsequently, Chen Yi's columns were racing southwest from conquered Nienchuang to join with the troops of Liu Bocheng in executing an encirclement of the Nationalist Twelfth Army Group, commanded by General Huang Wei. The Nationalist group, composed of eleven divisions and a mechanized column, totaling about 110,000 men, had been ordered up from Hankow in the southwest to cover the withdrawal of the Hsuchow garrison. Chiang Kai-shek, recognizing belatedly the untenable position of the Hsuchow garrison, had ordered its retreat to the cover of the Huai River line, the strategy proposed to him initially by his general staff and American advisers, which he had earlier rejected. Anticipating the maneuver, the Communists threw a blocking force of about 250,000 troops across the line of retreat to the south. Chiang then ordered the Hsuchow garrison to break out and go to the relief of Huang Wei's Twelfth Army Group, which had been encircled sixty-five miles to the southwest. Short of food and munitions, which were being supplied by air, the Twelfth Army Group was being decimated by a ring of Communist artillery. Responding to Chiang's order, the Sixteenth Army Group, which had been holding the southern sector of the Hsuchow perim-

---

*Claire L. Chennault, following his retirement in 1937 from the U.S. Army, went to China, where he formed the volunteer Flying Tigers for operations in support of Chiang Kai-shek in the war against Japanese invaders. During World War II, the general commanded the U.S. Fourteenth Air Force based in Kunming. At the end of the war, he founded CAT, a commercial airline, whose planes were leased in the Civil War to the Nationalist forces.

eter, moved out on November 27 but was quickly enveloped by the Communists and surrendered after six of its regiments defected. In the engagement
some 30,000 troops of the Sixteenth Army Group were killed or captured.
The commander, General Sun Yuan-liang, escaped dressed as a beggar.

The following day, with his forces disintegrating, the Nationalist commander in chief, General Liu Chih, flew out of Hsuchow to the safety of
Pengpu, a rail town on the southern bank of the Huai River. This was only
four days after he told me and other correspondents in our briefing in Hsuchow that he would never surrender the city. He took with him the Generalissimo's son, who turned over the command of the Armored Corps to his
deputy. Two days after their flight, Liu Chih's deputy, General Tu Yu-ming,
carried through the evacuation of Hsuchow. Huge gasoline and munitions
dumps around the city were blown up, sending up clouds of smoke hundreds of feet into the air. Outside the city, Tu formed up the remnants of
the Hsuchow force, which included the Armored Corps and the Thirteenth
and Second Army groups, into a column of some 250,000, including about
130,000 combat effectives. The column then moved south slowly, weighed
down by heavy equipment. It was made up of the combat effectives, thousands of lightly armed service troops, as well as families of army officers,
local officials, and students. The troops, buffeted by the sharp, cold winds of
the approaching winter, marched across the desolate plain alongside American six-by-six wheeled trucks, halting at times to fight off repeated Communist guerrilla attacks on their flanks.

Having taken Hsuchow on December 1, the Communist armies of Liu
Bocheng and Chen Yi pursued and struck the flanks of the retreating Hsuchow garrison, bringing it to a halt sixty miles from the city. In desperation,
Tu Yu-ming, the Nationalist commander, circled the huge column into a defense perimeter northwest of the town of Yungcheng, about a hundred miles
north of Pengpu, the safe haven on the Huai River to which he had hoped
to escape. Trucks were emplaced along the outer rim of the perimeter, and
the troops dug trenches behind them in the ice-crusted soil. The Armored
Corps and artillery were sited at the center of the perimeter to lay down protective fire. Within the perimeter, pelted by freezing rain and snow, the civilians who had accompanied the column huddled in improvised shelters in an
abandoned village. In desperation, Tu Yu-ming radioed the Generalissimo
begging for a relief column that would enable his troops to break out of the
encirclement.

Upon arrival from Hsuchow at Shanghai's Longhua Military Airport, I
became witness to another sort of mass flight. In anticipation of an imminent

Communist assault on the coastal metropolis, a civilian exodus had begun. Chinese who could afford the huge ticket prices were flying out on foreign-owned commercial airliners. Along the wharves of the Whampoa River opposite the towering buildings of the Bund, housing the great trading companies, foreign banks, and the swank Cathay Hotel, all manner of small ships were taking on passengers bound for Taiwan, Hong Kong, and the southern ports. The U.S. Navy transport *Banfield* was lying nearby with several hundred marines aboard to aid Americans if evacuation was ordered. But at that moment most of the 100,000 foreign residents seemed somewhat less inclined than the Chinese to leave Shanghai, reluctant to forsake the easy life they had enjoyed there. At the Shanghai Club, which boasted the longest bar in the world, and at the American and Diamond bars, I spoke to British, French, and American residents, many of them women, who were ignoring warnings of their consulates to leave if they had no compelling reason to stay on. British traders, like those of Jardine Matheson, were least ready to abandon their lucrative business. The American-owned *Shanghai Evening Post and Mercury* carried a speech by the British consul general, Robert Urquhart, in which he told businesspeople meeting at the Country Club on Bubbling Well Road: "Shanghai is home to us as a community, not merely a trading post, and we are not going to up and leave our community home at the first signs of an approaching storm. Does anyone suggest that if there is a change of government here, the new one will be so unreasonable that they will make civilized life and normal trading impossible? I have great confidence that the government of China will not fall into the hands of any but responsible men, who will have the interests of their country at heart. And we foreigners ask for nothing more."

The British consul general was thus keeping the colonial "stiff upper lip" despite daily signs that the metropolis of 6 million was becoming unmanageable. Overrun with desperate, starving refugees, the streets were in chaos despite the presence of thousands of troops striving to enforce martial law. The economy was disintegrating. On November 1, General Chiang Ching-kuo, one of the Generalissimo's sons, who had been put in charge of maintaining order, had resigned his post, declaring indignantly that the city had fallen into the toils of "unscrupulous merchants, bureaucrats, politicians and racketeers." In August, in events leading up to his resignation, Chiang had issued draconian economic reform decrees to curb currency speculation, hoarding, and black marketing. He had sternly enforced the regulations, executing some of the offenders on the streets as crowds looked on. But when his measures began to restrict the speculative business life of the city, Chiang encountered opposition from local titans. The general had the support of K. C. Wu, the ebullient, courageous mayor of Shanghai. But he ran afoul of Tu Yueh-sheng, the notorious leader of the underworld, a member of the Green Gang secret society, who was known to have political ties to Chiang Kai-shek. The irrepressible Chiang Ching-kuo also crossed his stepmother, Madame Chiang Kai-sheck. His agents discovered a huge hoard of prohibited goods in the warehouses of the Yangtze Development Corporation, controlled by H. H. Kung, the banker husband of Madame Chiang's elder sister. Chiang's agents raided the warehouses and threatened to arrest David Kung, the banker's son, who was in charge of the cache. Madame Chiang flew to Shanghai, and soon after, David Kung left for the United States, fleeing any reprisal in the scandal. Restraints on prices and wages were scrapped under the pressure of the local overlords the day before Chiang Ching-kuo resigned. The value of the currency plummeted thereafter. In a stunt to stabilize the currency, the Bank of China proclaimed it would sell 40 grams of gold to each applicant at the fixed price of 3,800 yuan an ounce. Some 30,000 people, frantic to exchange their paper currency before it became worthless, rushed to line up before the bank. Ten suffocated in the mad crush. The exchange offer turned out to be only a token gesture, since the bank's gold reserves had already been earmarked for transfer to Taiwan on Chiang Kai-shek's personal order.

In Shanghai, I filed my Hsuchow dispatches at the AP office and billeted at the Foreign Correspondents Club. The club occupied the top three floors of the Broadway Mansions, a high-rise hotel linked to the Bund by a bridge over Soochow Creek, a polluted waterway to the Whampoa River crowded with native sampans. Many of the club bedrooms were standing empty, since correspondents had begun to evacuate the city, not willing to risk being trapped in a Communist takeover. I met there with Fred Hampson, the indomitable AP bureau chief for China, who had decided to remain in Shanghai through what seemed to be the inevitable Communist occupation. Over drinks in the empty bar, I found Hampson preoccupied by how he could post a correspondent with the advancing Communist armies. At the time, there were no independent Western correspondents reporting from the Communist side. As he spoke of his frustration, Hampson dangled before me the irresistible bait of fame. I left him wondering how I could become that famous correspondent.

On my return to Nanking, I went to Harold Milks with a plan that I began to concoct on the plane, which I thought would get me back to the front and posted with the Communist forces. Tu Yu-ming's encircled Hsuchow garrison column seemed destined for annihilation, and I foresaw a quick advance thereafter by the Communists on Pengpu, the principal town on the Huai River. I knew that there was in Pengpu an Italian Jesuit mission. My plan was to enter the mission, wait there until the Communists occupied the town, then emerge and ask the Communists to allow me to cover their advance on to Nanking and Shanghai. I envisioned myself as the sole Western reporter covering the advancing Communist troops, filing dispatches over their broadcast radio for pickup by the AP monitor in San Francisco. I also thought of seeking an interview with Mao Zedong. Recalling the friendly reception given me by the Communist leadership in Yenan in 1946, I thought I would find the Communists amenable. Milks, a seasoned midwestern newsman, listened with a trace of skepticism but nevertheless agreed. I confided also in Audrey's father, Chester Ronning, who provided me with sage survival advice and a sack of Chinese silver dollars, acceptable currency in the Communist-held areas.

On December 12, 1949, Milks drove me in his jeep to Pukow, the terminus on the Yangtze River of the rail link to Pengpu and Hsuchow. Troop trains were arriving from the north packed with wounded soldiers and thousands of refugees. The trains were so overcrowded that some refugees came into the station clinging to the iron cowcatchers at the front of the steaming locomotives. Despite the freezing December wind, women dressed in ragged tunics over trousers, with babies on backs, sat on top of the train, beside their men folk clutching bundles of their remaining worldly possessions. One old bearded man hanging out of a vestibule was holding a straw cage filled with quacking white ducks.

Grinning soldiers in a crowded boxcar of one of the few trains going north, responding to my entreaties voiced in my poorly accented Chinese, hauled me aboard, and I found a place among them propped up against a sack of rice. The rice sacks, the soldiers told me with provocative leers, were stashed along the sides of the boxcar to afford some protection from the gunfire of Communist guerrillas who waited in ambush along the tracks. As the train jolted out of Pukow and rattled north, I peered out through a door left ajar and saw bodies of men, women, and children, looking like crumpled rag dolls, lying at the side of the tracks. Hands made numb by the intense cold, unable to hold on as they rode atop the moving trains coming from the north, they had toppled down. In the evening I gladly accepted a

bowl of cold rice sprinkled with piquant sauce offered to me by a young officer. Wrapping myself in a blanket, I spent the night half awake, suffering
the stench of unwashed bodies lying close together, staring into the darkness as the train jostled from stop to stop past flood-lit army blockhouses,
and beginning to wonder if I had been too adventurous.

At dawn we were in Pengpu, a rude market town with a population of
about 250,000 which traded the grain crops and livestock of Anhwei Province. Hoisting up my duffel, I jumped out of the boxcar into a frantic mob
struggling to get on the train, which was to return south. Women were carrying or pushing frightened children into the boxcars or climbing up the
side of the train to tie them to whatever metal protrusion they found on top.
I followed the soldiers, who opened a path through the crowds with swinging
rifle butts, to the small dingy station. There I found a rickshaw pulled by a
young coolie who took me at a trot over muddied streets to the walled compound of the Sacred Heart Jesuit Mission, a cluster of about twenty buildings around a redbrick Gothic church. As I paid the rickshaw puller, I asked
him if he feared the coming of the Communists. "No." he replied. "It will be
better. When the fighting stops, the rice will be cheaper."

Welcomed by a priest into the Catholic mission, I was received by Bishop
Cipriano Cassini, a kind, portly Italian in his fifties with a trim gray beard
who wore a black skullcap and a large crucifix over a long black gown that
swept the stone floor. His mission operated schools for the education of some
ten thousand Chinese boys, a nunnery, an orphanage for abandoned infant
girls, and a hospital. Cassini, who had come to China sixteen years earlier,
had been appointed bishop by the Vatican in 1936. He spoke Italian, French,
Chinese, and a few words of English, and we carried on our conversation in
fragments of several languages. Over strong black coffee, he listened sympathetically to my plan and told me: "You are welcome to share our bread and
shelter." He readily agreed to allow me to stay in the mission, not manifesting any concern that harboring an American might someday invite Communist retaliation.

In the afternoon, I called on General Liu Chih, the Nationalist commander in chief, who had fled Hsuchow on November 28. I found him in a
villa vacated by a wealthy rice merchant. The general, fleshy in a plain uniform, flashed a gold-toothed smile as he welcomed me into his map room,
heated by a coal brazier. "We are closing a trap on Chen Yi and Liu Bocheng," he said, pointing to his situation wall map. He had sent his Sixth
Army Group, commanded by General Li Yen-nien, and the Eighth Army
Group, under General Liu Ju-ming, a total force of eleven divisions, north

from the Huai River line with orders to smash the Communist columns against the anvil, as his interpreter described it, of the encircled Nationalist Twelfth Army Group, commanded by General Huang Wei. The Twelfth was trapped forty-five miles northwest of Pengpu. I left Liu Chih's headquarters less than convinced.

Two days later, on December 15, his troops decimated by Communist artillery, and after one of his twelve infantry divisions had defected, General Huang surrendered the remnants of his Twelfth Army Group. His forces compressed into a four-mile-square area, he had held out for almost three weeks. He was taken prisoner with his deputy commander, Wu Shao-chou. The next day, Liu Chih's Sixth and Eighth armies, which had advanced only seventeen miles, came under attack by Liu Bocheng's columns and turned back to Pengpu harassed by local Communist militia. Standing on the banks on the Huai River, I watched their tanks and truck convoys rattle back over the railway bridge, followed by long lines of weary infantry. One of the last trains arriving from the north brought a company of light tanks on flat cars which were sent south to a new defense line that was being prepared.

On December 16, I was told at the garrison headquarters that Tu Yu-ming's Hsuchow column was still holding out, awaiting help from the south. The following day, the Communist radio carried a message from Mao Ze-dong addressed to Tu Yu-ming: "You are at the end of your rope. For more than ten days, you have been surrounded ring on ring and received blow upon blow, and your position has shrunk greatly. You have such a tiny place and so many people crowded together that a single shell from us can kill many of you. Your wounded soldiers and the families who have followed the Army are complaining to high heaven. Your soldiers and many of your officers have no stomach for more fighting. Hold dear the lives of your subordinates and families and find a way out for them as soon as possible. Stop sending them to a senseless death." Tu Yu-ming did not reply.

On the morning of December 18, in the Sacred Heart Church, I watched more than a hundred Chinese children chanting hymns, kneeling to be baptized. Above them, in the sandbagged steeple, soldiers at the lookout post listened to the rites conducted by a Chinese Catholic nun. That afternoon, the people of Pengpu, observing that demolition charges were being placed under the 1,823-foot, nine-span bridge across the Huai River, gathered before the garrison headquarters to protest its destruction. The bridge, erected forty years earlier, had served to transform Pengpu from a mud village into a bustling commercial center by attracting trade from the countryside. When a garrison spokesman emerged to tell the townspeople that the bridge might have to be blown to hinder a Communist crossing, there were shouted protests. I heard one man call out that the bridge belonged neither to the Nationalists or the Communists but to the people. They knew how difficult it would be to repair the structure. They spoke of that day in January 1938 during the war with Japan when Chinese troops blew up the bridge to impede the advance of Japanese troops. It took the Japanese eight months to repair the bridge. The Pengpu garrison did not blow up the bridge, but the troops began on December 27 removing sections of the bridge for shipment south to Pukow, making it impassable to truck and rail traffic.

On Christmas Eve, I spoke to Harold Milks on the single telephone line out of Pengpu, dictated my dispatch, and told him if the Communists did not come soon, I would try to reach their lines by crossing to the other side of the Huai River. That night, Milks sent a brief dispatch describing me as "the loneliest Associated Press staff member in the whole world this Christmas eve." By wondrous chance, Audrey read the dispatch in Vancouver, where she was attending the University of British Columbia. Strolling with a friend along a Vancouver avenue, she saw a rain-sodden newspaper lying on the sidewalk with a large headline about the China Civil War. Picking it up, she spotted the box, written by Milks, at the bottom of the front page describing my lonely Christmas vigil in Pengpu.

In fact, I was not all that lonely. That afternoon at the railway station I ran into three newly arrived British newsmen. They were Patrick O' Donovan of the *Observer,* Bill Sydney of the *Daily Express,* and Lachie MacDonald of the *Daily Mail.* To welcome them suitably I shopped at a Chinese provision store and was delighted to find a bottle of Johnny Walker Black Label Scotch, for which I paid the equivalent of twenty dollars. In a bedroom of the mission, portraits of the saints looking down on us, I doled out the scotch into tea mugs. With cheers we downed the precious drink and then in unison spat on the flagstones. I had been taken. The bottle had been filled with stale tea and resealed. We managed, nevertheless, a Christmas drink with a bottle of Italian red wine contributed by an obliging priest. I accompanied O'Donovan, a burley Irish Catholic man, to midnight Christmas mass, during which he knelt in prayer beside Chinese worshipers and received the sacrament from the bishop. The unheated church was draped in festive red cloth and crowded with about two hundred worshipers, mostly Chinese, who came carrying bedding, since they intended to stay the night. The town was under curfew, and edgy sentries were patrolling the snow-covered streets. Before the altar an Italian priest set up a large book of Christmas music, verses rendered in

Chinese characters, and led the congregation in singing "Adeste Fideles." Christmas dawned to the sound of random shooting in the town.

On Christmas Day, Liu Chih sent a message urging us to leave Pengpu aboard his train. The Huai River line was not to be defended, and he was moving his headquarters south. My companions of the night decided to depart with him, and I went to the railway station to say good-bye. I watched them leave on an armored train with tank turrets affixed atop the cars, the locomotive pushing an open steel-plated car manned by machine gunners. I *then* felt very alone.

Growing impatient, I decided on New Year's Day to cross the Huai River and hike north to the Communist outposts. After being told twice by the garrison commander that I could not cross the river, I managed to negotiate a pass from a Nationalist officer who was beyond caring about the activities of a crazy American. A priest found two railway workers, eager to return to their homes north of the river, who agreed to carry my baggage. Dressed in a U.S. Army pile jacket and a brown wool hat, I set out on the morning of January 2 followed by the railway men bearing my duffel between them on a yo-stick, the quintessential bamboo pole. At the railroad bridge, an army lieutenant checked my papers, looked me over curiously, and then escorted us on the pedestrian walk across the span to the last outpost at Tsaolaochi, ten miles north of Pengpu. Beyond, he warned, lay no-man's-land, ruled by bandits who preyed on travelers. Unarmed, we would be vulnerable until we reached the first Communist outpost. North of that outpost, the Communists were in control of all the Huaipei Plain except for the flaming perimeter held by the Hsuchow column, ninety miles to the northwest of Tsaolaochi.

As we began walking along the abandoned Pukow Railroad, Nationalist Air Force planes droned overhead on the way to drop supplies to Tu Yuming's troops or strike at the encircling Communists. About five miles out of Tsaolaochi, we saw a barrier across the road controlled by men with guns. A peasant coming from the barrier mumbled something about "bad men." Bandits, I thought apprehensively. The armed men had seen us, and so it was too late to turn back. There were four of them in peasant dress. A sharp-faced man, oddly wearing a crumpled gray fedora, pointed an American Thompson submachine gun at me. When I asked him in Chinese, "Who are you?" he shouted back, "Who are you?" and thrust his gun at me. "I am an American correspondent," I said. He did not seem to understand and angrily shouted again: "Who are you?" He slipped the safety catch on the Tommy gun, and, as if in a trance, I watched his fingers wrap around the trigger. One of my baggage carriers cried out, "He is an American correspondent." The sharp-faced one lowered the gun and searched us for weapons. Suddenly, two soldiers in uniform stood up about 150 yards from the barrier. They had been covering the roadblock with a machine gun. We were in the hands of Communist militia. I showed a letter written in Chinese to one of the uniformed militiamen. It identified me and asked clearance to proceed to the headquarters of Mao Zedong for an interview. I also showed him a photograph taken of me posing with Liu Shaoqi, Zhu De, and other Communist leaders at the dinner in Yenan. The militiaman, a broad-faced peasant with a pistol strapped around his waist, looked blankly at the photo and the letter and shrugged.

Escorted by a half dozen militia riflemen, I was taken with the railroad men on a long march to a village where the militia headquarters was located. It was the area in which Nationalist general Liu Chih's Sixth and Eighth Army groups had come under attack by the militia during their futile effort to reach the encircled Twelfth Army Group. Decomposed bodies of soldiers still lay in the fields or in slit trenches and foxholes picked at by village dogs and flocks of cawing ravens. Peasants were fashioning mud bricks to rebuild walls and thatch roofs on houses smashed by artillery fire. Trees, once carefully husbanded near each cluster of huts, had been cut down during the fighting to clear fields of fire. We passed scores of wounded Nationalist soldiers, whom the Communists had released farther north, limping back to their homes in the south.

At the headquarters, the militia chief told me of their victory. Proudly, he thumped his chest with the flat of his hand as he also trumpeted that the peasants of the region now owned the land and the landlords had been dealt with. He spoke of the coming of Communist comrades many months before the Battle of the Huai-Hai. The village, like others on the Huaipei Plain, had slumbered without a dream of change until Communist cadres coming from North China and Shantung Province suddenly appeared. In teams made up of about a half dozen cadres, some of them students, they visited the villages, where they entered into discussions with the peasants about their grievances. Nothing was said about Marxist-Leninist ideology. The cadres heard complaints about corrupt officials and the local landlord gentry who owned about one-fourth of the land. Laws restricting rents to 37.5 percent of the crop tilled by tenants were not being respected, and there were landlords who charged as much as 60 or 70 percent. Some of the gentry, called "Big Trees" by the Communists, behaved as petty despots, their men beating peasants who failed to pay their rents or the usurious interest charged on loans. It was not uncommon for a landlord to take the daughter of a peasant who failed to pay his rent as a slave maid or a concubine. Village officials deferred to the landlord "Big Trees," and there were no restraints imposed by the provincial government as long as taxes were paid. Bolstered by the presence of the newly arrived Communist cadres, the peasants organized violent demonstrations against the ruling gentry. In the village where the Communist militia headquarters was now located, a landlord who owned more than 50 acres was denounced, humiliated at a trial, and stripped of his holdings. At a neighboring village, a landlord accused of killing one of his tenants was stoned to death. The middle peasants who tilled their own soil were left undisturbed, but all large landholdings were seized and distributed by the cadres to poor families, each adult receiving about one-third of an acre. Several weeks after the arrival of the party cadres, the first Communist army units came into the villages. The soldiers paid for their food, unlike the Nationalist troops, who angered the peasants by requisitioning supplies. Peasants were formed into so-called self-defense units. In the fall of 1948, when Chen Yi and Liu Bocheng's columns entered the region to make ready for the Huai-Hai campaign, hundreds of villagers were ready to carry supplies and dig trenches across roads to slow the movement of Nationalist troops. When I asked the local militia leader how his men had been able to do battle against tanks and artillery of Liu Chih's Sixth and Eighth army groups, he said: "These are our fields."

What had transpired in the militia leader's village illustrated how the Communists gained mass peasant support in many regions of the country. The indifference of the Chiang Kai-shek government to the plight of the poorer peasants provided fertile ground for Communist inroads. In June 1946 the Nationalist government had reintroduced a land tax, which was so indiscriminately administered that it aroused anger and despair among the poorer peasants. To support its military operations, the government also increased requisitions of grain despite warnings by provincial authorities that peasants in desperation were being driven to uprisings, banditry, and flight to the towns and cities. Belatedly, only when the Communists were on the brink of victory did the Nationalist government begin to seriously consider land redistribution programs designed to attract peasant support, but only token efforts were made.

During the Civil War the Communist land reform policies fluctuated with the tides of battle and were not implemented in either a uniform or orderly manner, particularly in the treatment of the landlords and the middle peasants. In travels to regions other than the Huaipei Plain, I spoke to Chinese who had experienced rampant terror, especially in Hopei and Shan-tung provinces after the issuance of the May 1946 decree by the Communist Politburo on land redistribution. Hundreds of thousands of landlords and at times also middle peasants were denounced, deprived of their land and goods, and many were stoned or beaten to death in the mass "speak bitter-ness" struggle sessions. The peasants were incited by party cadres of "left-ist tendency" who did not heed the more moderate policies instituted later, which granted landlords not convicted of "crimes against the people" the right to retain land on the scale of the average holdings and guaranteed pro-tection to middle peasants who tilled their own fields. In instances in which Nationalist troops reoccupied areas where the Communists had carried out land redistribution, the returning landlord "Big Trees" often wreaked the most brutal vengeance on peasants who had supported the Communists.

In later years, recalling the passion of the militia leader in the Huaipei village, I wondered whether the peasants who had rallied to the Commu-nists felt cheated when Mao collectivized their independent landholdings in 1952 and in 1958 herded them into giant People's Communes. Two years after Mao's death in 1976, the communes were completely dismantled. Under Deng Xiaoping, who had become China's paramount leader, peasants were given plots of land on thirty-year leases to farm in a relatively free market economy. Millions of peasants were lifted out of absolute poverty. But then the Huaipei militia leader would be shocked to know that, following Deng Xiaoping's reforms in the early years of the twenty-first century, Communist police would be beating and incarcerating peasants who were taking part in thousands of rural demonstrations protesting their exploitation by corrupt local officials, arbitrary seizure by developers of their allocated land, and in-dustrial pollution of their environment.

––––––––––––

My first night in the "Liberated Areas" was spent at the militia headquarters in a mud-walled shed, where I stretched out on sacks of *kaoliang* (sorghum) grain. With rats scampering about, I pulled my wool knit hat down over my chin and during the night endured several rodents treading across my cov-ered face. I was glad to see the morning and the militiaman who brought a feast of fresh hen's eggs, steaming hot brown *kaoliang* bread, and tea.

We marched north all the next day but stopped, at my request, at the vil-lage of Chungchou, where there was a Farmer's Bank, where I exchanged one of the silver dollars given to me by Ronning for 200 yuan of the Communist-issued currency. At sundown we came into a village where I was greeted by the commander of a unit of General Liu Bocheng's columns. It was my first contact on the Huaipei Plain with a regular army unit. The commander, who wore no badge of rank or unit identification, was a lean, powerfully built man with a friendly, compassionate manner about him. "We will escort you to Suhsien," he said. "You will go by horse tomorrow." He released the railway men who had accompanied me, telling them they could go wherever they liked.

The next morning, on horses led by one mounted rifleman and with another militiaman leading a horse laden with my baggage, we rode out of the village, passing through a cluster of boys with shaven heads staring wide-eyed at the first "foreign devil" they had ever seen. The commander waved good-bye. I would see him again and come to like him more than anyone else I met on the plain. We rode well away from the railroad so as not to risk being strafed. Nationalist fighters and bombers passed overhead on the way to or returning from the encirclement of Tu Yu-ming's Hsuchow column, seventy miles to the northwest. Each village seemed like the other as our horses picked their way across the monotonous plain, following paths through the fields and along the banks of irrigation ditches. At a village in which we stopped for the night, I shared a hut with my escort and soldiers who played cards and sang at fireside. One of the songs referred to Chiang Kai-shek as "a running dog of the Americans," and with a grin, one of the soldiers asked in a friendly fashion: "Why is Truman helping Chiang?" I simply smiled and shook my head. In the morning I was awaken by soldiers drilling outside the hut and singing: "On to Nanking and strike down Chiang Kai-shek." Speaking later to the soldiers in the campsite, I listened to them repeating the litany of political commissars who promised liberation of their families from ruthless landlords and corrupt Kuomintang village officials. I never heard any references to Marxist-Leninist ideology. At one meeting the common soldiers were being briefed by an officer on the strategy of the campaign. It was this sort of indoctrination by many thousands of political commissars which cemented the loyalty of the sons of peasants serving in the Communist armies. Nothing like it, as far as I knew, was done in the Nationalist forces.

We rode on the next day, and our journey took us through the eastern edge of the battlefield where General Huang Wei's Twelfth Army Group had been destroyed three weeks earlier. The battlefield was deserted and silent, except for the cawing of ravens perched on human body parts. The fields had been cratered by artillery fire. Demolished American-made vehicles, stripped of parts, lay half buried. Huang and thousands of his troops had been marched off to prisoner encampments in long lines. I saw no one mourning or caring for the fallen, their bodies lying in fields illuminated by the golden glow of a setting sun. The shrunken face of one of the dead sprawled beside the road, his body sniffed at by village dogs, haunted me for years. My escort told me that Liu Bocheng and Chen Yi's conquering divisions had marched north to join the encirclement of Tu Yu-ming's forces.

At dusk on January 5, we reached what was apparently the main field Communist headquarters, about ten miles southwest of Suhsien. Artillery fire could be heard from the nearby battlefield where the Hsuchow column was dug in encircled by some 300,000 Communist troops. I was taken first by my escort to a hut where I waited until a man named Wu, addressed as "Deputy Commissar" but dressed like the soldiers in a plain uniform without insignia, arrived and questioned me in Chinese. He was obviously a sophisticated, well-educated man but hard-faced and suspicious. When I tried to engage him with pleasantries, he would tell me nothing about himself except that he was from Hopei Province. "I cannot take responsibility," Wu said, "for allowing you to pass into the Liberated Area. Your case must be referred to my superiors." He left with my letter requesting that I be permitted to proceed to Mao's headquarters for an interview with the Communist leader. I was escorted to another peasant hut with a grain shed, in which I slept restively that night listening to the thud of nearby artillery fire. At dawn, I found myself under the guard of three soldiers, all armed with American carbines. They permitted me to walk out into bright sunshine. Out of a clear sky, a Nationalist fighter swooped down on a strafing run, its machine gun fire stitching across a nearby field. It did not occur to me to duck for cover, nor did it excite my guards, who presented me with a breakfast of duck eggs. All through that day, and into the night, I heard the heavy thudding of artillery fire. Then, at dawn, the guns fell silent. When I tried to leave the hut to learn what was transpiring, one of the guards blocked my way.

In the late morning, Wu entered the hut where I had spent the night and told me firmly: "In regard to your mission we ask you to return. This area is a war zone and it is not convenient for you to proceed." I interjected: "But if it is a question of danger, I don't care." Wu snapped back: "You don't care, but we do care about you passing through here." Shaken, I turned and walked into the grain shed and in frustration beat my fist against the sacks of grain stalks. When composed, I returned to face Wu. I asked if I could proceed via Shantung to Tsingtao, where U.S. Marines were based. He declined. When I asked for an explanation in writing, he shook his head and said: "It is enough that you have asked and we have refused." He said he did not know whether my request for an interview with Mao had been referred directly to the Communist leader. Stung by Wu's hardness, I said bitterly: "You know I came here to tell your side of the story." Wu's features relaxed. "You cannot help us," he said softly and then shaking his head impatiently added firmly: "The horses are outside the door."

In front of the hut there was an escort officer and two soldiers already mounted. Wu returned my typewriter and camera, taken from me when I arrived. As I mounted my horse, Wu came up beside me, put his hand on the saddle, and said gently, speaking in English to me for the first time. "I hope to see you again. Peaceful journey. Good-bye."

As we rode out of the village, there was no sound of gunfire, only an eerie stillness. I said to the escort officer: "Are the Hsuchow troops finished?" "Yes," he replied. "Just about finished." It was January 7. In the next days as we rode back toward the Nationalist lines, the escort officer told me what had taken place within the encirclement and was later detailed on the Communist radio. Tu Yu-ming did not reply to Mao's December 17 message, in which Mao guaranteed life and safety to all if he would surrender. Thereafter, conditions in the Nationalist camp steadily worsened. Airdrops by Nationalist transports made from above two thousand feet could not meet the needs of the thousands of trapped military and civilians. Two-thirds of what was parachuted drifted into the hands of the Communists. Horses were slaughtered for food. Soldiers scrounged for bark and roots in the fields. Lacking fuel for fires, women and children froze to death in crowded huts. Communist loudspeakers along the perimeter offered food and safety to the Nationalist soldiers if they would surrender. Panic spread among the Nationalist troops when word circulated that Chiang Kai-shek might order the bombing of the Armored Corps so the tanks would not fall into Communist hands. Just before the final artillery barrage opened on January 6, the loudspeakers boomed out: "There is no escape." The Second Army Group was the first to surrender, then the Thirteenth, and finally the Armored Corps. By January 10, the Communists had rounded up the last of the fleeing Nationalist soldiers. The Battle of the Huai-Hai ended with the capture of Tu Yu-ming, the commander of the encircled Hsuchow column, who attempted to escape in the uniform of an ordinary Communist soldier. His deputy, Li Mi, managed to escape. I later came upon him in Burma, where he was involved in a secret American Central Intelligence Agency operation. Tu Yu-ming survived as a prisoner and after the Civil War was granted comfortable retirement by the Communists, as were many other Nationalist officers. Lieutenant Colonel

Chen, who piloted the plane that took me to besieged Hsuchow, was permitted to return from Taiwan and resettle in Peking. I encountered him by chance in 2003 at his well-furnished apartment, brought there for drinks by our friend, his American daughter, Rose Chen. "You must be one of the American correspondents I took to Hsuchow," he exclaimed when I entered his Peking apartment, and we embraced.

On the journey back to Pengpu with my soldier escort, we followed the same line of villages. In every village the nights were alive with high-spirited soldiers singing patriotic songs. All seemed to have been briefed on the general strategy of the campaign and the impending assault across the Yangtze. The October 10 statement of Mao Zedong that it would take one more year to completely defeat the Nationalists was widely quoted. In one village, soldiers intensely curious about American technology crowded around when I demonstrated my typewriter and camera. One of them asked about automat restaurants in the United States. "Twenty years after all China is Communist, we shall have automat restaurants," he said. (It was this quote in the stories I wrote about my trek across the Huaipei Plain upon my return to Nanking that seemed to evoke the most interest in the United States.) Thinking of that soldier as I write: If he survived, what fun it would have been to observe his reactions to the present-day skyscrapers of Shanghai.

That first night on my return journey I lay awake in my hut, tossing about, unable to sleep, dejected by the rebuff at the Communist headquarters. Staring into the darkness, the spell of my trek across the Huaipei Plain fading, I began to accept that my venture had been out of time and place. The era of easy mixing of Americans with the Communists such as in Yenan during the days of the Dixie Mission and the Marshall negotiations in Chungking was ended. There would be no more jovial dinners with exchanges of toasts or friendly ideological debates. We were beyond that crossroads. Mao Zedong was bent on his revolutionary course, and he would not be diverted by American influence, or for that matter, by the Russians. When will we talk to each other again? I wondered.

We made seventeen miles the next day, and we were back at the headquarters of the sympathetic commander of one of Liu Bocheng's units. Sitting before a campfire, the commander asked me about the two-party system and the status of blacks in the United States. He told me he had been with the Communist forces since 1936 and had seen his wife and family only once since then. In the morning before I left, the commander wrote on the flyleaf of my diary in fine Chinese characters. "We would like to fight to the end with our American friends for democracy, freedom and happiness." He signed his name Tian Wuzhang without indicating his rank. Another day's journey and we were within five miles of the Huai River Bridge. My escort found two peasants to help with my baggage, and waved good-bye. I approached the Nationalist outpost at the bridge holding up a white handkerchief, and they took me in. I stayed the night in the Jesuit mission, said good-bye to the bishop in sadness, knowing that the Communists in occupation of Pengpu would never tolerate the mission for very long, particularly Jesuit schooling of the children. At the railway station, I forced my way into a boxcar packed with refugees and Nationalist soldiers who had discarded their weapons. On January 12 I was back in Nanking, where for the first time I was able to file to the AP my account of the final phase of the Battle of the Huai-Hai and my journey across the Huaipei Plain. I also reported from Nanking that Nationalist troops had evacuated Pengpu on January 16 after blowing up its railroad bridge, so treasured by the people of Pengpu, and looting the shops. A new defense line was established thirty miles north of Nanking.*

For the Communists, the Huai-Hai campaign lasted sixty-five days in a deployment of swift movement and entrapment of segments of the Nationalist armies. They had suffered 30,000 killed in combat. But in what was the

---

*In October 2008 I relived the Battle of the Huai-Hai. On the invitation of the editors of the *Xuzhou Daily*, I was invited to revisit the battlefield and tour the magnificent museum that had been erected there in commemoration of the Huai-Hai campaign. I was stunned by the appearance of Hsuchow itself (now Xuzhou in Pinyin). In November 1948, I had left a shabby, disordered city of 300,000 enduring artillery shelling by the besieging PLA. Now it was a metropolis of some 1.7 million people with a skyline of high-rise office and apartment buildings. On the tour I was accompanied by Audrey, Professor Li Xiguang, executive dean of Tsinghua University's School of Journalism, my daughter Karen, and my grandson, Torin. We were escorted with ceremony to the Memorial Museum of the Huai-Hai Campaign, a handsome, stone-fronted building opened in 2007. Before it stood a towering gold-colored monument, its base carved with figures of soldiers in combat. In the museum, crowded with Chinese tourists, there were digitalized tableaux of battle scenes and life-size figures of both Communist and Nationalist generals in strategy conferences. Some 20,000 of the 30,000 PLA soldiers killed in the Huai-Hai campaign were memorialized in photographs and digital images. Atop the museum there was a huge revolving depiction of a battle scene on painted canvas that had taken ten painters eight months to complete. I was asked to donate my notebook and copies of my dispatches for an exhibit. In January, on the sixtieth anniversary of the triumphant end of the battle, Chinese Central Television (CCTV), the largest network in the country, showed for six consecutive nights a six-part documentary of the Huai-Hai campaign. One of the episodes was devoted to an interview with me.

most decisive battle of the Civil War, the Communists had achieved total victory over a Nationalist force of roughly their own size but better equipped and in complete control of the air. They succeeded in eliminating fifty-six Nationalist divisions, including some of Chiang Kai-shek's best American-equipped and -trained troops and the Armored Corps, altogether comprising 555,000 men. The Communists took 327,000 prisoners. At least four and a half Nationalist divisions defected to them. The military equipment captured, much of it American, was beyond counting. The battle was the final blow that shattered the Nationalist Army. As I had observed in Manchuria, the Nationalist disaster on the Huaipei Plain stemmed directly from Chiang Kai-shek's strategic miscalculations. Rejecting all advice, he had elected to stand before the vulnerable Hsuchow salient, exposing his armies to piecemeal destruction. In selecting his field commanders, Chiang appointed generals personally loyal to him, rather than the most competent. Defeat became inevitable even before the first shots were fired on the battlefields. The way was now open, as Mao had predicted on October 11, for an attack across the Yangtze on Nanking, Chiang's capital, and Shanghai. It was the turning point of the Civil War.

7

THE JESUITS

In 1971, I was able to contact Padre Mario Francesco, the last of the Pengpu mission's superiors. He was living in Rome, and through Paul Hofmann, the *Times* bureau chief there, I received a letter from him with this account of what happened to Pengpu and the Jesuits after the Communists occupied the town in January 1949:

When the Communists first came, they preached freedom. For the first year, the people kept quiet because they believed them. Then the Communists made everyone sign statements asking if they had cooperated with the old government. Worse, everyone was asked to write his own autobiography many times and answer three terrible questions: One: What do you think of Communism? Two: Give the names of your friends and enemies. Three: What evil deeds have you done to the people? Then there began the wave of denunciations and executions of the so-called "enemies of the people."

The mission did not escape this process. The Communists didn't want to expel the missionaries outright but were determined to find "evidence" of their wrongdoings so that the people would denounce them or they would leave of their own accord. It was a process to try to break down the missionaries, and it was this continual harassment that in the end killed the Bishop. The Communists would come in day and night and ask for the mission's accounts. They had already frozen the mission's money in the banks. They first came to the mission on January 19, 1950, asking for one room, to put their agent in to report everything that went on in the mission. Later they took over the whole second floor of the mission headquarters to house foreign guests, such as a group of Russian engineers who came in to rebuild the bridge which had been blown up by the Nationalists. When there were foreign guests in the building, the priests were confined to their quarters and only allowed out for a short time when it was certain that they would not meet with other foreigners. Once there was a delegation from the Italian Communist Party—but there were no contacts allowed.

One evening a Chinese priest arrived at the mission by river boat without official permission. The police agent reported his visit and the Bishop had to spend three nights in jail as punishment. Worse, the Bishop was forced to buy an advertisement in the local paper to say he had been wrong to receive a visitor without authorization and that the Communists were good because they had kept him in prison only three days. There was no limit to the charity of the Bishop. When the Communists came, they took everything he had, and when he had nothing more to give, he died. He died in the mission, sitting upright in his room with his breviary in his hands, on June 13, 1951.

Things got worse when the Bishop died. The Communists tried to say that the Bishop had committed suicide, taken too much opium. But the missionaries were able to get a statement from the doctors that he had died of a heart attack. When the Bishop died the Communists closed the church, defaced its facade to make it look like a bank, removed Gothic decorations and turned it into a theater. The priests were forced to move out of their residence and went to the nunnery. The Bishop was buried in an area south of the compound near the seminary. Some 2,000 Chinese Catholics came to his funeral. The Communists asked for their names. It was at this point that the mission decided to burn all its records. At this time, too, the Communists banned baptism, but the priests did not heed this ruling. They opened two new chapels in the nunnery and received more Chinese Catholics than before. When the Communists took over the mission schools, I went to teach in the seminary.

The Communist line to the missionaries was: "We protect the mission, but the people want you to leave." At least 1,000 meetings were held with the people to try to get them to denounce the "foreign dogs." But the people, who had been cared for by the mission hospital and whose sons had gone to their school, steadfastly refused to denounce the missionaries.

Then the Communists tried intimidation. They called in one of the 40 Chinese nurses and told her that her father was to be shot but she could save his life. She was asked to testify that I had done some fault, to give the names of the best Catholics of the mission and admit that there was a section of the Legion of Mary (which to Chinese minds sounded paramilitary) in the mission, which wasn't true. She finally agreed so as to save her father, and was told to bring her photo and not to tell anyone about the police pressure. But she came to me crying and told me everything. I counseled her to tell the police that everything she has said was false—which she did. She was then forced to report to the police daily, but nothing happened to her father.

Finally, the police picked on a former seminary student who had been a soldier in the Nationalist Army and was working at the mission and took pictures of him with me, holding a Latin grammar book and next to a crucifix. To me the police pointed out Article 12 of the Chinese State Constitution that says those who keep traitors must suffer the same punishment as traitors. This was intended to frighten me and make me leave of my own free will. But I only laughed and gave the police my written answer: "If I have gone against Chinese laws, I must do penance in China." The police were very angry. Then they said that if I did not sign a statement saying, "I leave China freely," five Chinese would be put in jail. Only then did I agree to sign, but the five Chinese were put in jail anyway. This happened in January 1953. I was the last of the superiors in the Pengpu Mission.*

---

*The Communist Party took control of the Catholic Church on the mainland in 1957 with the creation of the Chinese Catholic Association. In 2008 the association had an estimated 7 million members. Peking and the Vatican have not had formal relations since 1951, when the papal nuncio was expelled from the mainland in reprisal for the Holy See's recognition of the Taiwan government. On the mainland several million Catholics, who accept the authority of the Vatican rather than the Communist association, worship in underground churches. They have at times been subjected to police harassment.

8

CROSSING OF THE YANGTZE

On my return to Nanking from the Huapei Plain in January 1949, I found the Nationalists and their supporters cowering in despair as they awaited a Communist onslaught. On Christmas Eve, Chiang Kai-shek had attended services at the Song of Victory Church, which his wife established for Christian members of the government. He sang carols in his guttural native Chekiang accent. The next morning he told subordinates he would announce his resignation on Chinese New Year's Day. There was reason enough for him to depart. Nationalist military strength had been reduced to 1.5 million troops, of which 500,000 were service troops, while the Communist armies swelled by Nationalist defections were now estimated by Western analysts at 1.6 million, virtually all combat effectives. In Washington Madame Chiang had found the doors shut when she arrived to plead for additional financial aid to rescue Nationalist China from its runaway inflation. In December 1947, the Truman administration had proposed a $1.5 billion program of aid over four years, but the Congress had reduced it to $338 million when it passed in April 1948. Following the shock of the fall of Mukden, Truman reminded Madame Chiang that the United States had already provided $3.8 billion in aid, much of it military equipment which was now in the hands of the Communists. Dean Acheson, who was shortly to succeed the ailing Marshall as secretary of state, shared the general skepticism and disillusionment with the Generalissimo. After General Barr's experience, there was no interest in Chiang's proposal that American officers, perhaps General Douglas MacArthur or General Mark Clark, join in staff direction of the Nationalist war effort.

On Chinese New Year's Day, the Generalissimo was driven in his Cadillac out of the Great Peace Gate to the Sun Yat-sen Mausoleum on a slope of Purple Mountain. Standing at the foot of the stairs, I watched Chiang, in army uniform, cane in hand, mount the white stone steps to the tomb of the founder of the Chinese Republic. At the entrance, Chiang bowed three times before the white marble statue of the seated Sun Yat-sen. Emerging from the tomb, the Generalissimo paused and looked out over his walled capital for the last time. Then, saluting and nodding to soldiers massed before the tomb, he walked down the steps leaning heavily on his cane, reentered his limousine, and sped back to the Heavenly Palace, where he issued his resignation statement. He named Li Tsung-jen as acting president but in fact did not surrender the key levers of military and financial power. A few days later, on January 22, he flew to Fenghua, his birthplace, a picturesque town in Chekiang Province near the southern coast. Ostensibly, the Generalissimo had retired in Confucian humility to the life of a country squire. In reality, he was feverishly preparing his retreat to Taiwan, one hundred miles off the Fukien coast. While planning to leave Li Tsung-jen behind to face the Communists, Chiang denied him control over the bulk of the armed forces. For military support, Li could count only on General Pai Chung-hsi, the Central China commander, based in Hankow, who commanded 350,000 troops. When Li pleaded for additional resources to defend the Yangtze River line, Chiang rebuffed him. The Generalissimo meanwhile ordered the transfer to Taiwan of the air force, the navy, and the best army divisions, commanded by generals personally loyal to him. American military aid shipments en route were diverted to the island. The government's reserve of gold and silver bullion and other foreign exchange, as well as thousands of ancient art treasures collected from leading museums, were shipped surreptitiously in a convoy of cargo vessels to Taiwan.

To secure the Taiwan redoubt, the Generalissimo clamped tighter military and police control over the restive 8 million Taiwanese. At the end of World War II, the Allied command transferred authority over the island, which had been a Japanese colony for fifty years, to the Chiang government pending conclusion of a peace treaty. The Nationalist troops sent to occupy the island accepted the surrender of the Japanese and then indulged in an orgy of looting. Nationalist officials seized public enterprises and land for their personal use. In protest, the Taiwanese, in February and March 1947, staged public demonstrations demanding that the governor, Ch'en I, who had been appointed by Chiang, immediately take action to restore order and curb corrupt officials in his administration. Ch'en's response to the appeals was to summon additional troops from the mainland to repress the demonstrators. Between 10,000 and 20,000 Taiwanese were massacred, including several thousand of the island's political and cultural elite. Reacting to the shock abroad, Chiang ordered Ch'en I executed in punishment for his excesses, but the Taiwanese population remained hostile to the mainlanders.

As Communist armies regrouped for a crossing of the Yangtze, I became aware of a strange game of secret diplomacy and political intrigue in play, involving the Soviet Embassy in Nanking. The action swirled about the lonely figure of the American ambassador, J. Leighton Stuart.

In November 1948, before leaving for Pengpu, I had called upon Ambassador Stuart in his villa on the edge of the compound housing the embassy chancery. What prompted my request for a talk was a visit to the political section of the chancery, where I was told privately by members of the Political Section that the ambassador was at bitter loggerheads with his embassy's minister-counselor, Lewis Clark. In the sitting room of his villa, over cups of jasmine tea, responding to my delicately put questions, Stuart told me that despite the opposition of his embassy officers he was actively continuing to seek a peace settlement that would bring Mao and Chiang into a coalition government and stop the killing in the Civil War. Stuart spoke more as the missionary he was before his appointment as ambassador than as a functionary obliged to comply with Washington's bidding. The policy he was pursuing was at cross-purposes with the instructions given the embassy by General Marshall, the secretary of state.

In December 1945, when Marshall arrived in China on his mediation mission, he had arranged for Stuart's appointment as ambassador, replacing Patrick Hurley, so as to make use of Stuart's knowledge of the country and personal influence with the Chinese. Stuart, born in China, the son of a Presbyterian minister, was then president of Yenching University, a missionary-supported school on the outskirts of Peking, often referred to as the "Harvard of China." Yenching faculty and students revered the seventy-year-old Stuart, a thin spare man with dark cavernous eyes under heavy eyebrows, as a saintly figure. Appointed ambassador, Stuart worked closely with Marshall in his failed effort to bring about a peace settlement based on a coalition government. Two months after the general's departure from China in January 1947, there was a switch in White House policy that threw Stuart into despair. In the wake of the Communist takeover of government in an internal coup in Czechoslovakia in February 1948, President Truman's pursuit of coalition government in China had become a painful political embarrassment, and the policy was abandoned. Marshall, who had become secretary of state, specifically instructed the Nanking embassy in August to dissuade the Chiang government from seeking a coalition. He told the embassy to impress upon the Nationalists "the pattern of engulfment which has resulted from coalition government in Eastern Europe." Despite these instructions, Stuart continued to explore the possibilities of coalition government, turning at times to the Soviet Embassy, which, as he told me, encouraged him to believe that Russian help in peacemaking might be forthcoming. In October, Marshall virtually reprimanded Stuart, instructing him to tell the Generalissimo that his mediation proposals were his own and did not have the approval of the State Department.

When I spoke to Stuart in November, he was bent on searching for ways to persuade the Generalissimo to retire so that Li Tsung-jen, then vice president, would assume full power and make peace with the Communists. Stuart's only ally in American Embassy circles was Philip Fugh, his longtime Chinese secretary and confidant, whom he regarded as an adopted son. I became friendly with Fugh, a friendship that continued with him and his family for many years. Fugh's influence with the ambassador, who was often operating independently, was deeply resented in the embassy chancery. Lieutenant General Albert C. Wedemeyer, after a visit to China on a presidential fact-finding mission in July 1947, speculated that Fugh was a spy. He retracted the damaging aspersion years later. Fugh was Stuart's principal contact with Li Tsung-jen, the acting president. In early January, Fugh met with Chang Chi-chung, a skillful political intriguer who was Li Tsung-jen's key intermediary in peace negotiations with the Communists and his contacts with the Soviet Embassy. Secretly, Chang had been in touch with Zhou Enlai, with whom he had an old personal tie. Fugh told Stuart that he had been informed by Chang that the Russians were advising the Communists to halt at the Yangtze. The Soviet historian Ledovsky does not believe that Stalin told Mao specifically not to cross the Yangtze but certainly cautioned him against further advances, which might invite American military intervention. Stalin certainly had something to gain by leaving China fragmented. Apart from the concessions he had wrung from Chiang Kai-shek in Manchuria, he was being further tempted by Chang Chi-chung, who traveled to Sinkiang to negotiate an agreement that would have given Moscow special trading rights, bringing the Central Asia province under Soviet influence. Mao would later make reference to Stalin's double-dealing at a secret Central Committee meeting in 1962, saying: "This was in 1945, when Stalin tried to prevent the Chinese Revolution by saying there should not be a civil war and that we must collaborate with Chiang Kai-shek. At that time we did not carry this into effect, and the revolution was victorious. After the victory they again suspected that China would be like Yugoslavia and I would become a Tito."

In seeking Russian assistance for negotiation of a peace settlement, Stuart had directly, and through Chang Chi-chung, contacted the Soviet ambassador, General N. V. Roschin, several times. Some of these contacts, I learned, were not reported to the State Department. Roschin repeatedly expressed

interest in a mediation effort. On January 10, 1949, Stalin sent to Mao a Nationalist memorandum, apparently forwarded to him by Roschin, in which
the Li Tsung-jen government requested Soviet mediation in the Civil War.
Stalin asked Mao for his comment on a reply which he had drafted implying his own interest in a peaceful solution to the Civil War and his concern
about the possibility of American military intervention. Mao was said, according to Chinese archival sources, to have immediately rejected the idea
of Soviet mediation. Nevertheless, Stalin seems to have persisted. On January 23, Li Tsung-jen informed Stuart that he had reached a tentative understanding with Roschin for Russian intercession. The Soviet price was a
pledge that Li would maintain China's strict neutrality in any future international conflict, eliminate American influence from China to the greatest
extent possible, and establish a new basis for effective cooperation between
China and the Soviet Union. When Li asked for Washington approval of this
negotiating approach, the State Department told Stuart to reject the idea as
"incredible."

At this juncture, the Nationalists suffered another military disaster. General Fu Tso-yi, who had become the commander of the Peking-Tientsin defense line in North China, had secretly been in contact with General Lin
Biao, whose troops were closing in on Peking. Seeking to avoid a destructive
Communist assault on the old imperial capital, Fu asked a Yenching University professor to arrange a contrived surrender by Fu that would not allow
Chiang to paint him as a traitor. Lin Biao acceded with a face-saving siege
of the old capital during which the Communists pumped a few 75-mm shells
into the city, mostly duds, so as not to damage its historical monuments, and
a Communist regiment marched in unopposed on January 23. Prior to surrender of the city, the tale is told, which I was never able to confirm, that Lin
Biao decided that it might be necessary to breach the city's thick sixty-foot-
high wall by blasting open the western segment in the ancient Chinese sector
with artillery fire. But before commencing the bombardment, his command
is said to have consulted with a noted archaeologist at Tsinghua University,
which is located just outside Peking, to determine whether any historic land-
marks would be destroyed. The expert replied that valuable Ming architecture would be demolished and suggested a more vacant target area elsewhere
along the wall.

The Generalissimo had violently opposed the surrender, but Li Tsung-
jen, as acting president, was in agreement. Li sent an envoy to meet with the
Communists in Peking, but the envoy, Ho Ssu-yuan, a former mayor of Peking, was kidnapped and killed by the Nationalist secret police. Li was re-

puted to have also been a target for assassination, but he escaped. After the surrender of Peking, Fu Tso-yi was rewarded by Mao with a ministerial position in the new Peking administration. The twenty-five Nationalist divisions under Fu's command were absorbed into Communist armies.

On March 2 the Nationalist cruiser *Chungking,* donated a year earlier by Britain and the pride of the navy, slipped away from its mooring at Shanghai and defected to the Communists. Nationalist bombers found it off the Manchurian port of Hulutao on March 20 and sank it.

Beleaguered on all sides, Li Tsung-jen sent a delegation to Peking on April 1 to negotiate for peace. On its arrival, the Communists handed it an "Agreement on Internal Peace," which stipulated eight conditions tantamount to complete surrender. When Li Tsung-jen received the document in Nanking, the acting president rejected it, asserting that the terms would give the Communists "military control of the entire nation." Chang Chi-chung, the head of the Nationalist delegation, then defected to the Communists.

At midnight April 20 the Communist ultimatum expired, and in an "Order to the Army for the Country-wide Advance," Mao Zedong and Zhu De, the army commander in chief, signaled to their forces that the moment had arrived for the crossing of the Yangtze and the envelopment of Chiang Kai-shek's capital. The order stated: "After the People's Liberation Army has encircled Nanking, we are willing to give the Li Tsung-jen Government at Nanking another opportunity to sign the Agreement on Internal Peace, if that government has not yet fled and dispersed and desires to sign it." On April 22, even as Communist troops embarked on the crossing of the Yangtze, Li Tsung-jen, accompanied by General Ho Ying-chin, the temporary premier of government, and General Pai Chung-hsi, went to Hangchow from Nanking for a conference with the Generalissimo, who had flown there from his Fenghua retreat. Li Tsung-jen pleaded for defense of the south by falling back on his native Kwangsi and Kwangtung. In a joint communiqué the conferees pledged unity and a "fight to the end" with Ho Ying-chin empowered to exercise unified command over the armed forces. But for Chiang the conference was only a delaying tactic. He was intent only on preparing Taiwan as his fortified refuge, where he had already transferred 300,000 troops as well as air and naval units. When the Hangchow conference ended, Li Tsung-jen and Ho Ying-chin boarded a plane for Nanking, not realizing that it was the eve of the fall of their capital.

9

THE FALL OF NANKING

During the night of April 20–21, 1949, Communist troops, jammed aboard thousands of junks, sampans, and motor launches, swarmed across the Yangtze on a 325-mile front to envelop Nanking. They met little resistance from the 350,000 Nationalist troops concentrated in the Shanghai-Nanking region. Chen Yi's Ninth and Tenth armies crossed on the east. Their crossings were facilitated by large-scale Nationalist defections. At the Kiangyin fortress, guarding the Yangtze narrows, about ninety miles downriver midway between Nanking and Shanghai, the Communists succeeded in bribing the commander, General Tai Yung-kwan, who turned his thirty heavy guns on Nationalist river gunboats, preventing them from blocking the Communist crossings. At Nanking, Commodore Lin Tsun defected to the Communists with his naval squadron. Shanghai, some 150 miles downriver on the Yangtze, was left isolated for a later assault by Chen Yi. The Second Field Army, commanded by Liu Bocheng, crossed upriver west of Nanking. In Central China, Lin Biao's Fourth Field Army also breached the Yangtze.

The massive Communist crossing of the Yangtze stunned Americans. Like hundreds of newspapers across the United States, the *Sioux City Journal* of Iowa published my dispatch under a banner headline. The dispatch said: "Chinese Communist troops slashed across the Yangtze today at a point near Nanking and the American Embassy warned Americans to flee the tottering capital while there is still time. The Embassy in telling Americans to consider leaving Nanking raised the possibility that the city may become a battleground. Chinese officials were leaving the city by every plane." The *New York Daily News* published my story in an extra edition under the banner headline "Red Troops Drive across Yangtze."

The crossings led to an unexpected bloody international clash. On the morning of April 20, the British frigate *Amethyst,* proceeding up the Yangtze to Nanking, came under the fire of Communist assault troops who were poised on the mist-covered northern bank waiting for the order to cross the river. The frigate was struck fifty-three times. Of its 183-man crew, 23 were killed and 31 were wounded. The *Amethyst* had been en route to Nanking to relieve the destroyer *Consort* on station there and to furnish protection and provisions to the British Embassy. The *Consort,* coming from Nanking, the cruiser *London,* and the frigate *Black Swan,* racing up from Shanghai to the aid of the *Amethyst,* also came under damaging Communist fire and withdrew to Shanghai without being able to succor the crippled frigate. The *London* suffered 12 men killed and 20 wounded in the Communist shelling. Medical teams traveling overland from Nanking and seaplanes managed to reach the *Amethyst* with help for the wounded. I was on the riverbank as the wounded were landed from small craft and spoke to them. But the vessel itself remained trapped for 101 days because the captain refused to sign a Communist document acknowledging responsibility for "criminally invading Chinese territorial waters." The frigate, which had been immobilized by Communist artillery, escaped under fire on July 30, using a passing Chinese vessel as a screen.

At dawn on the morning of April 23, I was awakened in the Associated Press compound by sounds of explosions on the Nanking riverfront. The previous evening I had stood alone on a quay in the river port illuminated by Nationalist flares listening to the distant thud of artillery fire. Before returning to the AP compound I filed a story saying that the Communists would storm across the river in a matter of hours to seize Nanking. I was alone with the story. Harold Milks, the chief AP correspondent, had left Nanking in March on three months' home leave, convinced the Communists would not take the city before his return. He left the AP compound with its two Chinese servants in my care. The explosions at the river port indicated that the Communists would be crossing there. I clambered into the jeep in the courtyard and drove to Chungshan Road, the city's principal thoroughfare, and headed north toward the river quays. I was startled to find that the Nationalist military checkpoints on Chungshan Road were unmanned. I would soon learn that the Nationalist garrison had abandoned the city and the municipal police had fled with them. The Nationalist Twenty-sixth Army, which had been ordered to reinforce the garrison, never arrived. Thousands of refugees and disheveled Nationalist soldiers were fleeing south on all roads. Many came from north of the Yangtze, which they had crossed in sampans and small boats during the night fleeing Communist artillery barrages. Driving past the city's Northwest and North gates, I saw they were ajar and unguarded. The new railway station, a towering building of glass and white stone, just outside the North Gate had been destroyed evidently by Nationalist demolition teams. The river port was ablaze with torched buildings and exploding fuel dumps. There were no Communist troops as yet in sight.

Pressing my horn and driving as fast as I could to elude fleeing Nationalist soldiers trying to flag me down, I headed back into the city steering through mobs roaming the streets. The palatial residences of Li Tsung-jen, Mayor Teng Chieh, and other Nationalist leaders had been looted. The mayor had tried to escape by car with 300 million yuan snatched from the city treasury but, as reported later in the Chinese press, was beaten up by his bodyguards and left stranded by his chauffeur with his legs broken. (By the next day, the gold yuan was selling at 1.5 million to one U.S. dollar, making the mayor's intended haul worth only $200.) Looters swarming in from the slums of Futse Miao, the old Chinese quarter, were going about their thievery laughing and shouting to each other. From upper floors of the villas, they were hurling sofas, carpets, and bedding to the lawns below, where they were hauled away on peasant carts or on the backs of excited men, women, and children. A grinning Nationalist soldier, who had thrown away his rifle, was making off with a lamp in each hand. An old woman, wearing a ragged black tunic, hobbling on tiny feet bound in the old custom, went off with four elaborately embroidered cushions. Looters had also ransacked the huge Executive Yuan and the Ministry of Communications buildings, stealing away with window sashes and everything else that could be moved.

Making my way through the crowds, I drove to the Ming Tomb Airfield in the southeastern district. The field was in pandemonium. Transports of the Chinese Air Force and the two Chinese Airlines, CNAC and CATC, were being loaded in frenzy and taking off in quick succession. In disbelief I watched a Nationalist general running about ordering soldiers to load his piano and other furniture aboard an air force plane. Members of the Legislative Yuan were boarding another plane, several carrying tennis racquets. "We shall come back," a bespectacled legislator said to me in a trembling voice. Soldiers were swinging bayoneted rifles to hold back sobbing civilians trying to force or bribe their way aboard the planes taking on Nationalist officials and their families. Philip Crowe, the chief of the American aid mission, who had suffered a heart attack, arrived at the field on a stretcher and was put aboard the last plane to leave by his friend, Chester Ronning. The Nationalist leaders had already left for Canton, the southern metropolis. Before Li Tsung-jen and his premier, Ho Ying-chin, fled at about 9 A.M. from a refuge in the Ministry of Defense compound, George Yeh, the acting foreign minister, telephoned Jacques Meyrier, the French ambassador and doyen of the diplomatic corps, to tell him that the government was leaving and asked that the chiefs of missions follow it to Canton. In early February, the Nationalist premier, Sun Fo, son of Sun Yat-sen, had gone to Canton, where he installed his ministerial offices, leaving Li Tsung-jen to negotiate with the Communists. But in March, Sun Fo had been ousted on a corruption charge and replaced with Ho Ying-chin. The French ambassador told the foreign minister that the chiefs of mission, apart from the Soviet ambassador, who already was in Canton, intended to remain in Nanking. The United States and other Western governments were retaining the option of establishing contacts with the Communists through their ambassadors in Nanking. Meyrier confided in Leighton Stuart that the Paris government was concerned about what impact Mao's military advance might have on Indochina, where the French were waging war with Ho Chi Minh. It was a prescient concern, since the positioning in 1950 of Mao's forces on the Indochina frontier would enable Ho to defeat the French.

At dusk, the mobs became more violent. They looted abandoned police stations for weapons. Shooting broke out as volunteer militia organized by an Emergency Peace Preservation Committee tried to restrain looters. Dead lay in the streets. Time bombs left by the Nationalists in ammunition and fuel dumps on the banks of the river exploded, lighting fires that reddened the skies. Nationalist artillery positioned near Dragon Hill in the southern suburb fired aimlessly over the city toward the northern bank evidently to cover the withdrawal of Nationalist Army units. Families in the diplomatic missions huddled apprehensively behind barred gates. In the American Embassy compound, young diplomats patrolled the grounds with flashlights. A platoon of marines had been stationed in the compound, but it had been flown out on April 20 to Shanghai on the orders of Vice Admiral Oscar Badger, commander of the West Pacific Fleet, to avoid possible clashes with the Communists. Six marines were left behind to protect the 200 embassy personnel. The Commonwealth missions were guarded by a security force of 250 armed turbaned Sikhs organized by Sardar K. M. Panikkar, the ambassador of India.

At 6 P.M., I picked up Bill Kuan, a Chinese reporter who worked for the Agence France-Presse, and after inspecting the two airfields, which we found wrecked, we headed for the Nanking Hotel to look for General Ma Chingyuan, head of the Peace Preservation Committee. Driving along Chungshan Road, we were halted by eight Nationalist soldiers standing in a line across the boulevard pointing their rifles at us. Their leader said they were the last Nationalist sentries on the Nanking riverfront and had left their posts at sundown. The eight climbed onto the jeep, hanging on to the hood and sides, and we drove to the Sun Yat-sen Circle in the center of the city, where they were dropped off. Kuan asked them where they were going. "Out the South Gate," their leader said. We watched them, the last of the garrison of Chiang Kai-shek's capital, disappear into the darkness.

In the dilapidated Nanking Hotel, which was flying the white flag of the Peace Preservation Committee, we found people composing poster slogans to welcome the Communists. We were told that the head of the committee, General Ma, was spending the night at the Cairo Hotel, and so we drove there. In a dingy bedroom we found Ma, a retired army officer in the company of an odd assortment of people. There was a Nationalist colonel in a snappy uniform who told us he had been ordered to remain behind to help negotiate the city's surrender. A handsome girl in a khaki shirt with the sleeves rolled up sat beside a bespectacled young man. They did not encourage questions, and I assumed they were of the Communist underground, which had surfaced in the city. All listened silently as Ma unburdened himself.

Ma told us that at midnight of April 22, he had been aroused by a telephone call from General Chang Yao-ming, the Nanking garrison commander, who said his troops were evacuating the city immediately and asked him to take control during the transition period. He promised to provide Ma with police and security detachments to maintain order. Ma, a balding sixty-five-year-old man, dressed in a black buttoned-up tunic, recalled that conversation bitterly. Sitting on the edge of a chair, hands folded between his knees, shaking his head, he repeated: "We don't have enough troops to protect the city from looters." Ma had been able to marshal a security force of only a few hundred soldiers, police, and volunteers to safeguard the city of one million people. He said he was trying desperately to bring the Communist troops into the city as soon as possible to protect the diplomatic missions and ward off attacks on public buildings and utilities by Nationalist saboteurs. He had managed to contact the Communists by radio and had informed them the capital was ready to surrender. Communist troops had already crossed the Yangtze to Shang Hsin Ho, about three miles from the city's Northwest Gate. As we left him, Ma said he intended to go with a delegation, including Chen Yu-kuang, president of Nanking University, and Nu Cheng-yuan, a professor at Ginling College, out the Northwest Gate to Shang Hsin Ho, where they would contact the Communists and escort them into the city. Kuan and I then went to the central telegraph office to file dispatches. When we emerged, we saw that the Judicial Yuan, an imposing yellow structure on Chungshan Road, was in flames. Speculating that the flames, casting a red glow on the clouds, might bring the Communists into the city more quickly, I slowly drove north on the boulevard toward the Northwest Gate, where we hoped to meet them. It was 3:20 A.M. Suddenly, I heard a shout in Chinese of "halt," and I stopped. From shrubbery on the sides of the boulevard, two soldiers with rifles aimed at us converged on the jeep. "Who are you and what are you doing," one of the soldiers said, beaming a flashlight on us. Kuan replied: "I am a correspondent of the French news agency, and he is from the American Associated Press." Shining his flashlight on my face and examining me intently, the soldier exclaimed: "American, American!" Then he said: "Do you know who we are? We are the soldiers of the People's Liberation Army." They were men of Chen Yi's army, the point on the first column into Nanking. We were about a mile and a half from the Northwest Gate. The soldiers asked us to follow and led us to an infantry officer leading a column of troops into the city. The soldiers sweating under full packs and carrying heavy weapons looked exhausted. Their officer kept shouting, urging them to keep moving. These were not the troops who had been scheduled to parade into the city at sunrise. The fires in the city had brought this column at forced march through the Northwest Gate to take control. Slowly moving at the lead of the Communist column was a civilian jeep carrying army officers and apparently members of the Peace Preservation Committee. The infantry officer questioned Kuan and me and then impatiently ordered us back into the city. Gratefully, I drove quickly back up Chungshan Road past the burning Judicial Yuan to the telegraph office, where Kuan and I flipped a coin to determine who would file first. Kuan won and sent a three-word flash: "Reds take Nanking." My own tightly written sixty-five-word dispatch followed. Immediately after the transmission of my bulletin, Communist troops severed the cable landline between Nanking and Shanghai. When Kuan's dispatch reached the Agence France-Presse desk in Paris, the editors waited for additional details, which did not come until morning when the radio transmission resumed. The delay denied Kuan a world beat and bestowed it on me. My own dispatch went out immediately on the AP wires. After the radio transmission resumed, Kuan and I began filing fuller dispatches. I woke my friend, Hank Lieberman, to tell him that the Communists had entered the city. He asked me to file three hundred words to the *Times*, which I did despite lingering resentments of the imperious Cyrus Sulzberger. By the time the sun rose over Purple Mountain, the Communists had occupied Chiang Kai-shek's capital. A Chinese Web site has carried through the years a photograph of Mao Zedong reading the front page of a Peking newspaper citing my AP dispatch reporting the Communist occupation of Nanking. Mao had come a long way from Yenan.*

*In the spring of 2009, Chinese newspapers published commemorative articles in celebration of the forthcoming sixtieth anniversary of the proclamation by Mao Zedong in Peking of the establishment of the People's Republic of China. On April 18, the Nanking newspaper *Jinling Evening News* published a front-page interview with the clerk of the telegraph office in General Yang's Lane who handled the dispatches of Bill Kuan and myself reporting the fall of Chiang Kai-shek's capital to the People's Liberation Army (PLA). Herewith is a translation of the article:

This is the indelible recollection by the former telegram translator and underground Chinese Communist Party member, Lu Liwei, who is 81-years-old, of that night when news of the liberation of Nanjing was first disseminated from here:

"April 23rd, 60 years ago, 10 P.M., there were explosions in the train station and at the airport. The entire city was lit up with flames and the atmosphere was permeated with fear. A little after 3 A.M. of the 24th, guards of the telegraph building heard a jeep coming. Everyone in the building tensed up, holding assorted weapons in hand: bricks, sticks, and clubs, in anticipation of a terrible fight against bandits. The sound of the jeep came closer and closer, and we all had our hearts in our throats. The passengers in the jeep turned out to be Seymour Topping of the Associated Press and Bill [Kuan] of the French news agency."

Lu took a quick look at the telegram by Bill. It was a three-word piece, "Reds take Nanking." The piece by the reporter from the AP, on the other hand, was much more extensive. It was then, that Lu realized that Nanjing had been liberated. Both telegrams were sent smoothly. Unfortunately the short piece by the French reporter was mistaken by the French News Agency as the title of a lengthy report, and the piece never got printed because the agency was waiting for the full report. During that long wait, Mr. Topping became the first journalist to report the liberation of Nanjing to the entire world.

10

COMMUNIST OCCUPATION

At daybreak I picked up Chester Ronning at the Canadian Embassy, and we drove to the Northwest Gate, where thousands of Communist troops in their padded yellow uniforms and flat peaked caps were marching into the city. They sat down in orderly lines on their bedrolls along the sidewalks, with rifles tilted over their shoulders, listening to briefings from political commissars and singing revolutionary songs. People from nearby houses brought them tea and hot water, which the peasants call "white tea." Nationalist army stragglers, their weapons thrown away, passed by unmolested. In celebration of their victory, Communist soldiers climbed onto the facades and roofs of government buildings and Chiang Kai-shek's former office in the Heavenly Palace to plant their red flags. In a last gasp of defiance, three Nationalist Mosquito bombers strafed the Ming Tomb Airfield trying to detonate the fuel and ammunition dumps there. They overshot the field and wounded some children at play nearby.

Students from Nanking University, some of them Audrey's old chums, together with students from the ten other colleges and universities in the city, were at the Northwest Gate, some in trucks, shouting welcoming slogans and cheering the columns of troops. But the students, neatly dressed and obviously middle class, were bypassed silently. The Communists were not yet accepting them as comrades, although they had been among the six thousand students who three weeks earlier had staged militant demonstrations demanding an end to the Civil War. The demonstrations had been put down violently by Nationalist gendarmes. Within weeks, many of the students who massed at the gate to welcome the Communists troops were put into ideological indoctrination classes and organized into work squads. They were typical of an entire generation of university students who were trapped ideologically during the Civil War. Hungering for an effective role in determining their country's destiny, they had been compelled to make a choice between aligning themselves with a Nationalist dictatorship or a Communist one. Many fell between the cracks and became tragic victims of the purges of the Civil War. Forty years later, their student successors, demonstrating in Tiananmen Square for reform and democracy, would fall victim to fatal gunfire when the Communist government summoned troops to reassert control.

By the afternoon of that first day of the occupation, I was in trouble with the military. Upon my return from the Northwest Gate, three soldiers entered my office as I sat at my typewriter. Liu, my number one servant, was with them. Addressing themselves to Liu, they asked what I did. "Oh! He sends messages to the United States," Liu said casually, not aware he was arousing Communist vigilance. "What does he say in these messages?" he was asked. I cringed as Liu replied: "He reports about everything." That did it. Within a few minutes, the house was surrounded by armed sentries. I could not leave, nor could my cook go to the market for food. Ronning, hearing of my plight, delivered food packages through the wrought-iron gate of the stone wall surrounding the compound. I telephoned an officer at the embassy and had him send a message to Fred Hampson in Shanghai: "Boy Scouts at my door." Hampson promptly included that in one of his dispatches. After two days, without explanation, the sentries vanished. Thereafter I was free to move about. I accompanied Henri Cartier-Bresson, the French Magnum photographer, as he worked the bylanes of the city, taking some of his great China photos. My dispatches were not censored. The only newspaper to publish in the city, one filled with laudatory articles welcoming the Communists, was the Catholic *Yi Shih Pao*. Xinhua, the official Communist news agency, began functioning immediately, staffed by journalists who two days earlier had been working for the official Nationalist Central News Agency.

Nanking was administered by a Military Control Commission headed jointly by General Liu Bocheng and Deng Xiaoping. Liu, designated as mayor, spoke reassuringly to the city inhabitants, directing his remarks particularly to the businessmen: "Members of the Communist Party announce unreservedly that we fight for Communism, that we plan eventually to materialize a Communist society. However, being believers in materialism, we realize that the revolution in its present stage belongs to the New Democracy. Under these conditions we should make friends with over 90 percent of the people and we oppose only the reactionaries who represent less than 10 percent." During the period of New Democracy, Liu said, "We will concentrate on the development of production by promoting private as well as public enterprises, giving equal attention to capital and labor." His remarks, apparently made in consultation with Deng Xiaoping, who chaired the Nanking Municipal Party Committee, were very much in keeping with what Liu Shaoqi had told me in Yenan would be the policy after victory in the Civil War. It was a policy that Mao Zedong would abandon at the onset of the Cultural Revolution in 1966 and which would not be realized until Deng Xiaoping came to power as the paramount leader in the 1970s.

In late April, Nationalist bombers based on Taiwan began circling over the city every few days. The bombers, B-24s, B-25s, and Canadian Mosquitoes, came in quite low, since the Communists had no antiaircraft shielding the city other than limited range .50-caliber machine guns. Many of the bombs seemingly intended for the utilities and plants along the riverfront dropped into the Yangtze River. It appeared as if some of the pilots were deliberately trying to avoid bombing their own people.

On April 25, the radio announced the fall of T'aiyuan, the walled capital of Shansi Province, which had been ruled continuously since 1911 by the warlord Yen Hsi-shan. Marshal Yen, called the "model governor" by Nationalist adherents, had run a prosperous quasi-independent province. He had built more than six hundred miles of excellent roads and two rail lines, also developing agriculture and the forests so that the province had become virtually self-sufficient in food. Behind the thirty-foot-thick walls of his capital, arsenals produced rifles, machine guns, light artillery, and ammunition. When Communist troops swarmed into Shansi in the fall of 1948, the marshal retreated into T'aiyuan. Shortly after the Communist siege began, I flew to the airstrip within the city on one of Chennault's CAT transports, toured the impressive defenses, and heard the marshal declare his intention to hold out. The Generalissimo, Yen's close ally, had begun a massive airlift by the civilian transports carrying about five thousand tons of rice into the city monthly. Although short of foreign exchange, the Chiang government spent some $300,000 a day to sustain it. The rice deliveries were insufficient, however, for the population, and thousands starved to death. Resistance ended on April 24 after Yen flew out to Canton, where the Nationalist cabinet had been installed in February. There, he succeeded Ho Ying-chin as premier on June 2 and went promptly to parley with his ally, the Generalissimo.

During May, there was little radical change in the cultural life of Nanking. The Communist-control commission imposed restrictions on the local press and schools only gradually. Most university students in general greeted the establishment of Communist power enthusiastically. They formed speaking teams which toured the city explaining the "New Democracy" to the people. On the streets they performed the *yang-ko*, or "seedling song dances," which I first saw in Yenan in the local Peking Opera House, performed under the auspices of Jiang Qing, Mao's wife. Each dancer, arms akimbo, would take three short steps forward and then three backward, with a kick as an added flourish, while cymbals and drums gave the beat. Couples would weave in and out under a bridge of arms. Communist soldiers taught the students the steps, and newspapers published words of the songs. One song went:

> Reactionaries who exploit the people deserve to be cut into thousands of pieces.
> They totally ignore the affections of the common people and want only to be dictators.
> Big landlords, big warlords, big compradors, big families—all conspire together, all conspire together.
> And, therefore, we poor people suffer.

Chen Yi's troops left Nanking soon after the occupation to join other units wheeling eastward to capture Hangchow and encircle Shanghai, which fell on May 25. Behind an enormous ditch and a ten-foot wall erected by thousands of civilians laboring under the command of the garrison, the Nationalists put up a brief face-saving defense of Shanghai. Tang En-po, the Nationalist commander, pledged to turn Shanghai into a "second Stalingrad." Chiang Kai-shek flew into the port city from his retreat in Fenghua, spoke of "total victory within three years," and hastily departed. Chen Yi's troops thereafter paraded into, rather than stormed, Shanghai. They rounded up 100,000 passive Nationalist soldiers.

Rail, telegraph, and telephone communication between Nanking and Shanghai resumed within a few days after the fall of the port. But the Nanking telegraph office declined, as it had for several weeks, to accept international traffic. I sent my dispatches out by phone, mail, or courier to the AP office in Shanghai, which retained international links. Communist officials did not attempt to impose censorship on the few American and French correspondents who remained in Nanking.

In the diplomatic compounds life had become very boring. With their sources of information dried up, diplomats had little to report to their home governments. Typically, the American ambassador, J. Leighton Stuart, made only one note in his diary on April 30: "Charades after dinner at Jones'." But in the next weeks, Stuart was to become the central figure in a series of history-making events.

11

HUANG HUA AND J. LEIGHTON STUART

A turning point in relations between the United States and the Chinese Communists ensued in May 1949 with the arrival in Nanking of Huang Hua, with whom I had become very friendly in Peking. What transpired would tend to freeze relations between Peking and Washington for more than two decades.

For the Communists the former Nationalist capital had become the only venue available for diplomatic contact with the Western nations, and in particular, the United States. To undertake the most critical demarche Zhou Enlai detached Huang Hua from work with the Politburo and dispatched him to Nanking as chief of the External Affairs Office of the Military Control Commission, the department responsible for relations with the foreign ambassadors. With the exception of General Roschin, the Soviet ambassador, who, on Stalin's orders, had complied with the Nationalist invitation to relocate in Canton, all the foreign envoys had remained in the city. Roschin's transfer to Canton was very much in keeping with the double game Stalin was playing with the Nationalists and the Communists. From the standpoint of diplomatic protocol, Stalin behaved punctiliously in ordering his ambassador to follow the Moscow-recognized Nationalist government to Canton. But it was also a maneuver that put him in position to salvage any possible gain from the wreckage of Nationalist China while accruing him additional leverage in his manipulation of Mao. Andrei Ledovsky, then the first secretary of the Soviet Embassy, and several other Russian diplomats were instructed to remain in Nanking as liaison and consultants to the Communist Military Control Commission. Ledovsky continued to be a useful source for me as he had been in Peking when he served there as consul general.

In recalling my conversations with Huang Hua in Peking, it was apparent to me why he had been selected for the Nanking mission. J. Leighton Stuart would be the key intermediary in any approach to the West, and in particular the United States, and Huang Hua was the logical choice to engage him. Huang Hua had been a student at Yenching University in 1935 when

Stuart was serving as president. He was well known to Stuart as the militant leader of the school's student council. They had renewed their acquaintance in 1946 when Stuart visited Peking and met with Huang Hua, who was then posted at Executive Headquarters, where I met him. These two were now to become the principal actors in a diplomatic critical interplay between the United States and the new Communist regime. My reconstruction of these events is based on talks in Nanking with the key figures at the time, the sole access given to me by Philip Fugh to Stuart's personal diary after the ambassador's death in 1962, conversations over the years with Huang Hua, and recollections in his book *Memoirs* published in 2008.

Zhou Enlai had reason enough to want Huang Hua to open exploratory talks with Stuart at the first opportunity prior to the formal founding of the government of the People's Republic of China, which was to take place on October 1, 1949. Although the American military advisory group had been withdrawn, the Communists were still fearful of U.S. military intervention in the Civil War. They were aware that American officials were in talks with Nationalist leaders on the possible creation of a new resistance base in western or southern China. On the Burmese border, Nationalist units were regrouping with covert American help. There was the possibility that the U.S. Navy would be deployed to block the invasion of Taiwan, which was being readied by General Chen Yi in the southern ports. The United States had just transferred four ships to the Nationalist Navy, supplementing other military aid en route to the Chiang Kai-shek forces on Taiwan. The Nationalists were urging a diversionary landing by American troops on the South China coast. Stalin had warned Mao of "the danger of Anglo-American forces landing in the rear of the main forces of the People's Liberation Army." Neither the Nationalists nor the Communists were aware that President Truman had in secret deliberations with his aides expressed adamant opposition to any such action.

Huang Hua was told in Peking by Zhou Enlai to proceed cautiously in his approach to Stuart. He was to call on him only as a private citizen and as his former student at Yenching. "Be careful. Keep in constant touch with the Central Committee" was his final instruction before Huang Hua departed for Nanking. "My understanding of his word," Huang Hua recalled in his *Memoirs,* "was that the Central Committee was concerned about the possibility of US armed intervention against the New China. It had, therefore, concentrated more than one million troops of the Second and Third Field Armies in the Shanghai-Nanking area."

Huang Hua made the rather risky overland journey to Nanking by train and by truck, bypassing areas still held by Nationalist militia. The first foreigner received by Huang Hua after he was installed in his office in the former Nationalist Foreign Ministry was Chester Ronning. Fluent from childhood in Chinese, Ronning had been asked by the diplomatic corps to represent them, since the Communists were insisting that all business be conducted in Chinese. Ronning was told that the ambassadors would not be entitled to the usual diplomatic privileges and immunities because their governments had no official ties with the Revolutionary Military Commission then ruling in Peking. This was later modified to allow diplomats to communicate by cable in cipher with their governments. Huang Hua, soon after arrival, agreed to meet with me. He was in army uniform rather than in the civilian tunic he had worn in Peking. He greeted me in Chinese but then, becoming less formal, chatted in English and told me that I would be free to carry on my work as a correspondent. After the fall of Shanghai, Huang Hua arranged a visit for me to the port city, where Fred Hampson was still holding the AP fort.

A few days after his arrival, Huang Hua contacted Philip Fugh, the American ambassador's personal secretary, and arranged to call on Stuart at his residence. Ostensibly, it was to apologize for a minor incident, an intrusion by Communists soldiers who stumbled into the ambassador's bedroom during the occupation of the city. But Stuart noted in his diary that the meeting with Huang Hua on May 14, which lasted an hour and forty-five minutes, "may be the beginning of better understanding." Huang Hua raised the question of U.S. recognition of the future Communist government on condition that Washington sever all ties with the Nationalist government. Stuart gave him a hedged reply with no firm assurance. Stuart, accompanied by Fugh, his secretary, paid a return visit to Huang Hua on June 6 at the Foreign Ministry, where arrangements were made for the ambassador to visit Shanghai for a Yenching student reunion. Two days later, Fugh telephoned Huang Hua to ask if the ambassador could visit Peking in keeping with his past custom of celebrating his June 24 birthday at Yenching University. Fugh said the visit might afford an opportunity for a meeting with Zhou Enlai. Huang Hua, indicating that Stuart would likely be welcome, referred the request to Peking, and the ambassador informed the State Department of the proposed visit. Huang Hua's message to Peking inspired a sequence of intricate political maneuvers. Lu Zhiwei, chancellor of Yenching, was asked, presumably by Zhou Enlai, to write a letter to Stuart inviting him to Peking. On June 28,

Stuart received a puzzling letter from the chancellor which already assumed that he would be making the trip. After a telegraphic exchange with Peking to confirm the contents of the Lu message, Huang Hua visited Stuart to tell him that Mao and Zhou would welcome him heartily.

Stuart had not received any response from the State Department about the proposed Peking visit and in the interim had been instructed to return to Washington for consultation. Now assured that Mao and Zhou would welcome him, the ambassador messaged Washington listing the pros and cons. While conceding that the visit might enhance the prestige of the Communists and might mistakenly signal recognition, he said the benefits would outweigh any negative effects. He said it would have a beneficial impact on Washington's relations with Peking and would strengthen the more liberal faction in the Communist leadership. A debate ensued within the State Department as to whether Stuart should make the Peking trip, with the majority of China specialists favoring taking up what they regarded as a significant gambit by the Communists for exploratory talks. Previously, on April 6, Dean Acheson, then secretary of state, responding to a request from Stuart to stay on in Nanking after Communist occupation, had authorized the ambassador to stay and undertake secret exploratory talks with the Communist leaders to better define their attitudes.

I was at work in the AP office on July 1 when J. C. Jao, my Chinese assistant, excitedly called my attention to a declaration being broadcast by Peking Radio. It was in the form of a self-interview by Mao Zedong, marking the twenty-eighth anniversary of the founding of the Chinese Communist Party in July 1921. In essence it defined the foreign policy line of China for the next decade. Mao proclaimed that China would "lean to one side" in favor of the Soviet Union. As if he were reflecting a debate which had taken place in Peking among the Communist leaders, Mao posed questions and provided his own answers. This is a translation of our recording:

> "You are leaning to one side?"
>
> "Exactly . . . We are firmly convinced that in order to win victory, and consolidate it we must lean to one side . . . Sitting on the fence will not do, nor is there a third road."
>
> "You are too irritating?"
>
> "We are talking about how to deal with domestic and foreign reactionaries, the imperialists and their running dogs, not about how to deal with anyone else . . . either kill the tiger or be eaten by him—one or the other."

"We want to do business?"

"Quite right, business will be done . . . When we have beaten the internal and external reactionaries by uniting all domestic and international forces, we shall be able to do business and establish diplomatic relations with all foreign countries on the basis of equality, mutual benefit and mutual respect for territorial integrity and sovereignty."

"Victory is possible, even without international help?"

"This is a mistaken idea. In the epoch in which imperialism exists, it is impossible for a genuine people's revolution to win victory in any country without various forms of help from international revolutionary forces, and even if victory were won, it could not be consolidated."

"We need help from the British and U.S. Governments?"

"This too, is a naive idea in these times. Would the present rulers of Britain and the United States, who are imperialists, help a people's state? . . . Internationally, we belong to the side of the anti-imperialist front headed by the Soviet Union, and so we can turn only to this side for genuine and friendly help, not to the side of the imperialist front."

I telephoned Ronning at the Canadian Embassy to tell him of the Mao statement. There was a lunch in progress, on the occasion of Dominion National Day, for the Commonwealth ambassadors, and Stuart was among the guests. Ronning broke the news to them. It shocked Stuart, who had counted on visiting Peking and hopefully reaching some kind of an understanding with the Communist leadership. It shattered what he referred to later as his "dream of a China peaceful, united and progressive, helped in this by American technical advice, and financial grants or loans."

Mao and Zhou Enlai clearly were affronted by the delay of more than a month in responding to their invitation to Stuart. Absent a reply from Washington and suffering a loss of face in the exchange with Truman, Mao had chosen to lay down the line of leaning to the side of the Soviet Union. Two days after the Mao declaration, Stuart received a message from the State Department saying that his proposal had been considered "at the highest levels," obviously President Truman, and under no circumstances should he visit Peking.

Stuart left Nanking on August 2 on the embassy plane. In Washington, the ambassador's public comments were screened by the State Department. No public mention was made of his invitation to Peking. The State Department announced on August 14 that the United States intended to retain its diplomatic relations with the Nationalist government. Four days later, Mao published an article, "Farewell, Leighton Stuart!" in which he described the ambassador as "a symbol of the complete defeat of the U.S. Policy of aggression." The declaration reflected resentment of Stuart's support of the Chiang Kai-shek government during his tenure as ambassador and Mao's loss of face over the curt dismissal of the invitation to Stuart to visit Peking.

Before Stuart left Nanking, I spoke to him about Mao's invitation. It was his view that he might have improved relations with Peking and laid the foundation for the establishment of normal diplomatic ties. On November 30, aboard a train going from Cincinnati to Washington, Stuart suffered a severe stroke, which incapacitated him. He lived in Washington from 1950 until his death in 1962 at the Chevy Chase home of Philip Fugh and his wife. It was there in later years that Philip Fugh gave me the sole access to Stuart's personal diary, which contained the details of his contacts with Huang Hua.

In his will Leighton Stuart asked to be buried in China beside his wife on the grounds of Yenching University. Stuart's ashes were kept in an urn in the Fughs' home awaiting the opportunity to fulfill his wish. The urn was passed after the deaths of Fugh and his wife to their son, John, who rose to become a major general and judge advocate in the U.S. Army. General Fugh told me that he had sought unsuccessfully for years to obtain Chinese government permission to have Stuart's remains interred at Yenching. It was evident that the Chinese have not forgotten the contretemps of the aborted Stuart visit to Peking. Rendering an evaluation of Stuart in his *Memoirs,* Huang Hua said: "Despite his popularity among some Chinese intellectuals, he was after all a firm believer in American First, and faithfully carried out the United States policy of backing Chiang Kai-shek in its fight against Communism . . . In the final analysis, Stuart and Secretary of State Dean Acheson tried to play the China Card in the worldwide U.S.-Soviet struggle, intending to draw China to the U.S. side. However, the wheel of history did not turn in the direction Stuart wished."

General Fugh, now retired and chairman of the Committee of 100, an organization of prominent Chinese Americans, continued to press for fulfillment of Stuart's wish. In 2008, Beijing relented and allowed Stuart's ashes to be interred on August 2 in a private ceremony in Hangzhou beside the summer home that the ambassador had maintained in the resort city. The ashes were shipped from Washington in a State Department diplomatic bag to avoid any possible mishap. The small ceremony was attended by the American ambassador, Clark Randt Jr., the mayor of Hangzhou, along with alumni of Yenching. After placing flowers on the grave, General Fugh said: "Now, after a half century, his wish has finally been carried out."

Looking back on the Stuart episode, I believe that the ambassador was correct in assuming that Mao's relations with Stalin were equivocal at the time Stuart was invited to Peking and thus provided an opening for the United States. As late as December 1949, Mao was not yet fully accepted into the Soviet camp. In January of that year, still uncertain of Mao's loyalty, Stalin had sent Anastas Mikoyan, a Politburo member, on an exploratory mission to Mao's provisional headquarters in North China at Hsipaip'o in Hupei Province. Mao assured him of his solidarity with Stalin and that he looked to Moscow primarily for economic aid. It was his intention, he told Mikoyan, to create "a people's democracy based on the worker-peasant alliance," under the leadership of the Communist Party. Nevertheless, speaking to his party's Central Committee in 1962, Mao recalled: "Later on, I went to Moscow to conclude the Chinese Soviet Treaty of Alliance, Friendship and Mutual Assistance [February 14, 1950], which also involved a struggle. He [Stalin] did not want to sign it, but finally agreed after two months of negotiations. When did Stalin begin to have confidence in us? It began in the winter of 1950, during the Resist-America Aid-Korea Campaign. Stalin then believed we were not Yugoslavia and not Titoist."

While Mao had been prepared to welcome Stuart to Peking, Huang Hua told me years later, the Communist leaders believed that American policy was set and there was little prospect for change. At best they hoped to deter further American intervention in the Civil War on behalf of Chiang Kai-shek. But this does not mean that a meeting with Stuart in Peking, which Mao and Zhou sought, could not have been extremely useful for both the United States and China. It might have led at least to the opening of channels of communication. As many China specialists in the State Department felt at the time, that was reason enough to accept Mao's invitation. Even in the absence of normal diplomatic relations, the Chinese had been disposed to maintain channels to cope with dangerous confrontations. If Americans had continued to talk to the Communists, many of the misunderstandings and much of the agony in Asia over the next decades might have been averted. Critical policy decisions dealing with the confrontations in Indochina and Korea during the 1950s and 1960s were made on both sides on a basis of incomplete information and mistaken assessments. It is likely that the entry of Chinese Communist "volunteers" into the Korean War in November 1950 could have been avoided. Not until 1971, with President Richard Nixon's diplomatic opening to China and the visit to Peking by Henry Kissinger, did the United States begin to acquire firsthand information upon which realistic assessments could be made of Chinese intentions.

———————————

Soon after Truman ruled out the Stuart visit in July 1949, Mao took action that had a decisive effect on the course of the French Indochina War and later on the American war effort in Vietnam. He agreed then to provide Ho Chi Minh with a major program of military aid.

Mao had been approached by Ho Chi Minh for such assistance as early as 1945. In that year Ho made the last of eight recorded appeals to President Truman for support in his struggle with the French for Vietnamese independence. Like the previous appeals, it went unanswered. Truman had already approved resumption of French control of Indochina. Ho then turned to Mao for help. From 1945 to 1949 there were only limited exchanges between Ho's League for the Independence of Vietnam, known as the Viet Minh, and the Chinese Communists. In March 1946, a Chinese Communist militia unit, the First Regiment, retreated from Kwangsi Province into Vietnam under Nationalist attack and in return for food and other help given to them by the Viet Minh trained some of their guerrilla units. But otherwise the relationship did not significantly broaden until Chinese Communist troops arrived at the Vietnam frontier in force in 1949. After the founding of the People's Republic of China on October 1, 1949, Ho sent envoys to Peking to renew his request for military aid and diplomatic recognition of his newly established Democratic Republic of Vietnam (DRV) in the North. Mao was in Moscow at the time negotiating the Sino-Soviet Treaty of Friendship, Alliance and Mutual Assistance. He cabled instructions to Liu Shaoqi, the party secretary, who was in Peking to comply with the requests. The Maoist regime formally recognized the DRV on January 5, and Liu set to work putting together a major military aid program. On Mao's urging, Stalin extended diplomatic recognition on January 30 with the understanding that China would take the lead in providing aid to the DRV. To make direct contacts with the Communist leadership, as Qiang Zhai, the Chinese American scholar, describes in his book *China and the Vietnam Wars, 1950–1975,* Ho walked for seventeen days from his jungle headquarters to the China border, arriving there on January 30. He then continued on to Peking, where he negotiated the terms of military aid with Liu Shaoqi. Liu appointed Luo Guibo, a senior

Civil War veteran, as the principal liaison and adviser to the Viet Minh. Beginning in April, the Chinese began shipping large quantities of weapons and other supplies to the Viet Minh. A Chinese Military Advisory Group (CMAG) was created to coordinate the work of almost three hundred Chinese advisers assigned to the Viet Minh army headquarters near the Indochina border, at an officers' training school and in the field at the divisional level. The advisers were instructed to train the Viet Minh in the tactics and strategy formulated by Mao on September 7, 1947, in his directive from his northern Shensi mountain headquarters to the People's Liberation Army. Supplemented by deliveries of Soviet weaponry, the Chinese program gave Vo Nguyen Giap, the Viet Minh military commander, the means to defeat the French and later to prevail in their war against the United States and its South Vietnamese allies.

In allying himself with Ho Chi Minh, Mao seemed to be motivated by two considerations: one was his ideological commitment to leftist revolution in Asia; the other was a desire to create a buffer in Vietnam against any American military thrust into China. Could Mao have been convinced through assurances conveyed by Leighton Stuart that there was no American intention to threaten the security of his regime? One can only speculate, but in my view and in the opinion then of the most respected China experts within the State Department, Stuart might have made a difference if he had been permitted to go to Peking.

On the day that Mao proclaimed the establishment of the People's Republic of China, October 1, 1949, Huang Hua summoned the diplomatic corps in Nanking to the Foreign Ministry. Speaking in Chinese, he informed them of the proclamation and invited their respective governments to recognize and establish relations with the newly organized government in Peking. His statement was received in complete silence by the assembled ambassadors. After an awkward interval, Keith Officer, the Australian ambassador, rose to say that his statement had not been understood and asked if Chester Ronning, could act as interpreter. Huang Hua agreed, and Ronning acted as the translator for the diplomatic corps. Following the ambassadorial meeting, India agreed quickly to establish diplomatic relations and transferred its ambassador in Nanking, Sardar K. M. Panikkar, to Peking. With the outbreak in the next year of the Korean War, Panikkar became a vital channel of communication to Foreign Minister Zhou Enlai. He conveyed the warning that Chinese troops would intervene if American troops crossed the thirty-eighth parallel into North Korea. If Panikkar's intercession had been taken seriously by the United States, the entry of Chinese troops might have been averted.

Audrey and I became friendly with Panikkar in Nanking, chatting often with him under the plum trees in his lovely garden about events in Asia. Born into the untouchable caste and then adopted by a Brahmin family, Panikkar, through sheer brilliance despite his humble origins, had achieved remarkable success in India's diplomatic service. Educated at Oxford, he was also a distinguished historian. Panikkar was sympathetic to the Chinese Communists as revolutionaries, but I found that his personal sympathies did not cloud his highly perceptive observations of the realities.

Like Panikkar, Ronning recommended to his government that Canada establish relations with the Peking government forthwith. T. C. Davis, the Canadian ambassador, had earlier left China, and Ronning was the chargé d'affaires of the mission. Ronning saw an opportunity to influence the evolving policies of the Maoist regime through the prompt opening of a diplomatic channel of communication. But Ottawa hesitated, according to Ronning's personal papers, until June 25, 1950, when he was informed that the Canadian government had finally decided to enter into negotiations for recognition. He was instructed to advise Huang Hua to that effect. But before he could comply, the Korean War erupted. Ottawa then told him that the war had introduced new factors affecting relations with Peking. Ronning was instructed to close the Canadian Embassy and return home, where he was to become the head of the Far Eastern Department in the Ministry of External Affairs. Following the declaration of an armistice in the Korean War, Ronning in July 1954 was sent to the Geneva Conference on Korea and Vietnam as the Canadian representative. There, Wang Pingnan, a member of the Chinese delegation, broached the question of Canadian diplomatic recognition. Ronning told him that normalization of relations was not possible while three Canadian Catholic missionaries were in prison and another was being denied an exit visa. Nine days later, the priests were released, but Canada did not make a move toward recognition until 1956, when Ronning was informed by Lester Pearson, the foreign minister, that Canada would recognize the People's Republic and he would become Canada's first ambassador. Shortly before the formal announcement was to be made, Prime Minister Louis St. Laurent and Pearson visited Washington to inform President Eisenhower of the decision. To their surprise, Eisenhower, who was embittered by the Chinese intervention in the Korean War, protested. Eisenhower told them that other nations would follow the Canadian example, and this might result in the People's Republic being admitted to the United Nations. If China were seated, Eisenhower contended, the American public would demand that the United States withdraw from the United Nations and might even insist upon the UN headquarters being removed from American territory. Once again, Canadian recognition was delayed, this time until October 13, 1971, when Prime Minister Pierre Trudeau finally established diplomatic relations with the Peking government.

———————

After the departure of Ambassador Stuart from Nanking in August 1949, the former capital shriveled as a news center, and the AP asked me to proceed to Hong Kong for reassignment. The opportunity to leave came after the Nationalists announced they would relax the coastal blockade to permit the liner *General W. H. Gordon* to call at Shanghai to pick up foreigners. The night before boarding the *Gordon*, Robert Guillain, the correspondent for *Le Monde*, and I strolled down the Bund to the Cathay Hotel, where we were to have dinner. We walked past the tall buildings, dark and desolate, which had once housed the foreign banks, great trading companies, and clubs. Many of the 100,000 foreign residents of the city had fled. Caretakers of foreign properties were standing by helplessly as the Communists took over their enterprises. The Communists were insisting that Chinese staff be retained on full pay in the transition period although business was at a standstill. When we entered the great dining room of the Cathay, it was empty except for several score waiters, all still attired in immaculate white jackets. We dined alone with seemingly dozens of waiters hovering over us. I paid the bill, putting the tip on a silver tray; I glanced up and saw eyes peering from all parts of the room at it. The waiters had depended in the greater part for their livelihood on tips. There had been no other guests that day. Growingly uneasy, Guillain and I hastened into the night.

The next morning as I passed through customs at the Shanghai quay, a Communist officer watching over the proceedings saw that I was declaring books. He stuck a hand into my trunk and came up with the grass woven paperback copy of Mao Zedong's *On Coalition Government,* in which Mao once again advanced the concept of "New Democracy," that had been presented to me in Yenan. "Where did you get this?" The Chinese officer exclaimed in Chinese. "In Yenan in 1946," I replied. The officer looked at me intently, ordered my trunk closed, and waved me and my baggage past the guards without further formalities. As the liner left the brown waters at the mouth of the Yangtze on September 25 and entered the blue of the East China Sea, one of the 1,219 passengers, mostly diplomats and foreign businessmen, mounted onto a deck bulkhead and shouted: "We are liberated." I turned away, leaned over the rail, and looked back to China. Monumental events were impending there. How soon, I wondered, could I find a way to get back to China?

12

THE PURGE OF MY CHINA DEPUTIES

There were two devastating postscripts to my early experience in China which have never ceased to anguish me. Both concern the Chinese journalists who worked as my deputies during the Civil War.

Shortly before I left occupied Nanking in September 1949, the Communists began to systematically tighten their ideological hold on the population. Virtually everyone was drawn into study and indoctrination meetings. Those attending were required to confess past sins and faulty ideological thinking and to pass judgments on the thoughts and activities of friends, neighbors, and business associates. As the so-called reeducation campaigns became more intense and onerous, there was a change in the private attitudes of many Chinese intellectuals who had welcomed the Communists to the city. The change was visible in the demeanor of J. C. Jao, my Chinese deputy in the AP office. A man in his late forties, Jao had earned a bachelor's degree at the University of Missouri's School of Journalism, class of 1924, went on to graduate studies at the University of Pennsylvania, and upon return to China worked for the Chinese Educational Mission in Peking. When he joined the AP as a part-time correspondent, he was the editor of the *Tsingtao Daily Herald* and was teaching at Shantung University in that port city. Tsingtao was the principal base of the some fifty thousand U.S. Marines who were landed in North China in 1945 to assist the Nationalist government in accepting the surrender of the Japanese forces. Jao covered the withdrawal of the marines to shipboard from Tsingtao in February 1949 and then went to Nanking to work as an assistant to Harold Milks, serving as an interpreter, translator, and an occasional writer of short dispatches. A tall, spare man, rather reserved in manner, Jao was an independent thinker and politically liberal.

Jao had awaited the arrival of the Communists with evident apprehension. In the days immediately before the occupation he would not venture out of the AP compound. I therefore was surprised on the morning after the Communist entry to find him in good spirits and hopeful about the future. Like many of his Chinese friends, Jao was caught up in the talk of "liberation" and impressed by the good conduct of the Communist troops. As the summer wore on, however, and the Communists began to tighten their controls, he began discreetly to voice sour observations. When I left Nanking, leaving him in charge of the AP office, he was distrustful of the Communists. In January 1950, on behalf of the AP he traveled to Peking seeking permission for me to return from Hong Kong to the newly established capital to open an AP bureau there. In a letter to Fred Hampson in Shanghai, reporting on his inconclusive efforts, he noted that he hoped that eventually an American correspondent would be appointed so that he could retire safely to the limited role of interpreter and translator rather than continuing as an identifiable writer. Some months later, after his return to Nanking, he was brought into a Communist indoctrination course and questioned about his background and ties with Americans. He wrote to Hampson saying he was resisting accepting a job with the Communists in which he would be required to write anti-American propaganda. Contact was lost with him soon after.

On February 21, 1951, the Peking government promulgated a drastic decree on the "punishment of counter-revolutionary offenses." By then a purge had already begun in the countryside and urban areas. The people were spurred to denounce "counter-revolutionaries," and executions of the accused began to take place following mass trials. Those executed included former Nationalist officials, landlords and other gentry in the countryside believed hostile to the regime, businessmen accused of antistate practices, intellectuals and others who had been associated with Westerners and suspected of ideological opposition to the Communists. The Korean War thickened the atmosphere of fear, suspicion, and denunciation. The purge was intended to eliminate any elements in the population who might in the future rise and collaborate with the United States and Chiang Kai-shek in efforts to unseat the Maoist regime.

In Shanghai, the *Liberation Daily* reported that J. C. Jao had been arrested in Nanjing on April 27, 1951, in a roundup of suspected "counter-revolutionaries" in several cities. Although he was no longer employed as a reporter by the AP, he was accused of being an "international espionage agent" who had spied for the news agency. On May 5 the *Liberation Daily* announced that Communist firing squads had liquidated 376 "counter-revolutionaries" in Nanjing, 293 in Shanghai, and 50 in Hangzhou. The Nanjing and Hangzhou executions were said to have taken place on April 29 following public trials attended by as many as 150,000 people. The report cited J. C. Jao as a typical "counter-revolutionary." We never heard anything from Jao, or anything about him, thereafter.

The Communists never disclosed the total number of those executed in the nationwide Campaign to Suppress Counter-Revolutionaries, which continued into 1952. In October 1951 it was announced that the people's courts alone had tried 800,000 accused counterrevolutionaries during the first half of 1951. In a speech on June 26, 1957, Premier Zhou Enlai stated that 16.8 percent of the counterrevolutionaries had been sentenced to death, most of them before 1952. This would mean that at least 134,400 had been executed in the first six months of the purge. Colonel Jacques Guillermaz, the distinguished Sinologist, who served as French military attaché in the Nationalist capital during the Civil War and later in Peking, estimated in his *History of the Chinese Communist Party, 1921–1949*, published in 1968, that a total of 1–3 million had been executed. Other independent experts have made estimates ranging from hundreds of thousands to several million. The estimate of more than 10 million put forward by Nationalist officials on Taiwan has not been accepted as reliable by scholarly researchers.

My other Chinese colleague who suffered the Maoist purges was Peter Liu, a tall, strikingly handsome man in his twenties, son of a Nationalist Foreign Ministry official and grandson of a high-ranking official in the Manchu imperial court of the Qing dynasty. A graduate of St. John's University in Shanghai, Peter spoke flawless English and was employed as a translator at Executive Headquarters in Peking in 1946 when I met him and asked him to do some translation work for me. When the International News Service transferred me to Nanking in 1947, I brought him along as my assistant, and he continued to report for INS after I resigned to join the Associated Press. After the Communists occupied Nanking, he was sent by them to the Peking Foreign Languages Institute for training in government work. When the Campaign to Suppress Counter-Revolutionaries was unleashed, he endured interrogations but managed to survive. In April 1957 Liu counted himself lucky when he landed a job with the official Xinhua News Agency. He was at work there during Mao's 1957 Hundred Flowers Campaign, a short-lived period of liberalization when intellectuals were invited to join in a "blooming and contending" critique of Communist Party policies. Liu was caught up in a "self-rectification" campaign in which all individuals were expected, in the light of their experiences, to recommend improvements in party and government operations. Liu, anxious to be counted among the true revolutionaries, took the invitation seriously and indulged within Xinhua in a public critique. The Hundred Flowers abruptly ceased to bloom on June 8, 1957, with the publication of an editorial in the official *People's Daily*. The critics had overreached themselves, and Liu was found to be among the sinners. It was the beginning of another Maoist purge, the Anti-Rightist Campaign, which would punish some 550,000 people who in speaking out had voiced inner feelings contrary to party policies. It was a campaign conducted on the instructions of Mao Zedong by Deng Xiaoping, who subsequently became general secretary of the Communist Party and later paramount leader of the country. Liu was denounced as a "bourgeois rightist" at so-called criticism and self-criticism meetings where his work with me for an American news agency was recalled. On March 8, 1958, Liu was put on a bus and taken through the gates of a compound enclosed by tall walls topped by electrified wire netting. It was the Peking Municipal Detention Center for Corrective Education through Labor. Liu was then thirty-three years of age, and he remained in that labor camp for twenty-one years.

In 2001, Peter Liu published an autobiography, *Mirror: A Loss of Innocence in Mao's China*. In his book and letters to me, he described how following the Communist takeover in 1949 he decided to remain on the mainland, rather than emigrate to Hong Kong or Taiwan. "I still wanted to dedicate my youth and abilities to the new-born Republic." However, in a postscript to his book he wrote:

> I was rehabilitated at the age of fifty-five after twenty-one years in the labor camp. This plus nine wasted years as a suspected spy made up three decades from the age of twenty-five to fifty-five years, the prime of my adult life, all ruthlessly trampled to smithereens along with the unreserved enthusiasm with which I flung all of myself into the embrace of my beloved motherland. I received an apology for a "mistaken indictment" on the day of my rehabilitation, but was refused compensation of financial losses caused by my salary cut. I was neither elated at the apology nor saddened by the refusal of a compensatory payment, because neither was of any consequence with the humiliation I went through and the losses I sustained. At seventy-two I am long past the age of ambitions and adventures.

The author is shown sitting in front of a map in the Associated Press compound in Nan-king, Chiang Kai-shek's Nationalist capital, shortly before the city fell to Mao Zedong's forces in April 1949. The author met the troops of the People's Liberation Army as they entered the Northwest Gate and sent the first news report on the Communist occupation of the city. Courtesy Associated Press

A Nationalist cavalry company retreating in November 1948 from Pengpu on the Huai River, the point at which the author earlier crossed the Nationalist lines to the front where Chiang Kai-shek's armies would be defeated in the decisive Battle of the Huai-Hai in January 1949. The author was held captive for a time by Communist troops during the battle. Photo by Jack Birns of *Life* magazine/courtesy University of California Press

Member of suicide attack squad of the People's Liberation Army heavily equipped with grenades in action during the Battle of the Huai-Hai. Courtesy author/Memorial Museum of the Huai-Hai Campaign

Defeated Nationalist commanding general, Tu Yu-ming, captured during the Battle of the Huai-Hai, is led away by Communist troops. Tu was appointed by Chiang Kai-shek despite the fact that he was held responsible for the major Nationalist defeat earlier in Manchuria. Courtesy author/Memorial Museum of the Huai-Hai Campaign

General Chiang Wei-kuo, the son of Chiang Kai-shek, commanded the Nationalist Armored Corps during the Battle of the Huai-Hai. Chiang managed to escape by air from the city of Hsuchow as it was being encircled by Chinese Communist forces. Courtesy Chinese government archives

The three leading field commanders of the People's Liberation Army in the Chinese Civil War (*left to right*): Generals Lin Biao, Liu Bocheng, and Chen Yi. Lin Biao was later accused of involvement in a plot to assassinate Mao Zedong. He attempted to flee in September 1971 with his wife and son to the Soviet Union, but his Trident jet crashed in the Mongolian mountains and all aboard were killed. Courtesy Personal collection of Jacquez Guillermaz/author/Memorial Museum of the Huai-Hai Campaign

On Chinese New Year's Day, 1949, with his armies collapsing, Generalissimo President Chiang Kai-shek went to the Sun Yat-sen Mausoleum on Purple Mountain in Nanking. As the author watched, Chiang mounted to the tomb of the founder of the Chinese Republic, bowed, and looked out over his capital for the last time. He then drove to the Heavenly Palace and announced his resignation, naming Li Tsung-jen as acting president. He later flew to Fenghua, his birthplace, where he prepared his retreat to Taiwan. Courtesy Associated Press

As Communist armies closed in on Shanghai, General Chiang Ching-kuo, a son
of the Generalissimo, ordered the public execution of captured Communist
agents and black market speculators in commodities. The author was in Shanghai in November 1948 when the crackdown began. Shown is the execution of
accused perpetrators in Chapei Park. The city fell to the Communists on May
25, 1949. Photo by Jack Birns of *Life* magazine/courtesy University of California Press

American Ambassador J. Leighton Stuart shown chatting with Generalissimo Chiang Kai-shek
in Nanking in 1947. Stuart attempted to negotiate an end to the Civil War. He was invited to go
to Peking to meet with Mao Zedong and Premier Zhou Enlai, but President Truman forbade the
trip. Photo by George Silk of *Life* magazine/courtesy author

Mao Zedong is shown in Peking's Tiananmen Square reviewing his troops in a victory parade celebrating the capture of Nanking and the defeat of Chiang Kai-shek's forces. Nationalist General Fu Tso-yi surrendered Peking peacefully to Maoist forces on January 23, 1949, after secret negotiations with General Lin Biao, whose troops were besieging the city. Courtesy Associated Press

Liu Shaoqi, head of state of China, was denounced as "taking the capitalist road" by Mao Zedong in a power struggle during the Cultural Revolution that erupted in 1966. He was purged from the Communist Party, placed under house arrest, and died of medical neglect in 1969. When Liu's collaborator, Deng Xiaoping, came to power after Mao's death in 1976, Deng rehabilitated his memory. Courtesy Associated Press

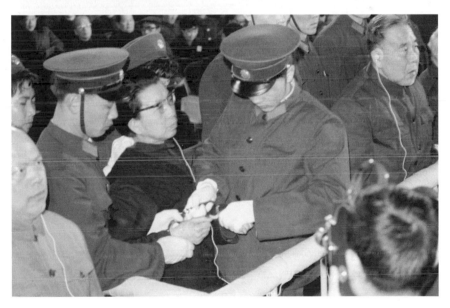

Jiang Qing, wife of Mao Zedong and the leading driving force in the Cultural Revolution, being handcuffed by policemen just after being sentenced to death at a political trial on January 25, 1981. She was accused of disrupting the country with violent excesses during the Cultural Revolution. Her sentence was later commuted, but she died in a prison hospital in 1991 by hanging herself in her bathroom. Courtesy Xinhua, Official Chinese News Service

Edgar Snow, author of the epic *Red Star over China* on the rise of the Chinese Communist movement, is shown in 1970 with Huang Hua, on a visit to Bo'an in Shaanxi Province, where Snow
interviewed Mao Zedong in 1936 with Huang Hua acting as interpreter. Bo'an was Mao's headquarters for a time during the Civil War. They are shown standing outside of Mao's old residence.
In 1976 Huang Hua was appointed foreign minister of the People's Republic of China. Courtesy
author, from private collection of Huang Hua

During the French Indochina War, the author traveled in 1950 with a Foreign Legion convoy to the Vietnam-China frontier. Shown at a French army post on the frontier are (*left to right*) Wilson Fielder of *Time* magazine, the French officer in command of the post, Carl Mydans of *Life* magazine, and the author. Courtesy Carl Mydans' personal collection

General Jean de Lattre de Tassigny, commander of the French forces in the French Indochina War that were defeated by Ho Chi Minh's Viet Minh, is shown in 1951. Shortly afterwards he returned to Paris, where he died of cancer and was given a marshal's funeral and honored at a massive parade. Author's collection/Official French Army photo

Graham Greene. This photo was taken in the author's Saigon apartment in 1951 when the British writer was doing research for his novel *The Quiet American.* Photo by Audrey Topping

Republic of Vietnam (South Vietnam) chief of state and former emperor Bao Dai (*second from left*) with U.S. chargé d'affaires Edmund Gullion during a tiger hunt in Vietnam's Central Highlands in 1950. Standing at right is Admiral Russell Berkey, commander of the U.S. Seventh Fleet. Lieutenant Commander Drake (*kneeling at left*) shot the tiger. Courtesy Associated Press

Ho Chi Minh, president of the Democratic Republic of Vietnam (North Vietnam), whose guerrilla forces defeated the French colonial army in 1954. Ho died in 1969, not living to see the ultimate victory in 1975 over the United States and its South Vietnamese allies, which resulted in uniting all of Vietnam under Communist leadership. Courtesy *New York Times*

Major General Charles Willoughby, intelligence chief for General Douglas MacArthur in World War II and the Korean War, is shown accepting the surrender of Japanese troops in the Philippines in 1945 by General Takashiro Kawabe (*second from left*). Willoughby's faulty intelligence assessments in the Korean War was a key factor in some of the worst American reverses in confronting Chinese Communist troops. Courtesy Associated Press

General Douglas MacArthur (*center*) being briefed on the advance of American troops in the Korean War after their successful landing on the Inchon Peninsula in September 1950. On his right is Vice Admiral Arthur Struble, Seventh Fleet commander. The bodies of three enemy North Korean soldiers lie in a gully in the foreground. Courtesy Associated Press

Chinese Communist troops crossing the Yalu River border into North Korea in October 1950 to confront General Douglas MacArthur's advancing divisions. The Chinese succeeded in driving MacArthur's United Nations' forces back into South Korea. Courtesy Xinhua, Official Chinese News Service

13
THE LAST BATTLE
HAINAN ISLAND

When the *General Gordon* entered Hong Kong's magnificent Victoria Harbor on September 26, 1949, the whistles of the other vessels sounded in welcome to the first ship out of Shanghai since the fall of the city to the Communists. Having been utterly vulnerable when the Japanese seized Hong Kong in 1941, the British were taking greater precautions as the Communists approached. The aircraft carrier *Triumph* and the cruisers *Belfast* and *Jamaica* lay in the harbor screened by destroyers and frigates. The colony's garrison was beefed up to about forty thousand service personnel, including crack army units, backed by artillery, tanks, and fighter planes. The troops were stationed in the New Territories two miles back from the frontier to minimize chances of a violent collision with the Communists. The British also clamped down on the fomenting of internal civil disturbances which might become a pretext for invasion of the colony.

Tillman Durdin, of the *New York Times,* an old friend, was waiting for me at the dock. That night we went to a Chinese restaurant, where we encountered Ian Morrison, the *Times* of London correspondent, and Han Suyin, a Chinese doctor, widow of a Chinese general. Morrison, a tall, good-looking Englishman, had sometimes picnicked with Audrey and me on Purple Mountain in Nanking. He was a superb correspondent, roaming East Asia from his base in Singapore. Born in Peking in 1913, he was the son of Dr. George E. Morrison, famous as "China" Morrison, also a correspondent for the *Times* of London and later political adviser to the Chinese government. An avenue in Peking was named after him, the thoroughfare on which I purchased my first postwar civilian suit in 1946. I had not met Han Suyin before, but I knew that she and Ian had become lovers. She was a slim, fine-featured young woman, born in China of a Belgian mother and a Chinese father. That night she was dressed in a vivid, luminous Chinese brocade dress. She and Ian looked exuberantly happy and were full of laughter when we paused at their table. I would not see Ian again. On August 3, Morrison and Christopher Buckley of the *London Telegraph,* accompanied by an Indian United

Nations official, Colonel M. K. Unni Nayar, were killed in Korea when their jeep ran over a mine.

Han Suyin wrote a novel, *A Many Splendored Thing,* the first of her many books, about her life with Ian in Hong Kong and later in China. The book included excerpts of eighteen letters Ian wrote to her from Korea. It was common knowledge among China hands and others that the central character of the novel, Mark Elliot, was modeled on Ian. It was a fascinating book. But like many of Ian's friends, I resented it because it bared the private emotions of a very reserved man and affronted his widow and children in Singapore. Years later, when I reread *A Many Splendored Thing,* I no longer reacted that way. The book had preserved a remembrance of Ian's humanity, insights, and grace. It conveyed also what it was like to be a reporter amid the agonies of the Korean conflict. In one of the quoted letters, Ian observed: "And now, through loving you, the Koreans are much less strange to me than my own race."

Soon after I reached Hong Kong, there was a letter from Audrey. We had been separated for eleven months, and I had not heard from her in many weeks. Her letter reassured me that our relationship had not changed. Her letters were coming more frequently after that happenstance, which I ascribed to a kindly Higher Being, that drew her to that discarded newspaper in Vancouver carrying the dispatch dubbing me "the loneliest Associated Press staff member in the whole world this Christmas eve." When the AP offered me leave if I would go to Fort Worth, Texas, to speak to a newspaper managing editors' convention, I agreed with alacrity and traveled a circuitous route to Texas via Vancouver, where Audrey was attending the University of British Columbia. At dinner she and I agreed to be sensible and delay our marriage until she graduated. I took her home to her women's dormitory. Five hours later I climbed out of bed in my hotel mumbling, "This is ridiculous." I took a taxi back to the dormitory and at 6:30 A.M. pounded on the door. A startled housemother in hair curlers summoned Audrey on my command. Audrey descended the stairs and agreed it was "ridiculous" and that we should be married at once. She checked out of the university while I flew to Fort Worth to speak to the newspaper editors. I then went on to Camrose, Alberta, Audrey's hometown, and on November 10 we were married in the home of her sister, Sylvia. The lead of an AP story reporting the marriage said: "One foreign correspondent is so confident that the Communists won't soon attempt an assault on Hong Kong that he is taking his bride back to that potential Far Eastern trouble spot." The story also quoted me as saying that a frontal assault on Hong Kong was unlikely. In fact, when we arrived in Hong Kong some days later, the British were worried about the Communists spilling over the border into the colony.

In Hong Kong, Audrey and I checked in at the flossy Gloucester Hotel, which we found we could not afford. Hotels were hard to get and rents astronomical. Hong Kong was booming commercially with the influx from the mainland of wealthy Chinese, many of whom had paid out fortunes in gold, jewels, or priceless antiques to unscrupulous airline pilots or ship captains to smuggle them out of China. Near Christmas time, running out of money, we moved to a small, less expensive Chinese hotel. Audrey had always treasured a tree at Christmas, so I went looking and found several that had been imported by a sharp Chinese merchant. He was selling them at outrageous prices to Western sentimentalists. The tree I bought was too tall for our small hotel room, and it stood bent against the ceiling, half blocking the entrance to the bathroom. I had to stoop beneath branches to get into the bathroom, and when inevitably a Christmas decoration went smash, I would hear Audrey sigh. On the second day, when we investigated why there was so much boisterous traffic in the corridors during the night, we learned we were living in a bordello. We fled in rickshaws, carrying our decorated Christmas tree, to Sunning House, a respectable but more expensive hostelry.

———

In January 1950, not happily, I left my bride in Hong Kong and flew in one of Chennault's CAT planes to Hainan. The island, only five hundred square miles smaller than Taiwan, off the southeastern China coast, was bracing for Communist attack. General Lin Biao's Fourth Field Army, which had fought over the length of China from Manchuria to Guangdong (formerly Kwangtung), the most southern province, was making ready for an amphibious assault across the ten-mile-wide Hainan Strait from the Liuzhou Peninsula. After crossing the Yangtze in Central China in April 1949, Lin's army had thrust through the heart of the country. Nationalist armies crumbled before him, at times under the shock of his hard-fighting columns, but more often because of mass defections or the incompetence of Chiang Kai-shek's generals. Only in General Pai Chung-hsi, the skilled and courageous commander of Central China, whom Chiang Kai-shek never counted among his personal retainers and therefore never fully trusted, did Lin find a worthy adversary. When Lin's troops marched into southern Hunan, Pai's divisions counterattacked and sent them reeling back to provincial capital of Ch'angsha. However, once again the personal rivalries and the jealousies of the other Nationalist generals came into play, frustrating his efforts to exploit the victory. Pai was not able to rally the other generals into a stable defense line to shield South China. Operating in tandem with the army of General Liu Bocheng, Lin Biao was able to roll up Southeast China and occupy Canton, the Kwangtung capital opposite Hong Kong, on October 11. As Communist armies advanced on Canton, Acting President Li Tsung-jen fled to Chungking. When apprised that Chiang Kai-shek was arriving to take command, nervously pleading a need for medical attention, Li fled to Hong Kong and then to the United States, taking with him a sack containing millions in American currency purloined from the Nationalist treasury. Chiang Kai-shek arrived in Chung-king (now Chongqing) in mid-November accompanied by his son, Chiang Ching-kuo, but they soon fled farther west to Chengdu, the provincial capital of Sichuan, as Communist forces under the command of Deng Xiaoping approached the city. Deng occupied the city on December 1 and was appointed by Mao Zedong as mayor and political commissar for party affairs.

In Chengdu, the Generalissimo gave over the defense of the city and command of the remnant Nationalist forces on the mainland to his son, Chiang Ching-kuo, who established his headquarters in the Chengdu Central Military academy. When advancing Communists troops laid siege to the city, the Generalissimo and his son, in the early morning of December 10, 1949, boarded an aircraft, named *Mei-ling* after Madame Chiang, and flew to Taiwan. There, Chiang Kai-shek reassumed office as president on March 15, 1950, with Taipei as his capital, still claiming sovereignty over all of China. The impending struggle for Hainan Island was to be the last major battle of the Civil War.

When I arrived in Haikhou, the provincial capital of Hainan, in January 1950, I found there were only a few foreigners left on the island. I was the sole correspondent. I stayed in a French Jesuit mission. On the first day, the French bishop, Dominique Desperben, took me up to the flat roof of his mission, where we looked out over Haikou, a dirty sprawling city of 250,000 people, in which most residents lived in old two-story buildings made of mud and white plaster. The Communist-held coast was visible across the narrow Hainan Strait. Nationalist Air Force fighters and bombers based on Hainan Island whipped low overhead, and we observed puffs of smoke where bombs were falling on coastal positions held by Lin Biao's troops. The planes were also striking within Hainan along the mountainous spine of the lush, green island at the guerrilla bases of the local Communist leader, Feng Baiju. Feng had held sway in the center of the island for more than twenty years, well before the Japanese invasion in February 1939. With his land reform program, he had drawn the support of many of the island's 2.5 million peasants. His political commissars administered villages only a few miles from some of the enemy Nationalist army camps. In anticipation of the coming of Lin Biao's troops, Feng's army of some twelve thousand had taken the offensive, seizing a section of the southwestern coast. Agents and arms were being landed there from junks which slipped by the blockading Nationalist Navy patrols during the night.

At the Nationalist military headquarters, I met with the top commander, General Hsueh Yueh, the former governor of Kwangtung Province, who was known as the "Little Tiger." The general, an energetic man, dressed in a flashy tailored American-style uniform, complained he was receiving only meager aid from Chiang Kai-shek. He was frantically trying to organize a defense force out of some 140,000 troops, about 80,000 of them combat veterans, evacuated from the mainland. About forty bombers and fighters were based at the Haikou Airport and at Sanya in the southern part of the island, both fields built by the Japanese, to strike at Allied positions in China and Southeast Asia. Nationalist gunboats were operating out of Haikou and Yulin, the excellent natural ports also developed by the Japanese.

Amid these preparations for battle, some three dozen foreigners were living fairly comfortably on the island, determined to remain no matter what the outcome of the impending battle. I visited the garden compound in Haikou of the American Presbyterian Mission, an oasis of order amid the decay of the city. There were ten women and four men in the mission, sturdy, dedicated people, who were supporting a church, schools, and a 180-bed hospital. With the Catholic missionaries, the Presbyterians administered a leprosarium where about 175 lepers lived, among them one foreigner, a man of German and French ancestry who was suffering the advance state of the disease. There were about 3,000 lepers on the island.

The most elegant foreign residents were the French consul, Hughes Jean de Dianous of Avignon, and his wife. Their fifty-two-year-old consulate, housed in a building constructed of yellow lava stone from the island's extinct volcanoes, was sited on a sliver of land separated from Haikou by a slender narrows. The couple commuted to the city by native sampan. I found them clinging to the ambience of their native land by offering the finest French wine and cuisine to their guests.

The consul's job was to report on Chinese activities that could affect Indochina. When I called on him, he was busy relaying pleas to Paris from the Nationalist government for the right of passage through Indochina of the remnants of General Pai Chung-hsi's army that were holding out against the Communists up against the border. From Haikou, the Nationalist Air Force was making two flights a day to drop munitions and other supplies to the isolated units, totaling some twenty-five thousand troops. Eventually they managed to cross the Indochina border at Mon Cay and were interned by the French, who confiscated their excellent American equipment. I visited the troops in Mon Cay in March 1950 and found them in good condition. Pai offered the use of the troops against Ho Chi Minh's Viet Minh guerrillas, but the French, fearful of Chinese Communist retaliation, declined. The troops that crossed into Mon Cay and other survivors who had escaped to Hainan were all that remained of Pai Chung-hsi's 350,000-man army. Three months before, it had been the single most powerful force remaining to the Nationalists on the mainland.

On Hainan, the governor of the island, Marshal Ch'en Chi-tang, received me for an interview at the Haikou Airport, where he was awaiting the arrival from Hong Kong of his young, pretty wife. The fifty-eight-year-old Cantonese marshal, a lively, outspoken man dressed in a brown tunic and white Panama hat, sat with me on the veranda of the airport's passenger shack gazing out to the Communist-held coast. The governor complained angrily about the sparse assistance he was getting from Chiang Kai-shek. "We have not received the money or supplies we need. Only some air force planes and navy ships have been sent to help us," the governor said. In lieu of funds from Taiwan, his government was turning out silver dollars at the provincial mint, but their silver content was diminishing rapidly. When Ch'en assumed civil control of Hainan the previous April, he found that the corrupt, inefficient Nationalist rule imposed after World War II had virtually wrecked the industrial foundation built by the Japanese. Of 170 factories erected by the Japanese, only about a dozen were operating. The port installations were a shambles, and steel rails of the new railroad had been hauled away. Little also remained of the projects initiated by the Japanese, which were designed to develop the rich mineral deposits and agricultural resources. It was estimated that the island could support more than triple its population of 2.5 million. Trying to salvage something from the wreckage, Ch'en reopened the high-grade iron mines and built a broadcast station, two hospitals, a weaving mill, and four schools. Now, bracing to resist a Communist invasion, he was reequipping troops of the island garrison and paying them with silver dollars from the mint.

I flew back to Hong Kong on February 2, the last correspondent to visit Hainan prior to the Communist invasion. The day before, the French bishop, dressed in his long black habit, had brought me again to the roof of the mission. The sun, a huge bright orange orb, was settling below the horizon as we looked out to mainland. The bishop tugged his long graying beard and said softly:" I have lived happily among the Chinese for thirty years, but now I am afraid."

In Hong Kong, there were new travel orders awaiting me from the AP. While in the United States on leave, I had been assigned to open a bureau in Peking as soon as the Communists would admit us. Following the negotiations of J. C. Jao, my former deputy in Nanjing, with officials in Peking, we speculated that it would be only a matter of months before I was granted a visa, although American recognition of the Maoist government did not appear to be an immediate prospect. The White House seemed more intent on withdrawing from the China morass than anything else. On December 23, an internal State Department policy paper was issued saying that the Communist seizure of Taiwan was anticipated and that American missions abroad should play down the importance of Taiwan to U.S. interests so as minimize the damage to Washington's prestige if it should fall. Secretly, Secretary of State Dean Acheson drafted a plan involving recognition of the Maoist government and withdrawal of American support from Chiang Kai-shek on Taiwan. It was conceived as a Cold War stratagem to lure Mao away from close alliance with Stalin. Hints dropped by Communist officials that the Maoist government was interested in trade and technical assistance from the United States suggested that the plan might win acceptance in Peking.

On January 5, 1950, President Truman issued a statement which seemed to make possible an accommodation with Mao. "The United States has no military bases on Formosa [Taiwan] at this time. Nor does it have any intention of utilizing its armed forces to interfere in the present situation. The United States Government will not pursue a course which will lead to involvement in the civil conflict in China. Militarily, the United States Government will not provide military aid or advice to Chinese forces on Formosa." Surprisingly, in what was in effect a rebuff to these American overtures, the Chinese Communists on January 14 arbitrarily requisitioned a part of the grounds of the American Consulate General in Peking. At the time, Mao was in Moscow seeking aid and negotiating a Treaty of Friendship, Alliance and Mutual Assistance. The sudden move in Peking might very well have been a gesture intended to demonstrate loyalty to Stalin and put to rest his suspicions that the Chinese Communists were open to dealings with the

United States. Acheson reacted by promptly ordering the withdrawal from the China mainland of the remaining diplomatic personnel on January 18, asserting that the action in Peking, and previous harsh treatment in Mukden of the staff of the American consulate during which Angus Ward, the consul general, was confined for a time, made it appear that the Communists were not interested in American recognition.

The AP Foreign Desk then cabled me suggesting that, since the Communists were ignoring my visa application, I visit "Saigon, Indonesia" for a month. Confusing Indochina with Indonesia might simply have been a typo, but it was indicative of how remote and out of the news Vietnam was at the time. Typical of virtually all American newspapers, the *New York Times* had published only one article on Indochina in 1942, seven in 1943, and four in 1944. A few days after my return from Hainan, Audrey and I flew to Saigon.

We were in Vietnam when word came that Hainan had fallen to the Communists after two failed amphibious assaults in March and mid-April. But on April 17, Lin Biao's troops swarmed onto the north coast landing from more than a hundred junks while another column transported aboard some sixty junks, landed west of Haikou. The Communist guerrillas struck from the interior. The Nationalist garrison retreated south to the port of Yulin, where some troops found ships to take them to Taiwan, the last Nationalist retreat. On April 21, having waited more than two decades, guerrilla chief Feng Baiju was the unchallenged ruler of Hainan, and on May Day he raised his red flag over Haikou. Within two years all the foreigners were gone, except perhaps for the lonely French German leper. The guns were silent now on the mainland with the Nationalists confined to Taiwan and its small offshore islands.

Reading the brief item in a Saigon newspaper, I reflected on my experience in covering the Chinese Civil War for three years from Manchuria down to that obscure island off the southern coast. How much of my reporting, and that of other American correspondents, had been digested by the people of our country? On leave in the United States four months earlier, I had found a vitriolic debate in progress on "Who lost China?" It had been touched off by the Republicans in the 1948 presidential campaign elections by their candidate, Thomas E. Dewey, who accused the Truman administration of failing to provide sufficient support for Chiang Kai-shek. Initially, I was simply flabbergasted and somewhat amused by this question of "Who lost China?" The answer seemed so obvious from the weight of documentation in the White Paper on China published on August 2, 1949, by the State

Department covering relations with China from 1944 to 1949, the reporting of General Barr on the incredibly inept performance of the Nationalist military, and what journalists, including me, had been filing to our publications for years. The record of Chiang's strategic bungling in military engagements with the Communists, his cronyism in the selection of inept army commanders, his tolerance of corruption, and the failure of the Kuomintang to carry out the political and economic reforms needed to rally the Chinese people to the banner of a democratic state—these were the factors unmistakably which enabled the Communists to come to power despite the two billion dollars of American military aid given Chiang. It was estimated that 75 percent of the arms provided the Nationalists had fallen into the hands of the Communists beginning with the collapse in Manchuria.

I was less amused by the hypocritical question of "Who lost China?" when Alan Gould, executive editor of the Associated Press, received a letter from Alfred Kohlberg accusing me of covering up Stalin's control of the Chinese Communist Party. Kohlberg, a wealthy New York importer of lace from South China ports, was a member of the "China Lobby," a group of American supporters of Chiang Kai-shek, notable among them Henry Luce, the publisher of *Time* magazine. Kohlberg took issue with the statement, which I had made in a widely published report, in which I had said: "All the dependable evidence we have points to the premise that Moscow does not have direct control over the Chinese Communists." In reply to Kohlberg, Gould stood by my record as an observer of China developments, pointing out that in the next sentence I had said: "Peking obediently follows Moscow's lead; almost certainly not on direct orders but rather because of ideological faith."

Other targets in the press, academia, and government were not as fortunate as I in the support they received from their superiors for their reporting. Fear of Stalinist aggression and Communist infiltration into the United States, the Communist coup in Czechoslovak in 1948, and the invasion of South Korea in 1950 by the North were among the factors that generated a public atmosphere of suspicion and insecurity which obscured undisputable facts. Spurred on by the China Lobby and later by the accusations of Senator Joe McCarthy, blame for the so-called loss of China was heaped on the revered General Marshall and leading academic China experts such as Owen Lattimore and John King Fairbank. The most knowledgeable China specialists in the State Department, among them John S. Service, John Davies, John Melby, and Edmund Clubb, were falsely labeled security risks or pro-Communist and accused of helping to bring about Mao's triumph through their criticism of Chiang Kai-shek's policies. China journalists, notably Edgar

Snow, suffered the Cold War umbrage. Careers were blighted or destroyed, and those individuals most qualified to provide guidance in the framing of an intelligent China policy were silenced or their voices muffled when they were most needed by the American people.

The fiction that the so-called loss of China could be attributed to pro-Communist bias was propagated on occasion even by someone as well informed as Dwight Eisenhower as he sought to cope politically with the impact on public opinion that McCarthy made with his broadsided accusations. In a speech in Milwaukee in 1952 while campaigning for the presidency, Eisenhower asserted: Two decades of tolerance for Communism reaching into high places in Washington had meant "contamination in some degree of virtually every department, every agency, every bureau, and every section of our government. It meant a government by men whose very brains were confused by the opiate of this deceit" resulting in the fall of China and the surrender of whole nations in Eastern Europe.

Over the next years, I found this distortion of Chinese history ever more excruciatingly painful. The politician most responsible for the collapse of Nationalist China, Chiang Kai-shek, was comfortably ensconced on Taiwan enjoying renewal of American military and economic aid. In January 1951, speaking in Taipei of his determination to retake the Communist-held mainland, Chiang Kai-shek said that past mistakes must be avoided if a successful invasion was to be mounted. The mistakes he cited were disunity and factionalism within the Kuomintang, incompetence, defeatism, selfishness, and lavishness. He made no direct reference to the failure of his own military strategy. Chiang remained president of the Nationalist government on Taiwan until his death there at the age of eighty-seven. Madame Chiang retired to an estate on New York's Long Island and died there in 2003 at the age of 105. In that year, when Audrey and I toured Chiang Kai-shek's palace headquarters in Nanjing, we were told by officials that the government was amenable to the interment of Chiang's remains there, as he wished, if the family and the government on Taiwan would approve of the reunification of the island with the mainland. Chiang's remains are buried in Taipei, the Taiwan capital, in an elaborate tomb modeled after that of Sun Yat-sen in Nanjing.

We may ask: What kind of a China would have emerged if Chiang Kai-shek had risen to his epic challenge and defeated Mao Zedong? On Taiwan, the Chiang government, spurred by conditional American aid, instituted economic reforms and built a prosperous society. After Chiang's death in 1975, it evolved from an authoritarian into a multiparty democratic state.

With competent governance, Chiang or his successors conceivably could have founded a democratic society on the mainland comparable to that which later emerged on Taiwan. Under a Communist government the people of the mainland are enjoying much improved living standards, largely as a consequence of the free market incentives introduced in the late 1970s by Deng Xiaoping, but promises of democratic reform remain unfulfilled.*

*On July 20, 1965, I reported from Hong Kong that Li Tsung-Jen, the Nationalist vice president and later acting president, had returned to the China mainland after sixteen years of exile in the United States traveling surreptitiously via Switzerland aboard a special plane to Peking. He had broken with the Chiang Kai-shek government on Taiwan, which earlier had formally impeached him as vice president and declared he would form a "third force." Welcomed at the Peking airport by Premier Zhou Enlai, Li pledged support for the Communist cause in the struggle with the United States to make up for his "guilty past." He was treated deferentially by Communist officials until his death in 1969 at the age of seventy-eight. Shortly before his death, according to Xinhua, he wrote a letter to the Peking government in which he said that the only way out for the Nationalist officials on Taiwan would be for them "to return as I did to the motherland to contribute their share to the liberation of Taiwan."

14
SAIGON

In early February 1950, just a few days after my return from Hainan Island, Audrey and I flew to Saigon in an old French commercial airliner and checked into the Continental Hotel. In our room, weary after the long flight, we had just sprawled on the large bed beneath mosquito nets and a ceiling fan that was barely stirring the sultry air when an explosion shattered the square beneath our window. We scrambled to look. There, on the other side of the square we saw a sidewalk café that had been blasted by a bomb. More than a score of rickshaw cabs were streaking away from the café. One of their drivers obviously had thrown the powerful bomb. French soldiers and sailors, dead and wounded, lay sprawled beside overturned tables and splintered glass within the café and along the sidewalk terrace. A badly wounded soldier clutching his groin stumbled into the street. This was our introduction to French-ruled Indochina, which for three years had been seething with the burning hatreds of colonial war and terrorism.

In the struggle against Ho Chi Minh's Viet Minh guerrillas in the jungles, mountains, and on the great river deltas of Vietnam, the French Union forces had suffered about 100,000 casualties, including 25,000 dead and captured. It was a war of surprise attacks on isolated French garrisons, of ambush and massacre, and ruthless retaliation with napalm air attacks and torching of villages suspected of harboring the Viet Minh. At night, the French remained in their fortified posts, and the Viet Minh became masters of the countryside. Millions of Vietnamese had been uprooted in the merciless warfare and flooded as refugees into Saigon, Hanoi, and the other French-held cities and towns. The world knew little or did not care very much about this vast human tragedy unfolding in a remote colony. Few foreign correspondents ventured into Vietnam to tell the story. Resident French journalists were subjected to military censorship. The war was overshadowed by events in China.

Under the French, Saigon was a much less safe place in which to live than the city I came to know in the 1960s, when it was policed by American troops. Viet Minh terrorists would throw an average of three or four plastic bombs each night into cafés crowded with French soldiers and sailors or into establishments that refused to pay taxes to their underground. Political assassinations were staged on open café verandas or on busy thoroughfares. No one was safe. I was nearby when Marcel Marshal Bazin, the dreaded chief of the political section of the French Sûreté police, was shot in the back while walking on a crowded street. Three Vietnamese policemen observed the killing without pursuing the assassins. Bazin had commanded the Sûreté shock force against the death squads of Battalion 905, the Viet Minh underground, which was terrorizing the city. His agents in retaliation for Viet Minh assassinations had been dumping the bodies of executed suspects on sidewalk corners to pressure the underground to desist. Shortly after I interviewed Jean de Raymond, French commissioner for Cambodia, he was murdered in his bedroom, struck on the head and stabbed in the throat, by a Vietnamese servant.

Yet stubbornly the French were resisting transforming Saigon into a barricaded city, as did the American military command in later years. Saigon remained a vividly colorful city of tree-lined boulevards with sidewalk cafés serving superb wines and gourmet food—a vibrant metropolis of 2 million encompassing Saigon and the twin Chinese city of Cholon. French soldiers in a mélange of uniforms—Foreign Legionnaires, African Senegalese, Moroccan Goumiers, and French paratroopers—thronged the streets, bars, casinos, and brothels. For the affluent, the friendly, opium-smoking Corsican who ran our hotel, the Continental, imported French prostitutes from Paris. There were lavishly furnished opium dens in Saigon and Hanoi whose patrons included occasionally prominent members of the French community. They would recline on the couches taking perhaps five or ten pipes, not the thirty or forty smoked by addicts, tended by Vietnamese girls in white diaphanous dresses who were available to those male patrons whose sexual desires were not quenched by the suppressant effects of the opium. Remote from the cement blockhouses and shanties on the outskirts of the city where most Vietnamese lived, the French *colons* dwelled in opulent style in luxurious villas.

I soon learned that much of that opulence was financed corruptly by covert manipulation of the piaster, the Indochinese currency. Fortunes were made by buying piasters—the official Vietnamese currency—on the black market and then obtaining authorization, usually through bribery from the French Office of Exchange, to remit the currency to banks in France at the official rate. The discrepancy yielded enormous profits at the expense of the French government.

Outraged Frenchmen told me that the Viet Minh had been exploiting this corrupt traffic to buy weapons, which were used in operations against French troops. The weapons were bought with hard currency from gunrunners operating out of Hong Kong and Bangkok. To obtain the hard currency, usually American dollars, the Viet Minh collected piasters from shopkeepers and restaurant owners through taxes, actually extortion. These piasters were then sold in Saigon to agents of a French syndicate at cheap market rate for hard currency payable in Switzerland. One of these syndicate agents, I learned, was a senior Chinese employee of the Bank of Indochina, which had semiofficial status. The syndicate made its profit by taking the piasters to the official French Office of Exchange in Saigon, where, with the connivance of French bureaucrats, the syndicate would obtain authorization from the office to remit the piasters at the official rate to France. The syndicate would make a profit of as much as 100 percent. I was told by my French sources that information about this traffic had been given to the French government by one of its intelligence agencies, Service de Documentation Exterieure et de Contre Espionage (SDECE), but the government refrained from taking action to avoid a public scandal that would damage it politically.

To bypass the military censorship in Saigon, Audrey and I went to Bangkok to file my story on this piaster racket. French agents who trailed me searched my room at the Oriental Hotel and obtained details of my story, apparently from my discarded drafts left carelessly in a wastepaper basket. Upon my return to Saigon, my French assistant, Max Clos, and I were called to the office of the Sûreté police chief. We found him in a state of great agitation, and to my astonishment, he began to plead for our understanding. He had assumed, incorrectly, that I knew his office was linked with the piaster traffic. He told me that income from dealing in piasters had been used in his office to pay his agents, and he showed us records of such payments to prominent personalities in Saigon. The Sûreté chief accused his SDECE counterpart of attempting to ruin him and said that the SDECE chief was obtaining funds by illegal sales of import licenses.

The French war effort was being undermined by this corrupt piaster traffic, and it was also having a cancerous effect on metropolitan France. The burden was shared by the United States, since Washington started picking up the bills for the French Indochina War in 1950 and by 1954 was paying about 80 percent of the costs.

This was the morass of corruption and deadly guerrilla warfare into which the United States plunged in February 1950. Just a few days after our arrival in Saigon, President Truman extended recognition to the newly created French-sponsored Vietnamese government headed as chief of state by Bao Dai, last emperor of the Nguyen dynasty. Truman also pledged military aid to the French in the war against the Viet Minh. The president put aside the traditional American reservations about French colonial policies and a pending post–World War II proposal by the late president, Franklin D. Roosevelt, to free Indochina from French colonial rule by converting it into a United Nations Trusteeship. Shortly before Truman made his commitment, Vietnam was incorporated with Laos and Cambodia into a new Indochinese federation with the three states granted limited autonomy within the French Union.

At the time of our arrival, there were only about a dozen Americans living in Saigon, most of them attached to the small U.S. Consulate. The American community in Indochina was made up largely of about 100 missionaries, most affiliated with the Christian and Missionary Alliance. The alliance had founded a church of some 50,000 members drawn from the 28 million people of the three Indochinese states. The missionaries, like Americans generally, were popular with the Indochinese, who deemed them anticolonialist, since the United States had recently granted independence to the Philippines. However, many French officials regarded Americans with deep suspicion. There was lingering anger about the support given in 1945 to Ho Chi Minh by agents of the Office of Strategic Services (OSS), the forerunner of the Central Intelligence Agency. Many French *colons* were convinced that the United States was intent on replacing France as the dominant presence in Indochina.

On February 9, 1950, Edmund Gullion, the newly appointed American consul general in Saigon, arrived and delivered a formal note to the Bao Dai government proposing diplomatic relations. On February 25, the consulate was raised to a legation, and Gullion was named chargé d'affaires, with the personal rank of minister-counselor. Almost immediately, the United States began to assemble in Saigon the panoply of intervention: large diplomatic and information staffs, economic and military aid missions. U.S. naval vessels called at the port of Saigon.

The AP had directed me to spend a month looking into vague reports of unrest in what was viewed as an obscure little country. But now, suddenly and unexpectedly, Indochina was thrust by the Truman commitment into American consciousness. I was directed to open a bureau, and I became the first American correspondent after World War II to be stationed in Indochina. Prior to my arrival French stringers covered news developments for foreign news agencies filing to Paris in French. Audrey and I stayed two years and witnessed the United States becoming mired in a struggle which was to evolve into one of the most painful episodes in American history.

I called on Gullion not long after his arrival at his office in the small consulate building just off Rue Catinat. Gullion, a polished thirty-six-year-old bachelor, son of an army officer and a career diplomat, received me in a friendly but guarded manner. He told me he thought American correspondents who had covered the Chinese Civil War were "defeatist" in their attitudes toward the anti-Communist struggle in Asia. Vietnam was not China, he said, and the French Army was not the Chinese Nationalist Army. The Truman administration was convinced that the French-supported Bao Dai government with American material support could bring about a military victory against the Viet Minh. Most important, the French Army would be an effective weapon for the containment of Communist China.

I left stunned by what Gullion had told me. I asked myself: Didn't we learn anything in China? Despite enormous American aid, the Nationalist government had been defeated by the Communists, who rode to power in part because of the ineptitude of Chiang Kai-shek but also because Mao Zedong had succeeded in rallying the peasant masses. Now we were plunging into another Asian bog by supporting a colonial regime that was struggling against an evidently popular nationalist movement.

It was also from Gullion, who was to play a pivotal and sometimes controversial role in the long-term development of Indochina policy, that I first heard of what in the State Department was called the domino theory. Four years later, President Dwight Eisenhower would articulate the theory publicly—that the loss of Vietnam to Communist control would lead to the loss of other Asian countries like a row of dominoes. This evolved into the rationale for U.S. intervention at the side of France.

What Gullion told me did not, in fact, square with what actually had transpired in the high councils of Truman's administration prior to his Indochina commitment. As Dean Acheson, who later became Truman's secretary of state, recalled in his memoir: "The U.S. came to the aid of the French in Indochina not because we approved of what they were doing, but because we needed their support for our policies in regard to NATO and Germany. The French blackmailed us. At every meeting when we asked them for greater effort in Europe they brought up Indochina. They asked for our aid for Indochina but refused to tell me what they hoped to accomplish or how. Perhaps they didn't know."

Robert S. McNamara, the U.S. defense secretary in the Kennedy and Johnson administrations, elaborating in his 1999 book *Argument with-*

out End on the Acheson recollections, added: "In this way, with almost no thought given to the fate of Vietnam itself, Truman, Acheson, and their colleagues in Washington struck a Faustian bargain by which the United States would eventually become the guarantor and underwriter of the unsuccessful French effort to reclaim its prewar colonies in Indochina. This was how U.S. involvement with Vietnam began: absentmindedly, almost as a kind of 'throwaway' in a grand bargain for the heart of Europe, to appease its defeated, temperamental, and proud French ally."

The Truman administration began as early as 1945 to yield to de Gaulle's pressure for restoration of French control of Indochina. Truman amended President Roosevelt's proposal for the transformation of Indochina into a United Nations Trusteeship leading to independence by adding a stipulation that it would be done only with French consent, something Paris refused to do. Early in 1946 American and other Allied naval vessels began transporting French troops, newly outfitted with American equipment, to Vietnam, where they took control of the cities.

The Truman commitment was made on the basis of scant information about what was actually transpiring on the ground in Indochina. The small American Consulate in Saigon, circumscribed by French suspicions, had provided only limited information to Washington. The Office of Strategic Services was withdrawn from Indochina in 1945 when the organization was dissolved by Truman to make way for the creation of the Central Intelligence Agency. Since then the CIA had made its assessments based largely on French and British intelligence.

The last American intelligence officer openly posted in Saigon was Lieutenant Colonel Peter A. Dewey, leader of a team of OSS agents. He was killed on September 26, 1945, in an ambush at a roadblock near the Ton Son Nhut Airport. In compliance with a British order, Dewey's jeep was not displaying an identifying American flag. Dewey was to have left Saigon that day, having been declared persona non grata by Major General Douglas D. Gracey, commander of the British occupation force for Indochina. These events stemmed from decisions taken in 1945 at the Potsdam Conference of the United States, Britain, and the Soviet Union, when it was decided that following the defeat of Japan Vietnam would be divided at the sixteenth parallel, with Chinese troops in control in the north and the British in occupation of the south, embracing Cochin China and its capital, Saigon. The arrangement was provisional with the understanding that the final disposition of Indochina would be decided after the war.

Dewey arrived in Saigon on September 4, technically in command of

Project Embankment, an operation to free 4,549 Allied prisoners, including 214 Americans held in Japanese prison camps near Saigon. However, Dewey had also been instructed by William "Wild Bill" Donovan, director of the OSS, to represent American interests generally in Cochin China. He was there when one of the great blunders of the postwar era took place. General Gracey's British occupation force began arriving on September 12. Unexpectedly, and without Allied authorization, in addition to his Gurkha troops, Gracey brought with him a small French infantry unit. The presence of the French troops immediately excited wild Vietnamese fears that the British were restoring French colonialism. Violent clashes erupted between the Vietnamese and French *colons*. Gracey almost immediately came into conflict with the Committee of the South, the representatives of Ho Chi Minh, who had taken over administration of Saigon from the Japanese prior to the arrival of British troops. Dewey raised the ire of the British commander by being in covert contact with the Vietnamese and openly manifesting support for their interests. He was then declared persona non grata by Gracey and told to leave Saigon. Before going to the airport and his death, Dewey sent a final message to Donovan: "Cochin China is burning. The French and British are finished here, and we [Americans] ought to clear out of Southeast Asia." It was a prescient message, which, if heeded, might have spared the United States and the Vietnamese people enormous grief.

The death of Dewey, a decorated officer who had served also in Europe with distinction during World War II, parachuting in covert operations behind German lines, evoked an angry outcry in the United States. Dewey had become the first American fatality of the Vietnam wars. An OSS investigation into his death concluded that Dewey had been ambushed and killed through being mistaken of a nationality other than American. The report stated: "If the jeep in which he was riding at the time of the incident had been displaying an American flag, we feel positive that the shot would not have been fired. A flag was not being displayed in accordance with verbal instructions issued by General Gracey." The general had insisted that flying an American flag would be an impingement on British authority. The foreboding in Dewey's final message to Donovan was realized within weeks after his death. On October 16, under attack by British and Japanese troops as well as French troops, released from their prisoner-of-war internment, the Committee of the South and its Viet Minh guerrilla forces withdrew from the Saigon area, and the war in Cochin China was on. General Gracey was later reprimanded by Lord Mountbatten, the Allied theater commander, for his unauthorized turnover of Saigon to the French.

For years speculative reports circulated that French or British agents might have been involved in Dewey's death. Dewey's body was never found after the ambush despite an intensive search. In March 2005, when Audrey and I revisited Vietnam, the mysterious circumstances were finally clarified. We returned in the company of Nancy Dewey Hoppin, the daughter of Colonel Dewey, and her husband, Charles, a lawyer. Nancy had been investigating the circumstances of her father's death tirelessly over the years and had sought unsuccessfully the location of his grave. The long-sought answers were obtained unexpectedly by her at a meeting near Saigon. Nancy was introduced by John McAuliff, director of the American Foundation for Reconciliation and Development, to Tran Van Giau, a historian and a former senior official, on the chance that he might provide more definitive information about Dewey's death. At the meeting, Tran Van Giau, who had been in command of Viet Minh military forces in the south during September 1945, cited a report he had received just after Dewey was killed. On September 26, Tran said, fighting was in progress around Ton Son Nhut Airport following a French attack three days earlier on the forces of the Committee of the South. Viet Minh guerrillas were forced to fall back after a failed attempt to take the airport. It was a band of those guerrillas that ambushed Dewey in his jeep at the nearby Chu-la T-junction. Tran said the guerrillas shot Dewey, thinking he was a French officer, and made off with the jeep and Dewey's body, which they threw into a river at Go Vap. Tran said he conducted an investigation upon receiving a report of the ambush and found that the officer who was killed was not French but was a member of the American OSS. Having provided the first definitive account of Dewey's death, Tran expressed condolences to the colonel's daughter, ending her long quest. In Hanoi, a Vietnamese historian and former diplomat handed me a photocopy of the letter sent to President Truman by Ho Chi Minh expressing condolences on the death of Dewey and friendship for the American people.

When I arrived in Saigon in 1950, the French were still unforgiving about the OSS operations, particularly about the activities of Lieutenant Colonel Archimedes L. A. Patti, who served as chief of OSS operations for Indochina in 1945. They accused Patti of undermining French authority and working to bring Ho Chi Minh to power, something that Patti vigorously denied in his memoir, *Why Vietnam?* written in 1980 after declassification of the OSS files. Patti did meet on a number of occasions with Ho Chi Minh and forwarded the Viet Minh leader's repeated appeals for friendship and support of Vietnamese independence to Donovan and the White House. In his conversations with Patti, Ho repeatedly emphasized that he was more the Nationalist rather than the Communist. In a clandestine operation on July 16, 1945, OSS agents designated the Deer Team parachuted into Ho Chi Minh's jungle camp near Kim Lung, where they trained and armed a cadre of Viet Minh guerrillas for action against the Japanese. One of them, a medic, Paul Hoagland, saved Ho's life by injecting him with quinine and sulfa drugs when he was critically ill with malaria and dysentery. OSS assistance was provided in return for intelligence information on Japanese operations and Viet Minh help in rescuing downed American airmen. When the war with Japan ended in August, the Deer Team accompanied Ho Chi Minh to Hanoi, joining Patti there as sympathetic observers of a mass rally on September 2 at which Ho Chi Minh proclaimed Vietnamese independence and established the Provisional Government of the Democratic Republic of Vietnam (DRV). In his inauguration speech in Hanoi, Ho quoted from the American Declaration of Independence. Earlier, Ho Chi Minh made use of the OSS radio network to transmit a proposal to the French government calling for Vietnam to enter into the French Union under a French president provided "that independence be given to this country in not less than five years and not more than ten years." The French ignored the proposal.

These overtures to the French were criticized by members of Ho's party who were agitating for more militant policies. Ho replied: "You fools! Don't you realize what it means if the Chinese stay? Don't you remember your history? The last time the Chinese came, they stayed one thousand years! The French are foreigners. They are weak. Colonialism is dying out. Nothing will be able to withstand world pressure for independence. They may stay for a while but they will have to go because the white man is finished in Asia. But if the Chinese stay now, they will never leave. As for me, I prefer to smell French shit for five years, rather than Chinese shit for the rest of my life."

The Chinese were in occupation of North Vietnam under the terms of the Allied agreement at the Potsdam Conference when Ho made this retort to critics. Chinese Nationalist occupation troops, many of them under the command of notorious warlords, had descended like locusts after the end of World War II on famine-stricken North Vietnam, systematically looting the country. In replying to his critics, Ho evoked historical Vietnamese fears of Chinese domination.

In February 1946, Ho Chi Minh wrote to Truman asking for support of Vietnamese independence in a step-by-step process similar to that by which the United States granted independence to the Philippines after World War II. The letter was the eighth recorded appeal to the president for friendship and recognition. Truman did not reply to any of the messages. When I toured

Vietnam in March 2005, Vietnamese officials and journalists reminded me of these rebuffs, which they historically term the first missed opportunity for peaceful settlement of the Indochina conflict.

In March 1946, Ho Chi Minh's provisional government signed an agreement in Hanoi with the French for the entry of Vietnam as a free state into the Indochina Federation of the French Union but without any guarantees of eventual independence. In June, however, the French, despite violent Vietnamese protests, unilaterally detached Cochin China as a separate state. Ho Chi Minh, nevertheless, persisted in attempts to reach an agreement, and in September he signed a modus vivendi understanding in Paris providing for a cease-fire in the guerrilla war in Cochin China and broad French rights throughout Vietnam. With the end of the British-Chinese occupation of Vietnam stipulated under the postwar Allied arrangements, French troops with American and British assistance took control of all major cities. In November armed clashes between French and Vietnamese forces erupted at Haiphong, and French naval vessels bombarded the city, killing thousands of Vietnamese civilians. Ho Chi Minh then rejected a French demand that all Vietnamese militia be disarmed, with security functions entrusted to French troops. When negotiations collapsed, Ho Chi Minh fled with his government into the jungles north of Hanoi. As the Viet Minh fell back on the Maoist strategy of protracted war, Ho appealed to Communist China and the Soviet Union for assistance. A founder of the Indochinese Communist Party in 1930, Ho had worked in the underground of the Comintern, the Moscow-based international Communist organization, on behalf of anticolonial movements since the 1920s. But in 1945 he had distanced himself from Stalin and Mao Zedong while seeking American recognition of his government and the possibility of economic assistance. Rebuffed by Truman and the French, he reentered the Sino-Soviet fold.

In turning to Bao Dai as a leader who might attract the loyalty of the Vietnamese people, the French gambled on a personality very different from that of their enemy, Ho Chi Minh, an ascetic who had spent most of his career in the revolutionary underground and in prison while struggling for Indochinese independence. Bao Dai's political career had been a checkered one. When the Japanese ruled Vietnam during World War II, he served as head of their puppet government and acquired a reputation as the playboy emperor whose interests resided more in female playmates and in hunting tigers than in politics. At the end of the war, when Ho Chi Minh's provisional government was briefly in control of Hanoi in 1945, he abdicated as emperor and agreed to serve as supreme adviser, a title that the Viet Minh bestowed with more than a little irony. Not long after, he fled to exile in Hong Kong. In 1949, desperate for a symbol to give legitimacy to their emerging dependent Vietnamese government, the French brought Bao Dai out of exile to become chief of state. In according recognition, the Truman administration, like the French, was looking to Bao Dai to rally Vietnamese democratic forces against the Communist-led Viet Minh.

Several weeks after our arrival in Saigon, Audrey and I traveled to Dalat, a beautiful mountain resort in Annam, to interview Bao Dai. The thirty-five-year-old French-educated emperor received us in his palace, a modernistic country house built with granite blocks furnished in Western style. It was guarded by a cordon of Vietnamese sentries and within by the secret police of the French Sûreté. Although he had abdicated, Bao Dai was still being treated as a royal monarch. The emperor, a heavyset man with black hair combed straight back, dressed in a gray American-style flannel suit, had just returned from a weekend hunt in the surrounding hills which abounded in tiger, elephants, and deer. I was the first reporter to be received since the founding of his government earlier in the month.

"The Vietnamese people want as complete independence as possible," Bao Dai told me. He said that the present status of his government represented a stage in its development and reflected the current political situation. Under the accords he had accepted, the French retained responsibility for defense and diplomacy, as well as legal, business, and cultural prerogatives for French subjects. The Vietnamese piaster was tied to the French franc. Bao Dai said he refused to recognize that a state of actual civil war existed within Vietnam, since his military forces were fighting "only against terrorism and banditry." Although entertained in the palace, we did not meet the empress, who was in Cannes, France, with their two children. But the emperor did not seem bereft of companionship judging by the bevy of beautiful Vietnamese and Eurasian women who were in attendance. His French advisers had not been able to persuade him to leave the pleasures of Dalat for Saigon or shed his playboy image. The emperor hosted a parade of American officials who listened sympathetically to his political woes but were unable to draw him more deeply into Saigon politics.

From the start, Bao Dai's regime was doomed to failure by the accords, which the French compelled him to sign. The agreement fell far short of the dramatic act of liberal statesmanship that might have placed Bao Dai's government on a solid political foundation and enabled him to attract support away from Ho Chi Minh. The French rejected the Vietnamese appeal for status in the French Union equivalent to that of a dominion in the British Commonwealth. In the grant of limited autonomy, there was no promise of independence or provision for the eventual withdrawal of French troops from the country.

French policy in effect bestowed upon Ho Chi Minh the leadership of the Vietnamese independence movement, and thus he attracted the sympathy or active support of the greater part of the population. His ideological leanings as a Communist were not a significant factor in his appeal. He consolidated control of the nationalist movement under his Viet Minh, a Communist-dominated political coalition, by sanctioning the purge of thousands of his Vietnamese political opponents. The executions and political assassinations were carried out largely in 1945 and 1946, usually by what were called Honor Squads, under the direction of Vo Nguyen Giap, the master military strategist of the Viet Minh.

When Audrey and I arrived in Indochina in 1950, Ho Chi Minh was the unquestioned leader of the Viet Minh–dominated jungle government. Although Ho's government had been recognized by Peking, I found a strange disinterest among the French about events in China. They spoke of the Chinese Civil War with detachment as if it were far away. They were not aware that Ho Chi Minh had gone to Peking and received an assurance of military aid. But soon thereafter, they learned painfully that the presence of Mao Zedong's troops on the Vietnam frontier and the military aid provided by Mao to Ho Chi Minh would ultimately result in their defeat.

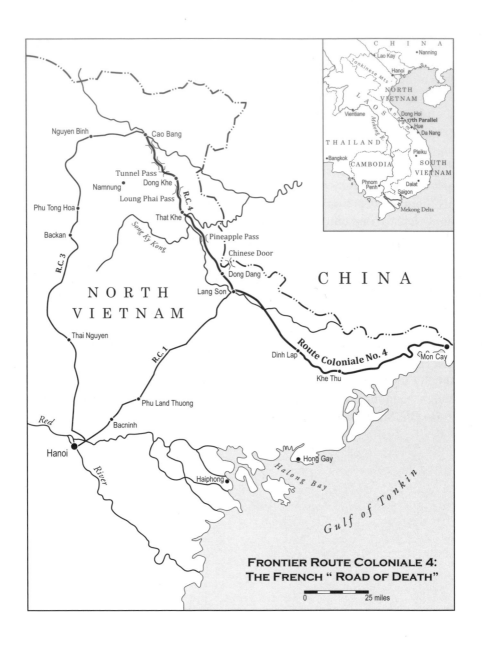

Inset map labels:
C H I N A
Lao Kay · Nanning
Tonkinese Mts
Hanoi
N O R T H
V I E T N A M
LAOS
Vientiane
Dong Hoi
Mekong R.
17th Parallel
Hue
Da Nang
THAILAND
Bangkok
CAMBODIA
Pleiku
SOUTH
VIETNAM
Phnom Penh
Dalat
Saigon
Mekong Delta

Main map labels:
Nguyen Binh
Cao Bang
Tunnel Pass
Namnung
Dong Khe
Loung Phai Pass
R.C. 4
Phu Tong Hoa
That Khe
Backan
Song Ky Kong
Pineapple Pass
Chinese Door
R.C. 3
Dong Dang
Lang Son
C H I N A
N O R T H
V I E T N A M
Thai Nguyen
R.C. 1
Dinh Lap
Route Coloniale No. 4
Mon Cay
Khe Thu
Phu Land Thuong
Red
Bacninh
Hong Gay
Hanoi
River
Haiphong
Halong Bay
Gulf of Tonkin

FRONTIER ROUTE COLONIALE 4:
THE FRENCH "ROAD OF DEATH"

0   25 miles

15
THE CHINA FRONTIER

By March 1950, Mao Zedong's forces had virtually consolidated their control of South China and had taken up positions opposite the line of French forts along the Indochina frontier. Chinese Communist commanders were entering into liaison with Viet Minh guerrillas operating along the border. The French were still uncertain as to how much of a commitment Mao Zedong would risk making to the Viet Minh. They were not aware that the Chinese were making preparation for the delivery in April of large-scale military aid.

In late March, I flew with Audrey from Saigon to Hanoi for an interview with General Marcel Alessandri, commander of French forces in Tonkin, Vietnam's most northern region. We stayed at the Metropole, a decaying French colonial hostelry on the edge of the Red River delta whose wine menu, high-ceilinged bedrooms, and bathroom bidets were about the only remnants of its former French colonial hauteur. Ceiling fans turned futilely above huge double beds encased in white mosquito netting. The netting spared us injury on our first night in Hanoi. We were asleep when an artillery blast from a nearby French battery interdicting Viet Minh infiltration onto the delta shook loose a large, heavy section of the ceiling plaster. It struck the netting, which sagged to within an inch or two of our heads.

The next morning, we met with Alessandri at his headquarters. One of the best of the French generals, the fifty-two-year-old officer who had spent almost all of his entire twenty-year army career in Indochina had just completed a sweep of the delta, driving most Viet Minh units out of the great northern rice bowl. He told us that his artillery was firing during the night on Viet Minh forces which had staged a lightning incursion onto the delta, and he expressed regret, with a slight smile, that we had become targets of our bedroom's ceiling plaster. Alessandri said he was planning an offensive against Viet Minh mountain positions along the border. The general said he had not seen any evidence that the Chinese Communists as yet were shipping arms to the Viet Minh on a major scale, but recently his troops had seized American rifles smuggled by gunrunners, probably based in Macau, to the Viet Minh via China. He was confident that his troops could repulse any counteroffensive by the Viet Minh to retake their positions on the Red River delta even if they were reequipped with weapons supplied by the Chinese. When I pressed the general for permission to visit the frontier, he was hesitant. Two large French convoys traveling along Route Colonial No. 4, the main supply road serving the border posts, had just been ambushed with heavy casualties. Finally, Alessandri relented and agreed to take me and two other American correspondents who had just arrived in Hanoi, Carl Mydans, the *Life* magazine photographer, and Wilson Fielder of *Time* magazine, to Lang Son, the principal fortress town on the frontier. Audrey, then four months pregnant, stayed on in Hanoi.

We flew with Alessandri to Lang Son in an old three-engine German Junker, dodging through cloudy mountain passes to a red-dirt strip, where we were met by a spit-and-polish Foreign Legion honor guard and taken straight to a meeting with Colonel Jean Constans, commander of the Frontier Zone. Constans told us he was attempting to seal off the frontier. His mission was to curtail the flow of Chinese arms to the Viet Minh and to block any attempt by them to descend onto the Red River delta for an assault on Hanoi. But closing what was known as the "Chinese Door" posed enormous strategic problems. Constans commanded four major French forts athwart the four traditional invasion routes from China into Indochina. On the western flank, isolated and supplied largely by air, stood the Lao Kay fort, which dominated a network of roads. The other three major forts were linked by R.C. 4, which had been dubbed "Rue du Mort" (Road of Death) because of repeated bloody Viet Minh ambushes. The highway bent along the China frontier for 150 miles from Mon Cay on the east coast through Lang Son to Cao Bang in the west. Fifteen miles to the northwest of Lang Son lay the outpost of Dong Dang, directly opposite the mist-shrouded mountain pass of Nam Quan. This was the historical invasion route. Traditionally, imperial envoys traveling from Peking had come through the Nam Quan Pass to Lang Son and then south down what became Route Colonial No. 1 to Hanoi and Saigon. Lang Son itself was a pleasant town of ten thousand inhabitants, constructed in the French provincial style with wide streets and low yellow-brown houses.

On our first night in Lang Son we dined at the Foreign Legion officers' club and listened to old songs of the legion over rounds of cognac. Two days later, with Constans's reluctant permission, in a jeep driven by Lieutenant Andre Wastin, a short, dark, cocky French officer, we set out for the China border. We were escorted by a weapons carrier loaded with ten heavily armed

Legionnaires, all Germans. We followed in the trace of a foot patrol that had been clearing the road of mines planted by the Viet Minh during the night. The road twisted through bare brown hills. It was ideal ambush country. Debris of clashes with the Viet Minh lay all about. There were lines of parallel trenches across the road, "piano keys" as they were called, dug by the Viet Minh at night and filled in by the French road clearers during the day. When we turned off the road for Chi Ma, an outpost on the border, the lieutenant halted the jeep and said to us: "Gentlemen. You must now make a choice, either our jeep goes ahead on the road, which often is mined by the Viet Minh, or the Legionnaires go first in their truck. If we go first in the jeep and hit a mine, one or two of us may be killed or wounded, but the Legionnaires will be able to beat off the Viet Minh who will attack after the mine explodes. However, if the Legionnaires go first and their truck hits the mine, we probably will be overwhelmed and killed by the Viet Minh ambushers. Now take your choice—which goes first, our jeep or the truck?" We exchanged glances: Carl Mydans, a short dynamic man, wise in the ways of war, who had distinguished himself in covering World War II, Wilson Fielder, the young, amiable *Time* magazine reporter, newly based in Hong Kong, and me. We nodded at each other and elected to go ahead of the Legionnaires' truck in the jeep.

At a fast, rattling clip we made it to Chi Ma. The French army post faced two Chinese Communist-held outposts, with a village in between. We walked through paddy fields to within thirty yards of the village gate, guarded by two Chinese soldiers. Mydans photographed the sentries as one of them looked us over with field glasses. We returned to Lang Son that night. Mydans and Fielder left for Haiphong the next day en route to Korea to cover the war. I never saw Fielder again. He disappeared in Korea during the battle for Taejon. He was last seen with an American Army unit that subsequently was overrun by the North Koreans. Mydans searched for days before he learned that Fielder's body had been found beside a road near a nameless village.

In Lang Son, I waited to join a convoy that was forming up for a dash along R.C. 4 southeast to Khe Thu on the Gulf of Tonkin. Beyond Khe Thu lay Hong Gay, the southern terminus of R.C. 4. On the suggestion of a French officer, I had sent a message to Audrey in Hanoi proposing she meet me at Hong Gay, which is situated on the extraordinarily beautiful Halong Bay on the Gulf of Tonkin. I did not realize then that I was launching Audrey on a journey nearly as dangerous as the convoy run I was about to make.

The mission of my convoy was to pick up arms, munitions, medical supplies, and the all-important *vin rouge* at the small port of Khe Thu for transport to Lang Son. From Lang Son the supplies would be sent north-west to key forts along R.C. 4. It was a tenuous supply line. Convoys trav-eled northwest from Lang Son infrequently since the thirty-six-mile run to the first outpost at That Khe was extremely hazardous. Beyond That Khe, except for the isolated fort midway at Dong Khe, the Viet Minh controlled the thirty-five-mile stretch to the terminus at Cao Bang, which was provi-sioned almost entirely by air.

Not long after dawn, our convoy formed up in the drizzling morning mist that hangs over Lang Son during the rainy season. I was in a jeep, which was mounted with a light machine gun, seated with a carbine across my knees beside the convoy commander, a cheerful, lean lieutenant of the French Ma-rines. The commander had insisted that I accept the carbine, which I did with some hesitation. As a former infantryman, I had no problem in han-dling the weapon, but journalists by custom usually worked unarmed. Led by a French sergeant, a patrol of ten Goumiers, Moroccan mountain fight-ers, brown-skinned bearded men, their soft-brimmed French campaign hats atop shaven heads, trudged past our fog-shrouded jeep and ahead of us down R.C. 4. The red clay road twisted for fifty miles through steep foothills to Khe Thu. Our convoy would have to reach the safety of Khe Thu before dark because the road belonged to the Viet Minh at night. Our jeep was the lead vehicle in the point detachment that was to clear the first six miles of road. We moved slowly behind the Goumiers' patrol, which scrutinized the hill-sides and checked the road for mines. Behind us came two armored person-nel carriers, each mounting a .30- and a .50-caliber machine gun covering two truckloads of Legionnaires. Three miles out of Lang Son, the detach-ment began dropping off files of Legionnaires, who climbed to the top of the ridges bordering the road to screen the passage of the convoy. French posts all the way to Khe Thu were sending out similar security patrols. Some of the posts were only small brick blockhouses, each manned by about six na-tive partisans. Others ranged from those with several watchtowers within a bamboo enclosure perched atop a hill to that at Dinh Lap, which was garri-soned with infantry, artillery, and tank units. The isolated posts were favor-ite targets for Viet Minh night raids made in overwhelming force. By day, when the French made retaliatory forays into surrounding territory, if they came upon deserted villages, indicating they belonged to the Viet Minh, the patrols would burn them and shoot the water buffalo in the rice fields.

Our advance detachment moved forward another mile before meeting the tank patrol from Loc Binh, six miles away. The road was open. From Loc Binh, the signal went back to the convoy. The Viet Minh were not on the

road, and once more with the morning, R.C. 4 southeast from Lang Son belonged to the French. At 10 A.M. the convoy, led by a truckload of Legionnaires and an armored radio vehicle, followed our advance detachment into
Loc Binh, a small town of clay-plastered buildings and a gray stone Catholic
church. Traveling at 200-yard intervals behind us came thirty-three civilian
and forty-five military trucks mounting machine guns. Another radio car
and a truck carrying Legionnaires brought up the rear of the column. The
convoy moved on slowly to Dinh Lap, the largest French post between Lang
Son and Khe Thu. Here were stationed the intervention troops with their
tanks and artillery. When the radio cars of a convoy signaled a Viet Minh
attack or contact was lost, the intervention troops moved swiftly to its assistance.

Southeast of Dinh Lap, the convoy passed from the land of the Thos, a
people of Tibetan origin, into the Nung country inhabited by mountaineers
closely related to the Chinese. With the foothills more densely covered with
jungle foliage, it was ideal ambush country and the most dangerous leg of
the journey. The convoy commander checked the grenades in the open glove
compartment of the jeep and the Tommy gun beside him with the safety off,
and I fingered my loaded carbine as I wondered what I would do if the Viet
Minh attacked. The Viet Minh attacks were very much alike, the lieutenant
said. They usually came within the large gaps between French posts with
hundreds of Viet Minh hiding in the thick roadside jungle growth. A convoy often would know it was under attack only after it had suffered its first
casualties. The convoy would speed up, but if a truck was crippled, blocking
the narrow road for the vehicles behind, anywhere from hundreds to thousands of Viet Minh would swarm down throwing grenades. Trucks would
be burned. French wounded would be killed. The Viet Minh would then disappear into the mountains, taking with them prisoners and captured matériel. They were usually gone when intervention troops arrived and the King
Cobra fighter planes from Lang Son came overhead.

At 5:10 P.M. our command jeep halted with its accompanying radio vehicle at the Na Peo outpost to drop off a truck with engine trouble. The radio
operator tuned into an English-language broadcast of the Voice of America.
Legionnaires gathered around to listen. One German, a baker by trade, asked
if he could settle in the United States after completing his enlistment. About
half of the Legionnaires were Germans who had signed up for the five-year
enlistment; only one-fifth were French, and most of the others were central
Europeans who did not want to return to their countries behind the Iron
Curtain.

Several miles beyond Na Peo, the heavy roadside jungle had been cleared away. The Viet Minh had attacked a convoy here. Twenty-five had been killed, fifteen wounded, and twenty-five men taken prisoner. Fourteen trucks were burned.

When our jeep entered Khe Thu at 6:10 P.M., a French Tricolor was flying over the post at half mast. There had just been a funeral for twelve soldiers; one of them a French warrant officer who had arrived in Indochina four days before. They had died two days earlier in a Viet Minh ambush eight miles south on Route No. 18. A detachment was going out in the morning to re-open the road. I went with the detachment.

The hills were steaming in a hot early morning sun when our detachment, a section of Legionnaires and a company of Nung partisans, reached the area where the small convoy had been ambushed. It was a "classic ambush," a French lieutenant told me. There had been thirty-five officers and men in four trucks who had been building a brick blockhouse at a ferry landing of the Song Ba Che River. The first truck, carrying a French lieutenant, a warrant officer, a sergeant, and three Moroccan privates, was going through a road cut lined with bamboo when ambushed. It was a complete surprise. The Viet Minh opened with one machine gun firing along the axis of the road, and three other machine guns blazed from the hillside, where more than two hundred Viet Minh were concealed. Everyone in the first truck was killed in the first hail of fire. The other three trucks halted at intervals of 100, 200, and 500 yards. Two men manning the machine gun on the second truck were picked off quickly. Several of the men in the second truck retreated to the next, where a defense was mounted. The Viet Minh charged down the road. They were repulsed, but only after they had reached the first truck and collected the weapons of the dead. Six Nung partisans stationed in a tiny nearby post were the first to come to the assistance of the convoy. Two were wounded by the Viet Minh. One of them dragged himself off, taking the bolt of his rifle with him so it could not be used by the enemy. The Viet Minh withdrew when they heard vehicles of the Khe Thu intervention force approaching. They carried off about twenty of their own dead.

"That is all that happened," the lieutenant said. "That is all that ever happens." Soon another convoy would go out to complete the building of the river blockhouse.

I returned to Khe Thu to spend the night, and the next morning with a French security detail I drove to Hong Gay, worried sick about Audrey. It was March 29.

Audrey had received my message five days earlier saying that I hoped

to be in Hong Gay on March 27. She had approached the French Information Service in Hanoi for help in getting to Hong Gay. Contrary to the advice given me in Lang Son, she was strongly advised against making the trip.
Viet Minh guerrillas were operating along the sixty-five-mile road between
Hanoi and Haiphong. The small riverboats, which plied between Haiphong
and Hong Gay, passed through hilly country where the banks were controlled by the Viet Minh. Determined, nevertheless, to go to Hong Gay, Audrey found a Vietnamese taxi driver in Hanoi whose fears about driving to
Haiphong were assuaged by a wad of bills. Perched on the back seat of an old
Citroen, dressed in slacks, all of twenty-one, with her blonde braids piled on
top of her head, Audrey was driven at high speed to the Haiphong port. She
checked into a decrepit French guesthouse and was lying in a four-poster
bed in her room when in amazement she heard familiar American voices. In
the adjacent room, she found Mydans and Fielder. After failing to dissuade
her from making the dangerous trip, the two took her the next morning to
the river dock. The boat to Hong Gay was a native craft, less than thirty feet
in length, pushed by a gasoline engine, and loaded with bags of rice, sixteen
Vietnamese, and a Frenchman carrying a submachine gun. The Frenchman
had been assigned to look after Audrey and was not at all happy about making the trip. The Vietnamese looked uneasily at Audrey's blonde braids, a
target that might draw fire from the Viet Minh.

As the boat slipped out of Haiphong port and upriver, the Frenchman
popped a conical Vietnamese peasant hat on Audrey's head and ordered her
down among the rice sacks. "Keep your blonde head out of sight," he said
as he crouched beside her. As the boat nosed through the narrow defiles for
the next six hours, the Frenchman kept his machine gun trained on the cliffs
towering above them. There were happy cries from the Vietnamese when the
boat entered Halong Bay, chugging through limpid waters afire with the intense colors of the sunset. In Hong Gay, at a French guesthouse fronting the
bay, Audrey waited for three days hearing rumors of a Viet Minh ambush
of a convoy— in fact the convoy that had preceded my own. That is where I
found her. She was in a screened-in porch munching bananas, the only decent food available. "Is that you?" she cried out. She tugged at my black beard,
and embracing, we told our stories. We remained in Hong Gay for several
days, boating on the magnificent bay amid the strange rock formations jut-
ting up like temple altars and huge idols carved by denizens of a forgotten
land now covered by the sea.

Flying back to Saigon, I came to jarring conclusions as I reviewed what I had observed on the frontier. In Saigon and Hanoi, American and French officials told me that the French troops had effectively sealed off the frontier except for small-scale infiltration by the Viet Minh. In fact, the Viet Minh could quite easily transit to China through the gaps between the forts on R.C. 4 over roads they now controlled. The isolated French forts and smaller posts were highly vulnerable to Viet Minh attacks and difficult to keep supplied, particularly in the rainy season. They might very well be overrun if the Chinese Communists elected to bolster the Viet Minh forces by supplying them with weapons and training their assault troops in safe havens on the China side of the border. The Viet Minh could thus be provided with an excellent base area from which to prepare a massive descent upon the Red River delta and Hanoi. The future course of the Indochina War was thus in effect being decided in Peking.

On June 19 I was back in Lang Son, where I found the military situation fundamentally changed. The French no longer thought that Mao Zedong, preoccupied with Korea and girding for an invasion of Taiwan, might exercise restraint. In April they had become aware by reports from intelligence sources and reconnaissance flights that the Chinese had initiated a large-scale program of military aid for Ho Chi Minh's forces. Roads leading to the Indochina frontier were being built or improved employing the labor of thousands, many of them captured Nationalist soldiers. On these same roads one day in the 1960s and 1970s Russian trucks would carry Soviet and Chinese arms and supplies to the North Vietnamese in the war against the Americans. A Chinese Military Advisory Group (CMAG), headed by General Wei Guoqing, had been established at Nanning in South China, with a staff of almost three hundred advisers. Thousands of Viet Minh were being trained there and closer to the border in centers at Yanshan, Longzhou, and Jingxi in Yunnan Province. Field hospitals had been erected to care for Viet Minh wounded. Viet Minh troops were beginning to return from the training centers uniformed, equipped with field kits, and fully armed with automatic weapons, bazookas, and other modern weapons, many of which were American arms captured by the Chinese Communists from the Nationalists during the Civil War. The guerrilla units were being reorganized into regular army divisions and regiments with political commissars and Chinese advisers attached.

Earlier, on May 25, Vo Nguyen Giap, the Vietnamese military commander in chief, had tested the French defense line along R.C. 4 by attacking and taking the post of Dong Khe, the strategic midway staging point, between

Cao Bang and That Khe. For the first time, Viet Minh employed antiaircraft guns, which scored hits on the French King Cobra fighter planes intervening in support of the post. Only about 10 percent of the garrison of four hundred French-officered Moroccan and Vietnamese partisan troops managed to escape. Two days later, a French parachute battalion airlifted from Hanoi was dropped on Dong Khe and retook the post. But I found that the Viet Minh strike had shaken the confidence of the French officers, who told me privately that the R.C. 4 defense line might become untenable. Fears were expressed to me by French officers of a debacle if the frontier force was not pulled back to more defensible positions on the Red River delta perimeter. Secretly, the plan for an offensive against the Viet Minh mountain strongholds, described to me by General Alessandri in March, had been ruled out by the commander in chief of French forces in Indochina, General Marcel Carpentier. A new plan was put in place that would precipitate the most significant battle of the French Indochina War. Over the vehement protests of Alessandri, Carpentier decided to withdraw the garrison at Cao Bang in a move designed to reorganize and consolidate the French defense line.

I was in Saigon when the Viet Minh roll-up of the French frontier line began on September 16, 1950, with the blow falling again on Dong Khe. Four Viet Minh battalions newly trained and outfitted in China and supported by heavy mortars and artillery struck at the post, defended by about 250 Foreign Legionnaires. The attack had been planned meticulously in conjunction with the chief Chinese field adviser, General Chen Geng, a veteran of the Chinese Civil War and a member of the Communist Party's Central Committee. The Legionnaires fought gallantly for sixty hours, retreating foot by foot to the southern section of the citadel while French fighter planes and bombers flying through heavy mists hit at the attackers. The Viet Minh were estimated to have suffered some five hundred casualties. On the morning of September 18, when a French Junker observation plane flew over the post, the firing had ended, the post was burning, and the Tricolor had disappeared from above the defense works. There was no radio contact. Only one officer and some twenty others managed to escape into the jungle. Dong Khe was a prelude to the most decisive battles of the French Indochina War.

On October 1, French troops executed a surprise thirty-six-mile sweep northwest from Hanoi and the Red River delta up through the rugged Tonkinese Mountains to seize Thai Nguyen, the principal political stronghold of the Viet Minh. Two flanking columns and paratroopers dropped north of the city and successfully enveloped the mountain communications center. It was an important psychological victory, but the French assault force did not seize the Viet Minh political leaders in the hastily abandoned town, nor did it divert the Viet Minh from their targets on the frontier. In fact, the operation served Giap well by tying up badly needed French troops—sixteen battalions, two squadrons of tanks, four groups of artillery, and most of the air force—which could have been usefully employed against him in the impending battle for the frontier.

To carry out his plan for a withdrawal of the garrison from Cao Bang, Carpentier had three choices: an airlift to Lang Son, a retreat southwest down R.C. 3 to Thai Nguyen, or a dash along R.C. 4 to the safety of the frontier post at That Khe. Overriding Alessandri's warning that it was an invitation to disaster, Carpentier chose withdrawal to That Khe.

On October 3, after blowing up their military stocks and a good part of the town, the Cao Bang garrison, comprising 2,600 troops, including crack Foreign Legionnaires and Moroccan Goumiers, set out southeast on R.C. 4 toward Dong Khe. Some 2,500 civilians, including all the women, children, and sick, had already been evacuated by air in late September, but some 500 civilian men weighed down with personal possessions accompanied the garrison. The Cao Bang evacuation plan, dubbed Operation Therese, called for a relief force of 3,500 Moroccan troops commanded by Lieutenant Colonel Marcel Le Page to fight northwest up R.C. 4 from That Khe, retake Dong Khe from the Viet Minh, then proceed north to the village of Namnang and meet the Cao Bang garrison there, whereupon they would undertake a joint withdrawal to the safe haven at That Khe. Both Le Page and the Cao Bang commander, Lieutenant Colonel Pierre Charton, complained repeatedly but to no avail that the plan was deeply flawed given the hilly jungle terrain and the vulnerability to Viet Minh attack. In fact, prior to the attack on Dong Khe, the chief Chinese adviser, Chen Geng, as Chinese archives would later reveal, had made plans with Giap to ambush the Cao Bang column if the French chose to withdraw overland.

The Cao Bang column reached Namnang, the rendezvous point, twenty miles from Cao Bang, at noon on October 4, and there Colonel Charton received a stunning message. Giap's battalions in overwhelming strength had been waiting in ambush on the heights above Dong Khe and had descended and shattered Le Page's column. Le Page's troops had been driven off R.C. 4 and were now trapped in the Cocxa jungle ravine southwest of Dong Khe. Charton was ordered to hasten down a jungle trail, the Quangliet, which paralleled R.C. 4, to the relief of the Le Page column. Charton in evacuating Cao Ban had ignored orders to destroy his heavy equipment, including artillery and motor vehicles, and make the dash down R.C. 4 on foot. Con-

fronted now with orders to move along the jungle trail, the garrison destroyed its heavy equipment and proceeded along the ill-defined Quangliet
jungle trail but soon came under repeated devastating attacks by thousands
of well-armed Viet Minh troops. Survivors of the Cao Bang column finally
joined the Le Page columns on October 7, but the combined force was overrun by the Viet Minh as they struggled to break out through the mountains
to That Khe. A few survivors made it to That Khe after days of wandering
in the jungle only to find that it had been abandoned and was in Viet Minh
hands.

Altogether, in the debacle of Operation Therese, the French lost six thousand troops, including some of the finest units of the French Army, and
enough equipment to outfit another Viet Minh division. The faces of the gal-
lant French soldiers I had known on the frontier paraded through my mind
as I wrote my dispatches. Unnerved, the French command undertook a pre-
cipitant wholesale abandonment of the frontier.

More than any other night, that of October 20, 1950, is burned indelibly
into my memory. It was the night I reported the fall of Lang Son, and it was
the night that Susan, our first child, was born. Cascading flares lit up the
skies over Saigon, and there was the distant thud of artillery fire as Audrey
in labor was wheeled on a cot into the surgery of the French military hospital. At the door of the operating room, I was listening apprehensively to
the distant crackle of small-arms fire when I heard Audrey cry out. Susan,
the first of five daughters, was born. The delivery was a harbinger of the violent world in which our family would live. The French doctor who cut Susan's umbilical cord wore a smock stained with the fresh blood of wounded
soldiers. Artillery fire was still puncturing the night. The French were laying down a protective barrage around a perimeter outpost under attack by
Viet Minh guerrillas. I left the hospital distraught on leaving Audrey and
our newborn baby girl, but Audrey typically urged me to go back to my typewriter, knowing that one of the most important stories of the war was taking
shape. I went directly to the little alcove in our apartment, which served as
my office, and checked with my assistant, Max Clos, who had been in touch
with his French military sources. French officials had revealed that Lang
Son had been abandoned, the evacuation being undertaken so hastily that
the military installations and the supply depots had been left intact. French
planes were at the moment bombing the depots, which contained enough
matériel to outfit an entire Viet Minh combat division.

As the French border posts fell, I reported in a dispatch to the Associated
Press that the Viet Minh had "won control of the North Indochina frontier

and ended French chances of winning a decisive military victory." Describing the loss of the frontier forts as "the turning point" in the war, I wrote: "Yielded to the Viet Minh is a near impregnable mountain base area with good trans-frontier connections to supply sources and training centers in Red China. This means that the Ho Chi Minh regime now has the space and means of preparing a full-scale military offensive against the principal French strongholds located further south. The purely guerrilla phase of the war in Indochina has ended."

Washington was not unaware of what would be the impact on French military prospects if Mao provided large-scale assistance to the Viet Minh. As early as March 27, 1950, the National Security Council estimated that "it was doubtful that the French Expeditionary Forces, combined with Indochinese troops, could successfully contain Ho Chi Minh's forces should they be strengthened by either Chinese troops crossing the border or by Communist-supplied arms and materiel in quantity." The secret memorandum NSC 64, recorded in the Pentagon Papers, the official history of the American role in Indochina, balanced this warning against the need to contain Communist expansion in Southeast Asia. The memorandum propounding the domino theory stated: "The neighboring countries of Thailand and Burma could be expected to fall under Communist domination if Indochina were controlled by a Communist-dominated government. The balance of Southeast Asia would then be in grave hazard."

The domino theory, which would be shown by subsequent events to be fallacious, provided a strategic rationale for meeting President de Gaulle's demands for assistance in Indochina in return for French military cooperation in Europe. Six weeks after the NSC 64 estimate was made, President Truman recognized the Bao Dai government and initiated his assistance program to the French with an allocation of $10 million for the year. The allocations mounted steadily to $1.06 billion in 1954, the year of the final French military collapse. When Chinese Communist "volunteers" entered the Korean War on October 25, 1950, the National Intelligence Estimate submitted to the president in December concluded that large-scale Chinese intervention in Indochina was "impending." Aid to the French in Indochina moved higher on the list of priorities. The French Union Army, made up of 130,000 troops, including a cadre of French soldiers, Foreign Legion units, African Colonials, and 50,000 Indochinese auxiliaries, were seen as the most reliable force for the containment of China.

Despite the loss of the frontier, the French were buoyed with the arrival on December 19, 1950, of General Jean de Lattre de Tassigny as the new commander. Anticipating momentarily a Viet Minh descent on Hanoi and the Red River delta, the French were in a panic. General de La Tour, who replaced General Alessandri as the commander in Tonkin, had ordered the evacuation of women and children from Hanoi. While pledging to defend the city, de La Tour began emptying military depots and trucking the matériel to the port of Haiphong to be shipped out. De Lattre, a World War II hero, sometimes referred to as the "French MacArthur," flew to Hanoi at this moment. The imperious general lined up the northern military commanders on arrival, questioned them, and reassigned several whom he found failing on the spot. He electrified the Expeditionary Force by declaring that they would "no longer give an inch." He took the risky decision of ordering the evacuation of civilians in North Vietnam halted. The passenger liner *Pasteur* at Haiphong, dispatched to bring out French civilians, was instead loaded with wounded soldiers and sent back to France two-thirds empty. The construction was begun of new fortifications at the mountain passes leading to the Red River delta backed up by mobile infantry-artillery teams.

On January 16, 1951, Vo Nguyen Giap initiated a general offensive toward Hanoi with an attack on Vinh Yen, at the western end of the Red River delta. He employed the "human wave" tactics which the Chinese had employed in Korea. De Lattre was prepared, his reinvigorated command having been reinforced with newly arrived American fighter planes and artillery. The Viet Minh were beaten back with more than 4,000 dead left on the battlefield. The French suffered some 400 dead in repelling the repeated attacks. Many of the Viet Minh panicked as they were caught for the first time in the open on the flat Red River delta by King Cobra fighter planes dropping napalm bombs. Two subsequent "human wave" drives were also repulsed in March and May. In June, on the advice of his Chinese advisers, Giap conceded in a radio broadcast to his army's political workers that Viet Minh troops were not yet ready for "the final phase" and ordered them to prepare for a "long and arduous war." Giap reverted to Mao's strategy of protracted war. For the French, de Lattre's stand before Hanoi was their army's finest hour in the Indochina War, but it was only a respite.

16

BURMA

THE CIA OPERATION

W hile posted in Vietnam in the spring of 1951, I became aware of frequent clandestine air movements through the Saigon airport to destinations outside Vietnam. Unmarked American-built transports were landing there, refueling under heavy guard, and then taking off for an undisclosed destination. In June, I learned that the planes were coming from Taiwan and were under charter from CAT, Claire Chennault's commercial airline, now based on the island. The pilots included a number who had flown in his World War II "Flying Tigers" squadron and others from the U.S. Fourteenth Air Force, which had been based in Kunming. The coordinating agency for the flights through Saigon was a "Sea Supply Company" with an office in Bangkok. The company, whose cable address was "Hatchet," represented itself as a commercial trading firm.

In July, leaving our infant daughter, Susan, in the care of a Chinese amah, Audrey and I flew to Bangkok tracking the story. I learned in the Thai capital that Sea Supply was a cover for covert operations by the Central Intelligence Agency. The unmarked CAT planes flying from Saigon were landing on a strip in eastern Thailand and then continuing on to Burma. We then flew on to Rangoon. From confidential sources in the diplomatic community in Rangoon, I began to piece together what was an incredible story. Three Chinese Nationalist Army columns, comprising some fifteen thousand men, had thrust about sixty-five miles into China's Yunnan Province from a refuge in northeastern Burma. They had retreated earlier across the China border into the Burma refuge pursued by Communist troops. The Nationalist columns had seized a base area, about 100 miles long, embracing the Kengma Airfield, some 200 miles southwest of Kunming. Chinese Communist troops were counterattacking, attempting to cut the Nationalist supply corridor to Burma.

The Nationalist units were commanded by General Li Mi, who had escaped from the Communist encirclement in the final engagement of the Battle of the Huai-Hai, which I had covered in January 1949. The CIA had flown Li from Taiwan into northeastern Burma, where he had reorganized the Nationalist Eighth Army's Ninety-third Division and other units which had fled across the border before the Communists' advance. Chiang Kai-shek had named Li as the ruling governor of Yunnan, an empty gesture because the province was largely in Communist hands. Transports, under charter to the CIA, flying via Indochina and Thailand, were bringing in arms, radio, and other equipment, as well as food and funds for Li. CIA liaison agents were operating on the ground with the Nationalists. The operation apparently had begun the previous May at the onset of the Korean War and was a diversionary action designed to harass the Chinese Communists more than anything else. However, it had unforeseen political ramifications. Mao Zedong was pointing to the Yunnan operation as further evidence that the United States was seeking to provide a base area for a future effort by Chiang Kai-shek to stage an effort to retake the mainland.

In Rangoon, I found the government of Premier U Nu in a state of alarm. It had appealed to the U.S. ambassador, David M. Key, for help in getting Li Mi's forces out of Burma. The Burmese Army had proved ineffectual. U Nu feared that Li's operations would provoke a Chinese Communist invasion of Burma or an internal Communist coup. Peking had declined to give U Nu assurance that this would not happen. The Burmese suspected American staging of the Li Mi affair and were convinced, quite rightly, that the operation would have required at least tacit White House sanction before it could be mounted. Ambassador Key repeatedly denied knowledge of American involvement, although he undoubtedly was aware of it to some degree. The Burmese government had imposed a ban on the travel of American officials north of Mandalay to the northeastern frontier areas. In Washington, State Department officials, except on the highest levels, were apparently not aware of the CIA operation, and officers in the field were authorized to issue flat denials in response to inquiries. Members of the staff of the American Embassy spoke frankly to me in confidence about what they knew about the operation. They were incensed and looked upon the whole operation as an act of folly from the standpoint of American interests. Relations with the neutralist Burmese government were in a shambles. The Li Mi forays could only have nuisance value, since sooner or later the Communists would mass overwhelming force to scatter the Nationalist columns. Li's troops would then be compelled to fall back into Burma, remaining a constant irritant to the Rangoon government and a provocation to the Chinese Communists. The U Nu government, afraid of arousing the Chinese, had suppressed news of the Li Mi operations. Not a line was appearing in the censored Rangoon press.

We flew to Singapore, where I filed my report to the AP. It evoked protests around the world on behalf of the Burmese but had little practical effects. Ambassador Key returned to Washington and, indignant over the CIA
involvement, resigned. When the Eisenhower administration came into office, the new ambassador, William J. Sebald, was confronted by the same di-
lemma. He was assured by the State Department that the CIA was not continuing to support Li, and he was ordered to reply in this vein to mounting
Burmese protests. The ambassador conducted his own investigation, which
soon revealed to him that the CIA was still involved.

Burma brought the matter before the United Nations in March 1953 and
again in September. In November of that year, an evacuation by air to Taiwan of some of the Nationalist units via Thailand got under way. However,
despite the announcement in Taipei by Li Mi on May 30, 1954, that the Yunnan Anti-Communist and National Salvation Army had been dissolved,
the evacuation dragged on for years, with repeated clashes between Burmese and remnant Nationalist troops. The sorry affair was protracted until
the Kennedy administration put an end to it by exerting strong pressure on
Chiang Kai-shek to complete the withdrawal. By that time the affair had so
embittered the Burmese that relations between Rangoon and Washington
remained poisoned for years.

The CIA operation reinforced Mao Zedong's stated belief that China
would not be secure from U.S. intrusion until American bases in countries
bordering China were removed. It hardened his resolve to aid Ho Chi Minh
in the struggle to oust the United States and its French allies from Vietnam.

17

THE KENNEDY BROTHERS IN SAIGON

John F. Kennedy arrived in Saigon on October 19, 1951, accompanied by his sister Patricia and his brother Robert Kennedy. JFK was then a congressman, Democrat of Massachusetts. I remember so well how boyish Bobby looked as he embarked from the plane, ducked under a wing, and smiled broadly at me as he followed Jack to the line of French and American Legation officials waiting to greet them. Bobby was then twenty-six and John Kennedy was thirty-four. The party was traveling on what was described as a study tour of the Middle East and Asia. They had been in New Delhi, where Prime Minister Jawaharlal Nehru impressed them with a seminar on the dynamism and the irreversible nature of the anticolonial revolution in Asia. The visit seemed of such a routine nature that I gave it only one paragraph in a dispatch devoted to reporting the return that day after a three months' absence of General de Lattre de Tassigny, the French high commissioner.

De Lattre had been in Paris pleading with a reluctant government for troop reinforcements. His only encouragement came, not in Paris, but during a trip to Washington, where he received assurances that American military aid would be accelerated. "The world has come to realize the importance of our fight in the defense of this part of the world," the general said at the Ton Son Nhut Airport. As for Jack Kennedy, to better identify the young congressman, unknown to most readers, an AP copy editor in New York added a sentence to my dispatch stating that the Massachusetts representative was the son of Joseph P. Kennedy, the former ambassador to Britain. Writers would describe that filial relationship in later years as one in which a son broke with his father on Indochina and other foreign policy issues. I had no reason to think that this visit by Kennedy to Saigon would have a profound impact on America's Vietnam policy over the next decade. Walt Rostow, who would become Kennedy's senior foreign policy adviser when he became president, would later write that the visit was Kennedy's "formative experience" in the making of Vietnam policy. At cabinet meetings, when Vietnam policy was being formulated, Kennedy would often refer to what he had learned during his Saigon visit as the rationale for his assumptions.

Kennedy was greeted warmly at the Saigon airfield by an old friend, Edmund Gullion, the counselor at the American Legation. They had become friendly four years earlier in Washington when Dean Acheson, the secretary of state, on Kennedy's request, had sent over Gullion, his assistant, to help the young congressman compose a foreign policy speech. After chatting with Gullion, Kennedy walked across the tarmac to where reporters were standing and asked for Seymour Topping. He had been told that I was the first American correspondent to be stationed in Saigon. "I would like to have a talk with you," Kennedy said with an engaging smile.

"All right," I replied. "I'll come to see you."

"No," he said. "I'll come to see you."

I noticed that Kennedy was pale and thin, his neck scrawny. He wore no hat, and his mop of unruly hair was badly in need of trimming. I later learned that in Japan he had come down with a life-threatening fever, temperature at 106, and had been taken to an American military hospital in Okinawa, where he recovered and then insisted on continuing the tour.

On the very day of their arrival, Gullion began briefing the Kennedy brothers on the political and military developments in Indochina. Seated in the evening in the rooftop restaurant of the waterfront Majestic Hotel, they glimpsed gun flashes as French artillery fired across the Saigon River to interdict sites used by infiltrating Viet Minh guerrillas to mortar the city. Gullion told the Kennedys of the recent French military reverses and then laid out what he believed to be the only policy that might contain Ho Chi Minh's surging Viet Minh. What Gullion said that evening constituted, in fact, an extraordinary turnabout in how he viewed French prospects in the Vietnam struggle. On his arrival in Saigon in February 1950, Gullion had told me he believed that the French army with American material aid could defeat the Viet Minh. But by early 1951 Gullion had conceded to me privately that he no longer believed in a French military solution. Gullion had become a strong advocate of transforming the figurehead Bao Dai regime into a truly independent government that could rally the Vietnamese people against the Viet Minh. He had come to accept that an appeal to nationalism rather than an ideological struggle against Communism was the central issue. He was allied with Robert Blum, the head of the American economic aid mission, in insisting that military aid should be channeled directly to the embryo Vietnamese National Army. Gullion contended that continuing to funnel aid through the French had the effect of reducing the Bao Dai government to "the role of a French protected anonymity."

Gullion and Blum were disputing with General de Lattre, who was adamantly opposed to direct aid to the Vietnamese. The high commissioner had accused the two of "fanning the fires of extreme nationalism. French traditionalism is vital here," he told them. "A new nation cannot be created overnight simply by giving out economic aid and arms." Complaining of Blum's close relations with the Vietnamese, he once exclaimed to him: "You are the most dangerous man in Indochina." Although de Lattre was to concede to me at the end of that very year that the Viet Minh could not be defeated unless a strong Vietnamese army was mustered, the general never approved of direct aid to the Vietnamese army, nor did he sanction full independence for Vietnamese generals in field operations. General Francis G. Brink, the chief of the U.S. military aid group, complained to me that he was so continually under French surveillance and so harassed that he found it difficult to do his job. He returned to Washington in a deep depression and soon after committed suicide.

Once, after I had sent a dispatch which reported a curt French postponement of a direct U.S. aid program leading the Vietnamese to complain that they'd been humiliated, de Lattre in a rage summoned me. Two of his military aides came to the door of our apartment near midnight and insisted that I accompany them to the high commissioner's palace. De Lattre was waiting with Donald Heath, the minister of the American Legation, who had arrived in July 1950, seated at his side. Heath, visibly embarrassed, had been harangued by de Lattre about my dispatch. I was in no mood to take abuse from de Lattre, since I was still smarting from a previous encounter in which the general had taken umbrage because I had interviewed Bao Dai and reported his aspirations for greater independence. When de Lattre accused me of undermining the French position, I retorted sharply, and a shouting match ensued, with Heath squirming between us. When I told de Lattre that I had stated the French position after exploring it thoroughly in a conversation with a senior French official, he expressed disbelief. The next morning he grimly lined up his cabinet and asked the members if any one of them had spoken to me. His senior political adviser confessed to having given me a background briefing. De Lattre exploded in wrath. Dubbed "*le roi Jean*" by his subordinates, de Lattre so terrified his deputies that it became very difficult to obtain interviews with them.

Gullion and Blum did not prevail on the direct aid issue or on other recommendations for rapid evolution of the Vietnamese government to palpable independence. In Gullion's words, Washington lacked or was unwilling to apply its leverage. The State Department retreated when the French government hinted that, if pressed too hard on the independence issue, it might withdraw entirely from the war, which was strongly opposed by much of the French public. There was also great reluctance to antagonize French officials at a time when French leaders were being urged to join in the creation of a European Defense Community, a proposal project which the French parliament eventually rejected in any case.

As the political and military situation deteriorated, Gullion became more open in his espousal of Vietnamese independence, and this brought him into sharp conflict, not only with the French, but also with his superior, Donald Heath, the chief of mission. A conservative career diplomat, Heath was much more solicitous of French interests and sensibilities than Gullion and also more the unquestioning executor of State Department policy. As Gullion persisted in voicing his views, relations between the two diplomats deteriorated to the point where Heath denied Gullion, his deputy, access to his exchanges of messages with the State Department. This was the extraordinary situation within the legation when Kennedy arrived on his ten-day visit.

―――――――――

On the afternoon of the day following Kennedy's arrival, there was an unexpected knock on the door of our apartment, located on Boulevard Charner, just opposite the flower stalls in central Saigon. Kennedy had mounted the narrow stairs of the shabby hallway to our door. He was alone. As he greeted Audrey and me, he said: "I'll only be a few minutes." We ushered him into our small lounge, which served as living and dining room, and he seated himself in an easy chair near the bamboo bar. He stayed more than two hours, asking questions about every aspect of the Vietnam conflict. He wanted to know what the average Vietnamese felt about the United States. I told him that Americans were the most popular of foreigners when we first arrived in Saigon, many of them citing the American grant of independence to the Philippines as a model for the French. But now we were resented and even hated by many Vietnamese because of our new links to the French. As for the military situation, I told him of my experience on the frontier, which had led me to report that there was no prospect of a decisive French military victory given Ho Chi Minh's control of the mountain passes to China. Having captured the leadership of the fervent nationalist movement, Ho had available to him a seemingly inexhaustible pool of recruits for his forces, which were being trained in South China, together with access to weaponry and other war matériel to outfit them. Kennedy asked if the Bao Dai government was given full independence, would that sway nationalists from Ho Chi Minh's side. I replied I agreed in most respects to what Gullion was telling him, but I was pessimistic, citing my Chinese experience, about the prospects of any Vietnamese government winning popular support while visibly dependent on the presence of France or, for that matter, the United States. In China, one of the factors which had accounted for Chiang Kai-shek's loss of popular support was his open dependence on the United States. For many Chinese it was a reminder of humiliating Western extraterritorial concessions. In the same sense, the Vietnamese associated any foreign dependence with their colonial experience.

At the end of what had been an intense discussion, Kennedy remarked: "I'm going to talk about this when I get home. But it will give me trouble with some of my constituents." Then he rose, peeked at our year-old Susan in her crib, and smiling told Audrey she looked like a Madonna out of a Botticelli painting. A legation car was waiting for Kennedy in the street.

When Kennedy left me, he seemed persuaded that only a truly independent Vietnamese government had any prospect of attracting popular support away from Ho Chi Minh. But evidently he did not grasp the full import of what I tried to impart about the critical advantage gained by Ho Chi Minh in seizing control of the frontier mountain passes. The Viet Minh access to a totally secure safe haven in South China for the training and equipment of their troops would prove to be a determining factor in the outcome of the French Indochina War and the American sequel.

After Jack Kennedy's talks with Gullion and me, the Kennedys dined with Bao Dai and came away unimpressed. Two days later they had dinner with General de Lattre. JFK posed challenging questions about French colonial policy that irritated the high commissioner. De Lattre was so indignant that he addressed letters of complaint to Ambassador Heath and his own contacts in Washington citing the congressman's "impertinence." Nevertheless, de Lattre arranged for the Kennedys to visit Hanoi and tour the fortifications guarding the Red River delta approaches to the city. A French colonel in one of the forts told them he was confident of victory against the Viet Minh but this might not be achieved during his lifetime. Bobby recorded this comment in his journal with exclamation marks.

Jack Kennedy arrived in Asia infected by the "Who lost China?" syndrome at home. His voice had been among those who charged that responsibility for the Communist conquest of China could be attributed to advice given the Truman administration by China specialists in the State Department. He was also critical of the opinions of two of the most distinguished

American China scholars, John King Fairbank and Owen Lattimore. In a speech before the House of Representatives on January 25, 1949, he accused the Truman administration of crippling Chiang Kai-shek's Nationalist government by delaying needed aid while pressuring it to enter into a coalition with the Communists. It was a contention, as regards the supply of military aid, which defied the facts. His Asian tour, and especially his talk with Nehru, spurred him to a reappraisal of what was transpiring on the continent. In the month following his visit to Saigon, Kennedy asserted in a speech:

> In Indochina we have allied ourselves to the desperate effort of the French to hang on to the remnants of an empire. There is no broad general support of the native Vietnam government among the people of that area . . . To check the southern drive of Communism makes sense but not only through reliance on the force of arms. The task is rather to build strong native noncommunist sentiment within these areas and rely on that as a spearhead of defense rather than upon the legions of General De Lattre, brilliant though he may be. And to do this apart from and in defiance of innately nationalistic aims spells foredoomed failure. To the rising tide of nationalism, we have unfortunately become a friend of its enemy and as such its enemy and not its friends.

In June 1953, now in the Senate, Kennedy was still hammering at the same theme: "It is because we want the war to be brought to a successful conclusion that we should insist on genuine independence . . . I strongly believe that the French cannot succeed in Indochina without giving concessions necessary to make the native army a reliable crusading force." He also modified his attitude toward China and retracted publicly his 1949 remarks blaming scholars and State Department officials for the collapse of the Chiang Kai-shek government in the Civil War.

Seen as the most influential adviser to Kennedy on Vietnam, Gullion found himself under fire within the State Department as the senator persisted in criticizing the prevailing policies of the Eisenhower administration. He was warned by associates that he might be risking his career by remaining so close to Kennedy. Gullion continued, nevertheless, to be a close friend and adviser to Kennedy all through his years in the Senate and after he entered the White House in 1961. When Gullion was returning from service as ambassador in the Congo in 1961, Kennedy thought of appointing him as ambassador to Saigon, replacing Frederick Nolting, but was dissuaded by the secretary of state, Dean Rusk. Gullion persisted, however, in impressing upon the Kennedy brothers his belief that creation of a popular Saigon government, supported directly with American military and economic aid, was the key to the solution of the Vietnam problem. It was a view that JFK first adopted in Saigon, and it would profoundly influence his shaping of Vietnam policy when he became president.

18
HANOI

In late October 1951, after two years in Saigon, we were packing to leave for London, my next assignment. The Council on Foreign Relations had offered me a one-year fellowship in New York, but Frank Starzel, the general manager of the AP, refused a leave of absence. In compensation, he allowed me to choose my next foreign post, and I elected to go to London. Larry Allen, a distinguished correspondent, having won the Pulitzer Prize in 1942 for his courageous wartime coverage of the operations of the British Mediterranean Fleet, arrived in Saigon to replace me.

I had just turned over news coverage to him when the Saigon correspondents were invited to an important news conference that General de Lattre would be giving in Hanoi. There were rumors of an impending major French offensive. Allen pressed me to accompany him. I demurred, having had enough of Indochina, but finally agreed reluctantly, swayed in part by a perceived need to back him up. He was new to Vietnam and of late had taken to partying too much. He was to become the model for the carousing American correspondent in Graham Greene's novel *The Quiet American*. Audrey, of course, insisted on coming along to Hanoi, intent on not missing the action and also because she would not be left alone on our second wedding anniversary. Leaving our infant Susan with the Chinese amah, we took off for Hanoi aboard the plane of a French admiral with other correspondents. When on takeoff the aircraft tipped and a wing just about scraped the ground, I appealed to the Lord—please not on these last days after so many close calls in this benighted country. The plane miraculously righted itself.

In Hanoi, we checked into the Metropole Hotel, not far from the small charming Restored Sword Lake. Hanoi was a vigorous, bustling city, but without the sophistication, luxurious languor, and brilliant tropical color of Saigon. The people were sturdier, more peasantlike in appearance. The buildings of crumbling yellow plaster bore the scars of the vicious street fighting between the French and the Viet Minh in 1946 which ended with the flight of Ho Chi Minh's government to his northern jungle retreat. With de Lattre in command, there was a new sense of confidence among the French.

At the Metropole, we encountered Graham Greene, with whom we had become very friendly. Our friendship began on the day of his arrival in Saigon in October. He had been in Malaya, where he did an article for *Life* magazine on the Communist guerrilla insurgency. His brother, Hugh Greene, who was with the BBC, was there on loan to the British government to develop an information program designed to inspire greater support among the Malayan population for the counterinsurgency campaign against the local Chinese guerrillas. The Anglo-American community in Saigon was easygoing and hospitable to newcomers, and Audrey went to Graham's door at the Majestic Hotel on the day following his arrival to welcome him bearing two dog-eared paperbacks of his novels—*The Power and the Glory* and *The Heart of the Matter*—to be autographed. Laughing, he invited her in and scrawled his autographs, noting with satisfaction that the condition of the books indicated that they had been well read. He then accompanied her by pedicab back to our apartment to meet me. Thereafter he became a frequent visitor to our apartment, usually in the morning, when he would sip our excellent French cognac with his coffee. Our apartment was a way station for visiting correspondents—Marguerite Higgins of the *Herald Tribune* and Homer Bigart of the *New York Times* among others taking time out from the Korean warfronts—and there Greene met Elaine Shaplen, the estranged wife of Bob Shaplen, of the *New Yorker*. Elaine was en route to Singapore, and he suggested that she meet his brother, Hugh. The meeting led eventually to marriage. The couple lived in London, where Hugh became director of the BBC.

When we joined Greene in Hanoi, he had just returned from Phat Diem, a Catholic community on the delta, ruled from a towering baroque cathedral by a Trappist bishop, Le Huu Tu. Greene had been in Phat Diem just after a French paratrooper battalion had retaken the coastal enclave from Viet Minh occupation. The Phat Diem episode was something of an embarrassment for Greene. In his July article for *Life* magazine, "Malaya, the Forgotten War," reporting on a brief visit to Phat Diem in January, he had described in glowing terms the bishop's militia as dedicated Christians capable of defending Phat Diem against the Viet Minh. "You see I wanted to say to my friends in Malaya, 'it can be done. An idea fighting an idea,'" Greene wrote. He did not know at the time that the bishop had been playing Ho Chi Minh and the French against each other, making a pretense of close ties with both. When the Viet Minh attacked Phat Diem, they met virtually no resistance from the bishop's vaunted Christian militia. The town remained briefly in Viet Minh hands until the French paratroopers reoccupied it.

Greene's classic novel on Vietnam, *The Quiet American,* which he completed in June 1955, was based on considerable field reportage by Greene in
1951–52. Its plot brilliantly captured the atmosphere of embattled Vietnam
and the character of many of the players in the struggle. Generations of
Americans have read the book as a faithful historical account of the French
Indochina War. In truth, however, the reader desirous of a factual political
and military history of the war must look elsewhere.

De Lattre had a large and attentive audience of correspondents, diplomats, and French officials for his much publicized news conference at the
Hanoi military headquarters. Gesturing theatrically before a large map, he
described how his troops were launching an enveloping maneuver on a key
Viet Minh center at Hoa Binh, the capital of the Muong tribe, about forty
miles southwest of Hanoi, on the fringes of the Red River delta. The town
dominated routes by which the Viet Minh were receiving rice supplies and
manpower from the south and central parts of the country. It was also the
key to the control of positions along the Black River to the north and east.

After de Lattre's press conference I left Allen to do the story and spent the
evening in a large, noisy Vietnamese nightclub with Audrey and Graham
Greene. When we returned to the hotel, I noticed a light under the door of
Allen's room and knocked. He welcomed me enthusiastically and showed me
the dispatch he had just filed. His lead said: "General de Lattre de Tassigny
today launched a major offensive to end the eight-year old French Indochina
War." I was horrified. I had seen too many such French operations end in
frustration, and even if the offensive succeeded, it would have hardly put an
end to the Indochina conflict. There was nothing to be done immediately to
put the forthcoming de Lattre operation into reasonable perspective.

Escaping the company of Allen the next day, Audrey and I accepted
Greene's invitation to a picnic. Greene mobilized a rickety taxi and gave directions to the Vietnamese driver. As we headed out, I struggled to contain
my anxieties, since I realized that Greene had chosen a picnic site on the Red
River delta where Viet Minh guerrillas operated quite often. Sprawled out
on blankets, we munched chicken sandwiches and drank white wine while
Greene talked about his latest book, *The End of the Affair.* Publication of the
book had just put him on the cover of *Time* magazine. He spoke of being unhappy about the last thirty pages and said: "Every author has a right to one
bad book." *Brighton Rock,* he felt, was his best book. We strolled to a nearby
Buddhist temple. Having paid the guardian monk the required sum, Greene
took a hammer and struck a gong to drive away the evil spirits. "I thought

you were Catholic," Audrey said, laughing. "I'm taking no chances," Greene replied.

During the picnic Greene's pale blue eyes lit up when we told him we had once been to a *fumerie* in Saigon with a senior French official and his wife and smoked a few pipes of opium for the experience. He was all for trying it himself. On the following evening we rounded up an acquaintance, a young American who worked for the local office of the U.S. Information Service, and the three of us followed him down back alleys to a door where a rapping code brought forth a Vietnamese woman in a white gossamer gown. She led us up a narrow stairway to a large open room with double-decker bunks and individual divans arranged between bamboo partitions. Reclining on the beds were both French and Vietnamese smokers. One could see that Greene, the eager novelist, his pale blue eyes alight, was devouring every detail. The four of us lay down on divans while attending girls heated opium paste over candles, kneading the paste into balls and tamping them into the bowls of long wooden pipes. We demonstrated to Greene how to inhale an entire smoke with a single draw, and he joined us in four pipes, a safe number for the occasional smoker. Enamored by this first experience with opium, Greene smoked thereafter on several occasions as noted by his biographer, Norman Sherry. Exhilarated, we returned to the hotel, where, although Audrey and I had a plane departing early the next morning for Saigon, we drank and talked until it was time to leave for the airport. Audrey recalls that in the last hours of our drinking bout, Greene was lecturing to me about journalism and I was commenting outrageously on the art of novel writing. Greene confided that for him writing a novel was something like squeezing a boil to empty it. He had to get it out.

We were in Saigon on November 14 when French troops entered Hoa Binh in the first stage of de Lattre's vaunted offensive. It was the general's last hurrah. I had been told in confidence in Saigon upon my return from Hanoi that he was seriously ill with prostate cancer and would be returning shortly to France for treatment. Despite my occasional altercations with him about news coverage, I had come to admire the general. In the year that he had been in Indochina he had thrown himself totally into the war effort and by his genius given the French Expeditionary Force its proudest moments. He was in Hanoi, directing military operations on May 30, 1951, when he received word that his son, Lieutenant Bernard de Lattre, a twenty-three-year-old infantry officer, had been killed. While commanding a company in the defense of Nihn Binh on the Red River delta, he had been killed by a mortar blast during a Viet Minh attack.

The general announced the death of his only child by saying simply in a brief communiqué that he had "fallen on the field of honor at four o'clock this afternoon." It was a time in the Indochina war when each year the French were losing in officers the equivalent of an entire class of Saint Cyr, the French military academy. After the collapse of the frontier forts, Bernard de Lattre had written to his father from the field in Vietnam: "What we need is a leader who leads, fresh blood, and new machinery. And no more niggling, small time warfare; and then with the morale we still have in spite of it all, we could save everything." His father did come, but he faced an impossible task after the fall of the frontier. While fighting a war already lost, he had to contend with a bitterly critical public at home, a government unwilling to give him needed reinforcements, and American critics whom he could not satisfy.

De Lattre left Indochina for Paris on December 19. I preceded him by several weeks and on arrival in the French capital called at the Quai d'Dorsay to meet with an old friend, Jean de Lipkovski, the head of the Indochina Desk, whom I had known in China when he was a diplomat with the French Embassy. When he began to talk about de Lattre's return to Indochina, I interrupted him to say that the general was critically ill with prostate cancer and I doubted that he would return. Lipkovski was stunned. "I must inform my minister at once," he said. The French government apparently had not been told of de Lattre's condition. When the general was operated on in Paris, there was no announcement of the nature of his illness. He died on January 11. Several hundred thousand people attended his funeral on January 15, many of them passing by his bier at the Hotel des Invalides. Under the Arc de Triomphe, France's monument to its military glory, President Vincent Auriol placed a marshal's baton on de Lattre's coffin. Earlier, in the presence of Madame de Lattre, both the French National Assembly and the Council of the Republic approved without opposition—the French Communists abstained—the bill conferring the title of marshal.

The offensive on Hoa Binh, de Lattre's last hurrah, was intended to provide a dramatic victory at a time when the French government was pressing the United States for an increase in assistance and just as the French Assembly was entering into a budget debate on Indochina. But the capture of Hoa Binh was a hollow victory. The Viet Minh had withdrawn to fight another day on their own terms. Eventually, the Viet Minh counterattacked, in January 1952, along the Black River, and General Raoul Salan, to whom de Lattre had turned over the high command, was compelled to yield the Hoa Binh salient. It was a major reverse for the French that would lead to their eventual defeat at Dien Bien Phu.

The climactic battle, which Viet Minh military commander Vo Nguyen Giap had sought vainly, came in the French surrender on May 7, 1954, at Dien Bien Phu in North Vietnam after a fifty-six-day siege. Of the 13,000 French troops defending the fort, some 3,000 were killed and the others captured. According to Chinese archives, the envelopment of Dien Bien Phu was planned by Giap in consultation with Wei Guoqing, a top Chinese adviser, who was receiving instructions as the battle progressed from the Central Military Commission in Peking. Most of the Viet Minh units which overran Dien Bien Phu were trained in Chinese camps and armed with Chinese- and Soviet-supplied weapons. With their new 37-mm antiaircraft artillery the Viet Minh put up a wall of fire around Dien Bien Phu which blocked the French defenders from receiving many of the airdrops needed for survival. The 37-mm weapons, which the Viet Minh used with deadly effect, were twin-barreled guns, manned by crews of five to seven soldiers, which could fire explosive shells at 150 rounds a minute, up to ranges of nearly two miles. The network of trenches dug around the French fort which allowed the Viet Minh to move close in on the French defenses were constructed under the supervision of army engineers sent from Peking. In the final assault the Viet Minh deployed two battalions armed with 75-mm recoilless cannons and Katyusha rockets newly arrived from China. The fall of the fortress near the Laotian border marked the end of French military power in Indochina, an event predestined in October 1950 by defeat on R.C. 4 and the loss of the mountain passes to China.

My most valuable gift to Larry Allen when I turned over the AP's Saigon Bureau to him in November 1951 was Max Clos, my French assistant, who one day would become one of France's most celebrated journalists. Clos, twenty-five years old, a black belt judo enthusiast, born in Ludwigshafen, Germany, joined the AP as a local staffer only three months prior to my arrival in Saigon. His only previous journalistic experience was working as a news editor for a French-owned Saigon radio station. He filed in French to the AP office in Paris, where his copy was translated into English for the wire.

He was green journalistically—I helped him in the shaping of his copy—but he mastered the techniques rapidly and served as an invaluable assistant, knowledgeable, courageous in the field, and independent in his reporting. Clos had had excellent French intelligence sources, and in one of his dispatches in 1952 he noted: "France is in her sixth year of war against the Viet Minh which is an armed nationalist group 20 per cent of which, according to neutral observers, is Communist while the politics of the other 80 percent relate only to their desire for independence from France." The reaction in the AP New York office was amusing given Clos's personal right-wing political bent. Questions were raised among executives as to whether he was "pinkish," since the AP then habitually described the Viet Minh simply as Communist-led. Alan Gould, the executive news editor, stood firmly by Clos, and he continued to work for Larry Allen. It was Gould, one of the finest editors of his era, who gave me license to write lengthy interpretive articles from China and Indochina, going beyond the usual news agency hard-news format. He recognized the need to enlighten average Americans about those obscure parts of the world in which the White House was making far-reaching commitments. Clos left the AP in 1953 to join the staff of *Le Monde.* He became a prizewinning correspondent covering wars in Tunisia, Algeria, the Congo, and Cuba. In 1955 he went to the staff of *Le Figaro,* the leading conservative French newspaper, where he rose to serve as its top editor from 1973 to 1988. When he died of cancer at the age of seventy-eight on March 9, 2000, President Jacques Chirac in a formal statement hailed him as one of France's most accomplished and eminent journalists. I mourned him as a friend and valued colleague who had given me unique insights into the thinking and behavior of the French *colons* at a turning point in Indochina history.

19

ON THE DIPLOMATIC BEAT
AND THE KOREAN WAR

When Audrey and I embarked for London after the difficult years in warring China and Indochina, we anticipated a somewhat more relaxed life. But there was no escape from the tensions of the Asian wars.

We lived in London in a maisonette on Prince Arthur Road near Hampstead Heath. There, two new daughters, Karen, born in 1952, and Lesley in 1954, both in Queen Mary's Nursing Home, entered the company of our Saigon daughter, Susan. Like the Britons, we suffered post–World War II food rationing and lack of central heating. We rented our maisonette from the Irelands, an elderly couple who lived on the top floor of the three-story townhouse. In doing her food shopping, wheeling a large English pram bearing two babies and leading Susan by the hand, Audrey would make the daily rounds with ration coupons in hand hoping to scare up some edibles. (Eating lunch at the AP canteen, I was developing a lifelong hatred for the only available vegetable, brussels sprouts.) One evening Mrs. Ireland clattered down the stairs, her long red hair flying, in pursuit of our black cat. As we looked on startled, she crawled under our kitchen table to snare the cat and emerged holding a lamb chop. She brushed it off and whispered to us: "Don't tell Mr. Ireland." Audrey unhesitatingly pledged secrecy, knowing how precious the morsel was given the limitation of one chop per week on the rationing coupon book. Then there were the penetrating fogs, commonly described as smogs. At the AP office on Farringdon Road, off Fleet Street, where I worked, the fogs sometimes forced their way through window apertures, leaving wisps hanging in the newsroom. One night, driving home through a dense fog, Audrey and I lost our way. It was one of the worst "killer smogs" of the time, a deadly mix of mist and soot mainly from coal hearth fires, which were causing hundreds of deaths from pulmonary diseases. Upon sighting a pedestrian, I stopped the car and, leaning out into the billowing fog, begged for directions to Prince Arthur Road. The man I hailed dashed from the sidewalk to the front of our car holding up a white handkerchief. Waving us on, our Samaritan ran ahead for several blocks guiding us to our street. I scrambled out of the car to thank him, but he had disappeared in

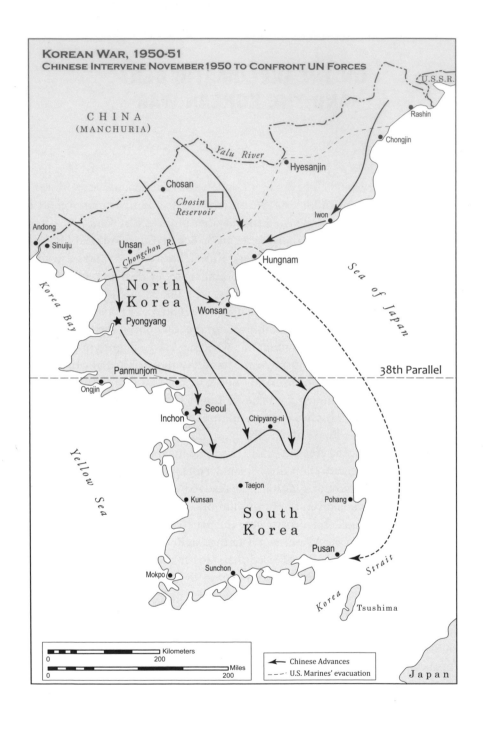

KOREAN WAR, 1950-51
CHINESE INTERVENE NOVEMBER 1950 TO CONFRONT UN FORCES

U.S.S.R.

CHINA
(MANCHURIA)

Rashin

Chongjin

Yalu River

Hyesanjin

Chosan

Chosin Reservoir

Iwon

Andong

Sinuiju

Unsan

Chongchon R.

Hungnam

Korea Bay

North Korea

Wonsan

★ Pyongyang

Sea of Japan

Panmunjom

38th Parallel

Ongjin

Seoul ★

Inchon

Chipyang-ni

Yellow Sea

Taejon

Kunsan

Pohang

South Korea

Pusan

Mokpo

Sunchon

Korea Strait

Tsushima

Kilometers
0   200

Miles
0   200

⟵ Chinese Advances

- - - U.S. Marines' evacuation

Japan

the fog. He was typical of the way the British behaved in a crisis. Knowing them made up for the discomforts of those early days in London.

During my first months in London, I worked on the AP desk, monitoring Moscow Radio, relaying cables from other foreign bureaus to New York, and familiarizing myself with the problems of covering of what then was the center of diplomatic activity. During my absences on the night trick, leaving the children under the care of a babysitter, Audrey would drive across the Heath to the studio of the noted sculptors Herman and Anna Nonnenmacher, with whom she was studying sculpture. Her lessons were fulfillment of a long-held ambition to enter into the arts. Audrey became a favored protégé of the Nonnenmachers, who were impressed with her talent. They arranged for two of her works to be exhibited at the Royal Institute Galleries, and later, Doris Lindner, a leading British sculptor, accepted her as a student. One of Audrey's exhibited works was a terra-cotta bust of me, which Lindner remarked "brought out the Neanderthal"—a comment that induced mixed feelings in me. The head was one of the works viewed by the famous portraitist Sir Jacob Epstein, who told Audrey she could become a great sculptor if she would leave her family and devote herself entirely to her art. Fortunately for me, Audrey did not abandon me, although she did subsequently continue her sculpting at an institute in Berlin and later in Moscow.

Soon transferred to the diplomatic beat, I then shuttled between covering the Foreign Office and diplomatic conferences on the European continent. In July 1954, I was in Geneva for the General Conference on Korea and Vietnam, attended by leaders of the belligerents in the two ongoing Asian wars and the major powers. I was to report on the final political spasms of the Korean and French Indochina conflicts. I benefited at the conferences by the presence in Geneva of two long-standing sources, who provided extraordinary insights into the highly confrontational negotiations between the Western and Communist blocs: Chester Ronning, my father-in-law, was serving as head of the Canadian Delegation, and Huang Hua, whom had I had not seen since our meetings in Nanking in 1949. His role at the conference on Indochina proved to be critical.

Following conclusion of the armistice in Korea on July 27, 1953, Huang Hua had served as the chief delegate to the negotiations at Panmunjom on outstanding problems, notably the exchange of prisoners of war. The negotiations lasted from late October until December 14, when Arthur W. Dean, the American delegate, in anger walked out complaining about Huang Hua's vitriolic denunciations of the United States' role in the conflict. When the Korean negotiations were transferred on April 26, 1954, to the forum of the

conference in Geneva, Premier Zhou Enlai, the head of the Chinese delegation, brought Huang Hua with him as an adviser.

The Korea segment of the conference, which was designed to forge a peace
treaty, collapsed shortly after my arrival in Geneva. The conferees were unable to agree on terms for withdrawal of foreign troops from the peninsula
through elections that would create a united Korea. Ronning placed much
of the blame for the failure of the conference on John Foster Dulles, the U.S.
secretary of state. Prior to the conference, Ronning told me, Dulles secretly
assured Syngman Rhee, the South Korean president, that the United States
would not agree at the conference to anything that he would find unacceptable. Rhee, who had opposed the convening of the conference, favored resumption of military operations against the North Koreans, hoping it would
give him control of the entire peninsula. Ronning also related to me how
Dulles had impeded progress at the conference by refusing to engage directly
with the Chinese delegation. At the reception opening the conference Ronning entered the ceremonial hall walking just behind Dulles. The U.S. secretary was greeted in Chinese with outstretched hand by Zhou Enlai, who
was standing near the door. Dulles, refusing to shake hands, brushed past
the Chinese premier, muttering "I cannot . . . " He then turned and strode
out of the room with hands locked behind his back. Shocked, Ronning hastened forward, grasped Zhou's hand, and greeted him in Chinese, mitigating the insult and loss of face. In the absence of formal diplomatic relations,
Dulles had decided not to shake hands with the Chinese leader. Zhou Enlai
never forgave the Dulles snub, nor did he forget Ronning's compensating gesture. At the closed final plenary session of the conference on June 15, when
all hope of an agreement had faded, Zhou Enlai proposed that the conference be adjourned only temporarily so that it could be reconvened whenever the chairmen decided a time was propitious for progress. He appealed to
the delegations not to extinguish the possibility of arriving at a peace agreement. Ronning for Canada, Anthony Eden, the British foreign secretary, and
other delegates were supportive of the proposal, but General Walter Bedell
Smith, the American delegate, rejected it, arguing that the conference was
never intended to be a permanent negotiating body outside the United Nations. Since consensus was required for any action, the conference ended
there, and the boundary between North and South Korea was frozen at the
thirty-eighth parallel as stipulated in the armistice agreement. It was an arrangement which has endured and served to isolate North Korea, spurring
its leaders to an enormous military buildup and toward efforts to develop
nuclear weapons.

Although I was not on the ground in the Korean War, as in Indochina, I became privy to the origins of the conflict, the developments which led to the intervention of Chinese Communist troops, and the miscalculations in the conflict on all sides which cost the lives of an estimated five million people. These fatalities included Korean civilians and combatants of the two Koreas, China, the United States, and the fifteen allied nations of the United Nations. American casualties alone, in the three-year war in which 300,000 ground troops were deployed, totaled about 54,000 servicemen dead, 103,000 wounded, and some 8,000 missing. Strangely, despite its enormous costs, overshadowed by the war in Vietnam, the Korean conflict all too soon became the "forgotten war."

In the war on the Korean peninsula, the coalition of American, South Korean, and other United Nations contingents suffered their most devastating defeat at an early stage when Chinese troops intervened and descended on them in overwhelming force. It was a reverse to be attributed in great part to a military intelligence failure on the part of General Douglas MacArthur, the supreme commander, and his G-2 deputy, Major General Charles Willoughby. I trace the roots of their failure to what I surmised in January 1948 during a visit to Tokyo when MacArthur was presiding in Japan as Supreme Commander Allied Powers (SCAP).

Posted then in Nanking for the International News Service, I was assigned to visit Tokyo to survey the post–World War II strategic situation in the Pacific. Upon my arrival in the Japanese capital there was a message waiting asking me to meet with MacArthur for an interview that I had not requested. I was told by the general's aides that the Supreme Commander Allied Powers wanted my impressions of developments in the Chinese Civil War. The general greeted me most cordially in his office on the roof of the Dai Ichi Building and then began questioning me about the evolution of the Civil War on the China mainland. I could see that the general, leaning back in his chair, sucking on his corncob pipe and gazing reflectively at the ceiling, was not intent on what I had to say. He interrupted me to lay out his own views, which took up most of our two-hour meeting. He said he had a solution for bringing about a Nationalist victory. "The United States should give Chiang Kai-shek five hundred bombers and maintain them," the general said crisply.

I listened to the general bewildered. The Nationalists had already been well supplied with American B-24 and B-25 bombers as well as Canadian

Mosquito strike aircraft. This unopposed air power had proven to be virtually ineffectual in combat operations against the Communists. After my meeting with MacArthur I discussed the China Civil War with Willoughby, his G-2. I found Willoughby, like MacArthur, lacking in understanding of what was transpiring on the mainland. Willoughby had an overbearing manner, redolent of his Prussian antecedents. Other members of MacArthur's staff in talks with me jokingly referred to him as "Sir Charles." Extreme right wing politically, an admirer of General Francisco Franco, the Spanish dictator, Willoughby was contemptuous of the Chinese Communist military. He dismissed Mao's armies and their commanders as comprising little more than a guerrilla force. It seemed to me that he was repeating the error he made when he underestimated the capabilities of the Japanese in the battle for Leyte in the Philippines. Looking now at yet another Asian army, he was underestimating the capabilities of the Chinese Communists. Two years later this miscalculation would bring MacArthur and Willoughby to the point of total disaster in battling Mao Zedong's intervention in the Korean War.

I was in Saigon in the early morning of June 25, 1950, when the North Korean leader Kim Il-sung gave the signal for the invasion of South Korea. The war seemed very distant and unrelated to Indochina even after President Truman, under the banner of the United Nations, committed American forces to the defense of South Korea with MacArthur in overall command. But the war suddenly took on new significance for Indochina on October 25 when Chinese troops intervened in great force. The Chinese struck after MacArthur's troops crossed the thirty-eighth parallel in pursuit of the collapsing North Korean army and advanced toward the Yalu River bordering China. In Saigon, French and American strategists saw the widening of the war in Korea as a likely prelude to a Chinese Communist invasion of Vietnam. Mao's divisions were already arrayed along the Indochina border. The last of the French forts had fallen that very month to Ho Chi Minh's Viet Minh, and the mountain passes were open to Chinese incursions. As documented in the Pentagon Papers, the National Security Council put forward contingent planning in the event of such an invasion that would have provided for allied naval blockade of China, bombing its lines of communication, and the deployment onto mainland China of Chiang Kai-shek's forces from Taiwan.

Despite these alarums, I was dubious that Ho Chi Minh would invite the Chinese troops in great force into North Vietnam. Advisers to train his Viet Minh? Yes, but not thousands of Chinese troops who might set up camp in the country indefinitely. For a thousand years, the Vietnamese had resisted any incursions by the Chinese, their traditional enemies. Still fresh for them was the memory of the looting of North Vietnam by Chinese Nationalist troops in the post–World War II occupation. The extent of lingering Vietnamese distrust of the Chinese would again manifested itself in 1979 when China and Vietnam fought a brief and inclusive war, with heavy casualties on both sides, over rival claims to the Paracel Islands, border demarcation, and the ousting by Vietnamese forces of the Peking-supported Pol Pot regime in Cambodia.

As events unfolded, Mao did not invade Indochina, but also he did not allow his distractions in Korea to diminish his aid program for Ho Chi Minh. If anything, Chinese material assistance to the Viet Minh was expanded. Given Mao's domestic problems, I could only assume that his intervention in Korea was impelled by what he saw as a serious threat by the United States to the security of his regime. The timing of the commitment could not have been worse for the Communists. Mao had not yet consolidated his mastery of the mainland. There were still possibly one million Nationalist guerrillas, dubbed "bandits" by Mao, still operating in scattered areas. The economy had been totally disrupted by the Civil War, and millions of hungry tattered refugees were crowded into the towns and cities. General Chen Yi was making preparations in the South China ports for an assault on the Taiwan redoubt of Chiang Kai-shek.

According to the testimony of Nikita Khrushchev, documented in the book *Khrushchev Remembers,* and considerable other evidence from Chinese and Russian archives, the initiative for the invasion of South Korea originated with Kim Il-sung, the North Korean dictator. He held that the South Korean army would collapse before the onslaught of his Soviet-armed forces. The Syngman Rhee government would then be swept away, allowing him to unify the peninsula under his control. Stalin gave his approval for the thrust into South Korea and in turn urged Mao to support the invasion militarily. Mao was hesitant. Relations between Peking and the Kim government in Pyongyang were not close. The quick response of the United Nations in condemning the invasion and pledging aid to South Korea together with the Truman commitment of American armed forces had surprised both Mao and Stalin. The military involvement of the United States in what earlier had seemed to the Communist leaders to be not such a risky endeavor compelled a reassessment by Stalin and Mao on what support they might render Kim without becoming involved in a wider conflict.

Early in the Korean conflict, on a contingency basis Mao began deploying troops behind the Yalu River bordering China for possible intervention while he awaited military developments on the ground. From the time U.S. forces under the command of MacArthur landed in Korea, Mao never discounted the possibility that the Americans might continue up the peninsula to the Yalu River with the aim of destabilizing his regime. Immediately he was concerned about the vulnerability of the power plants close to the Yalu River, which were of vital importance to the Manchurian industrial heartland. Mao was not relieved of his anxieties by the fact that the Truman administration, acting under the mandate of the United Nations, seemed to be exercising care to avoid a clash with China. What Mao found most alarming was MacArthur's liaisons with Chiang Kai-shek. On August 1, MacArthur had met Chiang on Taiwan. In a communiqué issued after the talks, Chiang spoke of military cooperation in defense of Taiwan, but he also added that victory over Mao on the mainland was assured. Chiang was then reassembling his forces in the hope that he might obtain American help for a return to the mainland. Seeking to cement his ties with MacArthur, the Generalissimo had offered three divisions for deployment in Korea, an offer that was declined on the advice of General Marshall and others who had little respect for the quality of Chiang's troops. Chiang's communiqué, which dismayed Truman and Secretary of State Acheson, who regarded it as provocative to the Chinese, had exaggerated the scope of the assurances of cooperation MacArthur had extended to the Nationalist leader. But Mao was not aware that this was the case or that Truman had directed the Seventh Fleet on June 28 not only to prevent any Communist attack from the mainland on Taiwan but also "any assault from Taiwan against the mainland."

In debates within the Chinese Politburo, a majority of its members, including Zhou Enlai and General Lin Biao, the conqueror of Manchuria, at various times expressed opposition to a foray into Korea, given China's internal problems and the danger of retaliation by the United States. Nevertheless, Mao persisted in reviewing the options. He cited the implications for China if the North Korean buffer state was overrun. Yet when he sent Zhou Enlai to Moscow, it was with instructions only to simply listen to Stalin's proposal for Chinese intervention, I was told by a Chinese official intimately familiar with the talks. But then, as Mao observed events in Korea, a second set of instructions followed while Zhou was still in Moscow in which Mao bent to Stalin on condition that the Russian leader provide additional armaments and cover by the Soviet Air Force for Chinese troops if they should cross into Korea.

On September 30, as Chinese troops massed along the Yalu, Zhou Enlai issued the first of several warnings to the United States. In a public statement, Zhou said: "The [Chinese] people absolutely will not tolerate foreign aggression, nor will they supinely tolerate seeing their neighbors being savagely invaded by the imperialists." Zhou then summoned the Indian ambassador, Sardar K. M. Panikkar, my interlocutor of Nanking days, to his Peking residence for a meeting on October 3, at which he formally communicated a warning that China would intervene if American troops crossed the thirty-eighth parallel. In his book *In Two Chinas*, published in 1955, Panikkar described the scene:

> Though the occasion was the most serious I could imagine, a midnight interview on questions affecting the peace of the world . . . Zhou Enlai was as courteous and charming as ever and did not give the least impression of worry or nervousness or indeed of being in any particular hurry. He had the usual tea served and the first two minutes were spent in normal courtesies, apology for disturbing me at an unusual hour. Then he came to the point. He thanked Pandit Nehru for what he had been doing in the cause of peace, and said no country's need for peace was greater than that of China, but there were occasions when peace could only be defended by determination to resist aggression. If the Americans crossed the 38th parallel China would be forced to intervene in Korea. Otherwise he was most anxious for a peaceful settlement, and generally accepted Pandit Nehru's approach to the question. I asked him whether he had already news of the Americans having crossed the border. He reported in the affirmative but added he did not know where they had crossed. I asked him whether China intended to intervene, if only the South Koreans crossed the parallel. He was emphatic. The South Koreans did not matter but American intrusion into North Korea would encounter Chinese resistance.

Panikkar immediately relayed Zhou Enlai's warning to New Dehli, where it was forwarded to the State Department. The decision as whether to heed Zhou Enlai's warning was put to Truman. At the time MacArthur was pressing his advance toward the parallel and was calling upon Kim Il-sung to capitulate. MacArthur was holding out the prospect of a united non-Communist Korea. The White House was told by both the CIA and British intelligence that Panikkar was biased in favor of the Chinese and that they evaluated his advice as unreliable. Earlier, when asked to address the question of the "threat of full Chinese Intervention in Korea," the CIA stated in a memo dated October 12, which was declassified and published in 2006: "The Chinese Communist ground forces, currently lacking requisite air and naval support, are capable of intervening effectively, but not necessarily decisively, in the Korean conflict . . . While full-scale Chinese Communist intervention in Korea must be regarded as a continuing possibility, a consideration of all known factors leads to the conclusion that barring a Soviet decision for global war, such action is not probable in 1950. During this period, intervention will probably be confined to continued covert assistance to the North Koreans."

Given these intelligence assessments, Truman dismissed the message from Zhou Enlai as a bluff, asserting that Panikkar had "played the game of the Chinese Communists fairly regularly" and that the Chinese warning was "probably a bald attempt to blackmail the United Nations by threats of intervention in Korea."

The Truman reaction to the Zhou Enlai warning would lead to one of the greatest military disasters in American history.

In the first weeks of the invasion, North Korean forces with a vanguard of Russian T-34 tanks had surged down the peninsula overrunning the ill-prepared South Korean army and the American Task Force Smith, made of up of elements of the U.S. Army's Twenty-fourth Division, hastily transferred from occupation duty in Japan. By August, the U.S. Eighth Army and South Korean forces had been forced to fall back into a perimeter around the city of Pusan in the southeastern corner of the peninsula. The allied perimeter defenses withstood heavy North Korean attacks while large-scale reinforcements of American, South Korean, and allied United Nations forces were being assembled. Massive American air strikes began to rupture the overly extended North Korean supply lines. In early September, MacArthur's forces broke out of the Pusan perimeter. MacArthur then undertook a brilliant, albeit risky, operation, dubbed "Chromite," which altered the course of the war.

MacArthur activated the X Corps under General Edward Almond, his former chief of Staff, comprising 70,000 troops of the First Marine Division and the Army's Seventh Infantry Division, augmented by 8,600 South Korean troops. The X Corps then executed an amphibious operation, landing on September 15 at the port of Inchon on the coast of the Yellow Sea, 150 miles northwest of Pusan, and deployed behind the North Korean lines. They encountered only light resistance from the surprised North Koreans. Kim Il-sung had given scant attention to warnings by Mao and the Chinese military leadership that the Allies might attempt such a landing at Inchon. The X Corps struck inland, recaptured Seoul, and moved to cut off the main body of the retreating shattered North Korean army.

In what was characterized as hot pursuit, MacArthur sent the South Korean Second Division across the thirty-eighth parallel into North Korea on September 30. Zhou Enlai had told Panikkar that China would not intervene if only the South Koreans crossed the parallel. MacArthur was then in receipt of an "eyes alone" message from General George Marshall, the new secretary of defense, stating: "We want you to feel unhampered tactically and strategically to proceed north of the 38th parallel." It was with this mandate, defying the Zhou Enlai warning about a crossing by American troops, that MacArthur took the fatal decision of ordering the First Cavalry Division of the U.S. Eighth Army across the parallel on October 7. The division in pursuit of the retreating North Korean army occupied Pyongyang, Kim Il-sung's capital, on October 20. While the Eighth Army advanced, the X Corps was trucked south to the port of Pusan, where its component First Marine Division and the army's Seventh Division, commanded by General David G. Barr, the former head of the Joint U.S. Military Advisory Group (JUSMAG) in Nanking, boarded transports with the mission of landing in a flanking operation at Wonsan, a North Korean port on the coast of the Sea of Japan. On October 24, just before the X Corps made its unopposed landing at Wonsan, MacArthur ordered the Eighth Army in the west and the X Corps in the east, making up two spearheads, to drive forward with all speed to the Yalu River to secure control of all North Korea. As to consideration of the possibility of Chinese intervention, ten days earlier, in a meeting with President Truman on Wake Island to reassess strategy, MacArthur assured the president, according to the transcript of their conversations, that of Mao's troops "only 50,000 or 60,000 could be gotten across the Yalu River. They have no air force. Now that we have bases for our air force in Korea, if the Chinese tried to get down to Pyongyang, there would be the greatest slaughter."

As MacArthur's forces thrust north, Chinese troops began infiltrating into North Korea. They were dubbed "volunteers" by Mao to maintain the fiction that China was not formally at war with the United States, which Lin Bao had warned in Politburo meetings might bring nuclear reprisal. The so-called volunteers actually included battle-hardened veterans of the Fourth Field Army as well as North Korean units which together had served under Lin Biao in his defeat of Chiang Kai-shek's forces in Manchuria. Suddenly, on November 1, at 10:30 P.M. as the Eighth Army made its way north toward the Yalu, the Chinese struck in overwhelming force, overrunning the Eighth Cavalry Regiment of the First Cavalry Division, which was occupying forward positions near the town of Unsan. As described in the annals of the U.S. Army Center of Military History, the Chinese came out of the hills

blowing bugles and firing at the surprised Americans. Withdrawing before
these "human wave" assaults, the unnerved men of the Eighth Cavalry abandoned their artillery and took to the hills in small groups. The elite regiment
lost more than eight hundred men, almost one-third of its total strength. The
Eighth Army, as other of its units came under attack, retreated to defensive
positions along the Chongchon River. Then, mysteriously on November 6,
the Chinese disappeared from the Eighth Army front and also on the east
where a marine battalion of the X Corps, leading the spearhead moving
north toward the Yalu, had earlier come under attack. There is no certainty
as to whether the Chinese withdrew simply to give MacArthur the opportunity to break off his advance toward the Yalu, as Huang Hua explained to
me in later years, or whether the withdrawal was actually a stratagem to lure
the Americans into a massive trap.

     Despite these shocking setbacks, MacArthur and Willoughby continued
to insist to Washington that the Chinese would not press their intervention
in any great force. The disappearance from the fronts of the Chinese troops
on November 6 was cited in support of their contention. According to the
U.S. Army Center of Military History, Willoughby estimated that the number of Chinese troops in the theater of operation was 35,500, while in reality more than 300,000 organized in thirty divisions had already moved into
Korea. This was a juncture in the war when expert knowledge of Chinese
strategy and tactics was desperately needed if MacArthur was to cope with
the threat. The single senior American military officer most qualified to provide that advice was General Barr. I had known Barr extremely well when
he headed JUSMAG in Nanking, both from his pre-1949 briefings and so-
cially. His daughter, Ginny Barr, was Audrey's close friend and a schoolmate
at Nanking University. In the year Barr spent in China as commander of
JUSMAG before its withdrawal at the end of 1948, the general had gained an
intimate knowledge of the operations of both the Communist and Nationalist armies, expertise which was evidenced in his comprehensive reports
to the Department of Defense. But as far as I am aware, Barr was not consulted by Willoughby or MacArthur in their strategic planning or enlisted
in advising their subordinate commanders on Chinese tactics and strategy.
He was in command of the Seventh Division when the Chinese intervened,
leading his troops up from the port of Wonsan toward the Yalu River.

     MacArthur was relying on air power to shield his troops when he ordered
the twin spearheads of the Eighth Army and the X Corps to resume their
push to the Yalu. Misled by Willoughby's intelligence assessments, MacArthur had failed to grasp that he was exposing his forces to the classic type of

entrapment which had brought victory to the People's Liberation Army in engagements during the Chinese Civil War. As MacArthur's troops moved north, Chinese armies were pouring across the Yalu bridges, employing well-practiced stealth tactics, marching only by night along mountain trails under perfect discipline to avoid detection, and taking up positions for a massive deadly assault.

As the Chinese were readying their assault, the X Corps' Fifth and Seventh Marine regiments of the First Division reached the hills overlooking the Chosin Reservoir near the Yalu and were joined in the area by the Thirty-first Regimental Combat Team, made up of units of the Seventh Division. One of the team's units slogging farther north entered Hyesanjin on the Yalu River on November 20. Hyesanjin, which in Korean means "ghost city of broken bridges," was the farthest point north reached by MacArthur's forces. In the army's official history of the Seventh Division, Colonel Herbert B. Powell, a regimental commander, is quoted as saying: "We swept through the city and took a good look around. Then we dropped back to a good hill position to wait for something to happen." They didn't have long to wait.

Suddenly, during two days of November 25 to 27, on a 300-mile front, with the bugles sounding once again, an estimated 300,000 Chinese troops swarmed down from the steep border mountain ranges which MacArthur had once described as too precipitous to shelter troops. They descended on surprised American and South Korean troops outnumbering them as much as ten to one. A wedge was driven between the Eighth Army and the X Corps. The Marines and the Thirty-first Regimental Combat Team of the X Corps were surrounded by three Chinese divisions. The Chinese mounted ferocious attacks at night and retreated during the day to escape the American air support, which alone prevented the surrounded units from being totally overrun. Ordered by MacArthur on December 5 to withdraw, the 25,000 U.S. Marines, and 100 British Royal Marines of the X Corps broke out of encirclement and fought southward toward the port at Hungnam, on the coast of the Yellow Sea, where ships of the Seventh Fleet were assembling to pick them up. The successful breakout was made possible by the holding operation east of Chosin of the Thirty-first Regimental Combat Team, but in the five-day battle the army unit was virtually destroyed as an integrated fighting force. In twelve days of running battles at times through blinding snowstorms over some fifty torturous miles to their embarkation point, the marine regiments managed to remain fairly intact, inflicting heavy casualties on the Chinese divisions, which sought to block their withdrawal. About 11,000 marines survived the retreat from Chosin, having suffered 561 dead,

162 missing, and 2,894 wounded. The Thirty-first Regimental Combat Team suffered the most devastating losses as they fought south to the port. A total of only about 1,050 of its 2,500 troops survived. Inadequately clothed for the Arctic-like temperatures, the army troops and marines suffered frostbite and other disabilities. Under the cover of naval gunfire, 105,000 troops of the X Corps were moved by landing craft out of the Hungnam port to waiting ships, the last of them embarking on Christmas Eve 1950. They were redeployed to South Korea to join the Eighth Army, which was in full retreat in the west.

General Barr was awarded the Distinguished Service Medal, cited for inspiring his men by personally braving enemy fire during the drive north to the Yalu. But the general was so distraught by the losses suffered by the Thirty-first Regimental Combat Team of his Seventh Division in the retreat from Chosin that he was replaced after New Year's Day by Major General Claude B. Ferenbaugh as commander of the Seventh Division.

On New Year's Eve, attacking once again through the snow with temperatures below zero, the Chinese shattered what remained of the United Nations front. A precipitous general retreat ensued of the Eighth Army and South Korean units in the face of an onslaught by swelling numbers of Chinese troops. Pursuing the fleeing Americans, the Communists captured Seoul in January.

While MacArthur's forces were being hacked severely in their retreat, the cost to the Chinese Communists in casualties was even greater. Out of apparent apprehension of being drawn directly into war with the United States, Stalin reneged on his agreement with Zhou Enlai to provide immediate and effective air cover. The Chinese troops were exposed to devastating attacks by the largely unopposed American Air Force. A few Russian-made MIG jets ventured into North Korea in early November but did not appear in some force over the battlefields until the first part of 1951. Some were piloted by Chinese trained by the Russians. Others were flown by Russians who kept radio silence to conceal their nationality. The MIGs proved to be less than effective in combat against the U.S. Air Force.

On December 3, MacArthur reported to the Joint Chiefs of Staff that the Chinese had committed what he described as twenty-six splendidly equipped and trained divisions against him with 200,000 troops in reserve. He was not sure that his forces could hold a line in South Korea. He complained that the South Korean forces had proven largely useless. Willoughby's intelligence had been faulty throughout in assessing Chinese capabilities, and now among his other errors he had made the mistake of identifying the Communist field commander as Lin Biao. The commander was, in fact, Peng De-huai, one of the most distinguished generals of the Long March, who had served as deputy commander in chief to Zhu De in the war against Japan and had led the First Field Army in sweeping up northwestern China during the Civil War. Lin Biao, who had questioned the wisdom of intervention in Korea, was offered the command but declined pleading ill health.

On December 30, when consideration was being given to possible withdrawal to Japan of the shattered American army, MacArthur was asked by the Pentagon to lay out his contingency planning. MacArthur startled the White House with his reply. According to his memoir *Reminiscences,* he asked for authorization to: "(1) blockade . . . the coast of China; (2) destroy through naval gunfire and air bombardment China's industrial capacity to wage war; (3) secure appropriate reinforcements from the Nationalist garrison on Taiwan to strengthen our position in Korea if we decide to continue the fight for that peninsula; and (4) release existing restrictions upon the Taiwan garrison for diversionary action, possibly leading to counter-invasion against vulnerable areas of the China mainland."

He added that these measures would assure victory in Korea and "save Asia from the engulfment otherwise facing it." The alternative to what he was proposing was defeat and acceptance of a "tactical plan of successively contracting defense lines south to the Pusan beachhead" as the only possible way in which "the evacuation could be accomplished."

MacArthur's proposals were rejected by the White House and the Joint Chiefs of Staff as impractical in strategic terms and a provocation which could lead to world conflict. When MacArthur pressed for authority to bomb targets in China, Truman refused permission. When the general made the disagreement public, the president fired him as supreme commander, and he was recalled to Washington.

General Barr reappeared in June 1951 to testify at the Senate's investigation of the White House's Asian policies and President Truman's recall of MacArthur. The general was stationed at the time at the Armored Center, the army's training school for tank commanders. Barr said he had favored MacArthur's proposal for "hot pursuit"—chasing of enemy planes into Manchuria—but endorsed the rejection by the Joint Chiefs of Staff of the general's more aggressive polices. He said that MacArthur's policies would have risked world war.

With MacArthur's recall, General Mathew B. Ridgway succeeded to command of the Eighth Army, which had been merged with the remnants of the X Corps. General Walton Walker, commander of the Eighth Army, had died in a jeep accident on an icy road. After months of inconclusive combat, the front stabilized around the thirty-eighth parallel, and Ridgeway opened truce negotiations with the Chinese and North Koreans on July 10, 1951. Negotiations at Panmunjom, which involved Huang Hua as the chief Chinese delegate, broke down four times. The Communists became more flexible in the negotiations after President Eisenhower warned that the United States might not be adverse to the use of nuclear weapons in the conflict. An armistice was concluded on July 23, 1953, with the thirty-eighth parallel as the line of demarcation between the North and South Korean forces pending negotiations at the Geneva Conference of a final peace settlement.

It had been a useless, enormously costly war with no gain on any side. In its origins, responsibility obviously rested in the first instance on Kim Il-sung and Stalin. In assessing the American role, MacArthur had made gross miscalculations, compounded by Willoughby's intelligence failures in assessing Chinese intentions and strategy. Truman shared in responsibility for having induced the entry of China into the Korean War. While he balked at any crossing of the Yalu River line, he gave MacArthur license to pursue the North Korean army beyond the thirty-eighth parallel. His dismissal of Zhou Enlai's warning transmitted through Panikkar as bluff, based in part on the highly questionable intelligence denigrations of the Indian ambassador's reliability as a channel of communication, was a fatal error. Based upon my own contacts with Panikkar in Nanking as well as assessments by Western diplomats who knew him well, such as Chester Ronning, there was no reason to question Panikkar's competence and reliability as a professional diplomat.

In retrospect, the analysis of the Chinese intervention in the Korean War, written by Richard W. Stewart for the U.S. Army Center of Military History, stated, "The initial warning attacks and diplomatic hints by the Chinese were ignored by the overconfident Far Eastern Command under General MacArthur. MacArthur's failure to comprehend the reality of the situation led the entire United Nations Army to near disaster at the Chongchon River and the Chosin Reservoir. Only the grit and determination of the individual American soldiers and Marines as they fought the major enemies of cold, fear, and isolation held the UN line together during the retreats from North Korea."

In a strange and unhappy aftermath to the Panikkar affair, I became entangled in controversy with him. Audrey, who also knew Panikkar well, received a disconcerting letter from him when we were living in Saigon, dated February 26, 1951, in which he complained that out of my "vivid imagination" I had attributed "Machiavellian activities" to him, and he asked that I desist. I wrote back denying that I had characterized him in this way. Most unfortunately, Panikkar had seen a published AP photo of himself with a very unfair caption that impugned his character, and he guessed erroneously that I had in some way contributed to it. The historical record shows that Panikkar was correct in every respect in the relay of Zhou Enlai's warning. I was convinced at the time that the branding of him by the CIA as unreliable was totally wrong and served only to confuse the White House at a most crucial decision-making moment. I never met Panikkar again, but a subsequent letter indicated that he had been mollified by my reply.

On October 25, 2003, by coincidence on the fifty-third anniversary of the crossing of the Yalu by the Chinese volunteers, I had a private talk in China about the Korean War with Huang Hua, who had been deeply involved at every stage in both the politics and diplomacy of the conflict. The talk took place in Hangzhou at the closely guarded compound known as Wang Village, on the shore of West Lake. Since the days of the Maoist regime, Wang Village has been reserved as a vacation retreat for top Chinese leaders. Audrey and I were overnight guests of Huang Hua and his wife, He Liliang, a former diplomat in the American Department of the Chinese Foreign Ministry.

Huang Hua, then ninety-one years old, shared his recollections with me in one of the luxurious reception rooms of the government hostel. Seated on a couch beside me, he sighed heavily and shuddered when I asked him about the Chinese intervention in the Korean War.

"The memory is so painful," Huang Hua said.

Stalin and Kim Il-sung asked Mao Zedong to support the North Korean invasion of the South. Mao and Zhou Enlai refused. We were not prepared, and we were still recovering from war against the Kuomintang and the Japanese. Mao warned Kim Il-sung that he risked having Korea cut apart by a landing of the Americans at Inchon. But he did not pay much attention. When the Americans were advancing north in October, we warned them through the Indian ambassador if they crossed the thirty-eighth parallel we would intervene. When they did cross, we waited until they came up to our border. We asked Stalin for air cover but he refused. He did not want to become directly involved. But we intervened, nevertheless, because we had to show the Americans that they could not come into China.

Huang Hua pointed out that after the first contacts with U.S. Forces the Chinese troops disengaged. He answered the question which arose then: If MacArthur had not pressed his advance, would the Chinese have returned, nevertheless, to the attack? Huang Hua said that the Chinese had disengaged to give the Americans an opportunity to break off their advance.

"The war was so terrible," Huang Hua said, closing his eyes for a moment. "Both China and the United States suffered so much. Even Mao's own son, Mao Anying, was killed. The commanding general, Peng Dehuai, tried to keep Anying safe. He made him his aide and kept him close at his headquarters. When the American planes bombed the headquarters, Peng Dehuai was in a shelter, but Anying was in the open. He was running to a shelter when he was struck on the left arm and side by napalm. He died of the wound. Our people were afraid to tell Mao of the death of his son. He learned of it only several days later when going through field reports. He was so overcome with grief that he had to lie down."

Mao's son was killed in November when Chinese troops were operating without air cover. The Russian-educated Mao Anying was at Peng Dehuai's headquarters as an interpreter in the day-to-day contacts with Soviet advisers.

In making arrangements for Anying to be buried in North Korea, Mao said in a public statement: "In war there must be sacrifice. Without sacrifices there will be no victory. To sacrifice my son or other people's sons are just the same. There are no parents in the world who do not treasure their children. But please do not feel sad on my behalf because this is something entirely unpredictable."

Mao had far more reason than the death of his son to bitterly regret his entry into the Korean conflict. The casualties suffered by American forces were horrific. But on the Chinese and North Korean side, the military casualties have been estimated several times what the United States suffered, mainly as a consequence of air strikes and concentrated artillery bombardment. The Chinese casualties were said to be 132,000 killed, 238,000 wounded, 8,000 missing, and 21,400 taken prisoner.

Beyond the human toll, the Chinese had other enduring reasons to regret the Korean conflict. Two days after the North Koreans attacked, reversing his hands-off policy, Truman decided to "neutralize" the Taiwan Straits by stationing units of the Seventh Fleet there, frustrating Peking's plan to "liberate" Taiwan. The status of Taiwan remains an issue in relations between China and the United States. It could reignite as an explosive issue if the island's government should unilaterally declare its independence. While this seems unlikely with economic ties between the mainland and the island flourishing, Peking has never renounced the possibility of an effort to take Taiwan by force should its policy of peaceful attraction ultimately fail.

20
GENEVA ACCORDS
PARTITION OF VIETNAM

After the collapse of the talks at the Geneva Conference on Korea in June 1954, I stayed on to cover the Indochina phase of the conference. Suddenly, in the most startling manner, I was thrust into the role of player as well as reporter in the negotiations on the future of Vietnam, Laos, and Cambodia. Once again, Huang Hua was the prime mover in propelling me into extraordinary events. On the morning of July 18, there was a telephone call from one of his aides. Huang Hua would like to see me immediately. The call came at a moment when there was apprehension at the conference that the Indochina conflict might become a wider war involving the major powers.

In Indochina, French Union forces were collapsing under the onslaught of Ho Chi Minh's divisions, which had been newly trained by the Chinese and supplied with modern weapons. The great French fort at Dien Bien Phu was surrounded by some 49,000 Viet Minh and on the verge of being overrun. France itself, its people recoiling violently from the war in which French Union troops had suffered 172,000 casualties, was caught up in a paralyzing political crisis. Pierre Mendès-France had become prime minister on June 18 with the promise that he would end the war by July 20 or resign. In his negotiations in Geneva with China, the Soviet Union, and Ho Chi Minh's delegation, Mendès-France had little bargaining power other than the threat of military intervention in Indochina by the United States. The Communist delegations at Geneva were aware that the United States was contemplating such intervention.

President Eisenhower had secretly reviewed, as recorded in the Pentagon Papers, the option of an air strike by two hundred navy planes in support of the Dien Bien Phu garrison. Thereafter, another plan was contemplated for intervention by navy and air force planes. The planes would carry out their strikes from bases in Vietnam which would be protected by the deployment of American ground forces. At one point aircraft carriers carrying nuclear weapons stationed off the Vietnamese coast were put on alert.

Attempting to dissuade the administration from intervention, John F. Kennedy stated in the Senate: "For the United States to intervene unilaterally and to send troops into the most difficult terrain in the world, with the Chinese able to pour in unlimited manpower, would mean that we would face a situation which would be far more difficult than even that we encountered in Korea." He reiterated the view that he had expressed shortly after his visit to Saigon in 1951 that he saw no hope for a Vietnam solution until the French granted the Vietnamese their independence.

On April 25, when Eisenhower was still undecided as to whether he could accept Dulles's recommendation that American forces be sent to the relief of Dien Bien Phu, Walter Bedell Smith, the American delegate at the conference, said to Chester Ronning privately: "No American boys are going to get bogged down in the jungles of Vietnam except over my dead body." On May 7, when Dien Bien Phu fell, President Eisenhower and Dulles were still discussing whether to urge the French to grant "genuine freedom" to its client Indochinese states as a condition for American military intervention. On May 20, the Joint Chiefs of Staff, in a memorandum to the Defense Department, commented: "From the point of view of the United States, with reference to the Far East as a whole, Indochina is devoid of decisive military objectives and the allocation of more than token U.S. Armed Forces to that area would be a serious diversion of limited U.S. capabilities."

On June 15, Eisenhower finally scrubbed plans for intervention, but the possibility that American forces might be committed was kept alive before the delegations at Geneva to provide the Western powers with added leverage in negotiating a settlement. It was a tactic successful to the point of persuading Soviet foreign minister Vyacheslav Molotov and Premier Zhou Enlai to nudge Pham Van Dong, head of Ho Chi Minh's delegation, toward compromise. Molotov knew that the United States had consulted with Britain and France on taking "united action" in Indochina. If American forces intervened, there was the possibility of a collision with the Chinese that might result in the Soviet Union being drawn into the conflict. Nikita Khrushchev was said to have expressed apprehension that the United States might mount a nuclear strike in Indochina and ignite a world war. Foreign Secretary Anthony Eden, head of the British delegation, was skillfully playing the role in negotiations with Molotov and Zhou Enlai of being the moderate statesman who was seeking a compromise that would deter the United States from military intervention.

When I went to meet Huang Hua in his hotel room, I did not realize that a high-stakes game was about to be played out among the great powers that afternoon which would shape the future of Indochina. I found Huang Hua agitated and eager to talk. We discussed the status of the conference negotiations for two hours, and it soon became obvious that the Chinese wanted to use me as an intermediary to get a quick message to the American delegation before the afternoon negotiating session, which had been summoned by Molotov. From what I gathered from Huang Hua, the Chinese believed that Dulles had instructed Bedell Smith to block an agreement at the meeting and that he had also persuaded Mendès-France to stiffen Western terms so that they would be unacceptable to the Viet Minh. The Chinese were plainly worried that the United States was preparing for military intervention in Indochina. Once again, they felt, their country might be drawn into combat with the United States, as in Korea, at a time when they were intent on devoting their resources to economic reconstruction. Like the Russians, they were also fearful that the United States might employ nuclear weapons. The Communist delegations were not aware that Dulles and Mendès-France at a meeting in Paris on July 14 had reached a secret agreement which fundamentally altered the stakes in the bargaining. Bedell Smith, who had been recalled, was to be sent back to Geneva, not to block an agreement as the Chinese feared, but with instructions to accommodate the negotiating position of the United States to a settlement based on the partition of Vietnam.

In the hope of reaching an agreement that afternoon, Huang Hua wanted me to convey the Chinese terms for an agreement to the American delegation even if I would do it in the form of a dispatch to the Associated Press. He was employing this device out of desperation because Dulles had barred any bilateral contacts between the Chinese and American delegations in the absence of diplomatic relations between the two countries. Immediately after our meeting, I wrote and filed my dispatch and at the same time gave a copy to the American delegation. I reported that the Chinese were prepared to sign an agreement, already approved in principle by Britain and France, based on the partition of Vietnam. I quoted Huang Hua as saying that a cease-fire agreement could be reached two days hence—when the deadline would expire for Mendès-France to either end the war or resign— if the Western powers would accept one "crucial" condition. "They must accept the barring of all foreign military bases from Indochina and keep the three member states out of any military bloc," Huang Hua said. "Refusal to join in such a guarantee could seriously deter a final settlement. On other important points in the negotiations we are in agreement or close to it. We are hopeful and believe there is time to reach a settlement by July 20."

The Chinese knew that the United States and France were consulting on the organization of a Southeast Asia Treaty Organization (SEATO) and concerned that South Vietnam, Laos, and Cambodia would be embraced in the pact and afford American base areas for possible future operations against China. "These efforts," Huang Hua said, "are a threat to any possible Indo-china agreement. Success or failure of the Geneva Conference may depend on the attitude of the American delegation in this regard." Huang Hua also asked for the stamp of American approval on any settlement. "We believe that the U.S. as a member of the conference should and is obligated to sub-scribe to and guarantee any settlement," he said. But he did not rule out an agreement if U.S. approval was not forthcoming. This was a crucial conces-sion on the part of the Chinese, since Dulles in his secret understanding with Mendès-France had committed the United States only to "respect" the pact, but not to be a signatory.

Prior to the afternoon session of the conference, Bedell Smith cabled the text of my dispatch to Dulles, as noted in the Pentagon Papers, describing its contents as "extremely significant." He reported that it had been provided in advance and that it "apparently represents the official Chinese Communist position and was given Topping in order that we would become aware of it." Bedell Smith added that he thought it particularly significant because he be-lieved Molotov wished to force the resignation of Mendès-France and "place on the shoulders of the U.S. responsibility for failure of the Geneva Con-ference and the fall of the French government if this occurs." Bedell Smith also reported on the background of my meeting with Huang Hua, which I had provided in the knowledge that Huang Hua was amenable, since he wished to have the quotes in my dispatch accepted as authoritative. When the conference resumed that afternoon, an agreement was sealed which was essentially in keeping with the understanding reached between Dulles and Mendès-France in Paris and in accordance with what Huang Hua had stip-ulated in his meeting with me. The United States did not join in the "Final Declaration," Dulles having balked at adherence to terms of the agreement which implied recognition of Communist sovereignty in regions of Viet-nam. But a unilateral statement was issued by Bedell Smith associating the United States with the accords, specifically in bringing about the restoration of peace in Indochina and attainment by Cambodia, Laos, and Vietnam of full independence. The statement in effect satisfied the Chinese condition that the United States subscribes to the accords.

After the signing of the Geneva Accords on July 21, I attended a champagne celebration given by the Chinese. Huang Hua introduced me to his colleagues as the author of the dispatch that had conveyed the Chinese position to the American delegation. It was an occasion for celebration by all parties to the accords, except very notably the Viet Minh delegation. Chinese and Soviet concerns had been met at the sacrifice of Viet Minh interests. When Ho Chi Minh sent Pham Van Dong, his foreign minister, to the Geneva Conference, his forces had already seized effective control of three-quarters of Vietnam, and French defenses in the rest of the country were collapsing. The price to the Viet Minh of winning these gains had been perhaps a half million casualties. In applying the coup de grâce to the French forces at Dien Bien Phu alone, the Viet Minh suffered 7,900 dead and 15,000 wounded. Now Ho Chi Minh was denied the victory in eight years of war because his allies, China and the Soviet Union, had backed off under the threat of American military intervention that might bring on a wider war.

In the course of the negotiations, the Viet Minh had been prodded into making major concessions. The Viet Minh had insisted at first on immediate national elections under Vietnamese supervision, which would have certainly brought them political control over the entire country. Instead they were compelled to accept a delay of two years and international supervision of elections. In the interim they were required to accept partition at the seventeenth parallel instead of, as they demanded, at the thirteenth parallel, which conformed more closely to the existing military dispositions. The Viet Minh no doubt had every reason to believe, as did Zhou Enlai and Molotov, that all of Vietnam would fall to them within two years. In that sense, the Viet Minh leadership was placated, although members of their delegation did complain privately to me that they had been cheated and expressed doubt that national elections would be held as scheduled in 1956. In fact, when the time arrived for the national plebiscite on reunification stipulated in the Geneva Accords, Ngo Dinh Diem, who had become premier of the Saigon government after the conclusion of the conference, refused to go through with it. He said a free vote was impossible in North Vietnam and held that South Vietnam was not bound by the accords, since they had not been signed by its government. Although the United States had pledged to respect the pact, Washington gave tacit support to the position taken by Diem. The feeling of Pham Van Dong that they had been cheated in 1954 explains in part their stubbornness years later in the negotiations in Paris with the United States on a Vietnam peace settlement. It also explains the reluctance of the Soviet Union and China to intervene to facilitate a settlement in response to American requests as well as the resistance of the North Vietnamese to any party acting on their behalf.

In August 1971, during the United States' efforts to end its involvement in the second Vietnam War, when Zhou Enlai was asked if he was interested in mediating in the Vietnam War, the Chinese premier replied: "We don't want to be a mediator in any way. We were very badly taken in during the first Geneva Conference."

21

BERLIN

COLD WAR

Life changed dramatically for the Toppings in 1956. The AP appointed me bureau chief in West Berlin, and I moved from London, where I had been preoccupied with monitoring the Asian conflicts, to coverage of the high tensions of the Cold War in central Europe. When we arrived in Berlin, it was a smoldering flashpoint in East-West relations. Under the terms of the postwar Potsdam Treaty, the city had been divided into four sectors: American, British, French, and Soviet. The Soviet sector had been converted by Moscow into East Berlin, capital of satellite East Germany. West Berlin was an isolated enclave lying within East German territory, garrisoned by eleven thousand American, French, and British troops and linked tenuously by some one hundred miles of rail and autobahn lines to West Germany. The Western sectors were under constant Soviet pressure, the rail and highway lifelines to West Germany, ceded to them under the Potsdam accords, being subjected to frequent Communist harassment. Nikita Khrushchev was demanding that the Western powers sign a German peace treaty under which they would surrender their sectors in Berlin and recognize the city as the capital of East Germany. With some crisis erupting almost daily either on the border of the divided city or along the corridor to West Germany, I was fortunate in leading a first-rate bureau in our coverage of the news. My deputy was Reinhold Ensz, a talented German-speaking American staffer. We were backed by a courageous crew of German reporters and editors who not only covered the news but also serviced the local newspapers with the AP international report.

Despite all the alarms, our family loved living in West Berlin. We found the Berliners typically independent, spunky, and cultured. We rented a pleasant house in suburban Dahlem from a stolid German landlord. Under the eaves of his attic we found a pile of flags of many nations to be displayed in turn according to which power ruled the city. At the American school Susan and Karen became accustomed to tanks of the U.S. garrison with guns on the ready lumbering by, although Karen, who was five, had to be assured on the first day that she would not be shot by the riflemen patrolling the grounds if she acted badly. Excitedly, the girls welcomed yet another sister, Robin, born in the American military hospital. Audrey divided her time between caring for our brood, writing, and pursuing her sculpting career at the arts center, the Hochschule für Bilden Kunst.

Free West Berlin was thriving with good hotels, casinos, nightclubs, and a vibrant cultural life. At the Schiller Theater we saw Arthur Miller's *The Crucible* and at the Municipal Opera House applauded the Berlin Philharmonic conducted by the young Herbert von Karajan. We became friendly with Lotte Lenya, the glorious singer and actress who fled Nazi Germany in 1933 with her composer husband, Kurt Weill. Visiting our home, she recalled the early thirties when she performed in Berlin under the direction of Bertolt Brecht. At his theater she gave her first performances as Pirate Jenny in *Threepenny Opera*, the lyrics written by Brecht. It was a role that later made her a star in the United States.

Under the four-power agreement, with my correspondent's license plate, I could pass through Checkpoint Charlie into Soviet-controlled East Berlin. Much of my reporting was based on what I viewed in East Berlin and circumspect conversations with sources when certain that police were not eyeing me. The East Germans opened the rest of their country to visits by Western correspondents only once a year for the international trade fair in Leipzig. Apart from news gathering, we made precious use of access to East Berlin to enjoy the Brecht Theater, where we saw a performance of *Mother Courage* and other plays by the great dramatist. One evening I took Efrem Kurtz, the distinguished American conductor, who often appeared with orchestras in Europe, to the East Berlin Opera. While we were driving in the misty night back to the West, my car was halted at Checkpoint Charlie by a Vopo, one of the dreaded East German border police. I became very uneasy when the green-clad helmeted guard leaned through the window and shone his flashlight into our faces. At the time Berlin was experiencing one of its recurring East-West confrontations during which access routes were sometimes suddenly closed. Curtly, the Vopo demanded our passports. I said to him in German: "We have been to the opera. This is Efrem Kurtz, the famous orchestra conductor." The Vopo, a young man, scanned Kurtz's face again, pulled out a pad from his pocket, and handed it to Kurtz. "May I have your autograph?" he asked.

Allied troops were on alert in Berlin during July 1958 as the on-and-off-again Soviet squeeze on the city tightened. East Germany had become increasingly aggressive in measures to stem the flow of tens of thousands of refugees from drab, depressed East Berlin into glittering West Berlin, most of them en route to free West Germany. Like the Allied commanders, I was always alert to the possibility that the Soviets might shut off indefinitely the access routes to West Berlin or let their East German puppets invade the Western sectors possibly touching off a war. To assess Communist intentions, I interviewed refugees, ventured into East Berlin to pick up gossip, and monitored the Eastern media. The United States was in tense confrontation with Walter Ulbricht's regime over its detention of nine American servicemen whose helicopter had strayed over East Germany and had been forced down on June 7, 1958. Ulbricht was insisting on direct negotiations with Washington for their release, something the United States was refusing to do, since it would constitute official recognition of East Germany.

Day after day, I pestered officials in East Berlin for an opportunity to see the American servicemen—five army soldiers, two artillery officers, and two helicopter crewmen—who were being held incommunicado somewhere in East Germany. Late in the night of June 30 the phone in my home rang and an unidentified voice said: "Please come to the Foreign Ministry in East Berlin tomorrow morning at 08:45."

When I turned up at the Foreign Ministry, I was greeted by a press spokesman, who said: "I am happy to advise you that your request to see your countrymen has been granted." Not unexpectedly, as we talked, in came a bevy of other correspondents. Looking them over, I became aware they were all from Communist newspapers published in East Germany and elsewhere in Europe. Among them was John Peet, a former Reuters correspondent, who had defected to the East. We were led to four limousines whose windows were curtained. A leer was all I got when I asked our destination as we drove south on the autobahn. Hours later, drawing a curtain aside to peer out at road signs, I saw we were approaching Dresden, the city which had been firebombed by the Allies during World War II, and soon after we drew up before an old villa. With a pretense of elaborate courtesy the press officer asked me, since I was a special "guest," to proceed ahead of the other correspondents. We were led into a bedroom on the upper floor of the villa, where abruptly I came face to face with the American prisoners, some of them only half dressed. Startled, they looked at me suspiciously. I pulled out my U.S. Defense Department accreditation card from a hip pocket and, holding it up, said: "Topping, Associated Press . . . may I see your senior officer?" Major George Kemper stepped forward. Before I could be silenced, I tipped him off that all the others were Communists, adding: "I suggest you and your group get together and decide whether you want to hold a press conference and, if so, what you would like to say." The correspondents were then herded to a lower floor and seated before a battery of press cameras.

The staging of the so-called press conference indicated that the East Germans were hoping the Americans would voice appeals to Washington to negotiate their release. When I asked permission to tell Major Kemper, who had been chosen by his comrades as spokesman, of the nature of the diplomatic exchanges, I was cut off by an East German official, who said: "No statements." However, as the conference went on, pressing loaded questions, I managed to convey to the soldiers what was at stake, that in effect they were being held for ransom, the price being diplomatic recognition. "That's enough for us," Kemper said. "You can tell them that we'll sweat it out as long as it takes." There were shouts from the other solders: "You're kidnappers . . . kidnappers." The East Germans reacted by shutting down the conference. My story, filed on return to West Berlin, describing the Dresden propaganda fiasco was front paged in non-Communist newspapers throughout the world. *Neues Deutschland,* the official newspaper of the East German regime, accused me of misrepresenting what had occurred. But interestingly, the Communist correspondents who witnessed the event did not in their accounts take issue with me.

My Dresden encounter became the centerpiece of the week's press section of *Time* magazine. Embarrassed by the widespread negative publicity of the Dresden affair throughout the world, the East Germans released the solders. My great reward came thereafter in the letters of thanks from the families of the servicemen.

In March 1959, Khrushchev toured East Germany to shore up the satellite state. I observed him in East Berlin on March 7 on a podium before a staged torchlight rally of some 100,000 people during which he demanded the withdrawal of Allied troops from West Berlin. He had just come from Leipzig, where he warned of the perils of a new war and declared that the Soviet Union would never permit the liquidation of Communism in East Germany. For the monster Berlin rally, the East Germans had erected a speaker's platform in an open square. It was torn down shortly before the rally began. The Soviet secret police had Khrushchev speak instead from a more secure podium with his back against a building wall. The incident was one of many indications of how shaky was the Soviet grip on the people of East Germany. At the time, Khrushchev was keeping a tight cap on the territory. About 400,000 Russian troops were garrisoned there reinforced by an East German army and security police totaling some 270,000. Khrushchev apparently was taking precautions knowing that many in the restive East German population were waiting for an opportunity to rise up. Soviet lines of communication across East Germany were not entirely secure. I reported that it was unlikely that Khrushchev would risk war by seizing Allied access routes to West Berlin or by violent intrusion into the city. I thought the real danger to peace, observing Khrushchev's tactical adventurism, lay not in any deliberate act risking war but rather in some miscalculation by him in dealing with the Western allies, particularly with the United States.

———————

Berlin turned out to be another way station in my career as a journalist. In the summer of 1959, the AP brought me home on leave and asked me to speak at a convention of newspaper managing editors on the West Coast. When Audrey, our four daughters, and I arrived in New York, there was a message from Manny Freedman, the foreign news editor of the *New York Times*, asking me to visit his office. I never made it to the AP convention. Freedman offered me a job, and I joined the *Times*. Since my rebuff by Cyrus Sulzberger in 1948 when posted in Nanking, I had not sought a job with the *Times*. I was happy with the AP, which I respected enormously. I went over to the *Times* for several reasons. It was evident that the *Times* had hired me to go abroad, where my main interest lay, and I felt the paper would give me more opportunity to write broader interpretive stories. Out of vanity I had also come to envy the greater attention and weight given by the governing decision makers to the reporting of special correspondents for the leading newspapers.

Stalwart and ready as always, Audrey took our youngsters by train across the continent to Camrose, Alberta, her hometown, parked them with her sister, Sylvia Cassady, and went to Berlin alone to handle the onerous chore of packing up while I reported for work at the *Times*. So much for the life of the wife of a foreign correspondent. When she returned with our children to New York, we rented a beach house on Bell Island in Connecticut and rediscovered America after an absence of thirteen years.

The *Times* had me tagged for posting abroad, but in keeping with the usual practice, I was to spend at least a year on the Metropolitan staff for familiarization, and also, spending the year on the Metropolitan staff was in fact a means of testing my skills. On my first day in the office I was summoned to meet with the managing editor, Turner Catledge. As I entered his office, Catledge, a courtly southerner, was chuckling. "Wes Gallagher just phoned to complain about us taking you from the AP," he told me. Gallagher was then general manager of the AP. Catledge asked me how much the foreign news editor had arranged to pay me. He nodded, still chuckling, and gave me a raise on the spot.

When I joined the *Times,* I told Freedman that I would go anywhere except Moscow. I had heard tales of how difficult it was to live in Moscow, and I thought going there with a big family would be too much of a burden. No correspondent with four kids had braved Moscow. My hesitations were overcome with the imposition of executive firmness and flattery, and I was earmarked forthwith for the Soviet capital. The paper wanted a Moscow correspondent with experience in covering Communist regimes. In preparation, I spent nine months on the Metropolitan staff on rewrite and as a reporter with very little time for Russian language lessons. The night before I was to leave for the Soviet capital in advance of my family, Freedman invited Audrey and me to dinner at his Manhattan home. The guests of honor were Catledge and his wife, Abby. Over drinks before dinner, the managing editor chatted about our assignment to Moscow and what life would be like there. "I would never send a correspondent with children to Moscow," he told us soberly, as he leaned nonchalantly against the living room mantelpiece. Audrey looked up at him astonished. "But Mr. Catledge, we have four children," she said, rather plaintively. Catledge frowned. "Well, I don't want to hear about it," he said with a shrug. The next morning I left for Moscow. Audrey and our daughters followed several weeks later.

When I became foreign editor in 1966, after tours in Moscow and Southeast Asia, I sent no correspondent abroad without my full awareness of family circumstances. Also, none went to posts such as Moscow, Tokyo, or Peking without adequate language preparation, which meant for some as much as a year of study at Harvard or some other suitable school. These policies paid off handsomely in more productive staff performance.

22
MOSCOW
THE SINO-SOVIET SPLIT AND THE
CUBAN MISSILE CRISIS

Working as a journalist in the Soviet Union was a consuming but rewarding experience. I was pitched into it on June 1, 1960, in fact, only a few hours before landing at the Moscow airport. Invited into the cockpit of the British airliner taking me to Moscow from London, I reported in my first dispatch what was entailed for a foreign aircraft to pass through the tight Soviet security air screen. On the following day, I attended the funeral of Boris Pasternak, in his little summer cottage surrounded by white birch trees in the artists' community at Peredelkino close to the Soviet capital. Invited with several other correspondents into his dacha, I paused at the bier of the seventy-year-old poet, who lay in an open coffin in the drawing room surrounded by flowers. As the celebrated pianist Sviatoslav Richter played Franz Liszt's "Consolation" and then a Tchaikovsky funeral dirge, KGB agents stood about in the room taking photographs of the mourners at this farewell to the 1958 Nobel Prize winner in Literature who had been a symbol of resistance to Soviet oppression. For accepting the Nobel Prize he had been vilified by the official Moscow Union of Writers as taking "thirty pieces of silver" from the West. His death on May 30 had been virtually ignored in the Soviet press, but more than a thousand people gathered outside his home on this day to render homage. The lips of many of them moved in unison as an actor from the Moscow Art Theater recited Pasternak's poem *Hamlet*. The coffin was carried into the garden lifted by many hands over the heads of the massed mourners. I followed the coffin as it was borne to the burial place on the crest of the hill. Although I knew Pasternak only from his poetry and his magnificent novel *Doctor Zhivago*, I instinctively joined in the outpouring of grief. I could think of no sadder introduction to this nation that I was to live in and cover for the next three years.

The pace of news coverage of the Soviet capital was demanding, intense, and highly competitive. I wrote at a battered desk in a tiny crowded office sitting opposite my fellow *Times* correspondent, initially Osgood Caruthers and later Ted Shabad. There was always a Russian guard at the gate of our shabby tenement building. During my first three months I covered an array of stories such as the trial in the Hall of Columns of Francis Gary Powers, the civilian pilot employed by U.S. intelligence who bailed out over the Soviet Union after his U-2 reconnaissance plane was shot down on May 1 by a surface-to-air missile. Powers pleaded guilty to the charge of espionage and was sentenced on August 20 to three years' imprisonment and seven years at hard labor.* Soon after there was the marvelous yarn of Strelka and Belka, the frisky dogs who orbited the earth seventeen times on August 20 aboard the second Soviet space ship, becoming the first living creatures to return safely from outer space. The epic space event took place the following spring, April 21, 1961, when I heard a broadcaster on Moscow Radio intone repeatedly: *Govorit Moskva! Govorit Moskva!* ("Moscow Speaks! Moscow Speaks!"). It was the call which Moscow Radio reserves for its most important announcements. On that morning, Yuri Gagarin became the first man to enter space. In a five-ton space ship named *Vostok* ("East"), Gargarin in 1 hour and 48 minutes had made a single orbit of the earth and landed in good shape. The flight, resounding evidence of the technological advance of Soviet society, brought a great outpouring of pride and happiness among the Russians. But the achievement also stood in glaring contrast to what was lacking in the everyday existence of the average Russian. Audrey recalls that on the day of the flight she could not find any eggs in the local open market or in the nearby shops. When I returned home from the Central Telegraph Office after filing a story on the epic space event, I walked up eight flights of stairs to our apartment because yet once again the elevator was not working.

Monitoring developments in the Cold War was my foremost concern in reporting from Moscow. Having observed Khrushchev's reckless tactics in Berlin, I arrived in the Soviet capital convinced that there was a real and ever present danger that he might ignite World War III through some miscalculation. It was extraordinarily difficult to ascertain and define what were the policies and intentions of the secretive men in the impenetrable Kremlin. Correspondents lived and worked encased within a complex of walls.

Audrey and I managed to surmount one such wall thanks to our four dauntless daughters. We were quartered in one of the so-called diplomatic ghettos for foreigners on Prospekt Mira in a four-room apartment shared with the girls' pets: five cats, an ailing pigeon, two goldfish, and two turtles. There was only one entrance to our walled compound, at which a Soviet

---

*Powers served one and three-quarter years of the sentence before being exchanged for the Soviet spy Rudolf Abel on February 10, 1962. The exchange took place on the Glienicke Bridge connecting Potsdam, East Germany, to West Berlin.

militiaman was posted. Neighboring Russian homes beyond the wooden wall were as remote to us as the moon. That was until the self-styled "Fabulous Four" consisting of Susan, now nine, Karen, seven, Lesley, five, followed by Robin, three, launched their breakout. The Fabulous Four pulled out boards in the wooden wall and looked into the eyes of Russian children in a playground. Without delay the Russian children taught our kids their first Russian word. It was *poyedem,* meaning "let's go, let's go and play." Not having any idea they were trespassing on forbidden territory, our girls crawled between the slats of the wooden wall and joined their new playmates. When the Soviet guards observed this commingling, they ordered our children to return to their ghetto space. Soon after, when the children continued to defy the rules, the wooden wall came down and a construction crew put up a stone replacement. But in their transcendent wisdom, the children were not to be separated. At the first snowfall, our children built snow steps while their Russian friends did the same on the other side, and soon they were chatting atop the stone wall. When the Russian children asked to visit our apartment, Susan did cartwheels to divert the guards while Karen led their pals across the courtyard. Thereafter, the militiamen seemed to give up and wink at this clandestine traffic. Our older daughters were relaying to us gossip of the neighborhood, telling of the joys and tears of Russian life in overcrowded apartments. Hidden in family cars they were smuggled by their pals to dachas on the outskirts of Moscow beyond the travel limit for foreigners. Consumed with curiosity about everything about them, the Fabulous Four ventured ever farther. Observing Susan as she took ballet lessons, the director of the Bolshoi School, Madame Golovkina, commented that she had talent and brought her into the school. Susan enthralled us with insights to the cultural world.

After a year, Susan and Karen, having acquired some grasp of Russian, asked if they could attend the Russian elementary school rather than the Anglo-American School for foreigners. They became the first American children in Moscow to attend a Russian elementary school. They donned the uniform of brown dress with white apron but were excused, given they were Americans, from wearing the obligatory red kerchief of the "Young Pioneers." At PTA meetings Audrey and I met parents eager to know us. The girls never complained about the lack of anything or having to sleep on double-deckers in a tiny bedroom overstuffed with clothes and toys. Audrey and I recollected with amusement how we'd been cautioned about going to Moscow with children. At times the Fabulous Four were more at home than we were. Tumbling about, they provided us with needed respites from the harshness of life in Moscow. After a year I noted in a letter to Clifton Daniel, the managing editor: "I am convinced that it is better to send a family here, rather than a single man. The family group provides a natural buffer against many of the strains." In our apartment we were guarded in discussing what we learned from diplomatic contacts or our Russian friends and neighbors. We lived with the knowledge that there were KGB listening devices secreted about and that our maid and the office chauffeur, however friendly, were assigned to us by UPDK, the government-run agency that serviced foreigners. One night a lighting fixture in the ceiling above the foot of the double bed in the small room where Audrey and I slept exploded and exposed a listening device. The KGB had been listening to some choice pillow talk.

The KGB unknowingly was instrumental in transforming Audrey from sculptor into a full-time journalist. When she went to a Russian store to buy clay and tools, she was turned away by the clerk, who said he was not permitted to sell art supplies to foreigners. A distinguished Russian portrait sculptor happened to be standing nearby when this exchange took place and offered the use of his studio to Audrey. She did her sculpting there happily until one day there was a telephone call to Audrey's language teacher from her Russian benefactor advising Audrey not to come to the studio. He explained that his friend had been arrested for associating with an American. Unable to continue sculpting, Audrey turned full-time to photojournalism, producing among other media work at least sixteen illustrated articles from Moscow for the *New York Times Magazine*—including such pieces as a cover story on the Russian cosmonaut Valentina Tereshkova, the first woman to enter space, and Robert Frost, the American poet, in conversation in a café with the leading Russian poet, Yevgeny Yevtushenko.

Less than two weeks after my arrival in Moscow, one of the most momentous developments in world politics began to unfold. On June 12 there appeared an editorial in *Pravda,* the official newspaper of the Soviet Communist Party, which denounced unidentified "revisionists and sectarians." On that day, picnicking at Uspenskaya, a sandy spit on the Moscow River, I sat beside Marvin Kalb, a CBS specialist in Russian affairs, and Max Frankel, whom I was replacing as the *Times* correspondent in Moscow, with a copy of *Pravda* spread on our blanket trying to divine just whom the vitriolic editorial was directed against. It was actually the first hint in the Soviet press of the veiled ideological polemics in progress between Moscow and Peking. We were to learn the polemics were harbingers of a dispute whose implications would alter the balance of power in the world. The Western nations would no longer be dealing with a monolithic Communist bloc. By 1969, the split would bring on clashes on the Siberian border between Soviet and Chinese troops. The Chinese would initiate construction of a nationwide system of air raid shelters against the possibility of a Soviet nuclear strike. The implications were also enormous for the United States. Seeking help in withstanding Soviet pressure on his borders, Mao Zedong eventually reached out for a new foreign support by mending relations with the United States embodied in the Shanghai Communiqué entered into with President Nixon in 1972.

In the weeks following publication of the puzzling editorial in *Pravda*, similar commentaries appeared in the Soviet press. I filed a succession of dispatches quoting the commentaries and speculating that the "monsters" being denounced were the leaders of the Chinese Communist Party. Every such dispatch was blocked by Soviet censors. The speculation about a Sino-Soviet rift intensified in November when a summit conference of leaders of eighty-one Communist parties was convened in Moscow. In open rebuff to Khrushchev, Mao did not attend, sending Liu Shaoqi, China's head of state, in his stead to lead the Chinese delegation. In late November, working with Arrigo Levi, a brilliant Italian correspondent for *Corriere della Serra*, I learned from sources in the conference that a severe ideological rift had developed with the delegations dividing and joining the opposing Chinese and Soviet camps. Liu Shaoqi, pursuing the Maoist line, was urging militant revolutionary action by Communist parties worldwide rather than reliance on Nikita Khrushchev's newly declared policy of "peaceful coexistence." The Khrushchev stratagem called for winning over the developing countries to the Communist bloc through political and economic attraction without necessarily resorting to violent revolution or war with the Western powers

On the evening of November 23, I went to the Central Telegraph Office, where Glavlit, the Soviet censorship office, was located and wrote a lengthy dispatch on the ideological split based on the leaks from members of the congress delegations. I had no real expectation that it would get through censorship. The dispatch reported in detail on the exchange of hostile polemics between the Chinese and Soviet ideological blocs. Khrushchev was gaining support for his policy from mainly the European parties, while the Latin American, North Korean, Indonesian, and Albanian delegations were leaning toward Liu Shaoqi. As required, I pushed two copies of my story through the green curtain which masked the censor's booth and waited. After several hours, my carbons, which in keeping with the usual procedure would show any penciled-out lines, were returned to me unmarked. I was astounded. The Russians had decided for the first time to allow the ideological dispute to be made fully public and had, therefore, passed my cable. My dispatch was already was en route to New York and the next morning led the front page of the *Times*.

At the moment, Western observers were not aware of the enormous price Mao was paying for daring to challenge Khrushchev. Five months earlier, in June, Khrushchev had summoned Communist Party leaders worldwide to a meeting in Bucharest during a congress of the Romanian Communist Party. Mao Zedong had refused to attend that meeting and sent Peng Zhen, the mayor of Peking, in his place. At the congress Khrushchev furiously denounced the Maoists, accusing them of "adventurism" and "deviationism," lumping them with their Albanian ideological allies. Peng Zhen responded by scornfully criticizing Khrushchev for blowing hot and cold in his exchanges with the West. He was alluding to the inconclusive encounter of the Soviet leader with President Eisenhower the previous month in Paris when the Russian broke up an East-West summit meeting by raging about the U-2 spy flight over the Soviet Union by Gary Powers. He characterized Khrushchev as "patriarchal, arbitrary and tyrannical." Peng's retort infuriated Khrushchev, and overnight the Soviet leader impulsively ordered termination of the Soviet aid program to China. Within the next month, 1,390 Soviet expert advisers were withdrawn from China, 343 contracts were scrapped, and 257 cooperative projects in technology and science ended. What I had been reading in *Pravda* about unidentified "revisionists and sectarians" was a reflection of the exchange of diatribes at the Romanian congress. The communiqué issued after at the congress emphasized unity in a new action program to attain world Communism but covered up the interparty polemics.

The Sino-Soviet split had its early origins in the Soviet Twentieth Party Congress in 1956 when Nikita Khrushchev denounced Joseph Stalin, who had died three years earlier, characterizing him as a paranoid tyrant. Mao had little reason to grieve for the Soviet leader. The Chinese Communists had been bullied by Stalin, and from 1927 to 1945 the Soviet dictator had wavered in his support of Mao in the struggle with Chiang Kai-shek. Speaking to the Eighth Central Committee on September 24, 1962, Mao confided that Stalin never trusted the Chinese Communists, believing them to be independent-minded Titoists except for the three-year period from the time of Peking's intervention in the Korean War until Stalin's death in 1953. Despite his differences with Stalin, Mao expressed irritation with the denunciation of

Stalin, long considered one of the heroic figures of the international Communist movement, by the upstart Khrushchev and his retreat from the concept of the militant struggle for attainment of world Communism. By inference, the castigation of the Stalin cult of personality was also seen as a criticism of the adulation of Mao in China. With the passing of Stalin, symbol of Soviet infallibility, the Chinese Communists had begun at the 1957 World Conference of Communist Parties in Moscow to challenge Soviet leadership of international Communism.

Despite the open break at the Moscow congress in November 1960, Premier Zhou Enlai attended the Twenty-second Party Congress in Moscow in October 1961. From the balcony of the hall, I watched the premier sitting grim faced among the other foreign Communist leaders on the stage of the auditorium of the new Palace of Congresses in the Kremlin as one Russian leader after another denounced the Albanians, the close ideological allies of the Chinese. It was, in fact, as the congress delegates knew, a proxy attack on the Maoists. Khrushchev accused the Albanian leadership of practicing the methods of the Stalinist cult of personality. Zhou Enlai rejoined with a call for a halt in the polemics, When his appeal went unheeded, the Chinese premier abruptly left Moscow while the congress was still in session. After Zhou Enlai's departure, Khrushchev stunned the congress delegates. Pressing his policy of de-Stalinization, Khrushchev read a decree that sent me running to a telephone. Khrushchev proclaimed: "The further retention in the Lenin mausoleum of the sarcophagus with the bier of J. V. Stalin shall be recognized as inappropriate since the serious violation by Stalin of Lenin's precepts, abuse of power, mass repressions against honorable Soviet people, and other activities in the period of the personality cult make it impossible to leave the bier with his body in the mausoleum of V. I. Lenin." A few days later Stalin's body was removed without ceremony from the mausoleum and interred near the Kremlin wall beside the graves of less distinguished revolutionary leaders beneath the plain marker "J. V. STALIN, 1879–1953." The day after Stalin's body was moved I strolled with our office translator through Red Square, near the Lenin Mausoleum, where groups of people stood about arguing heatedly about the justice of what Khrushchev had done. Questions were asked. "Why were we not told before?" Prior to Stalin's death in 1953, despite his cruelties, many Russians worshiped Stalin as a father figure. He had sustained the country during the Nazi invasion and had achieved victory in World War II. One of the people we spoke to was a uniformed serviceman, a pilot, who muttered: "I don't believe it. I would have died for Stalin in the war." When Audrey went to the Russian elementary school to pick up our daughters, Susan and Karen, she noticed that Stalin's head was missing in the portrait of members of the Politburo which hung above a portal.

After Zhou's abrupt departure from the congress, the Peking-Moscow polemics escalated rapidly, fragmenting the international Communist movement. Between June 1959 and October 1961, the Chinese-Soviet alliance in effect dissolved, thus eliminating the ideological restraints which had inhibited the reemergence of the historical national antagonisms between the neighboring giants.

One of the more inexplicable aspects of American policy in Asia during the 1960s was the disinclination to take cognizance or advantage of the Sino-Soviet dispute. Despite my reporting from Moscow on the ideological split, American policy makers continued to base their strategy in Asia on the theory that there existed a Soviet bloc, embracing both the Soviet Union and China, with the Kremlin as the directing center. It was not until the advent of the Nixon administration in 1969 that the momentous implications of the Sino-Soviet split began to be factored effectively into American policy making. By playing off one Communist giant against the other, Nixon was successful in managing the opening to China and obtaining concessions from the Soviet Union in negotiations on strategic arms limitation.

In March 1961, Khrushchev abolished prepublication censorship, which dated from czarist days, although its existence had been officially denied. Correspondents were called to the Foreign Ministry and told deftly by Mikhail Kharlamov, head of the Press Department: "From this day forward, correspondents will be able to use facilities both at the Central Telegraph Office in Moscow and in their offices, homes, and hotel rooms to phone directly." The abolition of censorship meant that I could file in much the same way as I would from any European capital. I would not have to worry about whether a dispatch would emerge from behind the green curtain or with deletions that would require rewriting to retain coherence. It also meant that in bitterly cold weather I would not have to trudge through the snow after midnight to the Central Telegraph Office to garner some important announcement from *Pravda* and push my dispatch through the green curtain.

The lifting of censorship had another special significance for me. Beginning in the late 1940s, with its correspondents in Moscow handicapped by censorship, the *Times* deemed it necessary to employ an expert on Soviet affairs in New York who would provide supplementary reporting and analysis. During my stint in Moscow, the expert was Harry Schwartz. Schwartz had never served as correspondent in Moscow, but he was fluent in Russian, had impressive academic credentials as an economist, and during World War II had been trained as a military analyst. His articles for the *Times* were based on regular perusal of some thirty-five Soviet articles and interviews with returnees from the Soviet Union. I found Schwartz's articles useful, but I had reservations about some of the conclusions arrived at far distant from the scene. The lifting of Soviet censorship, which I exploited at once by filing broader, more explicit analysis pieces, led to the transfer of Schwartz to another beat. I was no longer second-guessed by him.

Although censorship had been lifted, there was always the possibility hanging over correspondents of expulsion for what they were writing. Moscow was a vital post, and given the dangers of the Cold War, I was determined to stay on. Therefore, I avoided any snide reporting about the personal demeanor of Soviet leaders. The fact that Khrushchev got tipsy after too many vodka toasts at diplomatic receptions concerned me less than what he was revealing about his thinking and policies. Whitman Bassow, bureau chief for *Newsweek,* one of the ablest and most experienced of the Moscow correspondents, inadvertently stepped over the line in August 1962 and was expelled for writing "crudely slanderous dispatches about the Soviet Union." Bassow believed, as he explained in his book *The Moscow Correspondents,* published in 1988, that the ax fell on him most likely because of a humor feature which he tried to cable. It was a joke which he was told was circulating among Muscovites after Khrushchev ordered Stalin's remains moved to the Kremlin wall. The joke:

"A little boy asks his grandmother about Lenin."
"Ah, he was a great and good man."
"What kind of man was Stalin?"
"Sometimes he was good and sometimes he was very bad."
"And Grandma, what kind of man is Khrushchev?"
"When he dies, we'll find out."

The humor feature was not transmitted by the Central Telegraph Office, and that evening a television news commentator announced that Bassow had been expelled for violating "standards of behavior."

———————

In May 1961, I left Moscow on assignment to cover the Russian delegation at the fourteen-nation conference on Laos in Geneva. The conference had been convened at a time when the Cold War seemed close to turning into a hot one in Asia. The Geneva parley eventually reached an agreement in July providing for the establishment of a unified neutralist government under Prime Minister Souvanna Phouma. But shortly thereafter, the pro-Communist Pathet Lao faction broke away. It continued to dominate eastern Laos, safeguarding a key segment of the Ho Chi Minh Trail, the North Vietnamese supply route to the Vietcong in the south.

While in Geneva, Audrey and I attended a dinner given by Chen Yi, the then Chinese foreign minister, in honor of Chester Ronning, who was heading the Canadian delegation to the Laos conference. Ronning had asked Chen Yi if he could bring me, an American correspondent, to the dinner. Chen replied: "Of course, but only as your son-in-law." The Chinese delegation to the conference had not granted any interviews to American correspondents. Chen and I hit it off rather well. In command of the armies which had captured Nanking and Shanghai, he told me how he had enveloped Chiang Kai-shek's capital, and I told him what it was like covering the entry of his troops into the city.

There was also an interesting encounter with a Russian spy. One of my contacts in covering the Russian delegation was a Soviet official who obviously had the job of what we called "bird-dogging" American correspondents. He became particularly interested in me because I was the *Times* correspondent in Moscow and once in chatting with him I had mentioned that my mother was born in the Ukraine. One afternoon I strolled with him through the garden of the Palais des Nations, in which the negotiations were taking place, and he mentioned a memorandum which had been made available by the U.S. delegation to American correspondents. It dealt with matters relating to the American negotiating stance. It was officially classified as restricted, which meant, although not deemed secret, it was sensitive enough so that it would be made available only to designated individuals. The Russian asked with a broad smile if I would let him have a copy of the memorandum, since, after all, it had been distributed to many Americans. It was a KGB tactic. Once a target is sucked in by some minor exchange, then intimidation follows together with demands for higher-priority information. I told the friendly Russian with an innocent smile that I would be glad to ask the American delegation for a copy of the memorandum for his information. He turned pale and quivered. I never saw him again.

While the conference was still in progress, John F. Kennedy, the newly elected forty-three-year-old president, and Nikita Khrushchev agreed to meet in Vienna in June to discuss the East-West confrontations in Berlin and Indochina. Kennedy headed for Vienna with the burden of having suffered a major foreign policy reverse. The CIA-managed Bay of Pigs invasion of Cuba by Cuban exiles had been thrown back in April with heavy casualties. I went directly from Geneva to Vienna to cover the talks in the company of other *Times* reporters, among them Russell Baker, who was then with the Washington Bureau and later a popular columnist. Before leaving Geneva, Baker and I had drinks in a hotel bar with Joe Alsop, the superhawk Washington columnist, and we listened to him, as he stared at us over his outsized horn-rimmed glasses, hold forth on the need for Kennedy to disable the North Vietnamese by bombing Haiphong. It was reflective of the aggressive mood then among conservatives in the United States. Haiphong had not yet been bombed because of the danger of hitting Russian and other Eastern European shipping, although it was known the port was being used to supply North Vietnam with military matériel.

In Vienna I covered the Russian delegation while James Reston, the columnist and Washington bureau chief of the *Times,* looked after the American side. On June 4, I glimpsed Kennedy for the first time since our 1951 meetings in Saigon. He was coming down the stairs of the Soviet Embassy at the side of Nikita Khrushchev after two negotiating sessions with the Soviet premier. Kennedy looked rather exhausted. I didn't know at that moment that he had agreed, at the suggestion of his press secretary, Pierre Salinger, to see Reston privately in the American Embassy following the meeting with Khrushchev. After covering a press briefing by the Russian delegation, I was alone in an upper-floor room of the press hostel writing my dispatch when Reston walked in. "What are you writing?" he asked. I responded by reviewing the contents of the Soviet briefing. "Wait," he said. "I've just talked to Kennedy." Startled, I left my typewriter, perched on a chair, and listened raptly to Reston's account of his meeting with the president.

In a vacant room in the American Embassy Reston had waited for more than an hour for Kennedy to arrive. When the president entered, he sat down on a couch beside Reston, tipped his hat forward, and breathed heavily. Reston told me the president looked angry and was obviously shook up. Kennedy had been through two sessions with Khrushchev, which were much more contentious than he had anticipated. The Russian had handed him a virtual ultimatum contained in an aide-mémoire. The United States must sign a German peace treaty by December, which would in effect give legal status to East Germany and control over the access routes to Berlin. If the United States did not agree, the Soviet Union would sign a separate treaty and move unilaterally to dominate the access routes to Berlin. Kennedy responded by warning that the United States would fight to maintain access to its military garrison in Berlin. Kennedy told Reston he thought he knew why Khrushchev had taken such a hard line with him. He felt sure that Khrushchev thought that somebody who had made such a mess with the failed Cuban Bay of Pigs invasion lacked judgment and any president who made such a blunder and did not see it through thereafter had no guts. Kennedy told Reston there was now a need for him to demonstrate firmness and the place to do it was Vietnam.

The story which Reston filed to the *Times* that night served Kennedy well and was reassuring to the American public, but it puzzled me. He pictured the president as engaging in a calm manner with the Russian, writing that there had been "no ultimatums and few bitter or menacing exchanges" and that Kennedy had departed Vienna in a "solemn, although confident mood." The story was in keeping with the official American version of the dialogues. But in fact, the threats that Kennedy was subjected to by Khrushchev and his reactions were more accurately portrayed in Reston's memoir, *Deadline*, published in 1991. It was akin to what he had told me about his off-the-record briefing by Kennedy.

When Kennedy returned to Washington, he undertook emergency measures against the possibility of war over Berlin, including a doubling of draft quotas and a call-up of National Guard units and Reserves. In July, Kennedy asked Congress to approve a $3.25 billion military buildup and funds to make ready and stock fallout shelters as a precaution against the possibility of nuclear war. Kennedy was obviously putting on a show of strength to warn Khrushchev and to lay the basis for any future negotiation, but the magnitude of his response to the Soviet leader's threats surprised me. It seemed to me that at Vienna that there had been more theatrics on the part of Khrushchev in his meeting with Kennedy than realpolitik. Recalling my experience in Berlin, I doubted that Khrushchev would follow through on his threat to take over the access routes. I had reported from Berlin on verbal ultimatums one after another and repeated harassment of the autobahn and rail lifelines to West Berlin, but each time the Soviet leader had backed off from a possible military clash. In fact, by August, the ultimatum issued by Khrushchev in Vienna proved as empty as the ones he had put forward previously, and as a fallback Khrushchev conspired with Ulbricht to begin construction of the Berlin Wall.

In briefing Reston, without elaborating, Kennedy had said that Vietnam was the place he had to demonstrate firmness in the test of wills with Khrushchev. I found this puzzling. The test of wills in Vietnam logically was more with Ho Chi Minh and Mao Zedong than with Khrushchev. The

Russians were supplying some material aid to Ho Chi Minh's forces, notably surface-to-air missile (SAM) batteries, but the crucial decisions about
military strategy and politics were being made in Hanoi and Peking, not
Moscow. Ho Chi Minh's troops were being trained and armed with modern weapons in South China. Khrushchev himself was embroiled in a deep-
ening ideological quarrel with Mao.

According to what the Russians imparted at their Vienna briefing,
Khrushchev's emphasis had been on Berlin, not Southeast Asia. He had
proved amenable to whatever agreement on a coalition government headed
by Souvanna Phouma would be reached at the Geneva Conference on Laos.
This was not surprising, since the proposed settlement yielded to the Pathet
Lao continued control of the gateway territory in Laos to the Ho Chi Minh
Trail. As for Vietnam, the Russian historian Roy Medvedev later quoted
Khrushchev as having told Kennedy: "If you want to, go ahead and fight in
the jungles of Vietnam. The French fought there for seven years and still had
to quit in the end. Perhaps the Americans will be able to stick it out for a lit-
tle longer, but eventually they will have to quit too."

En route to Vienna, Kennedy had stopped off in Paris to meet with President Charles de Gaulle. Recalling the French military disaster, de Gaulle
warned Kennedy against becoming bogged down in Indochina. He told Kennedy that France would not repeat the mistakes of the past by sending troops
to Indochina, although his nation was a member of SEATO, which was committed to resisting Communist expansion. Two months earlier, at a meeting
in New York, Kennedy received similar advice from General Douglas Mac-
Arthur, who was quoted by Arthur S. Schlesinger, the historian, as telling
the president: "Anyone wanting to commit American ground forces to the
mainland should have his head examined."

Nevertheless, after his return to Washington, Kennedy tripled the number of American military advisers working with the South Vietnamese army,
authorizing them to accompany the troops on combat missions.

I was back in Moscow in October 1962 when my fear of some dangerous miscalculation by Khrushchev seemed to materialize with eruption of the Cuban
missile crisis. CIA spy planes had spotted some 22,000 Soviet troops and
technicians at work constructing missile sites. They were implanting forty-
two medium-range nuclear-tipped missiles with ranges of 1,100 miles. Another twenty-four intermediate missiles with ranges of 2,200 miles were en

route to the island aboard disguised Russian merchant vessels. In addition, Khrushchev had dispatched forty-two IL-28 nuclear bombers and twenty-four SAMs. Khrushchev intended with this massive nuclear capability to balance or outweigh the superior intercontinental missile capability of the United States and also that of the mid-range Jupiter missiles sited in Turkey. The Cuban base would also give him leverage in his confrontation in Berlin with the United States, France, and Britain.

As the crisis mounted, I recalled how Kennedy had been shaken by the aggressiveness and bluster of Khrushchev in their confrontation in Vienna and wondered whether Kennedy would show the Russian that he was mistaken in assessing the president as lacking in guts. Two images hovered in my mind. One was of the young Kennedy, who in Saigon had demonstrated toughness in his encounter with the bullying French general de Lattre. The other image was of his close adviser, Llewellyn "Tommy" Thompson, the American ambassador to Moscow who had been recalled three months earlier to Washington. Thompson had been at Kennedy's side in the meeting with Khrushchev in Vienna. A brilliant Kremlinologist, he was respected by Westerners and Russians alike. He was openly admired by Khrushchev, who gave a picnic for Thompson, his wife, Jane, and two daughters when they were returning to Washington. Embracing Thompson in farewell, Khrushchev teased the ambassador about the possibility of another international crisis. Thompson guessed he was referring to Berlin, given the Vienna confrontation. Like other correspondents benefiting from his incisive briefings, I had great admiration for Thompson. Audrey and I were quite close to the Thompsons personally. Our daughters took ballet lessons with his daughters, Sherry and Jenny, in Spasso House, the embassy residence. Once, the good-humored ambassador came to a masquerade party we hosted wearing a red wig, dressed in an old bathrobe, and carrying the cleaning lady's mop, all of which served to utterly baffle the KGB agents tailing his limousine and the Russian guards at the gate. I was grateful that this man of profound acuity and engaging personality was with Kennedy as the president faced off against Khrushchev. My concern as to whether Kennedy had guts enough in the confrontation with Khrushchev was soon dispelled when he imposed a naval blockade on Cuba to prevent the arrival of the Russian ships, and massed troops and planes in southern Florida for a possible strike at Soviet installations on the island.

At the height of the crisis, Moscow was a frightened city with Kennedy pictured in the Soviet propaganda as an ominous, threatening figure. Our older daughters, Susan, then ten, and Karen, eight, came home worried one afternoon after conversing with their Russian schoolmates, and Karen asked anxiously: "Kennedy doesn't want war, does he?" Attending a PTA meeting, we listened to a Soviet army general speaking to the parents about the missile crisis. Glancing at us and hesitating, he obviously skipped over pages containing anti-American diatribes. (When we were leaving the Soviet Union, the general sent us flowers and a note thanking us for allowing his children to be friends with our kids.) Near midnight, leaving our apartment to go to the *Times* office to await delivery of the official newspaper, *Pravda,* in which most major Soviet announcements were made, I would look at my four daughters sleeping in their double-decker beds and Audrey in the adjoining bedroom and persuade myself that it was beyond belief that Kennedy would loosen missiles that would obliterate us all. But fears that a missile strike was possible, if not likely, were in evidence not only in Moscow households but also in the subtle emanations from the Kremlin. Khrushchev and his cohorts were braced for an American strike on the Soviet missile bases in Cuba and girding for the possibility of a nuclear exchange between the two countries. Filing dispatches to New York via London on a shaky telephone line tapped by the KGB police, I reported the stark apprehensions of the Russian people as well as the pronouncements of their leaders and hints imparted by their subordinates. In Washington, Max Frankel, the State Department correspondent, was covering the American side in the exchanges with the Kremlin, and in turn, day after day, we led the front page of the *Times* under banner headlines. My only link to the home office was the shaky telephone line tapped by the KGB. Fortunately, I had at my side the second man in the *Times* bureau, the very able Ted Shabad, a fluent Russian-speaker and expert on the geography and resources of the Soviet Union. I felt driven by the need to report and interpret Soviet attitudes as faithfully and accurately as possible so that Americans would have the information and understanding required to cope effectively with Khrushchev's manipulations. It was a complex task in the environment of extreme tension permeating the two countries.

Once at a crucial juncture in the crisis when Kennedy was demanding that the Russian rocket-bearing ships turn about, I telephoned Manny Freedman, the foreign news editor, to report a rumor circulating in Moscow that Khrushchev was seeking a summit meeting with Kennedy. Freedman listened but then impatiently snapped: "We're not going to put up with that." His retort, more as an ordinary American than an editor, induced in me a feeling of estrangement. I wondered if some Americans viewed me as a messenger of the enemy. I never knew whether Freedman passed my tip to our Washington Bureau. In fact, on October 24, in a letter to Bertrand Russell, the British pacifist leader, Khrushchev had said that a summit meeting would be useful.

The crisis eased on October 28 when Khrushchev messaged Kennedy informing him that the Soviet rockets in Cuba were being dismantled and the other ships loaded with missiles recalled. In exchange Kennedy gave assurances there would be no invasion of Cuba, and in a secret deal negotiated by his brother, Robert Kennedy, the president pledged removal of the obsolete medium-range Jupiter missile bases sited in Turkey targeted on the Soviet Union. Llewellyn Thompson had early on suggested that Khrushchev might be looking for such a deal.

The enormous relief felt by the Russians was very much in evidence when Audrey and I attended a reception in the Kremlin on November 7, celebrating the forty-fifth anniversary of the Bolshevik Revolution. It was attended by about one thousand Soviet officials and foreign diplomats and was the first time that Americans had been invited to the Kremlin since the eruption of the missile crisis. At the reception in the gilded banquet hall of the Palace of Congresses, Khrushchev, vodka glass in hand, stood at the head of a phalanx of members of the ruling Presidium with the number two, Leonid Brezhnev, at his side. The Soviet leaders were clinking glasses toasting each other as if to demonstrate their solidarity. Circulating among the Russian guests, I detected near hysterical relief. A prominent Russian magazine editor whispered to me: "I thought a missile might come through my roof at any moment." Suddenly, to my consternation, I saw Audrey sidle out of the throng of Russian and foreign guests to a spot directly before the Soviet leaders, take a Leica out of her handbag, and begin photographing Khrushchev. I observed KGB agents converging on her from all parts of the hall. Journalists had been required on entering the hall to check their cameras, but Audrey had ignored the order. Unruffled by this blonde apparition standing before him, Khrushchev waved off the swarming KGB agents and posed smiling as Audrey continued to take photographs, which were published the next morning on the front page of the *Times*.

The incident seemed to break the ice, and led by Khrushchev and his wife, Nina, the Soviet leaders began to mingle with the guests. Surrounded by journalists, Khrushchev accepted questions from correspondents. Tension has not yet completely eased, he told us, but our rockets are out of Cuba. Grimly, he said: "We were very close—very, very close to a thermonuclear war. If there had not been reason then, we would not be here tonight, and there might not have been elections in the United States." As for Berlin, Khrushchev seemed to be backing off. "The Berlin problem is now assuming greater acuteness because Berlin is not Cuba," he said, but then added: "We do not want Berlin. We do not need it. We are asking for peace and a peace treaty." He spoke about the need for peaceful coexistence, compromise, and mutual concessions in East-West relations. Earlier in the day, Defense Minister Rodion Malinovsky, speaking before a military parade in Red Square marking the anniversary, omitted the usual Soviet warnings about Berlin which were sounded before the Cuban crisis.

As the evening wore on, Audrey made another approach to Khrushchev. With her friend Lucy Jarvis, an NBC producer, at her side, she asked if they could do a documentary for NBC on the Kremlin. The Soviet leader, who seemed charmed by her, agreed. (The NBC documentary was produced the following year.) Nina Khrushchev, who was standing nearby, invited Audrey to tea and consented to her bringing a camera. The next afternoon, in a small reception room of the Kremlin, with a few wives of ambassadors and members of the Presidium in attendance, Audrey chatted with Nina over tea and cakes about children and life in Moscow. The Cuban missile crisis thus ended, at least for the Toppings, with a tea party. In the summer of 1963, after ten days of hard negotiations in Moscow with W. Averell Harriman, then undersecretary of state, Khrushchev signed a nuclear test-ban treaty, which prohibited testing in the atmosphere and outer space. The Berlin crisis as such vanished.

At year's end, Kennedy gave another sort of party at Miami's Orange Bowl when he welcomed back the 1,113 survivors of the 1,300 exiles who landed on the shores of Cuba in the abortive Bay of Pigs invasion. The president ransomed them from Castro for $43 million worth of baby food and medical supplies.

In September 2001, Audrey and I visited Khrushchev's gravesite in the Novodevichy Cemetery, the most venerated cemetery in Moscow, where some of Russia's most famous writers are buried. I was then the administrator of the Pulitzer prizes and had been invited to Moscow by Genrikh Borovik, a former Soviet diplomat, to advise on the creation of a similar competition making annual awards to Russian investigative reporters. The foundation sponsoring the awards was to be named in memory of his son, Artyom Borovik, a celebrated pioneer investigative reporter, a courageous critic of Kremlin policies, and the best-known historian of the Russian defeat in Afghanistan, which he had covered as a journalist. Artyom, who as a child had played with our children when his father was at the United Nations, was killed in a mysterious plane crash at the Moscow airport in March 2000. At Novodevichy, where he was buried, we attended—just after the 9/11 terrorist attacks in the United States—a memorial church service at which we held candles as the Russian Orthodox priest intoned prayers for Artyom and for the 9/11 victims. Audrey and I then went to Khrushchev's burial plot. There was no one else there. It was a small plot headed by a black-and-white marble bust of Khrushchev which the sculptor Ernest Neizvestny said he had crafted in a style that would symbolize the ambiguity and contradictory nature of the Soviet leader's rule.

As for Castro, the Cuban leader emerged from resolution of the missile crisis enraged by what he denounced publicly as a deal negotiated behind his back. He rejected Kennedy's no-invasion pledge as meaningless and criticized Khrushchev's failure to demand American withdrawal from the base at Guantanamo and an end to the trade embargo imposed earlier by President Kennedy. However, I found him mollified by what amounted to a Soviet payoff in subsidies by Khrushchev's successors when I spent an evening with him in his Havana office in November 1983. Let me, in the next chapter, vault ahead in time, to say what that engaging meeting was like.

23

AN EVENING WITH FIDEL CASTRO

In November 1983, then as managing editor of the *Times,* I traveled through South America, visiting our bureaus, interviewing leaders of the strife-torn continent, and all the while hoping that Fidel Castro would agree to my repeated requests for a meeting. Since my days in Moscow during the Cuban missile crisis I had hoped for an opportunity to interview Castro about the aftermath of the confrontation with President Kennedy and his relations with the Soviet Union. I was accompanied on my Latin America tour by Bill Kovach, the enterprise editor of our National Desk. The circumstances were rather odd, but our invitation to visit Cuba did finally come through during the evening of November 23 in Managua, Nicaragua.

We had just interviewed Tomás Borge, a member of the ruling Directorate of the Sandinista Party, which was battling the American-supported Contra guerrillas. Borge had taken us to dinner in a shacklike house in a poor village on the outskirts of Managua, where we talked to the people and dined on pork, black beans, rice, and Coca Cola, and then back to the capital for drinks at a fancy bar at the Intercontinental Hotel. Suddenly, I was summoned from the bar at 10 o'clock to take a phone call from the Cuban ambassador. The next morning we were aboard a Cuban airliner bound for Havana. We lunched with Cuban officials in Havana at the Bodeguita del Medio, where there was a sign handwritten by Ernest Hemingway: "My Mogito in La Bodeguita, My Daiquiri in El Floridita." It was a lovely lunch sampling the Hemingway drinks, but our hosts did not reveal whether Castro would be seeing us. Two days passed marked by interviews with Cuban leaders and tours. Then, at 9:30 P.M., a phone call in my hotel room: "We will pick you up in a moment; the president is ready to receive you."

We were welcomed at the Council of State building by Alfredo Ramírez, the head of the American Department in the Ministry of External Affairs. We surrendered our cameras and tape recorder at the door, as requested, and a few minutes later we were ushered into Castro's spacious office, an oblong wood-paneled room. The president's large wooden desk piled with working files stood in a far corner before an overfilled bookcase. Fidel Castro greeted us as we entered. He was dressed in his familiar uniform, green combat fatigues, a short combat jacket with leather belt, and black zipper boots. His beard was quite long and rather straggly, but his hair with its silver gray streaks was well groomed. Castro waved us to beige leather couches arranged around a coffee table. We were seated with his aides: Alfredo Ramírez, Ramón Sánchez-Paridi, head of the Interest Section in Washington, and José Migar Barrenco, the secretary of the Council of State.

Castro, his manner warm and friendly, asked me to sit beside him, saying he would like to be able to look into my face. He apologized for inviting us to his office at such a late hour and added with a smile that possibly he had upset our plans; perhaps we would have preferred to go to the Tropicana, a large, splashy nightclub cabaret. Castro then invited questions, noting that he preferred to have our conversation kept out of the newspapers but that I was free to convey his views to associates. I am recording here condensed excerpts of Castro's remarks for the first time.

I began by asking Castro for his view of the tensions between President Ronald Reagan's administration and the Soviet leadership and their impact on Latin America, especially Cuba. Castro said that tensions were probably more severe than at any time since the Cuban missile crisis. He said the international situation had been aggravated in particular by the decision of the United States and its allies to deploy Pershing missiles in Western Europe. You can judge the reaction of the Soviet Union to the deployment of the Pershings, he said, by comparing it to the American reaction during the 1962 crisis when the Russians were implanting forty-two medium-range missiles on Cuban soil. The American reaction was violent. There developed the threat of war. Now, Castro said, there is a parallel. If Russian missile launchers had been implanted in Cuba, they could have hit American targets in only a few minutes. The Pershing missiles can reach targets in the Soviet Union in a few minutes. So there is reason for the Russians to be concerned—in fact, even more so, since the Pershings are fifty times greater in power and numbers. (The Pershing systems were scrapped following the ratification of the Intermediate-Range Nuclear Forces Treaty on May 27, 1988.)

Then, striking a characteristic pose, Castro stroked his beard, thought for a moment, and, gesturing with his forefinger, said: "However, you must understand that the struggle in Latin America began much before there was any East-West confrontation or, in fact, even before the Bolshevik Revolution." He said that the struggle for independence and freedom in Latin America would continue even if there was a détente between the Soviet Union and the United States. Even under conditions of détente, he thought it probable

that the United States would still resist the revolutionary struggle convuls-
ing Latin America. With a shrug, he said there was a possibility that détente
might even work to the disadvantage of Latin America.

I asked whether it was unrealistic for Cuba to adopt an attitude of hostility while living in the shadow of the United States. Castro retorted it was
not Cuba which had taken a stance of hostility but actually it was the United
States which had been hostile toward Cuba. He said that countries struggling
for their independence could not give up simply because they were living in
the proximity of the United States. He said the revolutionary struggle was
spreading throughout Latin America and he foresaw a day when even countries like Brazil would join and the United States would have to respect the
power of the Latin American nations. Despite all of this, Castro continued,
it was certainly possible for the United States to come to an accommodation
with Cuba and bring about flourishing economic relations. He asked me:
"You have diplomatic relations with China, which is a Communist country,
why not with us?" I pointed out that good relations had developed between
China and the United States for at least two reasons: China had become independent of Moscow and the United States thus no longer felt menaced by
a Sino-Soviet monolith. Secondly, the Chinese had given up attempting to
export revolution to the less developed countries.

Castro replied: As far as the export of revolution is concerned, it was true
that Cuba has assisted revolutionaries in various countries, although the extent has been exaggerated. He said it did not make any difference, in any case,
how much assistance you give to revolutionaries engaged in struggle unless
there is a real will to win and a need to bring about change in the country.
Those are the crucial and decisive factors, he said. He cited the American
programs of assistance to the Salvadoran Army and before that to the South
Vietnamese army. They failed, he said, because the revolutionaries had the
spirit and will to win and had roots among the people and in the country.

As regards Cuba's relations with the Soviet Union, Castro said, it was on
a mutual basis and at times it was the Cubans who took the lead in urging
Moscow to adopt policies. He said he remained grateful to Moscow for its
large-scale assistance dating from the Khrushchev era. He did not complain
about his treatment in the resolution of the missile crisis. Castro recalled that
when he first took power, he was isolated, under pressure from the United
States, and didn't know in which direction to turn. He said it was the Soviet
Union which came forward with the assistance he needed to build and preserve the Cuban nation—and the Cubans cannot overlook that fact. However, he stressed that Cuba retained its independence of action and that So-

viet military advisers were in Cuba solely to train his army in the use of new weapons. The Soviet military force was a remnant of what Nikita Khrushchev posted on the island prior to the 1962 missile crisis with the United States. At the time I spoke with Castro, he was receiving a Soviet subsidy of $4 billion annually, representing 25 percent of the small country's GNP. This included Soviet purchases of sugar and nickel at prices above market level. The subsidies ended in 1991 with the breakup of the Soviet Union.

In replying to questions, Castro stared intently into my eyes and often raised his hands in expressive gestures. Castro's personal interpreter was brought in after the first interpreter was worn out; she not only translated simultaneously but also mimicked Castro's inflections and expressions. Castro's remarks revealed a broad knowledge of foreign affairs and history, including that of the United States. He frequently cited names of relevant personalities, dates, and statistics. Speaking of the work of the thousands of Cuban teachers in Nicaragua, he said proudly that 93 percent of their pupils had advanced to the next grade. When two Cuban schoolteachers were killed by the Contras near the Honduran border, he said, twenty-nine thousand Cuban schoolteachers volunteered thereafter to go to Nicaragua. As he spoke tenderly about Nicaragua's schoolchildren, I thought, what a contrast. This is the same man whose dictatorial Communist regime had so brutally repressed political opponents.

At midnight, after the conversation with Castro had continued for more than two hours, ranging largely over issues relating to the civil wars in Salvador and Nicaragua, I was thanking Castro when he interrupted to say: "Well, it's not too late to go to the Tropicana." A tray of mojitos and daiquiris was brought in. For himself, Castro poured two drinks of Chivas Regal, saying he preferred scotch to rum. During our meeting, Castro smoked only one small cigar. He told us he had read everything that Hemingway wrote. In particular, he admired *The Old Man and the Sea* because Hemingway had written a novel "simply about a man and his thoughts."

24

PRESIDENT KENNEDY

When Kennedy assumed the presidency in 1961, in shaping his Vietnam policy, he had his experience in Saigon in 1951 very much in mind. He had remained persuaded that weaning popular support away from Ho Chi Minh's nationalist banner was the key to victory. The only instrument available to Kennedy for winning "the hearts and minds" of the Vietnamese people was the Saigon government. Success in Vietnam would turn on making that government stronger, more effective, and attractive to the Vietnamese people. This was his intention when, upon return from his confrontation with Khrushchev in Vienna, he tripled the number of American military advisers working with the South Vietnamese army.

From the Eisenhower administration Kennedy had inherited a client Vietnamese government headed by Prime Minister Ngo Dinh Diem. Diem had ousted the French puppet, Bao Dai, and his administration was nominally independent. To shore up the government, Kennedy framed a counterinsurgency plan that provided Diem with financial support for an increase of 20,000 in the size of the Army of the Republic of Vietnam (ARVN), which then stood at 150,000, and additional aid for the local Civil Guard, the counterguerrilla auxiliary. Later in the year, he augmented the program to bring the ARVN up to a strength of 200,000. Kennedy also deployed American Special Forces units, known as Green Berets, for covert action against North Vietnam. In return for this broad support, Kennedy asked Diem to undertake reforms that would rejuvenate the South Vietnamese military forces as well as a political action designed to inspire popular support. But not many months later he was told by his military and political advisers that Diem was failing despite this large-scale American support to transform his government into an effective countervailing force against Ho Chi Minh. In frustration, Kennedy approved in 1963 a CIA-inspired coup by dissident Vietnamese generals to topple Diem. The president had been persuaded that a competent replacement had to be found immediately for Diem, who among other things had become increasingly unpopular because of his repression of the Buddhists. The coup by the generals was staged on November 1, but as it went forward, unexpectedly and apparently without direct CIA complicity, Diem was assassinated.

Three weeks after Diem's assassination I was in New York, back from three years in Moscow and about to leave for Hong Kong to become the chief correspondent for Southeast Asia with oversight responsibility for our Saigon bureau. In preparation for the assignment I planned to go to Washington for background talks with officials. I thought of asking for an appointment with the president but then decided not to when I learned that four weeks earlier Kennedy had complained to the publisher of the *Times* about the reporting of David Halberstam, one of our correspondents in Saigon. At a meeting in Washington Kennedy had told Arthur Ochs "Punch" Sulzberger that Halberstam had become "too close to the story" and lost his objectivity. He urged Sulzberger to arrange his transfer. Sulzberger rejected the suggestion without hesitation. It was an odd and senseless suggestion, especially in the context of Kennedy's prior experience with the *Times*. In April 1960, the paper had been pressured by the Central Intelligence Agency to withhold a story by Tad Szulc reporting that an invasion of Cuba was imminent. The *Times* carried the Szulc story but omitted, at the insistence of the publisher, Orville Dryfoos, details which if published, he had been told, might imperil the operation. The Bay of Pigs invasion, which took place on April 17, was a disastrous failure resulting in 114 of the exiles killed and more than 1,100 taken captive. Kennedy berated the *Times* for disclosing the invasion prematurely with its publication of the Szulc story. But at a meeting in the White House of newspaper executives he told Turner Catledge, the managing editor, in a private aside: "Maybe if you had printed more about the operation, you would have saved us from a colossal mistake." Kennedy might very well have applied the same logic to Halberstam's perceptive critique of the conduct of the Vietnam War.

Several weeks after I took up my post in Hong Kong, I met Halberstam as he was returning home on leave following fifteen months in Vietnam. His scheduled leave had been delayed by *Times* executives so that it would not be interpreted as a transfer in compliance with Kennedy's intervention. On December 11, in a letter to Manny Freedman, the foreign news editor, dealing generally with plans for coverage of Southeast Asia, I said: "I have had an opportunity to talk to David Halberstam over the last two days. He seems to be in good shape. Halberstam expressed the wish to return to the Southeast Asia Bureau. I told him he would be welcomed after a period in New York during which he would be exposed to the practical problems of putting out the paper. If the staffing arrangements work out appropriately, I would like to see Halberstam back here. We would work well together."

The reference to Halberstam's need to become more informed about the problems of putting out the paper alluded to his ongoing battles with the Foreign Desk. Halberstam's great strength as a newspaper reporter was his ability to dig out facts, analyze them intelligently, and present them courageously. However, the quality of his copy in style and form was not always up to *Times* standards. Given his rather combative nature, he did not take well to editing or queries. Uncomfortable about the controversy surrounding him, the senior *Times* executives in New York did not offer Halberstam another Southeast Asia assignment, although he was nominated by the paper and shared the 1964 Pulitzer Prize for International Reporting with Malcolm Browne of the Associated Press. The pair was cited for "their individual reporting of the Vietnam War and the overthrow of the Diem regime." In approving the coup against Diem, Kennedy in effect accepted the view manifest in Halberstam's reporting, that it was self-defeating for the United States to continue to back the inept, corrupt dictator.

Halberstam's next assignment was to Poland, where his reporting on such sensitive subjects as the prevalence of anti-Semitism led to his expulsion by the Communist government on a charge of "slander." At a subsequent posting to Paris, where he was preoccupied personally with writing a novel, his performance was undistinguished. He resigned from the *Times* in 1967 to join *Harper's*. It was in magazine and book writing, beginning with his brilliant *The Best and the Brightest,* a massive volume on Washington's conduct of the Vietnam War, that he found contentment and fulfillment, until his tragic death in 2007 in a car crash.

On November 22, just before leaving New York for my new posting in Hong Kong, I was invited to the publisher's lunch on the fourteenth floor of the *Times* building. The police commissioner of New York was the guest of honor, and he was telling us how difficult it was to guard the president on his visits to the city when Clifton Daniel, the assistant managing editor, was called to the phone. Daniel returned, features taut, and said: "President Kennedy has been shot; he may be dying." Turning to leave, he said in a level voice, "Anybody who has work to do better go downstairs." I followed Punch Sulzberger, the publisher, to the elevators and down to the third-floor newsroom, which was in an uproar. Tom Wicker, who had been covering the president, was telephoning from Dallas.

Inexplicably, there was no advance obit for the young president. Arthur

Gelb, the deputy metropolitan editor, collared me. "Will you do the foreign policy section of the obit?" he asked pleadingly. I hesitated. Sequestered in Moscow for three years, I had not been able to keep abreast of all aspects of Kennedy's management of foreign affairs. But I agreed and took my place on the front rewrite desk beside Homer Bigart, the distinguished and tough veteran of the Korean War, who was writing the obit's domestic policy review. Copy boys were bringing stacks of clippings. At 2:30 P.M. Daniel, his horn-rimmed glasses perched atop his silver hair, came to the rewrite desk and, pausing before Bigart and me, said: "He's dead." Between then and 6:30 P.M. Bigart and I wrote what made up a page of the *Times.* Afterward we walked together to Bleeck's saloon on Fortieth Street. We drank and talked about Kennedy until Homer went into the telephone booth to call his wife, Jane. I elbowed up to the crowded bar to order another scotch and when I returned, I glanced through the window of the telephone booth and saw that Bigart, the indomitable war correspondent, was weeping. He was not alone. I left the bar and walked across Times Square. The lights were dimmed. In my room at the Astor Hotel, I lay awake thinking of the young congressman in Saigon and haunted by the question of how he would have finally dealt with the Vietnam imbroglio if he had lived. In the morning, before leaving for Washington, I scribbled notes about what I thought Kennedy would have done.

When Kennedy consented to the CIA coup to remove Diem, he was hoping for a replacement who would have the nationalist characteristics needed to attract popular support away from Ho Chi Minh. That imperative was born of the mind-set he developed in Saigon. The shock of Diem's assassination, only three weeks before his own assassination, ended the president's experiment. The fatal error lay, not in what Kennedy aspired to from his days in Saigon, but in the fact that when he became president it was too late in the ideological struggle. After more than two decades of political disappointments and revolutionary struggle, no Saigon government tainted by association with foreigners, French or American, could diminish Ho Chi Minh's nationalist appeal. At the time of Kennedy's death, Ho Chi Minh was gaining power, reinforced by an unending supply of recruits rallying to his nationalist banner and armed with full array of weapons coming over the porous China border. Paradoxically, if anything, Kennedy's policy of pressing devastating counterinsurgency sweeps, sometimes employing his Green Berets, had tended to turn more of the peasantry to support of Ho Chi Minh and his southern Vietcong allies.

Up until JFK's death, Edmund Gullion continued to be a close adviser to the president, persuading him to continue his support of the Vietnamese government. After the assassination, Gullion left the Foreign Service to become dean of the Fletcher School of Law and Diplomacy at Tufts University, but he remained in close touch with the Kennedy family. In the summer of 1965, the State Department called him out of retirement to serve as intermediary in a top-secret mission, code-named "XYZ." It was undertaken after Mai Van Bo, the chief of the North Vietnamese delegation in Paris, had made an informal overture hinting that there might be a softening of the forbidding preconditions, known as the Four Points, laid down by Premier Pham Van Dong for the opening of peace negotiations. Gullion met three times with Bo in Paris, but the channel abruptly closed when Bo failed to show up for a fourth meeting as the United States intensified its bombing of North Vietnam.

In February 1967, I visited Medford, Massachusetts, at Gullion's request to lecture at Fletcher. I found Gullion very distressed because Robert Kennedy was moving away from him on Vietnam policy and was adopting a militant antiwar position. Gullion himself was being harassed on his own campus by student antiwar activists. But he was persisting as a strong advocate of American support for the Saigon government's war effort. On March 2, Bobby, who had adhered to a stand similar to that of his brother following their Saigon visit, broke with the policies of the Johnson administrations and called for American withdrawal from Vietnam. Appealing for an end to the bombing of North Vietnam and the opening of negotiations with Hanoi, Robert Kennedy declared: "Under the direction of the United Nations and with an international presence gradually replacing American forces, we should move forward to a final settlement which allows all major political elements in South Vietnam to participate in the choice of leadership and shape their future as a people."

Later that year, speaking about Vietnam policy in an interview with John Stewart for an oral history, Robert Kennedy recalled the 1951 trip he made with his brother to Asia. The trip, he said, made a great impression on John, "a very very major impression . . . these countries from the Mediterranean to the South China Sea all . . . searching for a future; what their relationship was going to be to the United States; what we were going to do in our relationship to them; the importance of the right kind of representation; the importance of associating ourselves with the people rather than just the governments, the mistake of the war in Indochina; the mistake of the French policy; the failure of the United States to back the people."

The debate has never ceased about what course Kennedy would have followed if he had lived and served a second term. As for me, I believe that Jack Kennedy would have followed a course, possibly after the 1964 elections, similar to that proposed by his brother, with whom he had been very much in accord on Vietnam policy. He would have done so once he had concluded that it was simply too late to expect that any client government in Saigon could succeed in drawing a substantial number of the Vietnamese people away from support of Ho Chi Minh.

I had a second meeting in Asia with Robert Kennedy after our encounter in Saigon in 1951. Less than a month after his brother's death, Bobby, then attorney general, was sent to Southeast Asia by President Johnson to mediate in a violent dispute between Sukarno, the Indonesian president, and the leaders of the newly formed British-sponsored Federation of Malaysia. President Sukarno had denounced creation of the federation as "neo-colonialism" and was supporting anti-British guerrilla rebels in Malaya. The Kennedy mission was an important one of some urgency but also motivated in part by a desire to divert and reinvigorate the grieving Bobby. From my post in Hong Kong, I joined the traveling Kennedy party, which also included his wife, Ethel, in Tokyo. Kennedy was to meet there with Sukarno. I covered the talks during which Kennedy secured from Sukarno a tentative agreement to a cease-fire accord with Malaysian leaders.

Kennedy also spoke to an audience of thousands at Waseda University stadium, where he told the cheering Japanese students and faculty: "If President Kennedy's life and death and his relationship to all in our age group mean anything, it means we young people must work harder for a better life for all the people in the world."

Kennedy left for Korea on the evening of January 18, and I was with him aboard his U.S. Air Force transport. He planned to spend a day with American troops in Korea before continuing on to Malaysia and then to Jakarta for another meeting with Sukarno to cement the cease-fire accord. Airborne, the plane developed engine trouble and returned to Tokyo. A cable from the *Times'* Foreign Desk awaited me there. Proceed to Taiwan. France had broken ranks with the United States and recognized the Communist government in Peking. I was to cover the reaction of the Chiang Kai-shek government. I said good-bye to Kennedy at the Tokyo airport before his plane took off again for Korea.

In Tokyo, I had talked to Bobby about Saigon in 1951. With a sad half smile, he spoke of how important those days in Saigon had been for him and his brother. He said little about President Lyndon Johnson's Vietnam policy except to repeat rather wearily what his brother had said so often: There was no chance of winning the war unless the South Vietnamese government gained the support of the people.

Correspondents in 1957 at Checkpoint Charlie entry from the American sector of West Berlin to Communist East Berlin. *From left:* the author, who was then stationed in Berlin for the Associated Press, Joe Fleming (United Press), Ed de Fontaine (Army Radio), Terry Davidson (Reuters), Harry Gilroy (*New York Times*), unidentified officer, Gary Stindt (CBS), Russell Hill (Radio Free Berlin), Jeremy Main (International News Service). Courtesy author

In 1958 an American army helicopter with nine servicemen aboard strayed over Communist East Germany and was forced down. The author was allowed in response to his repeated requests to meet with the captive servicemen who were held in a villa in the East German city of Dresden. Topping is shown speaking to Major George Kemper while his comrades look on. The worldwide publicity given Topping's story was instrumental in obtaining their release. Courtesy Associated Press

U.S. Ambassador Lewellyn Thompson with Soviet leader Nikita Khrushchev, Jane Thompson, and Nina Khrushchev at a Benny Goodman concert in 1960 in the Moscow Sports Palace. Khrushchev, who hated jazz, left the hall during the intermission. Thompson subsequently was recalled to Washington and was at President Kennedy's side during the 1962 Cuban missile crisis. Photos by Audrey Topping

The author and Audrey Topping attended a Kremlin reception on November 7, 1962. It was the day Soviet Premier Khrushchev and President Kennedy resolved the Cuban missile crisis. Khrushchev told Topping that a thermonuclear war had been averted. Khrushchev is shown with Leonid Brezhnev (*center*), who succeeded the Russian leader when he was ousted by the Politburo in October 1964. Photo by Audrey Topping

In 1962 two of the author's daughters were outfitted in a Moscow department store for attendance at a Russian school. Shown from left to right are the sales clerk, Lesley, Karen (Audrey Topping standing behind her), Robin, and Susan. Karen and Susan in Russian uniform were the first American children to attend a Soviet elementary school. Courtesy *New York Times*

The author is shown with Fidel Castro after interviewing the Cuban leader in Havana in 1983. Castro stood by his alliance with the Soviet Union but also said he could not understand why the United States was refusing to recognize his government since Washington had diplomatic relations with China which was also a Communist country. Topping was then managing editor of the *New York Times*. Courtesy author/Photo by Cuban government photographer

The Topping family is shown on a boat on Hong Kong's Repulse Bay with their beloved Chinese junk, the *Valhalla,* in the background. The author was based in Hong Kong as the *Times'* chief correspondent for Southeast Asia from 1963 to 1966, dividing his time between China watching and covering the wars in Vietnam, Cambodia, and Laos. Courtesy author

American briefing in Saigon in 1964 during the Vietnam War. Author is shown at center. At his right is Pham Xuan An, a *Time* magazine correspondent who later confessed to be a spy for the North Vietnamese. Behind Topping on his right is Neil Sheehan of the United Press and later the *New York Times;* behind Topping on his left is Malcolm Browne of the Associated Press and later the *Times;* on Sheehan's right is Tillman Durdin of the *Times.*

Prince Norodom Sihanouk of Cambodia is shown on arrival at Phnom Penh airport in 1964 on the occasion of the Soviet delivery of jet fighter planes and other military equipment for his army. Audrey Topping is at right taking Sihanouk's photo. Courtesy author

The author was challenged in 1965 by Prince Sihanouk to check out press reports which he disputed of North Vietnamese bases on the Cambodia border with Vietnam. Topping traveled to the border jungle, led by Cambodian defense minister General Lon Nol, by helicopter, jeep, and on foot. Lon Nol is shown standing with cane while Topping (at center) checks maps. Lon Nol later ousted Sihanouk as head of state in a coup. Courtesy author/Photo taken by Cambodian military

Major James Reid, decorated U.S. military intelligence officer, at a base in South Vietnam in 1967 during the Vietnam War. Reid discovered how Chinese-made missiles were being secretly landed on the Cambodian coast and then smuggled to North Vietnamese troops attacking South Vietnam. Courtesy James Reid

Indonesian president Sukarno visited Washington in 1961. He is shown at the White House, where he met with President Kennedy and Vice President Johnson. Kennedy sought to wean Sukarno away from his ties to China and the Soviet Union with economic aid and support for the Indonesian claim to West Irian (Dutch New Guinea). The American overtures failed, and by 1965 Sukarno was allied with the Indonesian Communist Party (PKI) and had cemented his ties with China and North Vietnam. Courtesy Associated Press

Chinese premier Zhou Enlai hosted a reception in Beijing's Great Hall of the People in 1971 for Canadian ambassador Chester Ronning and his daughter Audrey Topping. The premier agreed at the reception to grant the author a visa to enter China. In 1966 Ambassador Ronning made two trips to Hanoi on behalf of the United States and Canada, seeking a negotiated end to the Vietnam War. Photo by Susan Topping/courtesy Audrey Topping

Audrey Topping riding in 1975 with the Kazaks while on assignment for the *New York Times* and *National Geographic* magazine in Xinjiang Province, western China. Photo by Chester Ronning/courtesy *New York Times*

Henry Kissinger visited former foreign minister Huang Hua in a Beijing hospital in 2008. On July 9, 1971, Huang Hua met Kissinger when he arrived on a secret mission to set up the visit of President Nixon. He escorted Kissinger to a meeting with Premier Zhou Enlai at which arrangements were made for the Nixon visit. Courtesy author, from private collection of Huang Hua

Audrey Topping's missionary grandparents: Rev. Halvor Ronning and wife Hannah with their three children Chester (Audrey's father, *far left*), Almah, and Neilius. This photo was taken in Xiangfan, Hubei, China, in 1899. Courtesy Audrey Topping

The author's parents, Joseph and Anna Topolsky, immigrants from Russia, shortly after their marriage in New York in 1916. As a young girl, Anna was witness to the pogrom murder of her mother by Cossack horsemen in a Jewish ghetto village in the Ukraine. Courtesy author

Menfolk of the author's family in a photo taken in Kobryn on the Polish-Russian border. Author's father, Joseph, is the boy at the left; Joseph's father is directly above him in cap and white shirt. Joseph immigrated to the United States in 1912 at the age of eighteen. One of two brothers he left behind and other members of his family were lost in the Holocaust. Courtesy author

The Topping daughters, who traveled the world with their working parents. *Clockwise from left:* Karen and Lesley, born in London; Susan, born in Saigon; Robin, born in Berlin; and Joanna, born in New York. In Moscow, Russians would jokingly accuse the Toppings of bias because they did not have a child born while stationed there. Photo by Patrick Vingo

25

OPERATION ROLLING THUNDER

In December 1963, Audrey and I were back to our old haunts in Hong Kong. It was to be our base for the next three years. We were hardly unpacked when I left for Saigon on the first of what were to be my frequent shuttle trips to Vietnam, Cambodia, Laos, and other crisis areas in Southeast Asia, such as Indonesia. Nostalgically, I booked into the Continental Hotel in Saigon and walked the familiar streets once traversed by French *colons* now crowded with Americans. Still brooding over the death of Jack Kennedy, I walked from the Continental down Boulevard Charner and mounted the back stairs of the seedy tenement as he had done, to my old apartment where we talked in 1951. A knock failed to bring any response. Gone was the bar on the ground floor where once Germans of the Foreign Legion in drunken binges sang as they did in Nazi days, "We're Sailing against England."

I was very much alone with the old ghosts. When I met with officers of the U.S. Military Assistance Command Vietnam (MACV), advisers to the Saigon government, none of them were very much interested in hearing about my experiences with the French Expeditionary Force in its war with the Viet Minh. Few knew anything about a French general named de Lattre. They were fresh faced, not like the French officers I knew at isolated posts gaunt and depressed after years of war in jungles and on the river deltas.

Shortly after he arrived in 1964, initially to become deputy commander of MACV, General William Westmoreland invited me to accompany him aboard a small plane on an inspection tour of bases manned by South Vietnamese troops and their supporting American units. Chatting with the general, I found him unassuming and open in stating his personal views about the course of the war. He mentioned that he had taken account of MacArthur's warnings after the experience of the Korean War of the dangers of deployment of American troops on the Asian continent. As we flew about the country, I told him what I had observed in the field during the French Indochina War. In covering that war, I never met a French line officer who was convinced that the Expeditionary Force, as Paris designated it, even with heavy reinforcements could defeat Vo Nguyen Giap's strategy of protracted

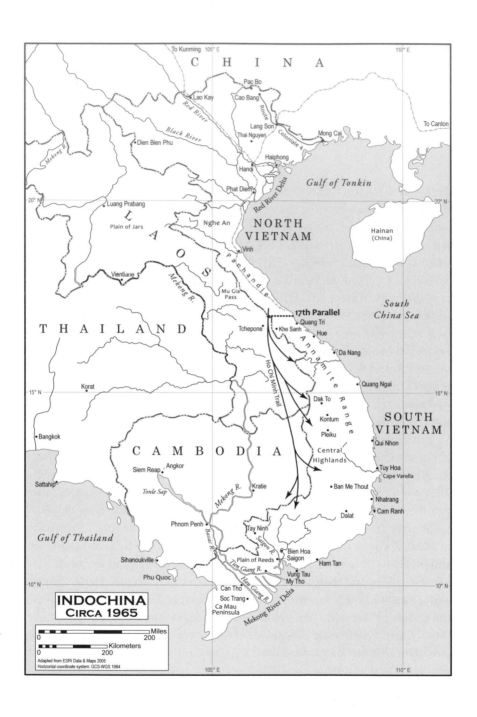

C H I N A

To Kunming   105° E
110° E

Pac Bo

Lao Kay
Cao Bang

Route

Lang Son
To Canton

Red River
Thai Nguyen
Mong Cai

Black River

Dien Bien Phu
Coloniale 4

Haiphong

Hanoi

Mekong R.
Phat Diem
Gulf of Tonkin

Red River Delta

20° N
20° N

Luang Prabang
NORTH
VIETNAM
Hainan
(China)

Plain of Jars
L A O S
Nghe An

Vientiane
Vinh

Mekong R.
Panhandle

Mu Gia
Pass
South
China Sea

T H A I L A N D
17th Parallel
Quang Tri

Tchepone
Khe Sanh

Hue

Annamite Range
Da Nang

15° N
Korat
Ho Chi Minh Trail
15° N

Quang Ngai

Dak To

Kontum
SOUTH
VIETNAM

Bangkok
Pleiku

C A M B O D I A
Qui Nhon

Central
Highlands
Tuy Hoa

Siem Reap
Angkor
Cape Varella

Tonle Sap
Mekong R.
Kratie
Ban Me Thout

Sattahip
Nhatrang

Dalat
Cam Ranh

Gulf of Thailand
Phnom Penh

Bassac R.
Tay Ninh

Saigon R.
Sihanoukville
Plain of Reeds
Bien Hoa
Saigon
Ham Tan

Phu Quoc
Tien Giang R.
Vung Tau

10° N
My Tho
10° N

Can Tho
Hau Giang R.

Soc Trang
Ca Mau
Peninsula
Mekong River Delta

INDOCHINA
CIRCA 1965

Miles
0   200

Kilometers
0   200

Adapted from ESRI Data & Maps 2005
Horizontal coordinate system: GCS-WGS 1984

105° E
110° E

war, adapted from Mao's concept. France had put 150,000 troops into the field, composed of some of the ablest professional soldiers in the world, and also excellent Vietnamese troops who knew the terrain meticulously well. Yet in the jungles and on the great river deltas the *"nettoyage"* campaigns of the French against the Viet Minh, similar to the American-devised "search and destroy missions" being mounted against the Vietcong, had not made a decisive difference. Unopposed air power also did not give the French any decisive edge. Most critically, when I traveled along the frontier with China, I saw that it was virtually impossible for the French to halt the southward movement of Viet Minh troops who had been trained and armed in the South China safe haven. Now, with Ho Chi Minh's forces solidly ensconced in North Vietnam since the 1954 Geneva Conference, Americans faced an even more difficult task than what confronted the French in their abortive effort to stem the infiltration into the South. Westmoreland listened patiently but then insisted that given the proper logistical base American forces could do what the French had not been able to do. American firepower was greater than what the French could muster, and that would be sufficient to defeat the Communists.

Two years later, in February 1965, I was back in Saigon at a time when it had become evident that firepower was not enough for victory in the war in South Vietnam. The Pentagon was fumbling for a new strategy to cope with the worsening military situation. The number of Vietcong guerrillas operating in South Vietnam had grown from about 5,000 in 1959 to an estimated 100,000 by the end of 1964. Efforts on the ground to block infiltration and the delivery of arms to the Vietcong from North Vietnam had failed. I was told that a decision was in the making as to whether a campaign of sustained bombing of North Vietnam should be undertaken. The stated goal would be to inflict so much damage on the North Vietnamese industrial infrastructure and military installations that Hanoi would desist from further infiltration of men and supplies into the South in support of the Vietcong.

On February 6, I lunched with a White House fact-finding mission at the home of Barry Zorthian, the public affairs officer of the American Embassy. The mission was headed by McGeorge Bundy, the special assistant for national security to President Johnson. It was Bundy's first visit to Vietnam, and he did not seem to have much knowledge of the country. The discussion over lunch centered on whether "to bomb or not to bomb." The mission had been sent to Saigon to confer with General Maxwell Taylor on his proposal, made with the concurrence of General Westmoreland, that a campaign of sustained bombing of North Vietnam be launched at once. Taylor

had urged President Johnson to break the will of the Ho Chi Minh government by inflicting "such pain or threat of pain upon the DRV that it would
be compelled to order a stand-down of Vietcong violence" in South Vietnam.
It was typical Taylor rhetoric, which I had heard before. During his tenure
in Saigon as ambassador, I thought his approach to the problems of Vietnam was demonstrably lacking in understanding of the native character, history, and culture of the Vietnamese. For one thousand years, the Vietnamese had successfully resisted the efforts of the Chinese and then the French
to break their will and compel them to bow down. There was no reason to
believe that the Americans would fare any better. Failure to take account of
such indigenous factors—which often determine why, when, and how an adversary will stand and fight—had already contributed to disastrous policy
misjudgments in China and Korea. When I was asked at the conclusion of
the lunch my view of the central question, I replied that it was doubtful that
the bombing would do anything but stiffen North Vietnamese resistance. If
undertaken, I added, at that time, just as the Soviet premier Alexi Kosygin
was visiting Hanoi, it would be dangerously provocative. Moscow in retaliation might increase its aid to the North Vietnamese, rather than acting as
a mediator in the Vietnam conflict as Washington hoped. When I remarked
to Bundy, who was sitting at my side, that the United States might eventually be confronted in Vietnam with the choice of withdrawal or accepting a
protracted struggle similar to that of the British on the Northwest Frontier
of India in the nineteenth century, he replied testily: "We cannot do that." It
was obvious that the mission was leaning to the bombing option. In fact, as
I learned later, at a White House meeting the previous September, a consensus had been reached that a measured bombing campaign designed to force
the North Vietnamese to halt their incursion into the South should probably start early in 1965.

    In the early morning hours of the day following the Zorthian lunch, I was
awakened in my room at the Caravelle Hotel by the persistent ringing of the
telephone. The Vietcong had mortared the compound of the U.S. Military
Assistance Command at Pleiku in the Central Highlands and also an army
helicopter base located four miles away at Camp Holloway. Eight Americans
had been killed and 126 wounded. Ten aircraft had been demolished. Soon
after dawn, I scrambled aboard the sole plane available at Ton Son Nhut airfield and flew to the hospital at Nha Trans, on the central coast, where the
wounded were being brought. In touring the crowded wards of the hospital
I spoke to the wounded, many of them badly hit by mortar fragments, and
glimpsed the dying behind the white screens. As I emerged, I encountered

General Westmoreland, who was being accompanied on his inspection by Bundy. Westmoreland told me they had been to Pleiku. Bundy looked pale and shaken as he made the rounds of the hospital with Westmoreland. It was one thing to press the buttons of war in the White House, but another to see blood on the ground. He had already telephoned President Johnson, and a decision had been taken to stage a reprisal raid on North Vietnam. By 4 P.M. that afternoon, forty-nine navy jets—A-4 Skyhawks and F-6 Crusaders from the Seventh Fleet carriers *Coral Sea* and *Hancock*—were bombing and rocketing the North Vietnamese barracks and guerrilla staging areas at Dong Hoi, forty miles north of the seventeenth parallel. Premier Kosygin was in Hanoi during these raids. Before the Vietcong attack at Pleiku he had told a cheering crowd of Vietnamese that the Soviet Union would "not remain indifferent" if acts of war were committed against North Vietnam.

Bundy returned to Saigon, boarded the president's personal Boeing Air Force One, and as the plane headed for Washington, he prepared a thirteen-page memorandum for Johnson, which said in part: "We believe that the best available way of increasing our chance of success in Vietnam is the development and execution of a policy of sustained reprisal against North Vietnam—a policy in which air and naval action against the North is justified by and related to the whole Vietcong campaign of violence and terror in the South." Two other reprisal raids for Pleiku code-named "Flaming Dart" came four days later. Flaming Dart initiated a sequence of events that transformed the character of the Vietnam War and the U.S. role in it. (In the 1990s during an exchange of views with Vietnamese leaders in Hanoi, Robert McNamara would be told, as he later related, that the Vietcong attack on the Pleiku barracks was taken on the initiative of a local commander, not on orders from Hanoi.) In Saigon, after the Flaming Dart reprisals, I attended a cocktail party in the home of an American general and found the military jubilant about the bombings. "We have a surgical instrument, with which we can do precisely what we want to the North," Brigadier General William DePuy, the deputy chief of staff, told me. Two days after Flaming Dart, President Johnson ordered commencement of "Operation Rolling Thunder." The sustained air war against North Vietnam was on.

In March, when it became evident that the South Vietnamese army could not provide adequate security for the American air bases engaged in Rolling Thunder, Johnson acceded to Westmoreland's request for the deployment of 3,500 marines. It was the start of a buildup that would ultimately put 550,000 American soldiers in Vietnam by 1969.

When the bombing started, the American public was told that the objective was to end the infiltration from the North. But this was not the case, according to a U.S. Senate study based on the revelations of the Pentagon Papers. The study said: "The rationale for the bombing was a mixture of complex and often conflicting objectives. The situation in South Vietnam seemed to be falling apart. The bombing of the North, it was hoped, would boost the morale in the South, show the determination of the United States, and break the will of the North to continue the aggression." The study added: "Target selection had been completely dominated by political and psychological considerations . . . Relatively little weight was given to the purely physical or more directly military and economic implications of whatever target destructions might be achieved."

In May 1966, I met with Westmoreland alone in his headquarters trailer in the field during an ARVN operational sweep against the Vietcong. He was a changed personality from the unassuming officer I had traveled with in 1964 in the small liaison plane. He was confident, assertive, and spoke of achieving victory in 1967. He had become something of a hero in the United States. He'd been displayed on the cover of *Time* magazine in January 1966 as "Man of the Year," and there was speculation that he might be the Republican nominee for the presidency in 1968. I asked him why he was so confident of early victory. He replied by describing what was termed by correspondents as the Westmoreland "meat grinder strategy," more delicately described by American officials as the "War of Attrition." The North Vietnamese, given the size of their country, would not be able to sustain the day-to-day casualties they were suffering in close combat with American forces. At that time, the United States was suffering in the range of more than one hundred fatalities each week, and in Saigon at the briefings, which the correspondents dubbed the "Five O'clock Follies," the American military was putting forward claims based on "body count" of huge Communist casualties. The misconceptions of Westmoreland's strategy were brought home to me vividly when I returned to a reunited Vietnam in 2005. After viewing the countless war memorials, I asked war veterans what enabled them to achieve victory despite their enormous casualties. The North Vietnamese and Vietcong suffered more than 900,000 dead compared with the American loss of 58,000 known dead. In Hue, Nguyen Van Luong, a member of the National Assembly, who commanded a force of one thousand North Vietnamese soldiers in the assaults on the U.S. Marines at the Dong Ha firebase in the Central Highlands, explained. He told me that his men fought for independence and freedom from the French and the Americans in the strong tradition of their ancestors who fought the Chinese invaders for more than one thousand years. He said the troops did not think of themselves as fighting for any political party or government. He echoed what I heard from Ho Chi Minh's people during the French Indochina War. It was history written in blood that Westmoreland never grasped.

The optimism Westmoreland generated in the United States evaporated in 1968 after the North Vietnamese and Vietcong in late January launched the Tet offensive, during which they attacked more than one hundred cities and towns, and staged an assault on the American embassy in Saigon. The attackers suffered heavy casualties, but by demonstrating the capabilities of the North Vietnamese forces, the offensive administered a political and psychological blow to the Johnson administration from which it never recovered.

26

SMALLBRIDGE

MISSION TO HANOI

As early as February 1966, as Rolling Thunder was entering its second year without evidence that North Vietnam was buckling under the onslaught, some thought was being given within the Johnson administration to the possibility of a compromise settlement with Ho Chi Minh. The Joint Chiefs of Staff were urging added pressure on North Vietnam through bombing of the oil depots near Haiphong and Hanoi "to bring the enemy to the conference table or cause the insurgency to wither from lack of support." Defense Secretary McNamara approved the bombing proposal of the Joint Chiefs in March, and President Johnson gave his approval in May but postponed the target date for the start of the operation to June 10. One reason for the delay was the White House reaction to a concerted effort by a number of world leaders to bring Hanoi and Washington to the negotiating table. The bombing had been creeping ever closer to the Chinese border, and there was concern that some miscalculation might spur Mao Zedong to intervene militarily in Vietnam as in the Korean War. Premier Zhou Enlai and Foreign Minister Chen Yi had warned through British and other intermediaries that any bombing of China would bring a response on the ground "without boundaries."

The cross-border routes from South China into North Vietnam were tempting bombing targets. They were being utilized to transport large quantities of Chinese and Russian weaponry and other supplies to Ho Chi Minh's forces, including the Soviet surface-to-air missiles (SAMs) and Chinese 37-mm radar-controlled antiaircraft artillery. The maneuverable 37-mm batteries were positioned to defend important communication lines along the Ho Chi Minh Trail, which were continuing prime targets of American air strikes. The Soviet and Chinese antiaircraft batteries had already brought down 400 American bombers and fighters, according to the Pentagon. Hanoi claimed that more than 1,000 planes of all types had been downed. Apart from the SAMs, the Russians were shipping tanks, artillery, and heavy infantry weapons to the North Vietnamese to supplement the small arms—mainly Chinese copies of Soviet weapons—being provided in large quantities by Peking. Soviet arms shipments to North Vietnam were transported by express freight trains from Siberia to Manzhouli in Manchuria and then on the Chinese trunk railroad south to Kunming and across the border to Hanoi. American bombers were targeting the North Vietnamese railroad segment which loops from Hanoi northwest to Kunming and northeast to Nanning, the principal transit depot for traffic down the Ho Chi Minh Trail. Deliveries of war matériel were also being made through Haiphong and smaller ports.

On November 30, 1965, I reported in the dispatch to the *Times* from Hong Kong that American bombers had attacked six bridges and two segments of the North Vietnam rail line. I also reported the presence of thousands of Chinese engineering troops at work on maintaining the rail system and repairing its bombed-out segments. U.S. intelligence services had become aware in June 1965 of the presence of the Chinese engineering troops. Reconnaissance aircraft had tracked the operations of the troops, easily identified because they wore their Chinese uniforms. In addition to performing engineering tasks, the Chinese were manning antiaircraft batteries and sweeping mines laid by the American navy in coastal waters. According to a study of Chinese archives recorded by Qiang Zhai in his book *China and the Vietnam Wars, 1950–1975,* the total number of Chinese service troops rotated into North Vietnam between June 1965 and March 1968 was more than 320,000, a force which peaked in 1967 at 170,000. The last contingent of engineering troops was withdrawn in August 1973. Chinese casualties, presumably by American bombing, totaled 1,100 killed and 4,200 wounded.

The Johnson administration apparently decided not to make an issue of the presence of Chinese troops in keeping with a policy of avoiding open confrontation with Peking. When I reported the presence of the Chinese troops in North Vietnam, the State Department reprimanded the consulate general in Hong Kong, accusing the staff of having leaked the information to me. Specialists in the consulate, concerned about the growing presence of the Chinese in North Vietnam, had, in fact, shared with me the intelligence information. In 1965 and 1966, the administration repeatedly conveyed to Peking through diplomatic channels that it was not contemplating an invasion of North Vietnam or any military action against China. Johnson's personal concern was registered in a conversation in July 1965 with General Harold Johnson, the army chief of staff. When the general discounted the possibility of a Korea-type incursion into Vietnam by the Chinese, the president retorted: "MacArthur didn't think they would come in either."

Among the notables counseling restraint in the bombing of North Vietnam were Secretary General of the United Nations U Thant, President Charles de Gaulle of France, and the prime ministers of Britain and Canada. Lester Pearson, Canada's prime minister, was under more pressure than the others to seek a peace settlement. Pearson had been supportive of President Johnson's Vietnam policies. Canada had been providing material support to the war effort, the nature of some of it unbeknownst to the public. Between 1965 and 1973, Canadian companies sold about $2.5 billion of war matériel to the Pentagon, including ammunition, aircraft parts, explosives, and napalm, much of it destined for the war in Vietnam. The herbicide defoliant "Agent Orange" was tested for use in Vietnam at the Canadian Forces Base (CFB) Gagetown in New Brunswick. American bomber pilots practiced carpet-bombing runs over Suffield, Alberta, and North Battleford, Saskatchewan, before heading out to Southeast Asia. In early January 1966, when his secretary of external affairs, Paul Martin, proposed a Canadian peace mission to Hanoi, confronted by the mounting unease among many Canadians about their government's involvement in Vietnam, Pearson proved very amenable. The mission, code-named "Smallbridge," was cloaked in secrecy. For the mission, Pearson selected Chester Ronning, Canada's most distinguished diplomat. At seventy-one, vigorous and active, Ronning had retired only several months prior to being recalled by Pearson. His last posting was in New Delhi as high commissioner to India. A close friend of both Pandit Nehru and Premier Zhou Enlai, he had been a key intermediary in defusing the dispute between India and China over rival claims to the border territory of Aksai Chin which had ignited armed clashes in 1962. Ronning was considered particularly suitable for the mission not only because of his connections to the Chinese, who were urging North Vietnam to fight on, but also because of the contacts he had made with Vietnamese diplomats at the 1954 Geneva Conference on Indochina as well as the 1961 Geneva Conference on Laos.

Ronning accepted the assignment, which called upon him not to act as a mediator but to explore what was needed to bring the United States and North Vietnam to the negotiating table. In preparation, Ronning flew to Washington to consult with Averell Harriman, ambassador-at-large, with whom he had collaborated when they headed their respective delegations to the Geneva Conference on Laos. Harriman gave his enthusiastic support to the mission and obtained the sanction of President Johnson. Ronning returned to Ottawa with State Department agreement to the mission following a meeting with William Bundy, the assistant secretary of state for Asian

affairs. Bundy was to become the key American player in what was to become one of the most controversial exercises in the diplomacy affecting the
Vietnam War.

Prior to Johnson's approval of the mission, several State Department officers had raised objections to the selection of Ronning as an envoy, citing his
advocacy of Western diplomatic recognition of the Peking government and
its admission to the United Nations. Pearson was asked for assurances that
Ronning would not during his mission dabble in the politics of the China
recognition issue. In an odd and rather ridiculous twist, there was a reference to me in these diplomatic exchanges. Knowing that Ronning would pass
through Hong Kong en route to Hanoi, the American consul general there,
Edward E. Rice, cabled Secretary of State Dean Rusk: "We shall do what we
can helpfully to influence Ronning's thinking if opportunity presents itself.
Incidentally, an American in Hong Kong who will have full opportunity to
affect his thinking is *NY Times* correspondent Topping, who is his son-in-
law." I came upon this reference in 1971 while perusing the Pentagon Papers
prior to their publication by the *Times*.

When Ronning arrived in Hong Kong in February 1966, he stayed in our
apartment in Repulse Bay Towers. No one, lastly me, intruded on Ronning
during his passage through Hong Kong with advice as to how he might conduct what had been staged as a top-secret mission. I learned only that Ronning had business in Southeast Asia with the International Control Commission (ICC), of which Canada was a member with India and Poland. The
ICC was created in 1954 to supervise the agreements reached at the Geneva
Conferences on Vietnam, Laos, and Cambodia. There was renewed interest
in the ICC because several governments were advocating the reconvening
of the Geneva Conference as a venue for Vietnam peace negotiations. While
awaiting a signal from Hanoi that he would be welcome, Ronning sailed with
us on our junk, the *Valhalla*, on the tranquil waters of Repulse Bay.

In Hanoi, Victor Moore, the Canadian representative on the ICC, obtained quick approval for the Ronning visit. Having suffered heavy casualties and bomb damage to their infrastructure, the North Vietnamese apparently were ready to talk peace. Traveling via Saigon and the Cambodian
and Laotian capitals, Ronning arrived in Hanoi on March 7, carrying a letter to Ho Chi Minh from Lester Pearson urging peace talks. He immediately
plunged into an exhaustive round of talks with government and Communist Party officials. During the initial contacts Ronning became progressively discouraged because the North Vietnamese adamantly adhered to the

Four Points, which had been laid down the previous April by Prime Minister Pham Van Dong, as the preconditions for the opening of peace talks. These stipulated: The United States must withdraw all troops and military equipment, dismantle its bases, and cancel its military alliance with South Vietnam; the internal affairs of the Vietnamese people must be settled in accordance with the program of the National Liberation Front (political wing of the Vietcong); peaceful reunification of Vietnam during which the two "temporarily divided" zones would not enter into any foreign military alliance or host foreign troops or bases. The unification problems were to be settled by the Vietnamese people in both zones without any foreign interference. Previous overtures by the United States for negotiations had been rebuffed because Washington would not yield to the demand that the Four Points be accepted as a basis for the opening of talks.

At the onset of the discussions in Hanoi, Ronning was given Ho Chi Minh's regards and apologies for not participating. The seventy-five-year-old leader said he was preoccupied with meetings of the Politburo, but it was clear, Ronning felt, he was overseeing the talks. Ho was quoted as favoring a return to the terms of the agreement reached at the Geneva Conference which provided for elections and reunification. For Ronning, the breakthrough came near the end of his four-day stay when he met with Prime Minister Pham Van Dong. The Canadian told Dong that his purpose was to obtain clarification of two of the preconditions for negotiations in his Four Points: withdrawal of all troops and acceptance of the program of the National Liberation Front in the South. Dong reiterated his stand on the Four Points but then said that developments since January had opened the way for a start on talks. However, he insisted on the precondition that "the United States unconditionally stop all air raids against North Vietnam." Ronning, startled by this unexpected turn, asked Dong if he was implying that the United States need only stop the bombing for informal talks to begin. As Ronning told me and later elaborated in his book *A Memoir of China in Revolution,* which he wrote in part while staying at my home, the following exchanges then took place:

> *Dong:* If the United States Government declares that it will stop all military action and attacks against the Democratic Republic for good, and unconditionally, we will talk.
>
> *Ronning:* Are you asking for cessation of military action against the DRV and if you get it, you are prepared to meet the United States to prepare the ground for ultimate negotiations?

Dong: To that sentence, I must add that an official statement must be made that [the bombing of North Vietnam] is unconditionally and definitely stopped.

Ronning: Are you limiting what you say to the territory of North Vietnam?

Dong: Yes.

Ronning: This has nothing to do with United States action in the South?

Dong: I have not mentioned it. Should I?

Ronning: Yes.

Dong: Our ultimate objective is United States withdrawal.

Ronning: Mr. Prime Minister, are you prepared to negotiate that issue?

Dong: All of the Four Points. The body with the authority is the National Liberation Front—two belligerents.

Ronning: Is that a precondition to talks, or can that be left for negotiations? Is there some possibility of starting informal talks between you and Washington if the United States accepts your proposal, leaving all issues with respect to South Vietnam for later negotiations—perhaps at a conference, so that talks leading to a ceasefire may start?

Dong: Our position embraces many aspects, but in brief, we can say that informal talks and a cessation of attacks against North Vietnam go together.

Ronning: To clarify your last point, your one requirement is an American declaration which definitely and unconditionally concerns cessation of action solely against North Vietnam?

Dong: Correct.

Ronning: We shall be glad to carry to the United States the proposal you make and your position.

Elated, Ronning returned to Ottawa thinking he was conveying a breakthrough in the diplomatic impasse, since the North Vietnamese had modified their position on the Four Points. Pearson and Paul Martin, his foreign secretary, were hopeful that Pham Van Dong's proposal would lead to peace talks. In Washington Ronning laid out the details of his meeting with Pham Van Dong to Bundy. The secretary treated the Hanoi proposal with suspicion. He saw it as a maneuver to obtain a halt to the bombing and felt that the preliminary talks which would follow would see a return by the North Vietnamese to insistence on adherence to the Four Points. But he said the State Department would give consideration to the matter. On Ronning's return to Ottawa, the Canadians waited more than six weeks for a reply from

Bundy. After being pressed by Martin in an urgent telephone call, Bundy notified the Canadian foreign secretary that a decision had been reached. Bundy told Martin that the bombing would be halted only if Hanoi reciprocated by terminating its assistance to the National Liberation Front. Specifically, the United States was asking that North Vietnam desist from infiltrating military supplies and fighters to the Vietcong. In formal terms, the State Department held to the position that the United States was not willing to stop the bombing as a "non-reciprocal precondition to the holding of discussions."

In early June, Ronning left for Hong Kong en route to Hanoi carrying the American reply. He was in despair, convinced that the North Vietnamese would reject the American counterproposal, but committed to salvaging what he could from his mission. The Canadians were not aware at the time that the Americans intended to commence bombing the oil depots near Hanoi and Haiphong on June 10. Nor were they aware, as Ronning embarked on his return journey to Hanoi, that Secretary of State Dean Rusk had sent a message to McNamara raising concerns about the timing of the bombing plan.

"I am deeply disturbed by the general international revulsion and perhaps a great deal at home, if it becomes known that we took an action which sabotaged the Ronning mission to which we had given our agreement," Rusk said. "I recognize the agony of this problem for all concerned. We could make arrangements to get an immediate report from Ronning. If he has a negative report, as we expect, that provides a firmer base for the action we contemplate and would make a difference to people like [British prime minister] Wilson and Pearson. If, on the other hand, he learns that there is any serious breakthrough toward peace, the president would surely want to know of that before an action which would knock such a possibility off the tracks. I strongly recommend therefore against the ninth or tenth. I regret this because of my maximum desire to support you and your colleagues in your tough job." Rusk sent a similar message to Johnson. The president agreed to postpone the air strikes.

When Ronning was passing through Hong Kong on his return visit to Hanoi, he confided to Audrey that he was once more en route to the North Vietnamese capital. He wanted Audrey to know of his movements, since she had managed to obtain a China visa and would be in Peking working as a correspondent for the *New York Times* when he was in Hanoi. I was not privy at the time to any of this. But by chance I had picked up Ronning's trail in

Vientiane, where I was covering the Laotian civil war between the American-backed Souvanna Phouma government and the Communist Pathet Lao. Ronning had boarded a plane of the International Control Mission for Hanoi on June 14. Tipped that he would be returning via Bangkok, I flew to the Thai capital and left a message for him at the Canadian Embassy. When Ronning arrived in Bangkok, he agreed to a late evening meeting in the balcony garden restaurant of the Oriental Hotel. At a secluded corner table, over the next two hours, I was told for the first time of the Smallbridge negotiations.

On his return to Hanoi, conveying the American reply to Prime Minister Pham Van Dong's proposal, Ronning met with Foreign Minister Nguyen Duy Trinh. The North Vietnamese evidently were anticipating a negative response to their proposal. During the long delay since Ronning's March visit, there had been leaks in Washington and an escalation of American military operations. When Ronning laid out the American terms for a halt to the bombing—essentially cessation of North Vietnamese assistance to the Vietcong in the South—Nguyen Duy Trinh rejected them summarily. He stood by the earlier proposal made in March that preliminary talks could take place if there was an unconditional end to the bombing of North Vietnam. But he did agree to Ronning's request that the Canadian channel be kept open for the possibility of further exchanges.

On the morning following our Bangkok conversation, Ronning left for Canada and I for Hong Kong. On the plane I wrote under a Hong Kong dateline the story of Hanoi's rejection of the American terms, attributing the report to unnamed sources. It was the lead front-page story on June 21 in the Times, even as Bundy was landing in Ottawa to hear Ronning's report. Bundy met with Ronning that night for seven hours in an Ottawa hotel. At the conclusion of the meeting, Bundy quickly messaged Rusk saying that in his view Ronning had found no opening or flexibility in the North Vietnamese position.

It was the signal that the Joint Chiefs of Staff were waiting for. The next day, the Joint Chiefs issued an executive order authorizing strikes on oil depots in the Hanoi-Haiphong area. It was to be a massive strike, but pilots were instructed: "At Haiphong avoid damage to merchant shipping. No attacks authorized on craft unless U.S. aircraft fired on, and then only if clearly North Vietnamese." Russian ships were making use of the harbor, and there was concern that one of them might be hit. Everything feasible was to be done to minimize civilian casualties. Bad weather delayed the air strikes. When they were finally carried out on June 29, the Seventh Air Force headquarters labeled them "the most significant, the most important strikes of the war." But the bombing effectively shut down the Canadian diplomatic channel to Hanoi.

Two years after Ronning returned from Hanoi with the North Vietnamese proposal for the opening of negotiations, President Johnson in effect took a first step toward accepting the terms of that proposal, which he had rejected previously. The bombing by that time had failed to break the will of the North Vietnamese, and American casualties were mounting. On March 31, 1968, Johnson announced that he had halted all air and naval bombardment north of the twentieth parallel. In the same speech he revealed that he would not run for reelection. Hanoi responded positively to the partial bombing halt, and preliminary talks opened in Paris. Formal negotiations commenced in early November after Johnson on November 1 ordered the cessation of all bombardment of North Vietnam.

In the two-year interval between the time that Ronning returned from Hanoi with the conditional offer to negotiate and Johnson's acceptance of similar terms which in effect meant cessation of the bombing, tens of thousands of Vietnamese and American lives had been lost.

After the death of Chester Ronning in 1984 at the age of ninety, Audrey and I happened to meet Bill Bundy at a reception in New York. He had by then retired from government and was serving on the Board of Directors of the Council on Foreign Relations. He told us he had felt guilty for a long time about how he had dealt with Ronning and handled his report when he met with him that June night in Ottawa. He said he should have given more weight to the proposal that Ronning had brought back from Hanoi. He had wanted to apologize to Ronning, but since that was not possible, he was glad that he could at least express his regrets to Audrey.

In his book *In Retrospect*, published in 1995, Robert McNamara discussed the Ronning mission:

> The Canadians considered Pham Van Dong's message a bona fide peace move; to them, it seemed an advance beyond Hanoi's earlier insistence on U.S. acceptance of the Four Points before negotiations. Many in Washington did not agree. They distrusted Pearson's and Ronning's prior open criticism of Washington's Vietnam policy and felt Pham Van Dong's words contained deliberate and clever ambiguities—for example, the

use of the word talks rather than negotiations seemed to imply only preliminary contacts, not substantive discussions. The president, moreover,
hesitated to stop the bombing again without some reciprocal concession
from Hanoi. Thus, the Johnson administration refused to authorize another pause. In retrospect, we were mistaken in not having Ronning at
least probe the meaning of Pham Van Dong's words more deeply.

Reviewing the years of bombing which continued intermittently into the
Nixon years even as inconclusive peace approaches were being made to
North Vietnam, McNamara commented in his book: "Of one thing I am
certain: we failed miserably to integrate and coordinate our diplomatic and
military actions as we searched for an end to the war."

The Senate study in October 1972 on the bombing of North Vietnam based
on the revelations in the Pentagon Papers concluded: "This study calls into
serious question the efficacy of strategic and interdiction bombing against a
highly motivated guerrilla enemy in an underdeveloped country. Bombing
appears capable of raising the costs of war to an enemy in such a situation,
but it cannot be depended on to weaken his will or to substantially reduce
his activity by interdicting his supplies. Compared to the damage to U.S.
prestige and the internal division created by the bombing policy, its meager
gains must be seriously questioned."

It was a statement that also had relevance to the record of failed bombing policies in Cambodia during the Nixon administration and the limitations as well as adverse effects encountered by the George W. Bush administration in the employment of air power in Iraq and Afghanistan.

27
CAMBODIA

From the 1950s the densely forested border regions of Cambodia were intermittently utilized by the Vietcong, and later by the North Vietnamese Army (NVA), as infiltration routes and bases for supporting operations in South Vietnam. To impede the Communists, the United States alternatively employed diplomacy, bombing, and covert incursions until finally, in frustration at failure to seal the border, President Nixon ordered the invasion of Cambodia in April 1970. American bombing incurred deep resentment among the Cambodian people. This became a major factor in the military victory in 1975 and ascendancy of Pol Pot's Khmer Rouge regime, whose genocidal purges would take the lives of about 1.57 million people.

Prince Norodom Sihanouk in the preceding twenty-five years was the central political figure in the struggle for dominance in Cambodia. The prince alternately juggled and played off the contending ambitions of the French, Americans, Vietnamese, Russians, and Chinese while striving to keep his country intact, neutral, and free of war. In the end he failed and languished in Peking in exile.

I first interviewed Sihanouk in May 1950. He was then king of Cambodia living in his Phnom Penh palace, an improbable mile-square fairy-tale cluster of golden edifices with tall spires and roofs inlaid with colored tiles styled in the architecture of the ancient Khmers. The twenty-eight-year-old monarch, educated in France, dynamic in personality, expert horseman, a patron of the arts with a penchant for writing poetry and composing music, received Audrey and me just several weeks after he had dissolved his government's cabinet and taken on himself the duties of the premiership. He would abdicate in March 1955 as king in favor of his father, Morodom Suramarit, taking the title of prince, so that he could function more freely in a new, broader political role. Sihanouk was then very much the hero and father figure in his country of 3.5 million people. It was a beleaguered nation, plagued by native Issarak guerrillas and infiltrating Vietnamese Communist forces.

In Phnom Penh, attired in a white linen suit, Sihanouk received Audrey and me at dinner in the Feast Hall and entertained us with his Royal Ballet. Audrey and I had just arrived in his capital from Saigon, where I was posted as the Associated Press correspondent. After dinner the king invited us into his luxurious private apartments, furnished in Western style, for a discussion. In retrospect, given how in the next two decades he would flip from political links with France and the United States to alliance with the North Vietnamese and China, the interview he granted proved most extraordinary. The king spoke to us of his dissatisfaction with the treaty he had been compelled to sign with France in November under which, like Vietnam and Laos, Cambodia was granted only nominal independence within the French Union. Under the treaty, France retained control of defense and foreign policy with special rights for French interests in the economic and cultural spheres. "I regard the treaty as only a basis for further negotiation toward greater independence for Cambodia," he said indignantly. But it was Ho Chi Minh, the king said, who posed the greatest threat to the future independence of his country. If his Viet Minh triumphed in Vietnam, he said, it "would mean the end of national sovereignty for Cambodia. The Ho Chi Minh government would set up a puppet Cambodian regime." He told us that some 3,000 Viet Minh had already infiltrated into Cambodia from Vietnam, occupying a broad zone along the border, and were receiving arms through a corridor to Thailand. Sihanouk's French-officered army of about 6,000 men was battling the Viet Minh and a faction of the Issarak Cambodian guerrillas who were allied with the Communists. Formed after the defeat of the Japanese in World War II, the Issaraks, whose name is a contraction meaning "League for the Independence of Cambodia," were operating in diverse groups: some working with the Viet Minh, others committed solely to fighting the French, and some simply as bandits. As a group they were the forerunners of the Khmer Rouge Communists, which, led by Pol Pot, would seize control of the country in 1975.

After our meeting with Sihanouk, we returned to Saigon in a French military convoy. The heavily armed truck convoy sped across the lovely, brilliantly hued Cambodian landscape and through the villages at frighteningly high speed to lessen the chances of being ambushed by marauding guerrillas. En route we stopped for several days in Siem Reap, adjoining Angkor, the ancient Khmer capital. We were the lone guests in the Grand Hotel, a hostelry dating from the nineteenth century. The hotel, adjacent to the magnificent temple towers of Angkor rising out of the jungle, was guarded while we were there by a cordon of French troops. In the morning we strolled through the imposing ruins of Angkor built by the Khmer Empire's King

Suryavarmen between A.D. 1113 and 1150 to honor the Hindu god Vishnu. We came upon a crumbled temple which was being reconstructed by Cambodian workers stone by stone under the supervision of a French archaeologist. We asked the archaeologist if they were rebuilding according to illustrations from some ancient scroll. He shrugged and laughed. "These are descendants of the Khmers," he said, "and they are fitting the stones in place only by their ancient instincts."

I returned to Phnom Penh in September 1951 for an interview with Sihanouk in his palace. The prince told me of his latest frantic efforts to maintain the integrity of his kingdom. Three battalions of his army, newly equipped with American arms, were combating mounting Viet Minh infiltration. The prince was reaching out to the United States for additional military assistance and also political backing in his stalemated negotiations with France for greater independence.

I soon learned in speaking to other Cambodian leaders that there was also something of an odd flap in relations with the United States which stemmed from a story published in March in Washington newspapers. The story reported that Sihanouk was sending a white elephant to President Harry Truman as a gesture of goodwill. In Washington, Truman as head of the Democratic Party was being teased about receiving the gift of an elephant, symbol of the Republican Party. The widely circulated story was funny to everyone except the Cambodians, who felt that the world was enjoying a bad joke at their expense. A senior Cambodian official, Sinn Choi, told me that the elephant affair might have unfortunate political consequences. He explained: "Many years ago, when Cambodia was one of the most powerful kingdoms of Asia, vassal states were required to send white elephants to the king as a form of tribute. So you can see," he said pointedly, "what sending a white elephant to President Truman might mean to the Cambodian people." Fearing protest demonstrations, Phnom Penh newspapers were told by the palace to stop printing Washington dispatches about the affair. While Sihanouk was sending an elephant to Truman, I was told privately that the original story published in Washington had no basis in fact. But given all the publicity, the king had decided, nevertheless, to send a young elephant, not white, to the president as a gesture of goodwill.

While checking rumors circulating in the capital that an elephant had already been shipped, I obtained, by means not to be disclosed, copies of the cable traffic between State Department offices in Indochina and Washington detailing the extraordinary saga of the elephant. The tale had a sad ending, but there were hilarious aspects which provided me with a welcome respite from reporting the horrors of the Indochina war. Herewith the exchanges:

March 8, 1951
From: American Legation Saigon
To: Don V. Catlett
U.S. Charge d'Affaires, Phnom Penh

All Saigon Newspapers carry White House announcement that King of Cambodia will send white elephant to President Truman on occasion of Cambodian Minister Nong Kimny's arrival in Washington. President quoted as being appreciative and intending to give elephant to Washington Zoo. Please confirm without giving any encouragement to Cambodians if offer and acceptance not yet firm.

Minister Donald Heath

March 8, 1951
Minister Donald Heath

Dear Mr. Minister:
I have just received your telegram regarding the story in the Saigon press and I must give a little background to clarify the situation. On February 3, Mr. Brady called me by radio from Saigon to say that the aircraft carrier U.S.S. *Windham Bay* was leaving Saigon that evening and that it could take an elephant which he understood had been promised as a gift to President Truman. After a morning of telephoning and conferences, it developed that his majesty, although most helpful, even to the extent of being prepared to give an elephant under the circumstances, had not previously promised one. It is still a mystery as to who promised it. In any case, it was impossible to find an elephant that day and the project was dropped. The aide of his majesty assured me if they could have advance notice, they would be glad to make an elephant available to us in the event that another U.S. vessel called at Saigon. Nothing was said about a white elephant.
Shortly after the receipt of your telegram, Prince Monissara came to inform me of the story in the Saigon newspapers. He asked me to make it clear that although his majesty holds to his promise of an elephant, he cannot give a white one, as they are non-existent, and in any case, have a particular significance to this country. The Cambo-

dian government is naturally embarrassed by the story and somewhat irritated by the jocular tone used in the Saigon press.

I, too, am embarrassed by this story, as the natural reaction of a Cambodian is to suppose that the so-called release from the White House was based on information from this legation, which is not the case. Would you please inform Washington that: (1.) His majesty has never promised a white elephant; (2.) His majesty has no intention of sending an elephant at the time Nong Kimny arrives; (3). Both the Cambodian government and myself would like information as to the sources of the story.

Sincerely yours,
Don V. Catlett

March 16, 1951
From: State Department
To: Saigon Legation

Elephant story probably evolved from item in Washington newspapers apparently based on conversation between State Department officers and Washington Zoo after receipt of Navy dispatch. Charge d'affaires at Phnom Penh should inform Cambodia: 1. No offer from Cambodian government of elephant white or otherwise transmitted to Charge d'Affaires or any authority to President. 2. No White House release was issued and no comment made by the President. For your information, Isthmian Lines offers free transportation Saigon to New York of elephant.

Acheson

June 11, 1951
U.S. Charge d'Affaires
Phnom Penh, Cambodia

His Excellency Neal Phleng
Minister of Foreign Affairs
Phnom Penh, Cambodia

I have the honor to enclose a letter from Minister Donald Heath addressed to his Majesty Norodom Sihanouk Varman accepting on behalf of President Truman the gift of an elephant which his majesty has graciously made. I am now attempting to make arrangements for transporting the elephant to the United States.

Don V. Catlett

June 11, 1951
To: American Legation, Saigon
From U.S. Charge d'Affaires, Phnom Penh

Isthmian Lines agent here has been instructed to arrange transportation from Phnom Penh to Manila where, it would be embarked on *Steel Worker* for United States. As elephant should be in Manila by June 30 only possibility get it there in time is embark elephant on *Felix Roussel* leaving Saigon June 17.

Catlett

June 11, 1951
Mr. John Getz
American Legation
Saigon

It is impossible to send the elephant to Saigon by river boat in time to embark him on the *Felix Roussel.* Truck seems the only answer.

The elephant is seven years old, about six feet high at the shoulders and weight I would guess 4,200 pounds. He is a male but is supposed to be pretty well behaved. As for food, he eats sugar cane (impractical for a long voyage), corn (although he should not be fed that as a sole item of diet), rice shoots and paddy.

The Cambodians can't seem to say how much he eats per day, but perhaps the zoo people in Saigon will know from his age and size.

Sincerely,
Don V. Catlett

June 17, 1951
From: American Legation, Saigon
To: Charge d'Affaires, Phnom Penh

Captain *Felix Roussel* refuses to take elephant. Investigating possibility of air transport from Phnom Penh to Manila.

Heath

[*Editor's note:* The plan to ship the elephant by air was abandoned after the Cambodians advised Catlett that the elephant would get airsick.]

July 2, 1951
Societe Indochinoise de Transports
Phnom Penh, Cambodia
Monsieur Catlett
Charge d'Affaires, American
Phnom Penh, Cambodia

Dear Monsieur:

Relative to our talk Saturday concerning the hiring of one of our trucks to transport a young elephant from Phnom Penh to Saigon. The undersigned is informed by a person who has worked several years with elephants that these animals are very insane and their mahouts (caretakers) are not always their masters. Considering these risks of damage to our truck without counting any other consequences, I regret I must withdraw my promise of providing you with transport for the elephant.

Sincerely,
V. Geiler

July 19, 1951
American Legation, Saigon
Charge d'Affaires, Phnom Penh

Dear Mr. Catlett:

Several worthy appearing projects and plans for transport of the elephant have fallen through, but we think that we finally have the answer. The French ship, *Darlac,* will leave Saigon July 26 with elephant and with his feed for 50 to 55 days. The ship will arrive in Singapore July 30 and the elephant will stay at the local zoo until Aug. 5. The elephant will leave Singapore on the *Steel Surveyor* on Aug. 5 with one stop at Durban, South Africa, will sail around the Cape, arriving in New York on or about Sept. 1.

Since the elephant must arrive in Saigon early on July 24, it may be necessary to transport the elephant by the Legation truck. (We hope the fears of the Phnom Penh truckers are groundless!)

Following the advice of the veterinarian, we are planning on sending the following foods with the elephant based approximately on 50 days of travel: 1,000 kilos each of rough rice, corn, rice, 2,500 kilos of rice straw and 100 kilos of banana trunks. A sturdy cage will be constructed here.

Is it too early to congratulate ourselves?

Sincerely yours,
Roman L. Lotsberg.

July 21, 1951
From: U.S. Charge d'Affaires, Phnom Penh
To: American Legation, Saigon

Elephant leaving Phnom Penh Sunday morning by truck. Mahout accompanying elephant speaks only Cambodian and is to be taken to Cambodian office in Saigon which will take charge of him and send him back to Phnom Penh.

Catlett

July 22, 1951
From: American Legation, Saigon
To: U.S. Charge d'Affaires, Phnom Penh

According all opinions mahout must accompany elephant to States. Present mahout has sick mother and refuses stay Saigon beyond tomorrow morning. Need mahout with passport latest early Friday.

Heath

July 26, 1951
From: U.S. Charge d'Affaires Phnom Penh
To: American Legation Saigon

Cambodian government has found mahout but question arises of incidental expenses on trip in addition to food and lodging on ship. For example will need warm clothing in New York while awaiting return vessel. If Isthmian Line or Legation can take care such expenses mahout willing to go. Cambodian government taking care of his family during his absence. Advise urgently whether he should proceed.

Catlett

July 26, 1951
From American Legation, Saigon
To: U.S. Charge d'Affaires, Phnom Penh

Send mahout with passport fastest means. Cost transportation, clothing available here. Cambodian Embassy will assume responsibility New York.

Heath

July 27, 1951
Miss Thelma M. Jensen
American Legation, Saigon

Dear Thelma:

I am sorry that we were not able to send the mahout down by this morning's plane because we had passport trouble. I'm also sorry about the original delay in finding a mahout, but the Cambodians didn't find one until Thursday morning who was willing to go to the United States.

With best regards and hoping that you and I have heard the last of l'Affaire du Elephant.

Don V. Catlett

July 29, 1951
From American Legation, Saigon
To: American Consul General, Singapore

Cambodian elephant arriving Singapore 30 July for transshipment. Mahout who speaks only Cambodian arriving Singapore via Malayan Airways today.

Heath

August 21, 1951
U.S. Charge d'Affaires,
Phnom Penh, Cambodia

His Excellency, Var Kamel
Ministry of Foreign Affairs
Phnom Penh, Cambodia

Excellency:

I have the honor to refer to our telephone conversation of today and to give as follows the information regarding the transportation of the elephant which was sent as a gift to President Truman by His Majesty Norodom Sihanouk.

The elephant was embarked on the S.S. *Surveyor* at Singapore on August 5, 1951 to proceed to the United States via the Panama Canal. All arrangements have been made to receive the elephant and to transport it from New York to Washington. There is accordingly no necessity for a representative of the Cambodian Legation to be present, but there will undoubtedly be some publicity given the arrival of the elephant and a Cambodian representative might be useful in this connection.

Don V. Catlett

Sept. 8, 1951
From: American Legation, Saigon
To: U.S. Charge D'Affaires, Phnom Penh

State Department informed Cambodian elephant died aboard ship off Capetown, South Africa, Sept. 6. Burial at sea. Mahout will be returned Indochina from United States. Please inform Cambodian government. Formal regrets will be pouched.

Gullion

Sept. 8, 1951
From: U.S. Charge D'Affaires, Phnom Penh
To: State Department, Washington

Norodom Sihanouk Varman, King of Cambodia, expressed regrets today when he heard of the death of the elephant he was sending to President Truman. The young elephant died on board a ship on the way to New York.

"I regret very much that the gift did not reach President Truman," the King said, and I shall have to offer another gift of value to the President, but one which is more transportable. I am thinking of offering him a statue from Angkor."

Catlett

The elephant story won great plaudits from my editors. It was published in the *New York Times* with the text of the exchanges of cables as well as in other newspapers across the United States, in many instances with bold feature headlines and accompanying cartoons. It was a very funny story, but I came to regret it. Sihanouk complained to the White House about the publication of his cables. The State Department investigated the leak, singled out the Foreign Service officer who had given me access to the cables, and reprimanded him for a breach of security. I was appalled.

When I returned to the United States in 1951, I went to the State Department and discussed the elephant affair with an assistant secretary of state. I told him that I had been given access to the cables without restrictions, but I had not told the diplomat that I intended to publish the text of the exchanges of cables. The secretary accepted my regrets and said he would lift the reprimand from the diplomat's personnel file.

In later years I recalled the story of the elephant in a journalism manual on ethics and in lectures to students at the schools of journalism at Columbia University and the University of Missouri, citing the mistake. The point: When a source provides confidential information which if published will endanger the source, the reporter has an obligation to inform the source of the intention to publish and to protect the source in every ethical manner possible. I also regretted very much what happened to the other victim: the elephant.

28

SIHANOUK BESIEGED

During the early 1960s, I revisited Cambodia several times, and as I wandered through the pleasant byways of Phnom Penh, I would at times recall the funny, tragic "*l'affaire du elephant*" with nostalgia. It marked for me one of the few periods of cordial relations between Prince Sihanouk and the United States. The relationship thereafter deteriorated into violent confrontation. Unexpectedly, I became directly involved in Prince Sihanouk's angry exchanges with Washington.

On August 6, 1965, the *New York Times* published a United Press dispatch quoting military intelligence sources in Saigon as saying that the North Vietnamese had moved the headquarters of their 325th NVA division from South Victnam to the extreme northeastern corner of Cambodia to escape bombing by American and South Vietnamese aircraft. The Cambodians denied the report, determined not to allow the United States or the South Vietnamese any pretext for crossing the border in pursuit. At this juncture, an invitation came to me from Prince Sihanouk through the Cambodian ambassador at the United Nations challenging me to check out the report of the presence of the 325th North Vietnamese division by touring the specified border area. It was in a region to which no Western observer had been for years.

My invitation arrived three months after Sihanouk, breaking diplomatic relations with the United States, had expelled the American military and economic aid missions. The prince acted five days after South Vietnamese planes bombed the Cambodian village of Khum Dar, a hamlet situated in open terrain two miles inside the border. Earlier, Sihanouk had protested repeatedly to Washington about bombing attacks on Cambodian border areas by American and South Vietnamese planes as well as ground incursions by South Vietnamese troops searching for Vietcong and North Vietnamese bases.

It was well known that Vietcong forces were slipping occasionally into Cambodian frontier areas to evade pursuit or to outflank some South Vietnamese position near the border. It was also evident that it was impossible even for a force twenty times the size of Sihanouk's army of thirty thousand to close the border entirely to such incursions. But if the report that the 325th Division had moved its headquarters into Cambodia was accurate, it would mean that the North Vietnamese for the first time had established a major operations base there. This would give the South Vietnamese and American forces cause enough for a large-scale cross-border strike.

I eagerly accepted Sihanouk's invitation—American correspondents at the time were barred from Cambodia—fully aware that it would be a tricky undertaking laden with propaganda pitfalls. Sihanouk was playing a game on both sides of the political divide. I had learned that Sihanouk, desperate to forestall any spillover of the Vietnam War into his kingdom, was secretly negotiating with the National Liberation Front (NLF), the political arm of the Vietcong, to obtain a guarantee of the inviolability of his country's borders. As an inducement he was dangling political recognition of the NLF.

General Westmoreland, learning of Sihanouk's invitation, strongly advised me against making the trip, warning that I would be used as a propaganda tool by the Cambodians, who he maintained were concealing Communist use of the border region for strikes into South Vietnam. Unspoken was the general's uneasiness about the possibility that I might report on the secret CIA and Special Forces reconnaissance missions being undertaken in Cambodia. I rebutted Westmoreland's advice, arguing that at a minimum it would be useful to survey the terrain features of the border region so as to assess the nature of the strategic problem. Westmoreland then provided me with one of his staff officers to brief me on the locations of suspected Communist operations. In fact, what I was embarking on turned out to be a prelude to the covert American B-52 bombings of suspected Communist sanctuaries in Cambodia, which would become a major issue in American politics.

In Saigon, my American briefing officer paced before a wall map pointing to forests near the Cambodian border where he believed major North Vietnamese and Vietcong bases were located. He traced the possible supply routes from these bases to where the Vietcong guerrillas were operating in South Vietnam. Above the twisting, poorly defined Cambodian border, largely hidden under thick jungle foliage canopy, U.S. reconnaissance planes crammed with electronic gear had been searching ceaselessly for evidence of North Vietnamese and Vietcong activity. The briefing officer quoted his South Vietnamese sources extensively but conceded that American intelligence independently had no hard evidence that there were major North Vietnamese bases in Cambodia. I then flew to Phnom Penh and spent my first days there interviewing the British and French military attachés. They told me that they had failed in many investigations to establish that there were major Vietcong or North Vietnamese sanctuaries in the Cambodian border region or that the country was a route for the delivery of equipment and supplies to the Vietcong. They did pinpoint areas for me where there might be such activity but noted that the forested regions were so impenetrable that they could not be sure of what might be going on there.

On October 4, I was driven with military escort to the coastal town of Sihanoukville, northwest of the Vietnamese border, where my guide turned out to be no less than the Cambodian defense minister, Lieutenant General Lon Nol, who two years later would stage a coup overthrowing Sihanouk as head of state. Lon Nol was waiting for me beside a helicopter in an open field outside the port town. The general spread out maps on which I pointed out areas I wished to visit. These were locations where Western briefing officers and the media had reported Communist activity. We then mapped out an itinerary through the border jungles and set out on a two-day trek by helicopter, jeep, and on foot.

By helicopter we surveyed the border between Krek and Minot, just to the north of the Parrot's Beak, which juts into South Vietnam's Tay Ninh Province. American intelligence officers speculated that the Central Office for South Vietnam (COSVN), the unit coordinating North Vietnamese and Vietcong operations in the South, was based in Tay Ninh Province. What was believed to be its key operational area was labeled Zone C, extending from northwest of Saigon to the Cambodian border. The zone was being heavily bombed by American and South Vietnamese planes. I asked Lon Nol to make an unscheduled visit to Krek so that I could travel along Provincial Route Number 22 to a border crossing where American intelligence had received reports of wheel marks indicating Vietcong traffic in and out of Zone C. Our helicopter landed at Krek, and by jeep we drove to the Cambodian army post of Trapcang, about two miles from the frontier. Beyond that point no Western observer was known to have been permitted to go in at least several years. The general, whom I found to be a rather nervous, emotional man, agreed to proceed after he called in an overhead cover of two Cambodian Sky Raider fighter planes, since we were entering an area which was repeatedly bombed and strafed by South Vietnamese planes. The road was passable for another mile and then ended at an old destroyed bridge. Escorted by armed peasant militia, we picked our way across the stream over a temporary footbridge made up of loose tree branches and then followed a foot path through the jungle until we came to the barbed wire fence of a small Cambodian army installation, Poste Smach, sixty yards from the frontier.

The old Route 22 was not passable beyond, and it was obvious that the tale of fresh wheel marks had no basis. That morning at Poste Smach we heard the sounds of bombs exploding nearby in Zone C. Militiamen at the post told me that it was the fourth such raid by South Vietnamese or American planes in ten days. Later I learned that the bombing we heard that day had been part of the start of a sustained campaign ordered by the Johnson administration in which, from 1965 to 1968, 2,565 sorties were flown by tactical aircraft dropping 214 tons of bombs along that section of the border.

At Bo Kheo, in the remote northeastern corner of the border, we made another unscheduled landing at my request, about twenty-five miles from the frontier, beside Provincial Route Number 19. We inspected an airfield which had been described in news agency reports quoting American intelligence sources as a Communist air base. We found the airfield heavily overgrown with brush. It obviously had not been used for years and could not have accommodated the North Vietnamese transport planes which the report said had been spotted landing there. Route 19 was cut and impassable for vehicles where it was shown on maps to cross the jungle-covered border. One intelligence report had said that forty trucks had been spotted on the highway crossing the border. From the air we surveyed the area in which the 325th North Vietnamese division was said to be operating. It was a dense, uninhabited, and trackless forest in the extreme northeastern corner of the border region. We saw no evidence of human activity, and there was no observable trail into the forest. It seemed most unlikely that any sizable military unit could be operating there.

As we moved along the border, we encountered groups of Vietnamese refugees who had crossed into Cambodia to escape bombing and strafing by American and South Vietnamese aircraft. Near the Cambodia frontier post at Oyadao, I spoke to a Vietnamese rice farmer, named Nguyen Dieu, whose family had fled with seventy-two other families from their village of Thangduc in Pleiku Province, about eight miles from the Cambodian border. A gaunt, fifty-one-year-old peasant, Dieu spoke with more fatalism than rancor about the death of his village and the flight of its thirteen hundred inhabitants after an attack by American jet planes on August 7. For Nguyen Dieu, the war against the Vietcong had been until that day a nebulous happening beyond the horizon of his rice fields, although he had felt the pinch when his two eldest sons were drafted into the South Vietnamese army. Beginning in May, however, Vietcong occasionally came into the village to buy food. The war closed in when the Vietcong emerged in force from the forests in July and besieged Duc Co, two and a half miles west of the village.

South Vietnamese troops and a U.S. Special Forces unit were then stationed in the post. To reinforce the besieged post a South Vietnamese paratrooper battalion was dropped into Duc Co. People in Nguyen Dieu's village could hear the sounds of battle only distantly. Suddenly, in August bombers appeared overhead. "They were bombing villages around Duc Co," Nguyen said. "Then planes bombed and fired their guns at my village. There were no Vietcong in Thangduc. People were killed. I do not know how many. Everyone began to run into the forest." Other villagers were killed and wounded in the forest by the planes which followed them bombing and strafing, but Nguyen did not know how many. He said he never saw any Vietcong after the bombing. In the forest, Nguyen gathered his wife and five of his children. Their fourteen-year-old daughter was still missing, but he decided to join the group of families which had elected to go westward to the Cambodian border. Between August 8 and 14, six groups of 73 men, 75 women, and 243 children crossed the frontier into Cambodia. They walked along Route 19, carrying a few household possessions, until it became a footpath into the forest on which they encountered Cambodian border guards. At the time there were reports from Saigon, apparently based on aerial observation, of Vietcong movement across the border. Fleeing refugees may have been mistaken for Vietcong. Near Oyadao, Nguyen Dieu built a lean-to from bamboo and straw to shelter his family and their dog, which followed them from Thangduc. "We do not want to go back until there is peace," he told me.

Our circuit along the border bespoke the obvious. As of October 1965, there were no major North Vietnamese sanctuaries in Cambodia, as I reported in a series of stories to the *Times*. Vietcong units certainly, as evidenced by what I was told at Oyadao, were ducking in and out of the border region. By observation it also seemed obvious that the bombing strategy being employed along the border would be of limited effectiveness in combating the Vietcong or halting North Vietnamese infiltration. Precise spotting of targets by aerial reconnaissance in the vast forests with their thick canopies of foliage was nigh on impossible. The electronic gear employed was of little help. This is what had impelled the American military to begin deployment of teams of Special Forces and the CIA, usually composed of a mix of American and Vietnamese, to reconnoiter into Cambodia. Over the years in the highly secretive operation more than one thousand such reconnaissance missions were undertaken by teams under the operational code names of "Daniel Boone" and "Silver House." The team members crossed into Cambodia in civilian clothes and without identification. They were told that if they were captured there would be no negotiation to obtain their release. Families of those killed or captured were told that they were lost in operations on the Vietnamese side of the border. This secrecy was, in part, political so as not to give substance to Sihanouk's complaints that his border was being violated.

When I returned to Phnom Penh from the frontier, I was received by Prince Norom Kantol, a courtly, soft-spoken aristocrat who was premier and foreign minister. He vigorously denied that Cambodian territory was being used by the Vietcong and said that the United States shared in responsibility for the hundreds of South Vietnamese incursions. "It is to be feared," he told me, "that these aggressions must be a prelude to an attack against our country in the near future." The prince, like other Cambodians I interviewed, was convinced, despite denials by American officials, that an invasion of their country by the South Vietnamese was impending. The worst fears of the Cambodians did come to pass in the next years. When I left Phnom Penh, I knew that Sihanouk and his countrymen would use every means open to them and make any alliance simply to shield their country from any destructive foreign intrusion.

During my interview with Prince Kantol, he told me that Sihanouk was absent, on a trip to their Communist allies. He had already visited Peking and was en route to Moscow. Kantol was not aware that the trip had resulted in a political disaster and that Sihanouk was on the way home in a state of rage. Upon arrival in Phnom Penh, Sihanouk took to the Cambodian Radio and made a two-hour speech, on October 17, in which he said that the Soviet Union had humiliated him in a manner that was "a virtual provocation for the rupture of relations between the two countries." He said that his long friendship with Soviet leaders had ended because of their curt cancellation of his scheduled state visit to Moscow. He described how the Soviet ambassador in Pyongyang, the North Korean capital, had handed him a note on October 8 that said the Soviet leaders were "very busy" and would be unable to meet him as planned. The Russians offered to allow him to cross Soviet territory on the way to other Communist countries in Eastern Europe and suggested that he arrange another visit to Moscow. The prince said the slight was "absolutely inexcusable and irreparable" and that he had called off his entire Eastern European tour, since he was no longer interested in visiting countries in the Soviet camp.

The Soviet snub was obviously a payback for the declarations made by Sihanouk in Peking in which he strongly endorsed the foreign policy and ideological positions taken by Mao Zedong contrary to those adopted by the Soviet Union. Sihanouk said that while in Peking he had been promised additional aid, including arms. The fallout with Moscow was costly to Siha-nouk. The Russians were the major contributor of aid, particularly for de-velopment projects. In professing neutrality, the prince had been using the Soviet Union, and to lesser extent, France, as a counterweight in his relations with China. Sihanouk was now more dependent than ever on China as his principal mentor and ally.

A fter my return to Hong Kong, I received a personal letter from Siha-nouk, written in French, dated December 5, 1965, which was indicative of the prince's continuing frenetic balancing act. He said in part:

> Certainly, the United States should be showing greater understanding of a country like Cambodia, which has succeeded despite American in-trigues [aimed at overthrowing its national government] in effectively keeping Communism under control internally. This is what the Admin-istration of your country attempts to do. In fact, through its brutal pol-icy, its lack of understanding of Asian realities, and its support of dictato-rial and unpopular regimes, it brings about the contrary effect. It creates Communists where they do not exist and multiplies them where they are not numerous. The breaking of relations between our two countries is not, therefore, a "contradiction," neither on my part (since I have no reason to reproach myself) nor on the part of the United States, which is less interested in containing Communism than in creating docile allies in its struggle against China.

The prince referred me to his signed editorial in the Cambodian maga-zine *Kambuja,* a copy of which he sent me, in which he accused the Central Intelligence Agency of attempts to topple him from power. Sihanouk was al-luding to a failed army coup attempt against him in February 1959. He said of the Johnson administration: "They have failed to understand that if Com-munism is to be contained they should assist in forging a cordon of states, strong in their nationalist convictions, irreproachably independent and gen-uinely free; states which have at their hand stubborn intractable leaders, as de Gaulle in France and (I will add without false modesty) Sihanouk in Cam-bodia."

I had already become aware of Sihanouk's list of heroes simply by stroll-ing through his capital, an attractive prosperous, city of a half million res-idents. He honored them ceremonially by anointing some of the principal thoroughfares, such as Charles de Gaulle Avenue, Josip Broz Tito Boulevard, and Jawaharlal Nehru Boulevard. Once, taking a walk along the tree-lined streets, I had paused at a small café on the Boulevard of the USSR for a cup

of tea and listened to a small string orchestra play the prince's latest musical composition, the *Bolero Twist*. I now assumed, after the debacle of his
canceled trip to Moscow, that the name of that pleasant boulevard would be
changed.

In early January 1966, I covered the three-day state visit of Charles de Gaulle
to Cambodia. I was one of several reporters in the large entourage accompanying the president. The occasion provided Sihanouk with what he regarded
as his greatest moment of glory. It was also an occasion when the United
States was offered an opportunity, which it did not exploit, to open peace
negotiations with the North Vietnamese. In a speech delivered before more
than 100,000 people in Phnom Penh's National Sports Stadium, the French
president appealed to the United States to withdraw its forces from Vietnam.
He said that the Vietnam conflict was threatening world peace and was "increasingly coming closer to China" and becoming "increasingly provocative
in the eyes of the Soviet Union." He said the opening of peace negotiations
depended upon acceptance by the United States of an advance commitment
"to repatriate its forces within a suitable and determined period." De Gaulle
spoke after meeting with Nguyen Thuong, chief of North Vietnam's diplomatic mission in Cambodia, in the Palais Khemarin within the Palais Royal
compound where the president was staying. His diplomatic aides took other
soundings with envoys of North Vietnam and the National Liberation Front.
The French diplomats told me later that Hanoi might find withdrawal during a period of two years from the issuance of such declaration by the United
States as an acceptable basis for the opening of peace negotiations.

In his speech in the Sports Stadium, de Gaulle, erect in a tan summer
uniform, spoke with sweeping gestures to an audience of thousands, which
cheered him wildly. Seated on a bench behind the rostrum, I followed his remarks in the official text and noted that he rarely departed from it, although
he hardly glanced at his own copy. In a voice laden with emotion, after citing
the friendship of France and the United States over two centuries, he urged
Washington to follow the example he set in withdrawing from rebellious
Algeria, France's former colony, saying: "In view of the power, wealth and
influence at present attained by the United States, the act of renouncing[,]
in its turn, a distant expedition once it appears unprofitable and unjustifi-
able[,] and of substituting for it an international arrangement organizing the
peace and development of an important region of the world, will not, in the

final analysis, involve anything that could injure its pride, interfere with its ideals and jeopardize its interests." The French president's emotional appeal did not move the Johnson administration.

From Phnom Penh I traveled with de Gaulle to Angkor. To celebrate the visit of his hero, Sihanouk transformed the temple enclave into a fantasy of light and sound, his Royal Ballet performing before the great temple. Upon leaving Cambodia, de Gaulle rendered homage to Sihanouk for his struggle to safeguard the territorial integrity of his country and its neutrality. Sihanouk, however, found in the next year that those twin goals were incompatible.

In 1967, in one of his ideological swings, after years of bitter animosity, Sihanouk turned once again to the United States. The situation on the ground had changed radically, and there was no longer any doubt that the North Vietnamese were infiltrating into Cambodia and had in alliance with the Khmer Rouge occupied large areas of the country, particularly in the northeast. Increasingly concerned, looking everywhere for help, the prince made overtures to the United States. In October 1967 he invited Jacqueline Kennedy to visit the temples at Angkor. I presumed he withdrew or apologized to her for his public remark uttered during one of his rages against the United States professing that he did not intend to mourn the death of her assassinated husband. Shortly afterward, Lyndon Johnson, hoping that Sihanouk would join in ridding his country of the Vietnamese Communists, messaged Sihanouk to the effect that Chester Bowles, the American ambassador to India, was available for a visit to Phnom Penh. Bowles had made a point of retaining good relations with Sihanouk. He had remained outspoken in his admiration of Sihanouk's independent spirit and his struggle to safeguard the neutrality and integrity of his kingdom. In 1962 he had visited the Cambodian capital and had been treated most cordially by Sihanouk. The prince responded to Johnson by extending a warm invitation to Bowles, and in January 1968 the ambassador flew from New Delhi to Phnom Penh. Sihanouk was not aware that his invitation was putting into motion a top-secret operation that would be code-named "Vesuvius."

Just prior to Bowles's departure for Phnom Penh, under the tightest security, a group of American officials and military left Saigon on two T-39 light aircraft for New Delhi to brief the ambassador on violations of the Cambodian border by the Vietnamese Communists. The group, led by Philip Habib, a veteran State Department negotiator, included Lieutenant General William de Pugh, the chief of army operations in Vietnam, and two military intelligence officers, Lieutenant Colonel William White and Major James W. Reid.

White and Reid carried with them briefing papers containing information collected in Cambodia by the Daniel Boone and Silver House teams in their cross-border forays. The papers also included data from air reconnaissance and radio intercepts, transcripts of interrogations of Vietcong deserters, and intelligence information gathered from the French rubber planter community.

Meeting with Sihanouk in Phnom Penh, Bowles displayed the maps and briefing books submitted to him in New Delhi by the Habib intelligence team. He proposed that whenever a bombing strike was to be made against North Vietnamese or Vietcong targets in the Cambodian border regions, the prince would be provided in advance with a data packet on the target area so that the prince could clear his people out of harm's way. Sihanouk agreed in strict confidence to receive what became known as the "Vesuvius Packets." But he specified that bombing must be restricted to areas uninhabited by Cambodians such as those in the northeast and asked for a guarantee that there would be no more American or South Vietnamese ground incursions. Bowles replied he could only convey the request on cessation of the ground incursions to President Johnson. It was a request never honored, but nevertheless, Vesuvius went forward in utmost secrecy.

Years later I was given the secret details of the Vesuvius operation by James Reid, a member of Habib's team, now a retired colonel of the U.S. Army Intelligence. Although the most junior member of the Habib mission, the young Major Reid became a key player in the unfolding Vesuvius operation. Reid was ideally suited for his clandestine assignment. He was fluent in French and while a Princeton exchange student at the Ecole de Sciences Politiques in Paris had gained a working knowledge of Vietnamese. When I met Reid, a tall, intense man, he was authoring elaborately illustrated art books and travel guides. He was a distinguished lecturer in cultural programs aboard cruise ships. The prize possession in his home in Hartsdale, New York, which was stunningly decorated with ancient and modern art objects, was an eighteenth-century bronze drum of Cambodia's Kha Hill tribesmen ferried discreetly to him out of Phnom Penh by the Australian military attaché.

Reid described to me for the first time the delivery and preparation of the Vesuvius Packets, to which he contributed information from his excellent French planter sources. One of the first of the packets, which were assembled in Vietnam by the intelligence wing of the MACV, contained information that the Vietcong had established a hospital hidden in the Cambodia border area to care for their troops wounded in Vietnam. Since the United

States had no diplomatic relations with Cambodia, delivery of the packets required intermediaries. Reid would deliver the packets to a contact at the American Embassy in Saigon. The ambassador, Ellsworth Bunker, in turn would pass them to the Australian ambassador, Noel St. Clair Deschamps, who would fly to Phnom Penh and deliver them personally to Sihanouk. The Australians were then representing the United States in the Cambodian capital. Prior to the Bowles mission, Deschamps had already delivered information to Sihanouk on Communist violations of the border.

Reid's most important intelligence coup was made possible by his contacts in the French community, notably rubber tree planters. When Reid first raised the question of cooperation with the French, General Westmoreland replied caustically: "Do you really believe we can rely on the French after what's happened here in the last 100 years?" But once persuaded by Reid, Westmoreland agreed in return for intelligence information provided by the planters to desist from the practice of cutting back plantation rubber trees beside trails which might serve as concealment for Vietcong ambushers. The arrangement enabled Reid to solve a puzzle bedeviling American intelligence.

It was known that food and medicine were being trucked at night from Sihanoukville, the Canadian port neighboring the Vietnamese border, with the connivance of Sihanouk and Cambodian army officers, to the Communist units operating in the border areas. Many of the supplies destined for the Communists were being unloaded from ships flying the flags of neutral countries such as Panama. But American agents could find no evidence that weapons or munitions were being unloaded and transported, particularly the devastating 122-mm rockets, bearing Chinese factory markings, used to bombard targets in South Vietnam. How were they being delivered?

This is Reid's story, told to me at his Hartsdale home, of how the puzzle was solved:

> I was invited to dinner in Saigon by the Marquis de la Garde, to whom I had been introduced by friends in Paris. I was in worn field fatigues— what a startling contrast to the elegant French. My dinner partner was Marie Georges Sauvezon, a charming, cultured French woman. She was the publisher in Saigon of the excellent French daily newspaper, *le Journal d'Extreme Orient*. At the dinner, Madame Sauvezon suggested that I come to her apartment the next day for drinks. "There would be," she said, "someone there with very interesting information."
>
> At her apartment the next day, Marie introduced me to a rubber

planter. His plantation was on the coast near Ha Tien, virtually on the Vietnamese border. He told me that one night he awoke at about 3 A.M. suffering from a headache. He went out on the terrace of his villa which was on a hill overlooking the coast. There was a full moon, and he made out movements near the beach. Intrigued, he dressed, went down, and walked several hundred yards along the hill where he was able to get a clearer view. What he saw astounded him. For there, stretching out to sea for hundreds of feet was a long line of coolies standing up to their waists in water, which was barely three feet deep in that area. Out beyond, in deeper water where the sea bed dropped sharply, was a large cargo ship, and from it a small boat was transporting weapons—apparently rockets—to the head of the human line. The first person on the line shouldered the rocket, handed it to his neighbor, and so on until it reached the shore. Apparently from that beach the weapons were transported across the border. Surveillance of the coast was tightened thereafter.

Reid left Vietnam in July 1968 for his next assignment, to attend Stanford University for advanced studies on South America before serving there as a military attaché. Prior to leaving he was presented with the Legion of Merit for "outstanding meritorious services" by General Creighton Abrams, who had succeeded Westmoreland as commander of U.S. forces in South Vietnam. The Vesuvius operation continued after his departure, although it is highly dubious that in making his compact with Bowles Sihanouk would have agreed to the magnitude of the massive B-52 bombings which ensued.

29

THE B-52 BOMBINGS

On the morning of March 18, 1969, Cambodia was shaken by sixty B-52 carpet bombings, forty-eight in the border region and twelve farther inland. The previous bombings by American tactical aircraft, which had been carried out intermittently since 1965, had failed to rid the Cambodian border region of North Vietnamese and Vietcong bases and safe havens. Communist cross-border raids had been very costly to South Vietnamese and American forces. President Nixon in response ordered the deployment of the long-range B-52s, which carried huge bomb loads, for strikes at areas where the Communist units were thought to be based. While the bombing by tactical aircraft had struck narrowly at suspected targets, the carpet bombing by the B-52s now devastated entire localities. The principal intended target was COSVN, believed to be the mobile command and control headquarters for Communist operations in South Vietnam.

In the first B-52 bombing foray, the pilots reported, from altitudes of about thirty thousand feet, that they had observed explosions which could have been ammunition and fuel depots. When a Daniel Boone reconnaissance team, of two Americans and eleven Vietnamese, landed by helicopter in an area where COSVN was thought to be operating, the team came under heavy fire, indicating that the carpet bombing had been less than totally effective. Five members of the team were killed and the leader wounded. The survivors were picked up by another helicopter in a hasty evacuation. COSVN—possibly consisting, in my view, of not much more than radios and maps in knapsacks carried by sandal-shod bearers moving from straw-thatched hut to hut—continued to be an elusive target.

The B-52 bombings were carried out covertly. The secrecy was such that William Rogers, the secretary of state, was excluded from the "need-to-know list" of American officials. On March 26 the *New York Times* reported that B-52 raids on Cambodia's Svay Rieng Province had been under consideration at the request of General Creighton Abrams, who the previous June had replaced Westmoreland. I was then supervising the Indochina coverage as foreign editor of the *Times*. The short article also stated that there were

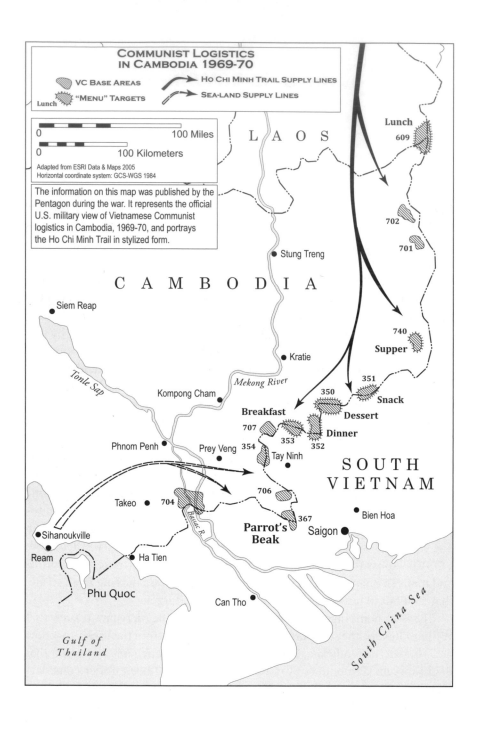

COMMUNIST LOGISTICS IN CAMBODIA 1969-70

- VC Base Areas
- "Menu" Targets
- Ho Chi Minh Trail Supply Lines
- Sea-Land Supply Lines

Lunch

0 — 100 Miles
0 — 100 Kilometers

Adapted from ESRI Data & Maps 2005
Horizontal coordinate system: GCS-WGS 1984

The information on this map was published by the Pentagon during the war. It represents the official U.S. military view of Vietnamese Communist logistics in Cambodia, 1969-70, and portrays the Ho Chi Minh Trail in stylized form.

L A O S

Lunch
609

702

701

Stung Treng

C A M B O D I A

Siem Reap

Kratie

Tonle Sap

Mekong River

740
Supper

351

350
Snack

Kompong Cham

Breakfast
707

Dessert

Dinner

Phnom Penh

Prey Veng

354
353   352

706

Tay Ninh

S O U T H
V I E T N A M

Takeo   704

Bien Hoa

Basac R.

367
Saigon

Sihanoukville

Ream

Ha Tien

Parrot's
Beak

Phu Quoc

Can Tho

Gulf of
Thailand

South China Sea

high State Department officials strongly opposed to the bombing. Among them were members of Henry Kissinger's own staff: Anthony Lake, who had served in Vietnam, Roger Morris, and William Watts. Eventually, the three resigned in protest. When questioned by a *Times* reporter, the presidential press secretary, Ronald Zeigler, said he knew of no such Abrams request reaching the president's desk. In fact, such a proposal had been made by Abrams to the Pentagon, which had then been referred to the White House. The bombings were staged after American intelligence officials thought they had pinpointed the location of COSVN in the Cambodian mid-border region, to the northwest of Saigon, west of An Loc, which had been designated as Base Area 353 and dubbed the Fishhook. Targets were selected on a basis of information received from a Vietcong deserter and aerial photographs.

The *Times* broke the story of the bombings on May 9, in a front-page article by William Beecher, the military correspondent in the Washington bureau. He reported that "American B-52 bombers in recent weeks have raided several Vietcong and North Vietnamese supply dumps and base camps in Cambodia for the first time, according to Nixon Administration sources, but Cambodia has not made any protest." Beecher reported that "Cambodian authorities were cooperating with American and South Vietnamese military men at the border, often giving them information on Vietcong and North Vietnamese movements." Evidently, the Vesuvius compact in some form was still operative, although the bombing had been extended from northeastern Cambodia to inhabited areas in the south in violation of the condition which Sihanouk contended he laid down at his 1968 meeting with Bowles. With an estimated fifty thousand North Vietnamese and their Khmer Rouge allies now in occupation of possibly one-third of Cambodia, Sihanouk, frantically looking westward for help, apparently was amenable to the bombing. Four months after the first B-52 bombing raid, Sihanouk restored diplomatic relations with the United States. In exchange he received a pledge that the United States would "respect Cambodia's independence and sovereignty within the present territorial borders." Yet still playing both sides against the middle in his struggle to preserve the integrity of his country, Sihanouk retained covert relations with Hanoi, hoping to limit North Vietnamese infiltration of Cambodian territory.

Beecher's exclusive story on the bombings did not at first raise a great furor. It was, however, one of a series of news breaks traceable to government leaks that spurred Kissinger into ordering FBI wiretaps as a means of identifying the sources. Four journalists and thirteen government officials became the targets of the wiretaps. As to just how he obtained his story,

Beecher broke a silence of thirty-six years when he spoke to a Harvard seminar in 2006. Reasoning that B-52 bombings had been carried out in Laos and in Vietnam along the Cambodian border, he laid out speculative scenarios for similar attacks against Communist base areas within Cambodia and presented them for comment to White House and State Department officials. He pieced together his story from what they told him and more substantively from what they would not deny. Commenting on Henry Kissinger's contention that the bombing operation was kept secret to safeguard American lives, Beecher observed during his seminar: "From whom was it secret? Not from the North Vietnamese on whose heads the bombs were falling. Not from officials of the Cambodian and South Vietnamese governments. It was a secret only from the Congress and the American public."

In January 1970, Sihanouk left Phnom Penh, accompanied by his wife, Monique, for a cure at a clinic on the French Riviera. He went from there on to Moscow to mend relations with the Soviet leaders, disrupted after their earlier snub of him. In his absence, in early March, Lon Nol, the defense chief, acting in tandem with Prince Sirik Matak, issued an ultimatum to the North Vietnamese and Vietcong infiltrators: Leave Cambodia or face attack. He also rallied anti-Vietnamese demonstrations across the country. Demonstrators destroyed the Vietcong and North Vietnamese diplomatic missions in Phnom Penh. Prince Sirik Matak shut down the smuggling from Sihanoukville of food, medicines, and other supplies to Vietnamese Communist units in the border areas, which had been carried on with the connivance of Cambodian army officers. Sihanouk had agreed to this smuggling operation, dubbed by American officers as the "Sihanouk Trail," in 1966 at the request of Premier Zhou Enlai when the American blockade of the Vietnamese coast and bombing of the Ho Chi Minh Trail were impeding deliveries by the Communists to their units in South Vietnam. Prince Matak then joined with Lon Nol in signing a decree ousting Sihanouk from power. The conspirators, who were in close touch with the sympathetic U.S. Embassy in Phnom Penh, cited Sihanouk's toleration of the Vietcong and North Vietnamese bases as one of the reasons for the coup.

Sihanouk was at the Moscow airport en route to Peking on March 18 when Soviet premier Alexei Kosygin, who was there to bid him farewell, informed him that he had been deposed by Lon Nol. When the Cambodian leader arrived in Peking, Zhou Enlai was waiting for him with a pledge of Chinese support if he would commit "to fight to the end." Sihanouk agreed. On March 21, Premier Pham Van Dong of North Vietnam flew to Peking to confer with Sihanouk on the prince's request. Secretly, they worked out an alliance providing for two thousand so-called advisers to be assigned to train and arm pro-Sihanouk guerrillas and the allied Khmer Rouge, use of Hanoi's supply network to deliver Chinese arms, and joint Cambodian–North Vietnamese military operations against Lon Nol's forces. Sihanouk told Wilfred Burchett, the leftist Australian journalist, that Pham Van Dong had given him an assurance that after victory Cambodia would be "independent, neutral and free of any Vietnamese presence." When Burchett told me later in the year of this compact, I thought back twenty years to the time when the young Sihanouk had told me that if Ho Chi Minh triumphed in Vietnam, the Communists would set up a puppet regime in his capital.

Sihanouk never forgave the Russians for continuing to maintain their embassy in Phnom Penh, where Lon Nol was in control, while refusing to recognize his government in exile in Peking. While living in Peking, Sihanouk conspired with the "Center," the leadership group of the Khmer Rouge, headed by Pol Pot, to gain its help in returning to power. He lived as a pampered guest in a garden villa of the old French Embassy compound, which had been taken over by the Chinese Foreign Ministry. I last saw him during a visit to Peking in 1971 at a banquet in the Great Hall of the People in honor of the visiting Communist boss of Romania, Nicolae Ceauşescu. Sihanouk was chatting with Mao's wife, Jiang Qing, when the military band struck up his composition *Nostalgia for China*.

The B-52 bombings begun in March 1969 of suspected North Vietnamese positions in Cambodia continued in what was code-named the "Menu Campaign." They were directed mainly against targets in the border region but were gradually extended much deeper into Cambodia, largely in the southwest. The Menu Campaign, initiated with the March 18 strike, which was code-named "Breakfast" —and the strikes that followed, "Lunch," "Supper," "Dinner," "Dessert," and "Snack"—ended in May after Lon Nol assumed power in Phnom Penh. A total of half a million tons of bombs were dropped.

In April 1970, the Nixon administration was confronted with these realities: The bombing campaign had failed to halt North Vietnamese infiltration into Cambodia. The military installations held by Lon Nol, now openly an American-supported ally, had come under attack by powerful North Vietnamese and Khmer Rouge forces. The Communists held five Cambodian provinces in the northeast. The Paris Peace Talks with Hanoi were stalled, and antiwar sentiment in the United States was mounting. At this juncture Nixon decided to invade Cambodia. In a television speech on the evening of April 20 he told the American people, masking the B-52 bombings and the incursions by U.S. Special Forces and those by South Vietnamese troops, that the United States had scrupulously respected Cambodia's neutrality. But now, an offensive by the Communist forces was threatening to take over the country, and the "will and character" of the United States was being challenged. He portrayed the Communist offensive as a lasting threat to the implementation of his program of "Vietnamization," under which American troops would be withdrawn in increments from Vietnam as their ground combat duties were handed to South Vietnamese forces. Nixon revealed that a joint American–South Vietnamese thrust into Cambodia was already under way with the aim of clearing out the North Vietnamese sanctuaries and destroying COSVN, which he described as the key control center for the Communist forces in South Vietnam. Once these objectives had been attained, he said, U.S. troops would be withdrawn.

Several hours before Nixon spoke, the invasion had begun with a spearhead of twelve South Vietnamese (ARVN) infantry and armored battalions totaling about 8,700 men crossing the border and attacking Communist border positions along the flanks of the Parrot's Beak, to the south of Fishhook. Three days later, "Operation Rock Crusher" was launched with eight American and six ARVN battalions crossing into Cambodia. A task force of 10,000 American troops and 5,000 ARVN, including armored units and mechanized infantry, penetrated deep into Svay Rieng Province, which embraced the Parrot's Beak, linking up with other units that had been lifted in by helicopter. By May 16, a total of 90,000 American and ARVN troops were engaged in search and destroy operations in the dense forests. In support of the ground operations, the allied air forces flew more than 14,000 attack sorties against North Vietnamese and Khmer Rouge troops and supply depots. B-52s based in Guam flew 653 bombing sorties. A U.S.-Vietnamese naval task force swept up the Mekong River opening a supply line to Phnom Penh which was being harassed by the Khmer Rouge.

Militarily, the Cambodian incursion, mounted over seventy-five days before the invasion force retired to Vietnam, was deemed a success to the extent that it attained its immediate objectives. Most large enemy units retreated inland before the onslaught, suffering 11,349 of their combatants killed and 2,328 captured according to the MACV count. The U.S losses were 284 dead, 2,339 wounded, while ARVN casualties were put at 800 dead and 3,410 wounded. Some 600 weapons and other supply depots were taken. COSVN was said to have been forced to displace west of the Mekong, disrupting its command and control of units in South Vietnam.

But it was a short-lived success for Lon Nol, who had been given no advance warning of the invasion. When Henry Kissinger finally sent Alexander Haig, his military aide, to inform him of the overall strategic plan, Lon Nol, the ever emotional general, was reduced to tears and panic upon being told that American troops would be withdrawn in July after completing their sweep of eastern Cambodia. A promise of material aid and air cover was small comfort to Lon Nol, who knew then that his forces would be shortly confronted by the larger Communist units which had retreated inland to escape the bombings. In practical terms, while the American invasion might have secured the western flank of South Vietnam, Lon Nol was being abandoned except for air support, which was of limited value.

Politically, the Cambodian invasion was a disaster for the Nixon administration. There were moves in Congress, affronted by the covert operations, to cut off funding for the Cambodian operations. College campuses exploded with massive antiwar demonstrations. The most violent was at Kent State in Ohio, where Sihanouk had once spoken to a receptive student audience. Students there hurled rocks at National Guardsmen who were using tear gas to contain the campus antiwar rally. The Guardsmen retreated before the barrage to a nearby hill. In the confusion that followed, sixty-one shots were fired into the crowd of students. When the field was cleared, two boys and two girls lay dead on the campus; eight other students were wounded. A photo of Mary Ann Vecchio screaming as she crouched over the body of a student became an icon of the antiwar movement.

It soon became apparent that the ground invasion, although it imposed heavy losses on the North Vietnamese and Khmer Rouge, had failed to effectively root them out. By 1972, an estimated eight thousand Cambodians resentful of American intervention, particularly the bombings, had rallied to the Khmer Rouge, and four North Vietnamese divisions had extended their control from the border region to much of the country. When there was an intensification of attacks on the Lon Nol forces, Nixon ordered a massive resumption of B-52 carpet bombing, which struck deeper into Cambodia and continued until 1973. The final phase of the bombing, aimed at containing a Khmer Rouge advance on Phnom Penh, blasted the densely populated area around the capital. The village of Neak Luong was hit, and more than 125 Cambodians were killed. The bombing of the village was labeled a targeting mistake, and for this error, the air force imposed a fine of seven hundred dollars on the bombardier of the B-52. The bombing ended on August 15, 1973, when Congress cut off funding amid widespread denunciation of Nixon's concealment of the extent of the bombing and some public calls for his impeachment.

A study conducted by Ben Kiernan and Taylor Owen in 2006 concluded that the United States from October 4, 1965, to August 15, 1973, dropped 2,756,941 tons of bombs in 230,516 sorties on 113,716 Cambodian sites. The tonnage compares with some 2 million tons of bombs dropped by the Allies during all of World War II. The Kiernan-Owen study was based on air force data released by President Bill Clinton when he visited Vietnam in 2000 which detailed the bombings of Vietnam, Cambodia, and Laos from 1964 to 1975. Clinton made the data available to assist in the retrieval of buried unexploded ordinance.

Estimates vary widely on the number of the civilian deaths resulting from the bombings. The Kiernan-Owen study cited the consensus estimate of 50,000 to 150,000 but projected the possibility of higher figures if other data were made available on the extent of the bombings.

In strategic terms, possibly the most deleterious effect of the bombing was the power that accrued to the Khmer Rouge as a consequence of the resentment it engendered among the Cambodian peasants. Many thousands of them rallied to the support of the Khmer Rouge. The population was also resentful of brutal repression under Lon Nol, particularly of the ethnic Vietnamese minority, which caused thousands of deaths. Another factor drawing support for the Khmer Rouge was the alignment of Sihanouk, a popular figure among the peasantry, with Pol Pot. At one point Sihanouk visited the Khmer Rouge in the field during their battle with Lon Nol's forces.

The surge of popular support for the Khmer Rouge opened the way for their victory march on Phnom Penh. Lon Nol, suffering from one of his nervous breakdowns, fled the Cambodian capital on April 1, 1975, to exile in Hawaii, leaving Prince Matak to face the incoming Khmer Rouge, who promptly executed him. U.S. ambassador John Gunther Dean decamped with his staff on April 12 aboard marine helicopters to a navy ship standing by in the Gulf of Thailand. Most foreign correspondents also left the city. Wes Gallagher, the vice president of the AP, ordered all members of his bureau to leave what had been one of the most dangerous assignments during the Indochina wars. Thirty-four correspondents had been killed in Cambodia or were missing. Twenty-five were lost in 1970 alone. In the spring of that year, after Lon Nol ousted Prince Sihanouk in his March coup, a bevy of correspondents descended on Phnom Penh. Venturing out of the capital, many were ambushed, presumably by Vietcong, North Vietnamese, or Khmer Rouge units. Some of those who were captured were released, but others were executed. Between April 5 and April 16, ten journalists who headed out to Parrot's Beak to cover the American invasion did not return. Among them were

two Americans, Sean Flynn, the son of the movie actor Errol Flynn, working as a photographer for *Time* magazine, and Dana Stone, of CBS News. In
the worst debacle, American and Japanese members of CBS and NBC television crews died in May when, disregarding a Cambodian Army warning,
they drove from Phnom Penh down a highway into a Communist ambush.
Those not killed immediately apparently were executed the following day.

Sydney Schanberg of the *New York Times* was among the few correspondents
who stayed on for the Khmer Rouge occupation of the Cambodian capital. Prior to taking up his post as bureau chief in Phnom Penh, we had cautioned him in New York not to take undue risks. "No story is worth a man's
life," he was told by James Greenfield, the foreign editor. Nevertheless, after
some hesitation, on the eve of the evacuation of the American Embassy staff,
Schanberg decided to remain in Phnom Penh. What happened to him and
his Cambodian assistant, Dith Pran, would become an epic chronicle in the
history of American journalism.

The Khmer Rouge entered Phnom Penh on April 17 and were welcomed
by flag-waving citizens who evidently thought that Pol Pot would be a gentler
master than Lon Nol. The Western press corps was no less sanguine. Typical of press reaction, four days before the Khmer Rouge took Phnom Penh,
Sydney Schanberg reported: "It is difficult to imagine how their lives could
be anything but better with the Americans gone." The *Times* carried Schanberg's dispatch under the headline "Indochina without Americans: For Most,
a Better Life." Schanberg added, however, in the same piece: "This is not to
say that the Communist-backed government, which will replace the American clients, can be expected to be benevolent."

On the first day of the Khmer Rouge occupation, Schanberg was given a
better sense of what could be expected. Years later I asked him for an hour-
by-hour account of what happened to him and Dith Pran, his Cambodian
assistant and photographer, on that day. This is what he told me:

> 5 A.M.—As I started to file the final page of my story for the paper of
> April 17, the teletype connection to Hong Kong broke and could not be
> restored. So Pran and I left the telegraph office and started driving cau-
> tiously around the city to see what was happening. Through the night,
> bitter fighting had raged on the edges of the city, setting whole neigh-
> borhoods on fire. Several mortar rounds fell not far from the telegraph
> office.

5:30 A.M.—Khmer Rouge guerrilla troops in black-pajama dress are entering the capital from all sides, by land, river boat and bridge. Government soldiers are throwing off their uniforms and hurriedly putting on civies. We retreat to the Hotel Le Phnom, where most of the press always stayed. Only about a dozen foreign journalists have remained in the capital.

6 A.M.—We listen to the radio as we pack our belongings and canned goods for a likely move to the French Embassy, which has been agreed upon as a sanctuary for foreigners. The victors have taken over the Government radio station and are telling Cambodians to lay down their arms because Angka ("The Organization") is their new Government. Leaving our suitcases where we can get them in a hurry, we go for a walk not far from the hotel to get a sense of whether there is major risk. We meet a few of the insurgents and converse with them through Pran without incident. But they are cold and distant. They tell us of the strict rules of behavior and suggest we should follow those rules. In the central part of the city, many Cambodians are hailing the Khmer Rouge conquerors showering them with flowers. Some people are hanging out of their windows shouting peace slogans. But there are harsher reports from other parts of town and rumors of a forced evacuation.

12 P.M.—Around noon, Pran, John Swain of the London *Times,* our Cambodian driver and I believing mistakenly it's safe enough . . . we make a foray to the main civilian hospital, Preah Keth Mealea, to assess the casualty situation there. The place is a charnel house. Only a few nurses were brave enough to report for duty—no doctors. Supplies have run out and there are lots of dead bodies. Many of the wounded are bedded out on the stone floors and blood drips down the staircases. We take some pictures but it's hard to look at it and we go down stairs, get in the car and head for the hospital's main gate. Our car is blocked. A Khmer Rouge squad is coming through the gate driving a captured armored personnel carrier. Pran at once tells us to do whatever our captors ask. He had recognized instantly their lack of inhibition about blowing us away. I remember thinking desperately, but without saying it: "For God's sake, Pran, stop arguing or they'll kill you." The Khmer Rouge push us into the armored vehicle through the hinged back door and Pran followed. I was able then to ask him what he was arguing about. He explained that the Khmer Rouge had told him and the driver to take off since they wanted only "the big people." The driver went off but Pran kept insisting to the Khmer Rouge that he had to stay with us and they finally let

him get into the armored vehicle with us. From inside the vehicle, Pran kept telling the Khmer Rouge we were Frenchmen who were there to tell the world about their victory, a refrain he repeated over and over for the next several hours. As we drove on, the Khmer Rouge stopped to pick up two captured men in civilian dress. Pran recognized both of them as officers in the small Cambodian Navy. One of them began to pray, putting the ivory Buddha he wore as a pendant in his mouth. The other officer handed me his wallet and asked me to hide it and thus hide his identity, assuming apparently that I as a foreigner had some magic. I took it and hid it under the sandbags on the floor. When we arrived at our destination—a Mekong River bank in the northern part of the city—the metal rear door was swung open and we were ordered out. Two soldiers stood on the bank, pointing their AK-47 rifles at us from their hips. I and I'm sure everyone in the vehicle thought we were going to be mowed down immediately and rolled into the river. But Pran leapt out of the vehicle and starting arguing for us again—and kept importuning the Khmer Rouge pretty much non-stop for the next three hours as we waited in the sun with our hands behind our heads, the guns pointing at us. And then, Pran quieted down. There was a command and the guns were lowered—and we were, in short, released. Some of our belongings were returned.

It was 3:30 P.M. As the three of us were leaving the riverbank I looked back and saw the two Cambodian officers sitting on the ground under guard, looking pale. One of them was still praying. To watch that was to see the dark bottom of helplessness.

4:30 P.M.—We got back to the hotel. A jeep was parked outside with two Khmer Rouge holding weapons topped by grenade launchers. An International Red Cross worker came out of the front door. He told us the Khmer Rouge had given an order that everyone had to be out of the hotel in 30 minutes. I asked him when exactly did they give that order. He said: "Twenty-five minutes ago." We grabbed our suitcases and began walking up the boulevard toward the French Embassy. The street was filled with Cambodians being herded out of the city. Sandals fell off their feet as they fled littering the ground. The Embassy's swinging gates were locked because throngs of Cambodians were trying to get in. We climbed over the seven-foot wall. The French told us Cambodians had to sleep outside, not in the Embassy building. I waited until dark and then brought Pran inside. A few days later, after our efforts to forge a British passport for Pran had failed, the Khmer Rouge ordered all Cambodians to leave the Embassy and join the agrarian revolution in the countryside. To avoid the crush, Pran and some friends left a day before the deadline and began walking up Highway Five. And his four-and-a-half years in hell began.

After thirteen days in the French Embassy compound, Schanberg and other foreigners were hauled in a Khmer Rouge truck convoy to the Thai border. On arrival in Bangkok, after recovering from the trauma of his experience, Schanberg went to the *Times* office and wrote a series of stories on what he had witnessed, which were published on May 19 on more than two pages of the *Times*.

With the occupation of Phnom Penh, Pol Pot, head of the Center, the leadership group of the Khmer Rouge, proclaimed the establishment of Democratic Kampuchea and took the title of premier. Immediately, he set about creating what he envisioned as a racially pure Khmer, classless, essentially agrarian society "cleansed of all foreign influence." To consolidate his absolute power, Pol Pot ordered the evacuation of the cities, which he viewed as potential centers of opposition. Their inhabitants were force-marched into the countryside, where they were herded into prison camps or into labor gangs. Schools, hospitals, factories, and monasteries in the urban areas were shut down. Executions ensued immediately of Cambodians who had served as officers in Lon Nol's army or as officials in his civilian administration. An estimated 20 percent of the population, about 1.57 million people, died in the holocaust at the hands of the Khmer Rouge in the years 1975 to January 1979 through execution, starvation, unattended illnesses, overwork, or other mistreatment. The Vietnamese and Chinese resident minorities were prime targets of Pol Pot's execution squads. The holocaust ended when a Communist Vietnamese army battling through Cambodia seized Phnom Penh in January 1979. The Khmer Rouge had been scuffling with the Vietnamese for years over rival claims to the Mekong Delta. Pol Pot fled by helicopter to a retreat in the jungle of northern Cambodia, bordering on Thailand, where he died in a hut in 1998 and was cremated on a funeral pyre of discarded tires and other junk.

Prior to Pol Pot's death, Sihanouk was witness to much of the carnage instigated by the dictator. Returning to Phnom Penh from Peking after the Khmer Rouge occupation of the Cambodian capital, he was installed by Pol Pot as a powerless head of state. But in the next year, on April 4, 1976, he was deposed, later denounced as a traitor to the revolution, and spent some time under house arrest. When the Vietnamese invaded Cambodia in December 1978, Pol Pot rehabilitated Sihanouk politically and dispatched him to New York to appeal to the United Nations for help. Sihanouk failed, and the Vietnamese occupied Cambodia for the next ten years. In 1993, Sihanouk was restored in Phnom Penh as king but later, in ill health, retired to self-imposed exile in Peking. He abdicated the throne in October 2004 in favor of his son, Norodom Sihamoni.

The Vietnamese seizure of Cambodia provided Dith Pran, who had saved Schanberg's life, with the opportunity for escape. During the Pol Pot repression, posing as a simple peasant, he had suffered beatings and starvation. Visiting his hometown after the Vietnamese invasion, he found that more than fifty members of his family had been slaughtered. Covered with graves, its wells filled with bones and skulls, the village land had become known as the "killing fields." Later, Pran was able to send a message to Schanberg through Eastern European journalists who were visiting the village where Pran was working under the Vietnamese as an administrative chief. In July 1979, Pran covertly made his way to the Thai border and crossed over to a refugee camp, where he contacted Schanberg through an American relief officer. Schanberg had been making ceaseless efforts to find Pran. When he was awarded the Pulitzer Prize in International Reporting in 1976 for "his coverage of the Communist takeover in Cambodia, carried out at great risk," he accepted the prize on behalf of Dith Pran and himself. Within a week after learning that Pran had reached Thailand, Schanberg found him in the refugee camp and brought him to New York. In Schanberg's book *The Death and Life of Dith Pran,* written in 1980, and in the 1984 film *The Killing Fields,* Dith Pran was lauded as a heroic, selfless holocaust survivor. From the time of his arrival in New York in 1980, where he worked as a photographer for the *New York Times,* until his death in a New Jersey hospital of pancreatic cancer on March 30, 2008, Dith Pran remained a passionate advocate and worker for human rights. In my many encounters with him at the *Times,* although he was treated as a hero, I found him to be the most modest of men.

30

THE INDONESIAN HOLOCAUST AND THE DOWNFALL OF SUKARNO

On the night of September 30, 1965, and in the early morning hours of October 1, life changed violently for the 107 million people of Indonesia. Before dawn six top army generals were murdered in a failed leftist coup that became known as the Gestapu. In the next days, the senior generals who survived the coup launched a massive retaliatory purge of the huge Indonesian Communist Party (PKI), which they accused of perpetrating the assassinations. President Sukarno, who had become allied politically with the Communists, was rendered powerless. He had been the unchallenged ruler of Indonesia for two decades. In the army purge and its aftermath, an estimated 500,000 to 1 million people were killed. The victims included hundreds of thousands of members of the Communist Party and those seen as associated with the PKI. Many thousands of others died in sectarian violence unleashed in the chaotic power struggle.

The elimination by the army of the PKI as a force in the southern archipelago, which extends for 3,500 miles over more than 17,000 islands, profoundly altered the balance of power in East Asia. It thwarted Sukarno's plans and those of his Communist allies for transforming Indonesia into a "People's Democracy" aligned in a "Jakarta-Peking-Hanoi Axis" which would dominate Southeast Asia. It also ended Sukarno's armed confrontation with the British-founded government of Malaysia, which he had opposed as nothing more than Western colonialism.

In July 1966, I traveled through the islands of Java and Bali piecing together a chronicle of the events leading to the Gestapu murder of the army generals and the horrific aftermath—one of the greatest massacres in history. The execution of Communists had not yet ended, and the jails were still crowded with the army's captives. Thousands were dying of maltreatment. Returning to Jakarta after touring the blood-drenched villages, I became a witness to the end game being played out in the ousting of Sukarno from power by the army. The political drama unfolded vividly for me as an onlooker at a strange evening reception given by President Sukarno on July

27 in the great hall of the Negara Palace for an assembly of Indonesian generals, government officials, and a few foreigners.

Under the crystal chandeliers of the great hall, President Sukarno stood in his stocking feet on a Persian carpet exhorting the Indonesian elite assembled before him to obey "all my teachings." A year earlier during the Independence Day celebration, I had watched in Merdeka ("Freedom") Square as more than 100,000 of his people cheered the "Great Leader" wildly as he proclaimed a new "anti-imperialist axis" linking Indonesia to China, North Vietnam, and North Korea. The United States, Britain, and other Western powers must "get out of the whole of Southeast Asia altogether," he had shouted.

Now, gazing wild-eyed about the glittering Negara Palace hall at the Indonesian officials, many of whom were deliberately slighting him by turning their backs or chatting with each other, the sixty-five-year-old president, flushed and infuriated, cried out that he still held supreme state authority. Out of him poured a storm of epithets about Western neocolonial plots and the need to continue Indonesia's armed confrontation with Malaysia. He reiterated his demands for adherence to policies he had put in place before the events of September 30: creation of the Jakarta-Peking-Hanoi Axis; rejection of all Western financial aid; and continued boycott of the United Nations, from which he had withdrawn his nation.

But as the palace scene conveyed, the political landscape had changed radically. The army under the command of General Suharto had assumed absolute power. The right-wing generals had put down the Movement of September 30, the political coalition of Sukarno and other leftist politicians, accused of inspiring the Gestapu coup.

Sukarno, once worshiped as a demigod by most Indonesians, was now a virtual prisoner, under close guard at his palace at Bogor, forty miles south of the capital. But still Sukarno clung defiantly to the outer trappings of power. The army hesitated to use force to eject him formally and publicly from the presidency, since in some regions of the islands the people still idolized him as the "Great Leader of the Revolution." Displacing him forcibly would risk civil war, army officers told me, even though they were denouncing and plotting against him. Thus the scene being played out on this night in the Negara Palace—full of hidden implications, expressed in the subtle Javanese style in whispers and glances—mirrored the historic juncture at which the Indonesian nation was poised in the struggle for ultimate power.

Standing erect directly before Sukarno's palace dais and looking up at him were General Suharto and the two other Indonesian leaders, who made up the triumvirate now effectively ruling Indonesia. They frowned and stirred uneasily, glancing at each other, as they listened to Sukarno's outburst. Sultan Hamengku Buwono IX, the leader of Central Java and the minister of economic affairs, did not betray his concern openly, although he was dismayed by the president challenging his plan designed to rescue the nation from disaster. Only a few people in the room knew that the sultan had privately approached the United States and the "Tokyo Club," a consortium of non-Communist nations to which Indonesia was heavily in debt. He had asked for a loan of $500 million to halt the runaway inflation and so retrieve the country from its economic disorder. The sultan had been told that until Sukarno ceased his hostile polemics and ended the armed confrontation with Malaysia, he could not expect Western countries to act on requests for large-scale aid. At the time, about 7,000 British and 2,400 Malaysian soldiers were fighting off raids into Sarawak and Sabah (North Borneo) by guerrillas armed and trained under Sukarno's direction. The appeal to desist from such guerrilla raids made to him personally by Robert Kennedy during their meeting in Tokyo in January 1964 had been unavailing.

Gazing up at the raging Sukarno, Adam Malik, the foreign minister, was less able to conceal his fury. By his antics, Sukarno was undermining Malik's plans for a rapprochement with the United States, ratification of the agreement reached in June in Bangkok to end the Malaysian confrontation, and his yet unannounced intention to reseat Indonesia in the United Nations. Malik, as he told me later in the evening, whispered to the impassive army officer at his right: "Shall I walk out or not?" The officer beside him was General Suharto, the army chief, who on March 11 had compelled President Sukarno to surrender executive power to him. "Be patient," the general replied. The peppery foreign minister shrugged and obeyed.

With a last angry glance about the hall, Sukarno put on his shoes and stalked out. It was his custom at some ceremonial occasions to take off his shoes while holding forth. General Suharto watched the president exit and then, turning to Malik, asked him to circulate about the room and advise the diplomats and other foreigners present to ignore Sukarno's tirade and reassure them that he would act within two weeks to restore de facto relations with Malaysia.

Several weeks before the palace episode, Sukarno had been publicly humiliated by the nation's People's Consultative Congress. The Congress was summoned by its chairman, General Abdul Haris Nasution, who alone among the seven senior generals targeted in the Gestapu putsch had managed to escape when the death squads descended on their homes. It convened as street demonstrations were being staged throughout the capital by Kami, the militant anti-Communist student organization, demanding the formal ouster of Sukarno as president. Responding to the outcry, the Congress scrapped the designation of Sukarno as "President for Life" and ratified the March 11 delegation of executive power to General Suharto. It approved of the army chief's dissolution of the Communist Party and the ban on propagation of Communism and Marxism-Leninism. Elections were to be held within two years. In foreign policy, the Jakarta-Peking-Hanoi Axis with its tie to North Korea was junked, and the country returned to its previous nonaligned status. As for the formal removal of Sukarno as president, General Suharto quieted the students by saying: "It is not yet time."

When Sukarno went to Merdeka Square on August 17, 1966, for his annual Independence Day speech, his reception was very different from what I had witnessed the previous year. This time, when he told the massed thousands: "I am your great leader . . . Follow my leadership, obey my directives," the crowd booed, and some one thousand students left the stadium shouting denunciations of him. In his speech, Sukarno unconvincingly deplored the killing of the six generals. The next day the Kami student groups, other mass organizations, and newspapers in West Java responded by demanding that Sukarno explain what he knew about the murders.

The September 30, 1965, putsch had its origins in the rivalries between two political blocs. One was the right-wing army generals, headed by General Nasution, the defense minister, and General Achmad Yani, the chief of staff. The generals confronted a coalition of leftist politicians led by Sukarno. The coalition embraced in the first instance D. N. Aidit, leader of the Indonesian Communist Party, which claimed a membership of 3 million. The party was affiliated with front organizations with a total membership of about 18 million, among them the highly militant Pemuda Rakyat, a youth organization of some 2 million, and Gerwani, a women's organization also of about 2 million. Affiliated also were some 12 million members of peasant and trade union organizations. Other key members of Sukarno's political coalition were Dr. Subandrio, the pro-Peking foreign minister, who was the president's closest adviser, and the chief of the Indonesian Air Force, Marshal Omar Dhani.

The alliance between Sukarno and Aidit had been forged four years prior to the September 30 crisis. It was then that Sukarno, impatient with the inefficient and corrupt political parties with which he had been associated, turned to the Communists. He was persuaded by Aidit that the PKI, while

leaning to Peking, would remain independent in the international Communist movement and that the party would be willing to share power with the
Nationalist politicians. A professed Marxist himself, Sukarno was drawn to
the Marxist-Leninist philosophy of the PKI. He saw in its dedicated leadership and its mass organization techniques the means of building the socialist
"Greater Indonesia" he had long envisioned. Steadily, up to September 30, Sukarno fostered the growth and influence of the Communist Party. He compelled the right-wing generals to accept his principle of "Nasakom," unity
based on a front of Nationalist, religious, and Communist forces. Under his
patronage, the Communist Party was able to set up the most pervasive political organization in the country. It took control of many local governments, successfully infiltrated the air force, and indoctrinated some army
officers. Sukarno brought Aidit and his chief lieutenants into his cabinet as
ministers without portfolio. Only the top army generals, notably Nasution
and Yani, blocked the formation of a Nasakom cabinet. Sukarno intended
that the cabinet would be one in which the Communists would rule as ministers with executive power preparatory to Indonesia's entry into a "Socialist stage."

In early 1965, Sukarno began to foster what he called the Jakarta-Pe-
king Axis and spoke of extending it to North Vietnam and North Korea.
Subandrio, the foreign minister, accompanied by senior military advisers,
arrived in Peking on January 23, just twenty-three days after Sukarno announced that he was withdrawing Indonesia from the United Nations. Subandrio met with Chinese leaders, including Chairman Mao Zedong, Premier
Zhou Enlai, and Liu Shaoqi, the head of state, and at the conclusion of the
talks, a joint statement was issued expressing "a mutual desire to strengthen
friendly contacts in the military field." The statement reaffirmed opposition
to the founding by Britain of Malaysia through the merger of Singapore and
Malaya, the policies of the South Vietnamese government, and the American stand in the Vietnam War. It was during those talks that Zhou Enlai
endorsed a proposal by Aidit for the creation in Indonesia of a "Fifth Force"
of millions of Indonesians in a People's Militia and offered to supply it with
100,000 small weapons. It would obviously be a force to counter the power
of the army and its right-wing generals. Chen Yi, the Chinese foreign minister, traveled to Jakarta to confer with Sukarno and attended the Independence Day celebration in Merdeka Square. I glimpsed Chen Yi as, with hands
clasped across his ample middle, he fell asleep in the hot sun while watching
a two-hour "People's Parade." In his speech that day Sukarno publicly put
forward the idea of a "Fifth Force" and soon after secretly dispatched Mar-

shal Dhani, the air force commander, to Peking to arrange the delivery of the arms promised by Zhou Enlai.

It was later that month that rumors spread that Sukarno, then sixty-four years old and troubled by a persistent kidney ailment, had become seriously ill, and both the army and the Communists began to prepare for a show-down over the anticipated succession. The army managed to stall the Su-karno-backed proposal for a political Fifth Force and blocked the delivery of the Chinese weapons promised by Zhou Enlai. The army leaders knew the PKI intended to employ Sukarno's proposed Fifth Force to broaden its power base in the country for an eventual bid for total power. They were aware that the PKI had begun secretly training its own militia at Halim Air Base near Jakarta, making use of a small number of weapons smuggled in from China and other clandestine sources. Hundreds of trainees were drawn from Pe-muda Rakyat, the Communist youth organization, and Gerwani, the Com-munist women's organization.

It was in this increasingly tense atmosphere that the September 30 Move-ment was born. Determined to go forward with the creation of the Nasakom cabinet he envisioned, Sukarno raged against the generals for obstructing his plans. Aidit and Subandrio together with other leftist politicians lis-tened attentively as did Marshal Dhani, who had arranged the secret train-ing of Communist militia near the Halim base. At the meetings a plan to eliminate those of the army who were opposing Sukarno's goals began to take shape. What the conspirators planned, I was told as I reconstructed the events, was not to be a coup d'état, that is, a seizure of total control of the government, nor was an immediate Communist takeover of Indonesia planned. Instead, the plotters intended to bring about a political power shift to the left. Those obstructing Sukarno's program for a Nasakom cabinet— that is, the top right-wing generals—were to be purged, somehow put out of the way. This move supposedly was also intended to forestall any possi-ble attempt by a newly formed Council of Generals to seize total power. The purge of the generals would upset the existing delicate power balance be-tween the army and the Communist Party, which Sukarno had previously fostered, but the president had been convinced by Aidit that the PKI would be content to share power. Was that an accurate appraisal of Aidit's inten-tions? In an interview in his Jakarta office, six weeks before Gestapu, I asked Aidit if his acceptance of Nasakom was a tactical move to gain power or a doctrinal adaptation of his Communist Party to Indonesian realities. "We remain Communist," Aidit replied, "but we have to be tolerant of national-ism and religion." But the PKI leader also said that his party would remain free to act as it deemed necessary. He did not exclude the possibility that it might follow the example of some European Communist parties and exploit creation of a national political front as a vehicle for the eventual assumption of supreme power.

The September 30 Movement conspirators who had become committed to serving Sukarno by purging his army opponents conferred secretly for weeks in Jakarta. Two of Aidit's aides participated, Supono and a mysterious "Sjam," who was believed to be Tjugito, a member of the party's Central Committee. Also drawn in were Mustafa Sjarif Supardjo, a brigadier general commanding a division in West Java, and Lieutenant Colonel Untung of Sukarno's Palace Guard. The plotters decided to go forward in their move against the generals on the night of September 30. Two days prior, Foreign Minister Subandrio left for the island of Sumatra on what was described as a speaking engagement. He would be safely distant if the plot went awry.

The command post for the purge of the generals was the Halim Air Force Base, which was under the personal command of Marshal Dhani. At about 10 P.M. on September 30, trucks loaded with troops arrived at the base, and shortly thereafter General Supardjo and Colonel Untung, who were charged by the conspirators with actually carrying out the coup, arrived by jeep. At about 3:30 A.M., seven squads made up of members of the Presidential Palace Guard and the Pemuda Rakyat, the Communist youth organization, under the command of Lieutenant Arief, set out in trucks to seize the seven senior army generals in their homes. Before leaving Halim, the squads were told in a briefing that a Council of Generals backed by the American CIA intended to overthrow Sukarno and the Great Leader's revolution. They were to arrest the seven generals, telling them that they were wanted immediately at the presidential palace for a meeting with Sukarno. The generals were then to be brought back alive or dead to Halim before being taken to nearby Lubang Buaja—the Crocodile's Hole—the area in which members of the Communist youth organizations had been undergoing military training.

At about 4 A.M., the squads descended on the homes of General Nasution, the minister of defense, General Yani, the army's chief of staff, and the other five generals. Although the generals had received warnings weeks before of the possibility of a move against them, the houses inexplicably had no special security arrangements. Sentries at the homes of Nasution and Yani were easily overpowered. Yani and two other generals who tried to fight off the attackers were killed, and three of the four other generals, among them Major General S. Parman, chief of intelligence, were taken alive. Those still alive and the bodies of the dead were taken in a truck to the Crocodile's

Hole. There, an apparently uncontrolled frenzy took place. The living generals were tortured and killed, and the bodies of all six were dumped at the site into the well, which was covered up with debris. Participating in the murderous orgy were members of Gerwani, the Communist women's organization. What transpired was evident by the condition of the severely mutilated bodies, which were discovered and brought to the surface by frogmen on October 4. The body of Major General Suprapto, a deputy chief of staff, who was taken alive to Crocodile's Hole, according to an official medical report, bore thirty wounds, including broken bones, bullet wounds, and knife thrusts. Some of the generals were said to have had their eyes gouged out.

Despite the elimination of the six, the purge was, in fact, badly bungled and fatally so for the perpetrators. The key target of the death squads, Defense Minister Nasution, the top general, escaped. When the raiders broke into Nasution's home, as his wife stalled them by slamming doors shut ahead of the intruders, the general slipped into the courtyard, climbed over a wall into the neighboring garden of the Iraqi ambassador, and despite a fractured ankle managed to limp away. In the melee the raiders shot Nasution's sister and his five-year-old daughter, who was in her arms. The child died later in a hospital. The PKI was to pay an incalculable price for the murderous assault on the Nasution family. It was General Nasution before all others among the generals who pressed for the subsequent massive purge of the Communists. He was present when the frogmen brought up the remains of his murdered fellow generals.

Sukarno arrived at Halim in the late morning of October 1 after spending some time at the house of Dewi, his Japanese wife. Awakened at 6 A.M. with news of the attack on Nasution's house, he set out for Halim, stopping over at the home of another wife, Haryati, before going on to the air base. According to the testimony much later before a military court trying Major Sujono, the commander of the ground forces at Halim, Sukarno first went to the operations command center and then to a house which had been prepared for him. Soon after, General Supardjo, the military chief of the plotters, arrived at Halim and went to President Sukarno to report. Major Sujono said he and others stood outside the house and watched through a window. He said he saw the president pat Supardjo on the shoulder, apparently approvingly. Supardjo then emerged from Sukarno's quarters and called out to Colonel Untung, saying: "The president has given his blessings and in a little while, a statement executed by the president himself declaring his support will be announced." Later in the day an announcement was made on Jakarta Radio of the formation of a Revolutionary Council. The broadcast, made in Untung's name, said that a number of generals had been purged to forestall a counterrevolutionary coup by the Council of Generals planned for Armed Forces Day, October 5. The broadcast did not cite any approval of the coup by Sukarno, who by that time must have been made aware that General Nasution had escaped.

The plotters made two fatal blunders. One was the failure to capture Nasution and the other their apparent decision not to put General Suharto, commander of KOSTRAD, the Strategic Army Reserve, on the list of those to be purged immediately. Suharto returned to Jakarta the morning of October 1 from a fishing trip and became aware of what was transpiring from the radio broadcasts of the Revolutionary Council. He learned that Colonel Untung had brought two Communist-infiltrated battalions, the 454th and 530th paratroops from Central and East Java, into the city on the pretext of participation in the celebration of Armed Forces Day. Their mission was to seize the radio station, which they did, and take control of Merdeka Square in the center of the city. One phase of the plot went awry with a comic aspect. Only the senior officers of the two battalions knew of the plot, and they neglected to tell the troops of the agreed password for effecting liaison with the allied Communist groups. When the Communist youth units summoned to the capital arrived at Merdeka Square and shouted the password at Untung's battalions, the puzzled troops responded by arresting the lot. The youth group was unarmed, since Colonel Untung had been unable to deliver arms, as promised.

General Suharto acted decisively as soon he became apprised of what was transpiring in the capital and at the Halim Air Base, where Marshal Dhani had assembled his forces. Suharto went to his KOSTRAD headquarters and rallied loyal elements of the armed forces and police. He managed to persuade the 530th Paratrooper Battalion brought to Jakarta by Untung to defect to him while the colonel's other battalion fled to Halim to join Dhani's troops. Suharto located General Nasution, who was still being hunted by the death squads. He put Nasution under protective guard and offered him command of the army. When the injured defense minister declined, he took command himself. Later, he would nudge Nasution aside entirely as he took full political power. By 8 P.M. Suharto was in control of Jakarta and preparing to move against the Halim base. His problem became more complex when he learned that Sukarno was there. He contacted the base and asked that the president leave before he attacked. Sukarno delayed, uncertain as to where he should go. The plotters urged him to go Madiun, a city in the western part of the province of East Java where the 1948 Communist uprising took place, apparently thinking that with the presence of Sukarno they might be able to reorder their forces. Sukarno was dissuaded by others who felt he would be endangered, and when Sukarno's wife Dewi arrived at Halim, he left with her in her car for his palace at Bogor. At dawn, Suharto's commandos assaulted the base and after brief skirmishing occupied it. Before the base fell, Marshal Dhani flew off to Madiun, while the remnants of his troops fled hoping they could make their way to Central Java.

On the morning of October 2, the official PKI newspaper, *Harian Rakyat*, committed a monumental blunder which provided the army with public justification for its bloody purge of the Communist Party. The newspaper was circulated on the streets of Jakarta with an editorial registering approval of the Gestapu plot. Apparently, the paper had been printed and circulated before the editors became aware that General Suharto had already in effect put down the September 30 Movement. The editorial stated:

> It has happened that on the 30th of September measures were taken to safeguard President Sukarno and the Republic of Indonesia from a coup by a so-called Council of Generals. According to what has been announced by the September 30 Movement, which is headed by Lieutenant Colonel Untung of the Tjakabirawa battalion, the action taken to preserve President Sukarno and the Republic of Indonesia from the Council of Generals is patriotic and revolutionary . . . But, however, the case may be [that] this is an internal Army affair. On the other hand, we the people, who are conscious of the policy and duties of the revolution, are convinced of the correctness of the action taken by the September 30 Movement to preserve the revolution and the people . . . We call upon the people to intensify their vigilance and be prepared to confront all eventualities.

The editorial effectively sealed the fate of the PKI leadership. Before his escape to Madiun, Dhani provided Aidit with a plane for a flight to Jogjakarta in Central Java. The PKI leader had arrived at Halim before midnight and had been present in the morning when General Supardjo briefed Sukarno. Aidit landed in Jogjakarta at 2 A.M. on October 2. Just before his arrival, Brigadier General Katamso, the army commander for the city, and Colonel Sugigsono, his deputy, were assassinated, and pro-PKI elements had taken control. Aidit told the local PKI leaders that Sukarno would arrive in the city soon to address a mass demonstration. Presumably, he expected Sukarno to proclaim his support for the September 30 Movement. But with the failure of the putsch in Jakarta, the Communists soon lost control of

Jogjakarta to the army, and Aidit fled the city. In Surabaya, the big coastal city in East Java, another PKI stronghold, there was no Communist move of any consequence to take control. I was told there that a lieutenant and a squad of six men did go to the unguarded radio station, where they broadcast a "Revolutionary Proclamation." When the surprised army commander in the city became aware of the Gestapu coup, he arrested the lieutenant, who was subsequently shot.

On November 21, Aidit was captured near Solo, forty miles northwest of Jogjakarta, and executed the next day. When I traveled through East Java in July, I interviewed the army commander, General Sumitro, and asked him about the execution of the Communist leader. He would only say for the record, "You can be sure of one thing. Aidit is dead." I was given, however, by members of his staff details of Aidit's last hours. On November 21, 1965, at 9 P.M., the Indonesian military police ripped open a bamboo cupboard in the corner of a shabby bungalow near a railroad track, on the outskirts of Solo. They confronted a crouching fugitive, who arose, faced the guns, and said: "I am Aidit." The Communist leader was interrogated briefly by a military police major and then asked to write a statement. He wrote until nearly 3 A.M. and then told the major: "I want to go to Jakarta. Can you help me?" The major replied that he was agreeable but they would first have to go to Semarang, the regional military headquarters. From there they could go by plane to Jakarta. Aidit was then put in a jeep and driven northwest on the road to Semarang. In the hills near Boyolali, the major halted the jeep at a desolate spot and told his prisoner to get out. Aidit was said to have exclaimed: "What is this? This is not legal!" Before he was shot, Aidit was said to have shouted: "Long Live the PKI." He was buried in an unmarked grave. The details of Aidit's execution and his last testament were not officially published.

When General Suharto assumed full executive control of the country on March 11, he promulgated a ban on the Communist Party. It was only a gesture for the record, since the massive purge of the Communists had already begun in late October. Commando units were then sent knifing through the Communist strongholds in Central and East Java. General Sumitro, the East Java commander, told me that Suharto had issued a detailed order in mid-November that the Communist Party should be destroyed "structurally and ideologically." Staff officers had visited the area commanders in early December to make sure the instructions had been understood and executed. "Most local commanders did their utmost to kill as many cadres of the Communist party as possible," the general said. Recalling the 1948 Communist uprising at Madiun, which was also crushed by the army, Sumitro repeated what

I had heard from army officers throughout Java: "They tried it at Madiun, and again in Jakarta, and we are not going to let them try it again." Sumitro added: "The PKI was able to make a coup in Jakarta, but they did not move all over the country because they had no weapons. If Aidit had been allowed to organize his Fifth Force and equip it, he would have moved to take over in Central and East Java."

Whatever the degree of complicity and intentions of the PKI in the September 30 Movement and in the Gestapu killings, and whatever Aidit may have planned, the end effect was that it gave the army the rationale for carrying out the total destruction of its long-standing political enemies. In Jakarta, the army executed members of the PKI's Politburo and Central Committee. Njoto, the deputy chairman, was arrested by military police as he was leaving Subandrio's home in Jakarta and later shot, as was the third ranking member of the Politburo, Mohammed H. Lukman. Among others executed, accused of being ringleaders in the attempted coup, were General Supardjo, Colonel Untung, and Marshal Dhani. Foreign Minister Subandrio was sentenced to death, but the sentence was commuted, and he spent the next twenty-nine years in prison.

Estimates of the number of people killed in the aftermath of Gestapu ranged from 500,000 to 1 million. My own estimate was 750,000, based on authoritative surveys conducted by university student organizations in October 1966 and checked by my Australian assistant, Frank Palmer, with Suharto's aides and army sources. But it will never be known precisely how many thousands of members of the PKI, their sympathizers, and families were killed. My estimate includes thousands murdered in criminal sectarian violence, many of them members of the large Chinese community, which was despised by many Indonesians. Many murders were committed by Indonesians who exploited the purge-incited chaos to exact vengeance in personal vendettas or simply for material gain.

Foreigners resident in Indonesia for decades were unable to make sense of the nature of the violence in all its hideous aspects. They spoke to me of how it seemed to be completely at variance with the gentle nature of the people, particularly the Balinese. Some said the populations may have been inflamed by highly colored stories of sexual mutilation of the slain generals. One of Indonesia's most distinguished writers, recalling his own moment of blood anger, said: "There is a devil in us and when it gets loose, we can run amok en masse." Many who participated in the killings of Communists justified their acts by saying, "It was them or us." I heard stories in cities and towns alleging that graves had been dug by the Communists before September 30 to receive the victims of an impending coup d'état. Lists were said to have been seized from Communist Party files naming army officers, religious leaders, local officials, and foreign missionaries to be executed. Boxes of instruments to pluck out eyes in the torture of prisoners were said to be found in the possession of Communists. Some of the stories seemed to have been spun out of a need to rationalize the mass killings. I did not come upon any persuasive evidence that the Communists possessed large stocks of weapons or were planning an immediate general uprising.

As I traveled through Java and Bali, there seemed to be no end to the killing. Many Indonesians whose relatives and friends had been slain were intent on collecting blood debts. The jails were jammed with people charged by the army with association with the PKI. The attorney general, Major General Sugiharto, told me he hoped to release about 120,000 detainees, many held in overcrowded prisons on bare subsistence rations, by the end of the year. At Solo in Central Java, Colonel Wibhawa said he had arrested 10,000 people in his region alone and was "still mopping up."

Army leaders told me that most of the killing of Communists was done by the aroused population. But in my tour of the former centers of Communist influence, I found either that most executions were carried out directly by the military or that the army incited the populations to do the killing. At some centers near Solo the military was staging executions without trial of selected Communists. The military executed its condemned by shooting, but the population was left free to behead victims or disembowel them with knives, swords, and bamboo spears, often with prior rituals of extreme cruelty. In the Banyumas region of southern Central Java, the politically inspired killings had evolved into guerrilla class warfare, with debtors eliminating their creditors, and rural tenants killing landlords.

In East Java, where estimates of the number of killings ranged from 100,000 to 300,000, most of the executions of Communists took place in the district of Kediri, which had been dominated politically by the Communists. The systematic execution of Communists was organized by the military commander, Major Willi Sudyono. His brother, Lieutenant General Sutoyo, was one of the six generals killed in the Jakarta putsch. There were religious as well as political motives for the population's participation in the killings carried out in Kediri, the center of Muslim religious instruction in East Java. Even before September 30, there had been clashes between Communist youth groups and Ansor, the youth organization of the Muslim Scholars Party. In the purge of the Communists, most of the killings were done by army-trained squads of Ansor, mainly youths in their teens and early twenties who were students at the Muslim university and religious schools in the Kediri district. Haj Marcus Ali, the fifty-seven-year-old religious leader of the district and a top leader of the Muslim Scholars Party, told me that Ansor had "fulfilled the command of the army" and that the "killings were the will of God." He said that 20,000 Communists had been killed in the Kediri district. Asked if there had been any resistance in the villages, he said he knew of fifteen members of Ansor and one army man who had been killed in the mop-up. He said he had two complaints against the Communists: they had offended Muslims, and they had taken "one-sided action" in their enforcement of land distribution and crop-sharing laws. In Central Java, where estimates of executions ranged from 50,000 to 300,000, members of the Nationalist and Muslim Scholars parties had also joined the army as executioners.

Apart from the Jakarta area, there was no mass killing in West Java, where there were no major centers of Communist influence. But reports from Sumatra and other islands of the archipelago, which I did not visit, told of purges that took many thousands of lives. In North Sumatra, I was told, hundreds were massacred in the Medan region, among them many Chinese merchants and their families. Mobs swept into the Chinese quarters, looting and killing.

On the idyllic island of Bali, when I arrived, the smell of death no longer hung heavily in the villages built with red-stone Hindu shrines at their centers. Once again, the people were going out to fish in the sea where not long ago hundreds of bodies floated on the waters torn at by the creatures of the depths. Maiden dancers, their black tresses plaited with fragrant white blossoms, danced entrancingly to the drums and gongs of the gamelan orchestras and tossed petals of hibiscus to me. Balinese smiled gently in response to my questions, saying that the terrible happenings were a "family affair" and they hoped American tourists would come back again, now that the Communists were gone. Yet the wounds festered amid the beauty. The prisons in Denpasar were still crowded. It was easy to rent a house because so many houses had been used by the army as depots for the rounding-up and execution of Communists. The Balinese, fearful that the spirits had not been exorcised, would not live in them. In Negra, there was one house where 300 Communists were said to have been shot. The well in the garden was stuffed with bodies. Children whispered about the fate of their teachers. Some 2,000 teachers were said to have died in the massacre. Most of the island's teachers, unable to live on their monthly pay because of the inflation, had joined Communist organizations seeking relief from their poverty.

No one knows precisely how many men, women, and children were slain on Bali. Estimates ranged from 20,000 to 100,000. Foreigners who lived on the island were convinced that about 50,000 of the population of 2 million had been killed. The army began its round-up of Communists at the end of October 1965, and it continued until mid-January. The army had required Communist Party officials before September 30 to hand over lists of members of the party and its affiliate organizations. Most of those on the lists were subsequently hunted to be killed. When I asked Parwanto, the prosecuting attorney of the Bali government, if there was any legal basis for the killings, he replied: "It was a revolution."

Most of the killings were carried out by army-selected civilian executioners who were known as Tamins. They were young men who were given loose black shirts and black trousers to identify them. They operated in teams, usually by night, and apparently met little or no resistance from the terrorized villagers. There were reports, which I could not confirm, that whole villages were wiped out. One responsible Balinese told of what happened to his typical village of about two thousand persons. Twenty-seven Communists had been killed there. The village headman, who was a member of the party, hanged himself. Others took poison. Some escaped. That evidently was the pattern for the several thousand villages on Bali.

The largest scale of killings occurred in the Jembrana Regency in the western part of the island, a center of Communist influence. There, the palace of the rajah of Negara, one of the eight traditional kings of Bali, was destroyed because he had allowed PKI members to meet on his grounds. His son, the pro-Communist governor of Bali, was in jail in Jakarta at the time. Eyewitnesses said the rajah's retainers were dragged from the palace to have their bowed heads crushed by rocks hurled by the mob. The rajah died as his palace was being sacked by the mob, and members of his family were slaughtered.

Describing the Ansor squads, a Christian pastor said: "We always wondered if they would eventually turn on us." The pastor told of listening in helpless agony to the cries for help in the night as Ansor squads pursued fugitives through the streets, and hearing the thud of great peasant sickles as the executioners slashed their victims to death. Toward the end of the mass killings, when whole families were sometimes put to death at one time, the Ansor executioners began to wear masks. There were often instances where men were killed who were mistaken for Communists or denounced because of some personal grudge. Old scores were settled under political pretexts. On the first day of the mass killings, one army officer in civilian dress cheerfully left Kediri city carrying a machine gun to shoot squatters who had refused to get off his untilled land.

After the interview with the Christian pastor I returned to the hotel where I was staying, an elegant hostelry built for tourists vacant except for Frank Palmer, my assistant, and me. I lay awake that night unable to shut out the ghastly accounts of the massacres. The stories of the descent of the Tamins on the frightened people in villages evoked vividly for me the memory of what my mother, Anna, had told me of the pogrom carried out by Cossacks against the Jews in her Ukrainian village. My mother was born in the ghetto village of Zamerhover. Her father, Morris, was a peddler. He would hitch up his horse cart, go out to the countryside where he would buy vegetables from the peasants, and then sell them to the people in the village. The family lived in a small cottage heated by wood in a brick wall stove. One morning mounted Cossacks raided the village. They were looking for loot, and they were seizing young men for the czar's army. Gazing out the cottage window, my grandmother, Pearl, saw that her sixteen-year-old son, David, who had been standing by the road, had been seized by two Cossacks. As my mother, then six years old, watched through a window, Pearl ran out, tore David from their hands, and he ran off. But Pearl was then struck down by baton-wielding Cossacks and trampled by their horses. The family carried her into the cottage, where she died with my mother weeping at her bedside. She was not the only Jew who died in the pogrom that day. What moved men to inflict such atrocities on innocents? It was a question I asked myself repeatedly that night and then over the next years as genocidal massacres were carried out in Cambodia, Yugoslavia, Africa, and the Middle East.

I did not detect any visible signs of remorse among those who did the killings in Bali, what until then was seen as the "island paradise." During religious festivals in Bali the young, black-clad executioners bowed before chanting Hindu priests who cleansed them of the taint of the blood of the tens of thousands they had slaughtered. The executioners marched proudly in parades. Their black garments were the vogue for many youngsters.

Amid all the carnage, I still came upon plain evidence in Central and East Java of continuing support for Sukarno, which gave the army reason enough for hesitancy in abruptly ousting him. Driving east out of Jakarta, passing through prosperous West Java, the army's political stronghold, I entered Sukarnoland. Here in Central Java and in East Java, where some 50 million of Indonesia's 107 million people lived, I found that the mystique of the "Great Leader" still prevailed. The rice paddies and plantations were tilled mostly by subsistence-level farmers, and although his Communist allies were no

longer in power, the farmers continued to look to Sukarno as the father figure. After the army purge the regions had come under the control of the Nationalist and Muslim Scholars parties. The two parties, as a buffer against
domination by the army, had joined in tacit political alliance with the beleaguered president.

Driving along the roads bisecting the farmlands and wending about the
mist-capped volcanic mountains, I saw signposts everywhere bearing slogans hailing Bung Karno—"Brother Sukarno." His photograph hung on
arches in the villages and on the bamboo walls of the peasant huts. They
were displayed in the limestone houses of officials and in the Chinese shops
of Jogjakarta, Solo, and Surabaya. Educated Indonesians in those cities told
me they knew of Sukarno's collaboration with the Japanese in World War II,
his assignment of Indonesians to the death labor camps, his political links
to the Communists, and his notorious dalliance with women. Yet, they said,
Sukarno had given them an ideology, a national identity, and the dream of
a "Greater Indonesia," which made him the linchpin of the some three hundred ethnic groups living in the vast archipelago. In Surabaya, a professor
of medicine said: "Sukarno is like a great mystical tree and we need him." In
Jogjakarta, a prominent and well-informed Indonesian said: "If something
happens to Sukarno in Jakarta, there might be civil war." Sukarno's continued influence extended beyond to the island of Bali, where, I was to learn,
the people were swayed more by the fact that the president's mother was Balinese than by the vagaries of his politics.

In the aftermath of the Gestapu, Sukarno exploited to the hilt this continued reverence for him. In his private sparring with General Suharto and
Foreign Minister Malik, he sometimes hinted that he might incite civil war
in Central and East Java if he was crowded too much by the army. Once,
Malik recalled, he had angrily snapped back at the president: "All right, go
to Central Java and start a civil war, and see who will win." Yet General Suharto continued to move cautiously, fearful of civil strife, weighing a constitutional solution whereby the president would accept a figurehead role and
bestow legitimacy on an army-run regime. The army did not challenge the
president directly to explain publicly his role in the plotting of the September 30 Movement and the Gestapu. Even some of his enemies who knew the
answer remained silent perhaps because they felt that preserving the image
of the founder of Indonesian independence was more important than exacting vengeance. Certain facts were plain. Sukarno wanted the generals Nasution and Yani and their deputies out of the way so he could replace them
with pliant military men who would not obstruct his plans for a Commu-

nist-led Nasakom cabinet that would bring about his socialist "Greater Indonesia." The president knew that Aidit, Subandrio, and other leftist politicians, Dhani, and some army officers loyal to him personally were planning action to satisfy his wishes. But the secret is buried as to whether he intended that the seven targeted generals be killed.

In 1967, the People's Consultative Congress, faulting Sukarno for failing "to meet his constitutional responsibilities," ousted him from the presidency and replaced him with General Suharto. The Congress heard Suharto testify that Sukarno was not "the direct instigator or the mastermind" behind the Gestapu plot. But Sukarno was found guilty to the extent that Suharto was able to keep to keep the "Great Leader" under house arrest until his death in 1970.

There have been suggestions that the U.S. government and its agencies played a clandestine role in bringing about the Communist debacle. There is no question that the CIA in cooperation with British and Australian operatives was providing support and encouragement to the anti-Sukarno factions before September 30. There was reason enough for the opposition to Sukarno, given his confrontation with Malaysia and the anti-Western policies he was fomenting elsewhere in Southeast Asia. The Johnson administration was concerned that Sukarno's pro-Communist stance in the southern arc might eventually affect the American war effort in Vietnam. According to CIA documents, declassified in later years, the American Embassy may have been involved in the transfer of funds to anti-Sukarno factions in the army. There was also a suggestion by some academic researchers, which I found naïve, that the CIA, which kept lists of the membership of the PKI, had turned them over to the army for use in the purge. The PKI operated mainly in the open as a legal political party enjoying the encouragement of Sukarno. The leadership was well known to the army. The army had kept a wary eye on the membership of the PKI and its affiliated organizations from the time of the Communist uprising in Madiun in 1948. The CIA officers, who operated under the cover of the embassy, did not have to use cloak-and-dagger methods to obtain the names of those in the leadership. They needed only to buy a subscription to *Harian Rakyat,* the official PKI newspaper, which did not hesitate to publish names. During the purge of the Communists, the army and its collaborators did raid local offices to obtain lists. I detected no evidence in Jakarta or in the former Communist strongholds in Central and East Java or in Bali of any direct American involvement in the political confrontation leading up to the Gestapu coup or in the army counterthrust and purge of the PKI. Marshall Green, the American ambassador, making a point of staying clear of the confrontation, confined himself in retrospect to stating in a meeting with correspondents: "The United States military presence in Southeast Asia emboldened the army, but it had no decisive effect on the outcome. It is perhaps better to look at it in negative terms. If we hadn't stood firm in Southeast Asia, if we hadn't maintained a military presence, then the outcome might have been different."

Ironically, Sukarno in death exacted revenge against Suharto, his warden. In 2001, his daughter, Megawati Sukarnoputri, was elected president of Indonesia. Her pedigree was undoubtedly a factor in her victory. In the years prior to her election she became a symbol of the resistance to Suharto's autocratic and corrupt rule and played a part in forcing his resignation as president in 1998. Suharto was charged with embezzling as much as $15 billion in public funds on behalf of his family and friends. His trial on corruption charges was suspended in September 2000 when judges ruled that the former president was not medically fit to stand trial. His lawyers successfully withstood the pressure for a trial up until his death on January 27, 2008. As he lay dying in a Jakarta hospital, a parade of Indonesia's elite, including President Yudhoyono, visited his bedside in what seemed to be a compassionate spirit of forgiveness for the years of his corrupt and brutal repressive rule. It was recalled that Suharto had given Indonesia some years of economic stability following the turmoil of Sukarno's demise. As for Sukarno's daughter, Megawati, her fame was short lived. After an undistinguished term of office as president, she was defeated in 2004 in a landslide election by a former general, Susilo Bambang Yudhoyono. Her defeat closed the book on the faded Sukarno mystique.

31

CHINA WATCHING

THE CULTURAL REVOLUTION

During the years I served as chief correspondent, Southeast Asia, for the *New York Times,* 1963 to 1966, I spent about half my time reporting on China from my base in Hong Kong and the balance covering the wars in Vietnam, Laos, and Cambodia, as well as developments in other countries of the region. It was in Hong Kong that I first detected the gathering storm of the Cultural Revolution in mainland China.

In Hong Kong, Audrey and I lived with our four daughters in a hillside apartment overlooking the magnificence of Repulse Bay. I would be away usually for three weeks or a month on my reporting swings through the region, mainly in Indochina. I would then fly back to Hong Kong for reunion with the family and my China-watching job. Audrey, who was editing the *Mandarin Magazine,* a periodical distributed worldwide by the Hong Kong Mandarin Hotel, would be waiting patiently. Relaxing on our balcony with Charlie, our Australian cockatoo, which Audrey had rescued from a Chinese opium peddler on Cat Street, we would gaze out over the bay to the faintly visible islands off the China mainland. Weekends, Ah Liang, our boat boy, would bring our red sailed Chinese junk, the *Valhalla,* into the bay, and we would picnic on board with the comfort of a jug of Portuguese rosé wine imported from Macao and water-ski pulled by the speedboat of a close friend, Dr. Dawson Grove, distinguished veteran of the 1941 Battle of Hong Kong.

Audrey treasured the *Valhalla,* which she named after the settlement founded in 1911 by her grandfather, a Lutheran minister, in a valley of the Peace River District of northern Alberta. She came upon the thirty-three-foot hull of the *Valhalla* in a small shipyard and hovered over Chinese shipbuilders as they made it seaworthy. She adorned it with a phoenix, a dragon, and other good-luck carvings which she found on the prow of an ancient junk that had been cast up on the shore of a deserted island. We entertained a parade of interesting visitors aboard the *Valhalla,* Teddy Kennedy and his wife, Joan, among them. Inevitably, I talked with Kennedy about my days with his brothers in Saigon.

Hong Kong was the chief observation post for hundreds of China watchers, an array of diplomats, intelligence agents, propagandists, academics, and journalists. The nations, such as Britain, France, and India, which formally recognized the People's Republic of China had the advantage of embassy observation posts in Peking, but their diplomats enjoyed only very limited access to the closed Chinese society and were restricted in their travels. More information was available in Hong Kong about internal developments in China than what the diplomats in Peking managed to gather. The few journalists, citizens of countries with diplomatic relations, who were posted in the Chinese capital fared no better than the diplomats.

My office, which I shared with our resident correspondent, Ian Stewart, was just up the hill from one of our most important sources of information, the U.S. Consulate. The staff of the consulate, with its huge China-watching team, was much larger than the staffs of most American embassies. To supplement the central China press, whose articles were distributed abroad by Xinhua, the official Chinese news agency, the consulate obtained smuggled copies of provincial newspapers and magazines forbidden for export. Mainland radios were monitored. Refugees, who came by the hundreds every month, and travelers were painstakingly interviewed. American diplomatic posts around the world and the various intelligence agencies reported on the movement of Chinese officials, ships, and planes. Information also came from high-flying U-2 reconnaissance planes, financed by the CIA and piloted by Nationalist Chinese Air Force personnel based in Taiwan. Apart from official American sources, Stewart and I worked the other foreign consulates and intelligence agencies, interviewed refugees and travelers, and with the help of our Chinese staff studied the mainland press. On my travels around the China periphery I picked up tidbits of information. Nightly, from 9 P.M. to midnight, Stewart or I would check the English version of Xinhua for important Peking announcements. Thereafter, the monitor of the Reuters news agency would telephone us if an important news break developed. With a thirteen-hour lead time over New York, we were often called out of bed to write for the first edition at three or four in the morning.

In analyzing the flow of China information, the experience I gained in my three years in Moscow was of inestimable value. China watching was not unlike Kremlin watching. The Chinese Communists patterned the makeup of their print press and radio broadcasts on the Soviets, using similar Marxist-Leninist jargon and techniques in signaling the official line to the Communist faithful abroad. Repeated omission of a name, for example, from published guest lists at Peking receptions or a change in the order of mention at other functions could be the first hint of a reshuffle in the leadership or a purge. The China watcher who could read the code would often be the first to detect seismic tremors of a political upheaval.

In February 1966, I detected such tremors. I reported in a dispatch from Hong Kong to the *Times* that the Chinese Communist leadership seemed to be "laboring under a severe strain in an atmosphere of uncertainty in Peking." The last official appearance of Mao Zedong had been on November 26, 1965. In the next few weeks, I learned that Mao had slipped out of the capital with his wife, Jiang Qing, repairing to her old haunts in Shanghai. Soon hints appeared in the press of what they were plotting. It was a power play targeted against Liu Shaoqi, the head of state, and Deng Xiaoping, the secretary general of the party. These were the two leaders of the faction that had nudged Mao out of the seat of supreme power. Liu Shaoqi, whom I had interviewed in Yenan in 1946 when he was serving as Mao's deputy, had in April 1959 replaced his boss as head of state. Rebelling against Mao's failed economic policies, the Central Committee had elevated the more pragmatic sixty-one-year-old Liu Shaoqi to the management of the government. Although Mao remained as Chairman of the Communist Party, he was relegated ostensibly to the work of resolving theoretical pursuits, while Deng Xiaoping, allied with Liu Shaoqi, took day-to-day control of party affairs.

Mao had been suffering this displacement for six years, complaining that he had become a "dead ancestor," respected but not consulted. Intent on restoring Mao to supreme power, Jiang Qing, defying the bars to her involvement in politics imposed earlier by party leaders, marshaled an aggressive radical clique in Shanghai, which would become known as the "Gang of Four," to undermine Mao's opponents. Only a few weeks after I reported on the strains manifest in the leadership, Jiang Qing and her young supporters launched their first attacks in the press on Liu Shaoqi and Deng Xiaoping. The attacks were opening shots in what was to become known as the "Great Proletarian Cultural Revolution." The term "Cultural Revolution" was to become common usage in China and abroad, but in the years I covered this shattering political upheaval, I never thought of it to be either a revolution or cultural in the sense of having roots in Chinese tradition. What it constituted in reality was an internal power struggle that rent China for a decade—1966–76.

Opposition to Mao was rooted in the national disasters stemming from his economic policies, which he put into effect during 1958–59. These policies were based on Mao's revolutionary thesis that the masses through "socialist education" could be spurred ideologically to a "high tide" of endeavor. This "tide" would be the driving force in the Great Leap Forward, a gigantic production effort in factories and home workshops, designed to hasten the industrialization required for the realization of Communism. In tandem with this industrial surge, Mao undertook an intensive program of agricultural collectivization. In 1952, Mao had reneged on a promise given to the peasants who rallied to him during the Civil War in response to his cry "Land to the Tillers." With collectivization, they were deprived of the distribution to them of land which had been confiscated from affluent landlords. The peasants were herded into cooperatives whose output was bought by the state at fixed prices. Then, in a further step, Mao merged those cooperatives, embracing about 99 percent of the peasantry, into 24,000 giant farm units. These so called People's Communes pooled land, houses, agricultural implements, and farm animals. On average each comprised about 2,000 households, with laborers divided into brigades and teams. In 1958, Mao's supporters claimed this twin mass approach had achieved fantastic increases in industrial and agricultural production. But as results were checked out more closely in 1959, disillusionment set in. As a consequence of the forced pace, severe production dislocations had developed. The population, pummeled by Maoist propaganda, was emotionally and physically spent. With agricultural and industrial production in sharp decline, the Central Committee ordered a retreat from Mao's policies. But the change came too late. The disruptions in production, which continued into the "bitter years" of 1960–62, took the lives of millions in widespread famines. Estimates of the total number of people who died as a consequence of the Maoist policies ranged from the official Chinese toll of 14 million to projections by independent scholars of more than 30 million.

Mao's failed policies could in some degree be attributed to what I observed in Yenan in 1946. For the Maoist leadership, as nearly as I could detect then, total victory in the Civil War with Chiang Kai-shek seemed such a distant possibility that little, if any, attention was being given to practical planning as to how an impoverished nation of half a billion people would be governed. As late as 1947, a year in which Chinese Communist armies triumphed in a series of critical battles, the leadership was still estimating that at best it would take another four years to gain control of the mainland. When the turnabout in the war came at astonishing speed following the victories in Manchuria and Central China and his troops marched into Peking on January 31, 1949, Mao was ill prepared to cope with the basic economic and social problems confronting him. There appeared to be no prospect of obtaining American economic support or obtaining substantial aid from the Soviet Union, which was struggling itself to repair the massive destruction of World War II. Operating since the 1930s on the run in the hinterland, although quite widely read, Mao lacked experience in the administration of large urban areas, let alone a nation. As a revolutionary, he had performed a historic service for the Chinese people by breaking down the old semifeudal structure that existed under Chiang Kai-shek, so that a new modern China could eventually emerge. But as he took the seat of power in Peking, Mao was unable in thought and action to make the transition from guerrilla revolutionary to statesman. To consolidate his power and eradicate all opposition, he launched a series of monstrous purges that took the lives of millions. Confronted by enormous economic problems, Mao instituted a fumbling regime that relied on inept ideological incentives and strategies, some of them based on the guerrilla "mass line" of Yenan days.

In May 1971, at a banquet given in the Great Hall of the People by Zhou Enlai for her father, Chester Ronning, Audrey asked the premier: "When you and Chairman Mao were in Yenan, did you imagine that in a few years you might be governing China?" Zhou replied: "When we were in the caves of Yenan, it all seemed simple. All we had to do was win. It was after victory that we had our big problems. We are still learning how to govern a country." He was clearly alluding to Mao's failed policies.

As early as 1959, Mao was subjected to thinly veiled attacks by party critics. They suggested that he had become feeble minded and that his revolutionary romanticism was no substitute for modern statecraft. The yearning within the Communist Party for pragmatic governance rather than rule by Maoist ideological fantasy surfaced publicly on June 16, 1959. On that date, the party organ, *People's Daily,* published an article entitled "Hai Rui Upbraids the Emperor," in which a mandarin of the sixteenth-century Ming court tells Emperor Jiajing: "For a long time the nation has not been satisfied with you. All officials, in and out of the capital, know that your mind is not right, that you are too arbitrary, and that you are perverse. You think that you alone are right. You refuse to accept criticism and your mistakes are many." The article was written under a pseudonym by Wu Han, deputy mayor of Peking, who was also a historian. It appeared to many as a bold attack on Mao.

Two months later, a frontal assault was made on Mao at a Central Committee meeting convened on Mount Lu in Jiangxi Province by Peng Dehuai, who had risen to become Minister of Defense after leading Chinese forces in the Korean War. The general and his supporters complained that Mao had set up the agricultural communes "too soon and too fast and they had gone wrong." The dissidence was also an expression of dissatisfaction within the military. A new professional army leadership had arisen which was impatient with Mao's political controls. The army leaders were critical of his split with the Soviet Union, which had choked off their major source of modern weaponry and the know-how they sought for development of a nuclear-missile arsenal.

Mao struck back at his critics by purging Peng Dehuai and his army chief of staff, Huang Yongsheng. In place of Peng, he appointed Lin Biao, the Civil War hero, who readily accepted Mao's thesis of "man over weapons," declaring that Mao Zedong Thought was a "spiritual atom bomb" mightier than any weaponry that might be supplied by the Soviet revisionists. At first, Liu Shaoqi did not come out openly in support of the critics led by Peng Dehuai. Mao's critics, whom I termed the "pragmatists" for want of a more precise description, did not as yet comprise a well-organized opposition group. But as the country struggled with the after effects of the Leap, the pragmatists became progressively bolder in challenging Mao. The struggle burst into the open again in January 1961 when the Wu Han article reappeared in *Peking Literature and Art* in the form of a historical play, *Hai Rui Dismissed from Office*. The play criticized Emperor Jiajing for having dismissed Hai Rui for telling him unpleasant truths. In a country where historical allusions have been used in adversary politics for centuries, it was plain that the emperor was Mao and Hai Rui was Peng.

On November 10, 1965, the Shanghai radicals mounted their counterattack on Mao's detractors with the publication in the Shanghai newspaper *Wenhui Bao* of an article denouncing Wu Han as the author of *Hai Rui Dismissed from Office*. The writer was Yao Wenyuan, a young literary critic, who had been working with Jiang Qing in her campaign to bend literature and the performing arts to a more radical emphasis based on class struggle. In his article, written under Jiang Qing's guidance, Yao accused Wu Han of being a dangerous class enemy who distorted history. Wu Han was lumped together in a "Three-Family Village Black Gang" with Deng Tuo and Liao Mosha, senior officials of the Peking Municipal Committee who had written a series of articles in the Peking press that were also considered veiled criticisms of Mao. They were accused of seeking to block Mao's effort to heighten the class consciousness of the masses and school them in the need for pressing forward with class struggle. In the framework of this seemingly theoretical debate, the decisive power struggle was launched.

At this juncture, Liu Shaoqi was in strong position. He controlled the party organization through Deng Xiaoping and much of the state apparatus, and his adherents were in charge of much of the media. Most of the intellectuals, including artists, literary writers, educators, and scientists, were weary of the Maoist ideological strictures. They leaned to the pragmatists, who accepted the classics and were tolerant of some deviation from the ideological strictures in contrast to Jiang Qing's view of culture as a tool that should be devoted totally to "socialist education" of the masses. At his side in the confrontation with the pragmatists, Mao had Premier Zhou Enlai, who stood ready to pick up the reins of government from the oppositionist head of state. With his appointment of Lin Biao as defense minister, Mao could also count for support on a strong faction in the army. Grouped around him ideologically were other radicals opposed to Liu and Deng's "right opportunist line," which they asserted would lead to a revival of capitalism. As proof that Liu and Deng were "capitalist-roaders," the radicals pointed to the introduction by the two leaders of material incentives for workers such as payment for overtime, piecework, and merit bonuses rather than relying on the Maoist vision of "socialist education." Liu had fostered these incentives as part of his program to repair the damage done to production by Mao's Great Leap. They were not much different from the reliance on incentives in the "New Democracy" policy that Liu described to me in Yenan. Liu favored the collectivization of agriculture but at a slower and more measured pace than Mao's mass hurried approach known as "rash advance." Rather than plunging ahead as Mao did in the Leap, Liu favored waiting upon industrialization that would produce the tools needed by the farmers for more effective production.

Fundamentally, the confrontation between the radicals and pragmatists was a struggle about who would govern China and how, not so much about basic Communist tenets. Their common goal was the eventual transformation of China into a classless Communist society. In Yenan, I had observed the close ideological affinity of Liu and Mao and their common acceptance of the tactical need to make economic and other compromises in a period of New Democracy on the road to their Communist utopia. Both spoke of a bourgeois-type revolution to precede the socialist stage. To the extent that there was an ideological divide at the onset of the Cultural Revolution, the argument was more on transitional methodology and timing in getting to the Communist utopia than on fundamental doctrine. The Maoist accusation that the pragmatists were retreating from Communism to capitalism was little more than a sloganeering cover designed to facilitate the destruction of their opponents in their reach for ultimate power.

As the Maoists arrayed themselves for a showdown battle, Liu Shaoqi made a fatal tactical error. On March 26, 1966, he left Peking on a scheduled state visit to Pakistan and Indonesia. On May 3, Xinhua broadcast an editorial from the army newspaper, *Liberation Army Daily,* calling for vigilance against "anti-Party, anti-socialist" intellectuals. The substance of the editorial and its terminology convinced me that a major purge was under way, and I cabled a dispatch to the *Times* saying: "A widespread cultural purge with clearly stated political overtones is underway within the Chinese Communist Party." I also reported that Zhou Enlai had made a speech on April 30 in which he stated: "A socialist cultural revolution of great historic significance is being launched in our country. This is a fierce and protracted struggle as to who will win, the proletariat or bourgeoisie, in the ideological field." Calling for the eradication of "bourgeois ideology" from all fields, the premier said: "This is a key question in the development in depth of our socialist revolution at the present stage, a question concerning the situation as a whole and a matter of the first magnitude affecting the destiny and future of our party and country."

The morning after I filed my dispatch, May 4, signaling the eruption of the Cultural Revolution, I was stunned to receive a casual message from the Foreign Desk of the *Times* saying that my story had been held over for lack of space. In great agitation, I telephoned the editor on duty and told him that my dispatch signaled the onset of momentous events on the China mainland. He consulted with Harrison Salisbury, then an assistant managing editor, who immediately saw the significance of the dispatch. It was on the front page the next day. Zhou Enlai later recalled that the Cultural Revolution was launched definitively on May 16.

In Liu's absence while in Pakistan, the Maoists struck effectively at his supporters. The "Black Gang" trio of the Peking Municipal Party Committee, which had parodied Mao, was ousted. The purge was then extended to Peng Zhen, the mayor of Peking, a close ally of Liu; Lu Ping, the president of Peking University; and the staff of the central and municipal media. The Maoists then turned their attention to the provinces where Liu's people exercised firm control.

In early June, I experienced the frustration of an American Hong Kong China watcher. I took my wife to the Kowloon railway station and put her on the train to Guangzhou while I stayed behind to report from a distance the erupting power struggle on the mainland. American correspondents were still barred from China, but Audrey, a Canadian citizen, identifying herself as a housewife, had obtained a three-week tourist visa for a tour of seven cities. There were no objections forthcoming from the Chinese when it became evident to them that she was working as writer and photographer for the *New York Times Magazine.* Draped in cameras, she bade me farewell with a pixie grin and boarded the train for Guangzhou. On her travels, she encountered the first evidence of the Cultural Revolution in Nanjing when her visit to the university there that she had once attended was canceled. The Nanjing radio announced that Guang Yaming, the rector, had been purged because of his "ignoble and villainous conspiracy to suppress the revolutionary movement in the university." She came upon the onset of the violent stage of the Cultural Revolution upon arrival in Peking on June 16. The Cultural Revolution was unfolding, and violent Maoist demonstrations were erupting on the streets of the old capital. When she checked into the Peking Hotel, she asked for a front room overlooking Chang'an Boulevard, the city's major thoroughfare, but despite her protests was given a back room without a view of the action in the streets. Never shy when on the job, Audrey decided to telephone her father in Hanoi, who had told her in Hong Kong that he would be staying at the Metropole Hotel. When the Metropole telephone operator responded by telling her that she did not know the ambassador's whereabouts, Audrey said firmly: "This is his daughter. I am calling from Peking. Ambassador Ronning is there on a special mission, so please call your leader Ho Chi Minh and ask him where Chester Ronning is." The operator, who spoke English, said: "I will call you back in fifteen minutes." On the dot, a Peking Hotel clerk banged on the door to announce that Ronning was on the phone. Audrey chatted with her father about doings in Peking and Hanoi, and the ambassador, who was on his "Smallbridge" mediation mission, also inquired about the well-being of our two older daughters, who were attending a missionary school on Taiwan, and about Charlie, our pet cockatoo. After the ambassador hung up, the Peking Hotel clerk returned bowing—obviously the telephone call had been monitored—to escort Audrey to a far more luxurious front room with a balcony view that enabled her to photograph the chaos in the streets below. Giant processions of young demonstrators with cymbals and gongs sounding and fireworks exploding were parading before the Central Committee Building, shouting "Long Live Chairman Mao."

Descending into the street and working alone—her Chinese guides too frightened to accompany her—Audrey photographed the turbulence. When a group of Red Guards encircled her and tried to seize her cameras, she fled to the protection of the nearby International Club, where fortunately a friend, Colonel Jacques Guillermaz, the French military attaché, who was watching the demonstrations from the front of the building, was able to shield her. Observing the processions, Audrey did not know, or for that matter neither did the young marchers know precisely, what Mao had set in motion. But within a few days, the government began canceling the visas of tourists, businessmen, and other foreign visitors. Audrey made it back to Hong Kong with her film and notes, which became a cover story in the *New York Times Magazine*. Almost at once, the gates to the country were slammed shut as officials braced to cope with an internal upheaval.

Mao reappeared in Peking on July 18 as the capital gradually was coming under Maoist control. The Eleventh Plenum of the Central Committee was summoned into session on August 1 to give formal approval to the Cultural Revolution as units of the People's Liberation Army were ordered by Mao to move into strategic positions around the city. Returning to Peking, Liu attended the closed Plenum, where he was criticized and soon found himself isolated. In early August, Mao was still confronted by party and government cadres in the provinces who were resistant to his radical ideology and loyal to Liu and Deng Xiaoping. To cope with them, the Maoists put into play their most potent weapon, the figure of Mao as the "father" of the Revolution. In their struggle with the Maoists, the pragmatists had been caught up in a contradiction that was to bring about their downfall. Their infighting with the Maoists had not detracted from their continuing surface adulation of Mao. The Mao cult had become so much a part of the Communist mystique that even his critics felt compelled to continue outwardly to render obeisance to the Chairman. At the 1959 Mount Lu Central Committee meeting, when an official declaration critical of his Leap policy was contemplated, Mao threatened to go to the countryside and rally the peasantry in support of his polices by launching civil war. The Central Committee backed off, as was indicated by the absence of any official rejection of Mao's policies. His public image of infallibility remained unblemished. Unaware of the inner-party dispute, the bulk of the population, especially the youth who had been thoroughly indoctrinated in schools, held to an unflagging worshipful attitude toward Mao. Exploiting his patriarchal role, Mao turned to the youth to carry the Cultural Revolution to the provinces. On August 5, he wrote his own "Big Character" wall poster, "Bombard the Headquarters," a call for militant action by young "shock forces" against his enemies. Hundreds of thousands of copies of the Mao wall posters were placarded all over the country. The "shock forces" mobilized around the country responded by marching in demonstrations denouncing the bourgeois "monsters and ghosts" who had supposedly infiltrated into important party and government posts as well as the schools and were betraying the great leader's ideology.

On August 18, at a rally of nearly 1 million students in Peking's Tiananmen Square, Mao accepted the red armband of a middle school group associated with Peking's Tsinghua University, on which was emblazed "*Hong-weibing*" (Red Guard) in gold characters. It was a militant group which had denounced and humiliated members of the eminent Tsinghua faculty who had been branded as too moderate in their revolutionary outlook or influenced by Chinese classical thought or foreign ideas. Thus, Mao designated the name and shaped the tactics of the diverse youth groups being formed in middle or secondary schools and colleges all over the country.

On the rostrum in Tiananmen Square a strange and tragic game was played out on the day of the mass rally. Liu Shaoqi, although he had been berated at the Central Committee Plenum, was permitted to stand on the platform even as Lin Biao, freshly anointed by Mao as his new "closest comrade-in-arms" and heir apparent, was invited to address the massed students. Unleashing what was to become the most shocking and destructive phase of the Cultural Revolution, Lin Biao called upon the youth to sweep away the "Four Olds"—old ideas, old culture, old customs, and old habits, which did not conform to socialist society.

Within a matter of days after Lin Biao issued his call, squads of Red Guards roamed China's cities destroying what they thought were vestiges of the old culture that were bourgeois or foreign. In Guangzhou, the privately owned little shops and stands were closed and denounced as antisocialist. Buddhist temples and Christian churches were closed and defaced. Pre-Revolution historical monuments were smashed. The homes of "Black Elements"—former landlords, accused counterrevolutionaries, or bourgeois families—were sacked, their antiques destroyed. On the streets, visiting Overseas Chinese were stripped of foreign-made clothing and humiliated. On college campuses faculty members were paraded with dunce caps, women with long hair were shaved, and the apartments of elderly couples were broken into, their precious antiques hauled into the streets and destroyed.

For the next two years, China was tortured by this uncontrolled paroxysm, an admixture of ideological fever and factional struggles for power, subsiding and then raging anew. Millions of Red Guards marched through Peking hailing Mao and embarked on rampaging tours of the country. By early 1967, they had paralyzed party and government offices. The army was compelled to take over administration of the provinces and protection of factories and utilities. Amid the chaos, rival coalitions of Red Guards, party cadres, and workers—all waving the red Maoist flag and Mao's "Little Red Book" of sayings—became locked in mortal combat.

Guangzhou, in keeping with its tradition of being at the center of revolution, was the scene of one of the worst of the collisions among Maoist factions. In early 1967, the East Wind and the more radical Red Flag groups fought pitched battles. In the fighting with iron bars and arms looted from army arsenals, thousands were wounded and killed. City services were disrupted, and crime was rampant. Encouraged by leftists in Peking, the Red Flag faction raided installations of the Guangzhou military garrison for arms. In Chongqing the contending factions employed machine guns and flamethrowers purloined from the city's arms factories. The casualties mounted into the thousands. In August, as clashes between the radicals and the army multiplied throughout the country, Mao toured five affected provinces and authorized military clampdowns. Gradually order was restored, although sporadic outbreaks continued into 1968.

During this madness, and when I returned to China in 1971 and again in 1980, I pieced together in interviews with Chinese officials the details of what had happened during the Cultural Revolution to Liu Shaoqi and other major figures whom I had come to know during the Yenan period. Liu disappeared from public view after his appearance on the rostrum in Tiananmen Square on August 18, 1966. Soon after, he and his wife, Wang Guangmei, were placed under house arrest in Peking. Liu Tao, their eldest daughter, denounced them in a "self-examination" article that was published in the December 1966 issue of a Red Guard organ at Peking's Tsinghua University. It was not unusual during the Cultural Revolution for children to denounce parents who were deemed guilty of what Lin Biao termed "old" thinking. Liu Tao accused her mother of acting like a "queen" and said her father had given her "sinister instructions" on many occasions during 1965. "I am of the opinion that my father is really the number one power-holder taking the capitalist road within the party," she wrote.

> For more than 20 years he has all the time opposed and resisted Chairman Mao and Mao Zedong Thought, carrying out, not socialism, but capitalism, and taking not the socialist road, but the capitalist road. In the current Cultural Revolution movement, he suppresses the revolutionary movements, enforces bourgeois dictatorship, brings white terror into play, and adopts the attitude of disregarding Chairman Mao. Really this simply cannot be tolerated, as Vice-Chairman Lin Biao has said. He never trusts the masses, but fears them and their movements to such an extent that he resorts to the suppression of the masses and their movement. Liu Shaoqi is actually the hangman responsible for the suppression

of this Great Proletarian Cultural Revolution, and if his road is followed, China will necessarily change color.

While under house arrest, Liu and his wife, Wang Guangmei, were paraded, cross-examined, and humiliated at Red Guard demonstrations. At one mass meeting, Wang, a highly cultured woman, was jostled about draped with a necklace of ping-pong balls symbolizing the pearls she had worn during the state visit with her husband to Indonesia before the Maoist denunciation of them.

At the Central Committee Plenum of October 1968, Liu and Deng Xiaoping were branded "Capitalist-roaders Number One and Two" and formally ousted from all their party and government positions. Denounced at the Plenum as a "traitor, renegade and scab," Liu was exiled to Kaifeng, Henan Province, in Central China, where he died in 1969 in an isolated cell, denied the medical care he needed for treatment of pneumonia and diabetes. Deng Xiaoping was banished by Mao to Jiangxi Province, where he was to spend three and a half years as a factory worker. In the next years, Deng would be restored as vice premier with the aid of Zhou Enlai only to be denounced once again by the Maoists in 1976 after the death of the premier. But shortly thereafter, with the demise of the "Gang of Four," he would regain power as the paramount leader of China, and he would then exact vengeance for what was perpetrated against him and his comrades.

32

FOREIGN EDITOR

In the first seven months of 1966 I had reported on momentous events in China, Indochina, and Indonesia. Before the year was out, I was to be involved in yet another momentous story, but in another role. In August, after three years in Southeast Asia, I was transferred from Hong Kong to Bonn. On arrival in the German capital, Audrey and I stuffed the brood into the Schaumburgerhof Hotel, the four kids, three cats, two turtles, and Charlie, the Australian cockatoo. I was not too happy about my assignment to Bonn, despite the hint from Sydney Gruson, then the foreign news editor, that I was being positioned for greater things in the paper's hierarchy. I was bored by the prospect of a second time around in Germany. Although important as the capital of West Germany, Bonn still seemed pretty much of a sleepy backwater compared with the seething divided Berlin I had known in the 1950s.

On our first day in Bonn, I took Audrey out to the swift-flowing Rhine to see the heavy barge traffic so as to rid her of a lingering dream. In Hong Kong, she had frantically researched—despite my shrugs—the possibility of transporting our beloved Chinese junk, *Valhalla,* from Repulse Bay to a mooring at Bonn. Our first week was preoccupied with putting our older daughters, Susan and Karen, into school, outfitting them with lederhosen and bicycles, buying a car, and renting a house. The night before we were to move in, I awoke to the ringing of the wall telephone in an alcove of our hotel room. I became fully awake when I heard the voice of Clifton Daniel, the managing editor, in his courtly southern drawl with a slight tease, saying: "Mr. Topping, would you like to become foreign editor of the *New York Times*?" I mumbled: "Just a moment," and sticking my head into the adjoining bedroom, called out to Audrey: "Do I want to be foreign editor . . . go back to New York?" Audrey replied with typical aplomb: "You do," turned over, and went back to sleep.

I gave up the life of a correspondent reluctantly. I did so only because I came to accept that after traveling abroad as a reporter for twenty years it was time to put my experience to use as an editor. I did not forswear the role of foreign correspondent entirely. Over the course of the next twenty years, as foreign editor and later managing editor, I seized every opportunity to write for the daily newspaper and the *New York Times Magazine*. Traveling every continent, I interviewed such personalities as President Nicolae Ceauşescu of Romania, Prime Minister John Vorster of South Africa, the Shah of Iran, Fidel Castro, Premier Zhou Enlai, Prime Minister Golda Meir of Israel, and King Hussein of Jordan. Audrey accompanied me as a freelance photojournalist and writer as she had in Asia and in the Soviet Union. There were also weeks when I was left behind in New York to mind the kids while she sallied abroad. She worked for the *New York Times* and the *National Geographic* magazine, among other publications, and also did television documentaries for NBC on the Kremlin and the Forbidden City in Peking.

Daniel asked me to be in New York to take up my new job as foreign editor within ten days. Only a few days short of our two-week sojourn in Bonn, we left for the airport in a taxi convoy—my wife, pregnant with our fifth daughter, our other four daughters, cats, turtles, and the talking cockatoo. A bewildered taxi driver asked me: "Is this a traveling circus?" I nodded with a straight face and a sigh. At Kennedy Airport, upon our arrival well after midnight, a customs official surveyed our motley caravan incredulously and waved us through, not taking account of a current ban on the importation of parrots, and without checking our wicker and rattan cases loaded with contraband Chinese goods obtained in Hong Kong. Our destination was a village unknown to us called Scarsdale, recommended on the telephone by our former China colleague, Henry Lieberman, as a decent place to live.

Two days after arrival, upon checking into the *Times* newsroom, Clifton Daniel informed me I was to be fully briefed by Sydney Gruson, the departing foreign news editor. Moments later, Gruson, wearing a bright bow tie and carrying a suitcase, bustled in and ushered me into an adjoining room. Gruson told me with a sigh of his troubles with the Internal Revenue Service, and as I listened waiting rather impatiently for my briefing, he suddenly glanced at his watch and cried out: "Good God! I've got to get to the airport," and left for Paris, where he was to become publisher of the international edition of the *Times*. I walked back into the newsroom and sat down at my new desk. I was the foreign editor of the *New York Times,* with a staff of more than forty correspondents stationed around the world. Fortunately, I had been in most of the places where we had bureaus, and so the transition sans briefing by my predecessor from the field to the Foreign Desk was not overwhelming. I was given full control of the international news operation. Cyrus Sulzberger no longer had oversight responsibility for the foreign staff. The publisher, Arthur O. Sulzberger, had in 1955 stripped his cousin of that function when he was recycled from chief correspondent to columnist. Cyrus Sulzberger still roamed the world writing for his column, "Foreign Affairs," but he could no longer dictate to the staff in his imperious style. That pleased me immensely, recalling his cable of 1948 denying me a job with the *Times*. In tacit recognition that I was in full control of international operations, my title was changed from foreign news editor to foreign editor.

My first major challenge as foreign editor was not long in coming. On the morning of December 15, a copy boy dropped a cablegram on my desk. I glanced at it and then seized it and studied it. I walked across the newsroom and placed it on the desk of Harrison Salisbury, then an assistant managing editor, and said: "Does this say what I think it does?" Salisbury examined it. There was something of a garble in the transmission. "Yes," Salisbury said, "I think it does." I exclaimed: "You're in." A visa to North Vietnam awaited Salisbury in Paris. For months, circling the periphery of the Communist bloc, he had explored every means to gain entry into embattled North Vietnam. He was not alone. While covering the de Gaulle visit to Cambodia, I encountered Wilfred Burchett, the leftist Australian correspondent who had close ties to the North Vietnamese. I sought his help in getting visas for Salisbury and me. Salisbury got the nod. To pick up his visa Salisbury left for Paris, with only Daniel, the managing editor, Turner Catledge, the executive editor, a few other need-to-know people, and me privy to his undertaking. John Oakes, editor of the editorial page, later complained about not being included in those briefed. In Paris Salisbury found that the message from Hanoi concerning the visa had been mislaid in our Paris office and so was delayed for the better part of a month in reaching me. Salisbury traveled to Vietnam via Phnom Penh, Cambodia, and Vientiane, Laos, aboard a plane of the International Control Commission and arrived in Hanoi on December 22. From that day to January 17, Salisbury filed some of the most significant and controversial dispatches of the Vietnam War.

On arrival in Hanoi, Salisbury set out at once to learn the results of the American air strikes on North Vietnam that had occurred on September 13 and 14. The North Vietnamese contended that the center of Hanoi had been bombed. The Pentagon denied it, saying the bombers had hit legitimate targets in the industrial outskirts rather than the urban areas. In his first dispatch, filed on Christmas Eve after viewing a number of sites where houses had been damaged by bombing or rocket fire inflicting civilian casualties, Salisbury stated: "Contrary to the impression given by United States communiqués, on-the-spot inspection indicates that American bombing has been inflicting considerable civilian casualties in Hanoi and its environs for some time."

The first site that Salisbury visited was in the area of Pho Nguyen Thiep Street in the Hoan Kiem quarter of Hanoi, a three-minute drive from the old Metropole Hotel, so familiar to me from my stays there in the 1950s. He reported that about three hundred thatch and brick homes and huts along the Red River embankment, possibly a quarter of a mile from Nguyen Thiep Street, were hit on December 13. On that site, he reported, four persons had been killed and ten injured, most of them while at work or hiding in a large shelter. The damaged houses lay along the western approaches to the key Paul Doumer (Long Bien) Bridge, and Salisbury speculated that American pilots possibly were aiming at the approaches to the bridge just outside the Hanoi city limits. Salisbury also inspected a house on Hue Lane in the Halba Quarter that had been hit on December 2, and he reported the death there of one person and the wounding of seven others, including two children. Perhaps because he had been witness to the destruction of the German blitz of London in World War II, he cited the casualties and damage in Hanoi as relatively light.

His reporting rendered its great impact in its implication that the Pentagon had been lying and misleading the American public in asserting that the so-called precision bombing had not hit the urban areas or caused civilian casualties. Salisbury also interviewed Premier Pham Van Dong, quoting him as declaring that North Vietnam was ready to fight for another twenty years to prevail in its "sacred war," an assertion that undercut predictions made by the Johnson administration that the North Vietnamese would bend to American power.

The Salisbury dispatches, published at a time of bitter divisive debate in the country over the administration's conduct of the Vietnam War, produced an enormous uproar. The Pentagon and the State Department challenged the credibility of Salisbury's reporting. Arthur Sylvester, the Pentagon press secretary, referred to the *New York Times* as "The new Hanoi Times." His office conceded that some of Salisbury's observations might prove to be correct but charged that his reports, which lacked attribution, were based on North Vietnamese propaganda. Secretary of State Dean Rusk made a late-night phone call to Arthur Sulzberger, asking the publisher pointedly if Salisbury was asking the right questions. "I hope so," Sulzberger replied. After the call, Sulzberger telephoned Daniel and asked him to contact Rusk and obtain from him any questions that he would have Salisbury put to the North Vietnamese. Rusk furnished a list of questions which were sent to

Salisbury unmarked as to their source, but it arrived too late. When Salisbury returned to the United States, he met with Rusk and reported that Pham Van Dong had indicated, as the Vietnamese premier had conveyed more explicitly earlier to Chester Ronning, that Hanoi might be more amenable to peace negotiations if the United States halted the bombing of the North unconditionally.

The *Washington Post* among many others in the media questioned the reliability of Salisbury's reports, asserting that his casualty figures, which lacked attribution, were similar to those contained in Communist propaganda pamphlets. Daniel retorted in a statement: "It was apparent in Mr. Salisbury's first dispatch—and he so stated in a subsequent dispatch—that the casualty figures came from North Vietnamese officials. Where else could he get such figures in Hanoi?" Very privately, Daniel summed up the uproar in a memo to executive editor Catledge, who was abroad, noting that "the Publisher was perturbed" about Salisbury's dispatches, and detailed how he was handling the nationwide fire storm which they had ignited. "Getting into Hanoi was a journalistic coup," Daniel said. "Harrison, as might be expected, very promptly dug up some interesting facts that weren't known before. He disclosed that there was considerably more damage to civilian areas than Washington was quick to acknowledge that this was so. At the same time, he obviously gave comfort to North Vietnam by affording an outlet for its propaganda and the point of view, and comfort to those who are opposed to the bombing, and opposed to the war . . . and as you know, Harrison has complicated matters by failing in his first dispatches to attribute casualty statistics and other controversial information directly to those from whom he received it. I asked him in a telegram to do this, and he has subsequently complied . . . The desk was instructed not to print anything without attribution or, if the attribution was obvious, as it was in most cases, they should simply put it in."

Daniel, who had begun to read Salisbury's dispatches before they were published, instructed editors in another memorandum to do "everything we can in coming weeks to balance the Salisbury reports." The *Times* then ran a front-page story by Hanson W. Baldwin, our military analyst, who was one of the most vociferous critics of Salisbury's reporting. He quoted Pentagon sources describing Salisbury's accounts as "grossly exaggerated." On all sides, by Washington officials and the media, the challenges to Salisbury's reporting centered on lack of specific attribution.

In one of the most frustrating turns of my career as foreign editor, I was absent from New York when Salisbury did his reporting. I was at home in

Scarsdale on Christmas Day and then left on a long-planned first tour of our bureaus in Eastern and Western Europe. After my return to New York on January 24, I was apprised of some of the details of how Salisbury's dispatches had been handled by the Foreign Desk. But it was not until September 2007, more than forty years later, that I learned for the first time precisely what happened on the Foreign Desk on Christmas Eve when Salisbury's first dispatch landed. Possibly to avoid embarrassing some of the desk editors on duty that night, the full account had been withheld from the top editors.

I learned the full story when I met with Evan Jenkins, who had been on the Foreign Desk on that Christmas Eve and handled Salisbury's copy. Jenkins thereafter had become one of my assistant foreign editors and later became a senior editor on the paper's central News Desk. At our reunion he was consulting editor, the chief copy editor, of the *Columbia Journalism Review*. There was a standing joke between me and Jenkins, an old friend, that he had spoken to me after midnight more often than my wife. When I served as assistant managing editor and later managing editor, Jenkins, working on the News Desk during what is called in newsroom jargon the "night trick," would call me if there was a major news break or a question of changing the front page of the newspaper.

I met Jenkins, at his suggestion, at a bistro near the Columbia campus, where he told me his untold story. Salisbury's first report from Hanoi arrived late Saturday, Christmas Eve, after the close of the first edition. The article was published in the late editions of Sunday, Christmas Day, and evoked no manifest stir, possibly because it had not made the first edition, which was the edition normally distributed in Washington. The dispatch was not seen in the capital until the next day. Yet there was another reason why the dispatch did not immediately evoke controversy. The copy editor assigned to handle Salisbury's first dispatch was Evan, who had joined the *Times* only six months earlier from the Long Island newspaper *Newsday*. As he read it, he became deeply concerned by the lack of attribution for some key aspects of the dispatch. He found himself confronted with both journalistic and personal dilemmas. Here he was, editing the work of not only one of the *Times*'s most brilliant and experienced reporters—Salisbury had won a Pulitzer Prize in 1955 for his reporting from Moscow—but also someone who was an assistant managing editor. Ironically, one of Salisbury's routine duties in the newsroom was to provide Clifton Daniel, the managing editor, with a postmortem of the previous day's paper for the purpose of spotting and culling out just the kind of flaws that Jenkins now saw in the Salisbury dispatch. Fully aware that the dispatch, once published, given the heated

debate in the United States on Vietnam policy, would draw the most critical inspection, Jenkins balked at signing off on it. Consultations then took
place with many-sided implications. Jenkins pointed out to his supervisor
on the desk, Cleve Mathews, that Salisbury was reporting details about the
American bombings that he could not possibly know through personal observation yet he had not attributed the reports. Jenkins had just been advised by another supervisor, the desk slot man, as he was handed the Salisbury dispatch for editing: "Evan, it's my experience that the best way to deal
with Salisbury's copy is to hook the paragraphs, fix the syntax, and otherwise leave it alone." Agitated, Jenkins told Mathews that he would rather
quit than put the dispatch into the paper in its existing form. Mathews then
took the copy to Larry Hauck, the editor in charge of the paper that night.
He was a member of what was known then as the Bullpen, composed of the
most senior news editors. When Hauck came to him on the desk rim, Jenkins pointed out several of the flaws in the copy. Hauck said: "Edit the damn
thing the way it needs to be edited." Jenkins then inserted phrases in the
dispatch which made it clear that much of the information about casualties
and damage Salisbury was reporting came from the North Vietnamese. He
also bracketed in a paragraph which quoted a State Department acknowledgment, issued just two days earlier, that the possibility of accidental bombing could not be ruled out. The changes made the story acceptable in keeping with the *Times*'s journalistic standards.

Two dispatches from Salisbury, which Jenkins did not edit, arrived subsequently on Monday, December 26, one having been filed the day before but
delayed in transmission. Both were published in the paper of Tuesday, December 27, but this time the "leave it alone" approach apparently prevailed,
and there were no insertions of attribution.

Waiting for me in late January upon my return from my trip was a rather
anguished note, dated Monday night (December 26) from Jenkins. It turned
out that he had not read the second and third dispatches, had not edited
them, and had not seen them until late that night. In his memo, with a tear
sheet from the Tuesday paper attached, Jenkins said: "I am enclosing sam-
ples of what I consider to be unfortunate reporting. In the places I've encircled, it seems to me Salisbury is reporting conclusions and not known fact."
But he added: "I ought to make it clear that I'm inclined to accept almost everything he said, including the conclusions."

After our talk that September afternoon in 2007 when he told me his
story, Jenkins sent me four documents. One was a recap of what he told me.
With it was a clip of Salisbury's first dispatch with penciled markings of

the editing done by him. Another was a copy of the Monday, December 26, memo he sent me, which had been lost in the files of forty years ago.

Despite the challenges to his reporting, Salisbury's dispatches swelled the growing public opposition to the war and heightened distrust of the claims of progress being made by the White House and the Pentagon. The historian Barbara Tuchman would later comment in her book *The March of Folly: From Troy to Vietnam*, that after Salisbury's reporting from North Vietnam, "Johnson's ratings in the polls for handling of the war slid into the negative and would never again regain a majority of support." But the attribution issue probably cost Salisbury a Pulitzer Prize, an accolade which I believe he deserved for his enterprise and the substance of his reporting. Turner Catledge was serving on the Pulitzer Prize Board when Salisbury lost out in the voting. The board turned aside the 4–1 recommendation of the International Reporting Jury and voted 6–5 against the Salisbury entry. In his memoir *My Life and The Times*, Catledge, who had recused himself from the deliberations in keeping with the board's conflict-of-interest rules, said he believed that members of the board who were supporting the war had voted against Salisbury for political reasons. However, he conceded that the *Times* had made an editorial slip in that Salisbury provided no attribution for the figures on civilian casualties in his first dispatch, making himself vulnerable to his critics. He argued that apart from personal observations, the information in Salisbury's dispatch obviously could come only from the North Vietnamese. He noted that the rest of the fourteen dispatches which Salisbury filed from Hanoi and the eight from Hong Kong were adequately attributed. Catledge himself erred in his memoir. The lack of attribution which drew fire was not in the first dispatch, edited by Jenkins, but in the two that arrived next, which were published as filed.

The fourth document which Jenkins sent me was a copy of a letter he sent on December 16, 1996, to John R. MacArthur, the publisher of *Harper's*, in connection with an article MacArthur was writing for the *Columbia Journalism Review*. It said, in part: "Topping, who had finished a foreign correspondent's career when he became foreign editor earlier in 1966, was also nominated for a Pulitzer prize that year for a series reporting on the slaughter of supposed Communists in Indonesia. I remember that it was very good. I was the grunt editor on that one, too. The Pulitzer advisory board, having rejected Salisbury even though he should have been a shoo-in, could hardly give the prize to another *Times* entry. So the prize for 1966 went to a *Christian Science Monitor* correspondent [John Hughes] for his coverage, as it happened, of the slaughter in Indonesia."

Three months after I met with Jenkins, I was devastated when I received a message from David Jones, the former national editor of the *Times,* informing me that Jenkins had died of cancer. Evan had not told me that he was terminally ill. He had arranged to meet with me before his death, evidently because he wanted to be sure that I knew and perhaps would record the full details of what happened that Christmas Eve in the *Times* newsroom. At a memorial gathering several days after Evan's death, I recounted his story to his family and friends. I told them that Evan was the kind of editor that made the *New York Times* a great newspaper.

―――――――――――

On November 30, 1966, two months after my appointment as foreign editor, I wrote to Clifton Daniel in effect asking for a mandate to undertake a major reform of the foreign news report and restructuring of the desk. In my memorandum to him, I said: "As the world becomes more complex, our reporting tasks multiply and the competition for space increases correspondingly. To fulfill our function as the paper of record, we should progressively become more selective as to the detail we publish. We must also develop appropriate forms of summary reporting if we are to open space for the growing number of subjects that demand attention. The social, intellectual and technological revolutions are moving nations more than politics and our report does not adequately reflect that perspective. Too much detail is slipping into papers, which is of ephemeral interest and does not significantly inform or stimulate our readers."

The mandate I requested for change was forthcoming from Daniel, who had been a correspondent in London and Moscow and saw the need for reform of our foreign news operations. A significant paring of the foreign report, which I instituted immediately, was to dispense with the lengthy texts of diplomatic notes exchanged among nations, which had been a hallmark of the *Times* as the paper of record but, I felt, added very little to our readers' understanding of events.

My reshaping of the report began in 1967 with a restructuring of the Foreign News Copy Desk in New York. The Foreign Desk I inherited was staffed with editors who seemed to function in the most routine, dispirited manner. I ruled strictly against copy editors tampering with the substance of a story, but I expected them to do more than correct punctuation and spelling. There was often a need to go back to correspondents on their stories to close gaps, question unsubstantiated assertions, fix the structure of a piece, or ask for follow-ups. But treated often by *Times* executives as little more than a collection of hacks—not an unusual attitude toward copy editors at many newspapers—our Foreign Desk editors often hesitated to engage with reporters in the field. Curious about these faceless people on the rim, I asked each to submit a detailed personal résumé. To my delight, I found these unknowns were possessed of an extraordinary range of talents and expertise. While earning a living on the copy desk, some were employed part-time as teachers or writers and editors at other publications. One of the most outstanding of the editors was Allan Siegal, who handled the critical late-night trick. Siegal left the paper for a time to join ABC, but I was instrumental in bringing him back to the Foreign Desk. It was an act I look back at with great satisfaction. Siegal eventually became an assistant managing editor serving as the longtime arbiter of style and standards in the copy editing of the paper. Looking to exploit my newly discovered resources on the Foreign News Desk, I assigned each of the copy editors to work as an area specialist and arranged opportunities for them to do independent research. Enjoying greater mutual respect, editors and reporters began working more closely together. The copy showed very marked improvement, and there was a greater flow of story ideas.

In June 1968, following the restructuring of the desk, I distributed a lengthy memorandum entitled "Foreign Desk Guidelines" designed to govern the content of the report and asked all correspondents to comment. It covered everything from the techniques of interpretive reporting, to the structure of stories, to closer collaboration with the copy desk. At the core of the guidelines was the statement:

To survive in the competition with electronic media, news magazines and the suburban press, which are attracting an increasing share of public attention, we must offer something more. If we are to remain the leader in foreign news reporting, we must add new facts and dimensions to our coverage. Specifically, what can *The New York Times,* with its unique staff, resources and public service tradition, do to better serve the reader? Governments will determine in large measure whether mankind can solve its great problems of security, law and material wellbeing, and, therefore, we should remain deeply concerned with the conduct of governmental affairs. However, we can be less preoccupied with the daily official rhetoric of the capitals. We should report more about how the peoples live, and what they and their societies look like, how their institutions and systems operate. Our report should reflect more fully the social, cultural, intellectual, scientific and technological revolutions, which, more than the political, are transforming the world society. And to comprehend, our readers must have more than sophisticated interpretive writing.

To give correspondents more latitude I developed the concept of the "Takeout," a new form of special article ranging in length from one to three columns written to add perspective, depth, and understanding to a subject. It did not require a strong spot news peg and therefore broadened coverage in such underreported regions as Latin America and Africa. The staff responded extraordinarily well to the new approach incorporated in the guidelines, and the report took on a more comprehensive and modern cast.

The final stage in the transformation of the report was completed when a tall, smiling, very likeable man began browsing about my desk. He was Walter Mattson, the paper's newly appointed production manager. He was doing what the previous publisher, Arthur Hays Sulzberger, had forbidden. To guard the independence of the News Department, Sulzberger erected what was dubbed the "Chinese Wall." It separated the News Department from the Editorial Department, which produced the opinion pages, and also barred business executives from the third-floor newsroom and any interference with the news report. Mattson, who eventually became president of the paper, was the first business executive to venture over the wall, and I was his first collaborator. I had been railing against the hodgepodge manner in which the foreign report was presented in the paper. In keeping with tradition, the foreign report was printed in the first pages of the main section followed in order by the national report, metropolitan news, financial, and sports. However, the foreign stories were simply dumped into the paper, being positioned haphazardly between ads according to the requirements of the Advertising and Production departments. Mattson offered a solution. He persuaded his advertising and production colleagues on December 12, 1968, to grant me a choice display space fixed across the top of page 3 and arranged for other fixed "holes" in following pages. The new layouts improved the presentation of the foreign report immensely. This design was adhered to through the following years. During those years I moved up in 1969 to become assistant managing editor and deputy to Abe Rosenthal, the managing editor. In 1977, I became managing editor when Rosenthal was appointed executive editor in charge of both the News Department and the Sunday Department. Working as team with Arthur Gelb, the metropolitan editor, Louis Silverstein, the highly talented staff designer, and on the business side, Mattson and John Pomfret, the general manager, we transformed the daily *Times* into a four-section paper. It was made up of a first section containing foreign and national news, the editorial page, and a facing Op-Ed page; the second section was devoted to New York metropolitan news; the third was made up of alternating sections devoted to lifestyle, culture, and sports; the fourth, to business under the title Business Day. This four-section paper became a model for newspapers throughout the country. Attracting new readers and advertisers, it made the *Times* highly profitable after a period in the 1970s when it was close to operating at a loss. The transformation was made possible by the courage and vision of the publisher, Arthur Ochs Sulzberger, who agreed to invest heavily in the changes although the *Times* company was then under the most severe economic strain.

This design of the Times changed radically in 2009 under executive editor Bill Keller. Page 3 of the first section was given over to the continuation (called "jumps" in newspaper parlance) of stories beginning on the front page. The introduction to the foreign news report was moved to a page further inside. This switch was part of a broad reconfiguration of the paper in which pages were shifted and sections merged in order to reduce production costs and open premium space for advertising. The four-section design was abandoned. The *Times* like virtually all newspapers was suffering financially by the migration of advertisers and readers to the Internet. Viewing the paper from my retirement observation post, I accepted the urgent need to reduce costs and attract more advertising. I was grateful that the changes did not impact on the essential quality of the foreign news report. Nevertheless, I was pained by the decision to relegate the introduction to the foreign news report, long regarded as the "jewel" of the *Times,* to a less prominent position. I was more troubled by the change in the character of the front page which accompanied the structural redesign.

From 1970, serving then as assistant managing editor, to 1987, when I re tired as managing editor, I chaired the 4 P.M. news conference at which the front page of the paper is designed. Seated with Rosenthal, who became executive editor in 1977, together with other senior news editors and the departmental chiefs, we made up the front according to a traditional format. What we judged to be the lead, the most important story of the day, was positioned in the far right column, with the story second in importance generally as the off-lead in the far left column. Stories were then positioned down the page in what we considered to be the descending order of importance, allowing at times for a news analysis piece or an interesting feature at the bottom. The Associated Press reported daily on the makeup of the front page, which many newspaper editors across the country used as a guide in composing their own front pages.

Under Bill Keller's editorial direction, the front page evolved from its traditional hard news format into a page given over in great part to stories with a feature-type approach. Apart from the lead fixed in column 6 on the right side, stories were positioned in no consistent recognizable order. On the bottom of the page, there were brief referrals ("reefers") to articles and editorial commentaries on inside pages. Whatever may have been gained by this "soft news" approach in competition with Internet Web sites which give priority to hard late-breaking new, the front page of the print edition of the *Times,* in my view, suffered the loss of an important attribute. It no longer serves the public as the oft-quoted daily guide to what *Times* editors gauge to be the most important events of the day. The AP no longer reports daily on the makeup of the *Times* front page.

My tenure as foreign editor ended in 1969 when I moved up to the job of assistant managing editor. This move pitched me into the center of a succession dispute which threw the hierarchy of the paper into turmoil. In July 1969, when the succession crisis was moving toward resolution, I was at the Foreign Desk one afternoon just outside the executive editor's office when Scotty Reston emerged and walked past me silently to a nearby book stand on which rested an unabridged dictionary. I looked at Reston uneasily and wondered if I should speak to him, try to mend our relations, which had deteriorated. I had long admired Reston for his work as a columnist in Washington, sharing a view held by many that he ranked with Walter Lippmann as one of the most outstanding journalists of his generation. My relations with Reston had become somewhat strained several weeks after he came up from Washington to replace Turner Catledge as executive editor. I was at a dinner in August 1968 in Connecticut when I received word that Soviet bloc armies had invaded Czechoslovakia to eclipse the "Prague Spring," a period of liberalization introduced by Communist Party leader Alexander Dubček. I drove back to the office and found Reston with several news editors debating what they should do about coverage. I listened impatiently for a several minutes and then said: "Okay, amateur night is over. I'll take it from here." Reston stalked way furious. I later regretted this arrogance on my part. But on this particular morning Reston was cool to me for reasons that went far beyond the irritations of that incident. His demeanor related to the succession dispute.

The affair began with decision of the publisher to appoint A. M. Rosenthal as managing editor. Before becoming assistant managing editor, Abe had served as metropolitan editor, and earlier as a correspondent performing brilliantly in Poland, India, and Japan. For his reporting from Poland he was awarded a Pulitzer Prize in 1960, the citation taking note of the fact that he had been expelled by the Communist regime, not for erroneous reporting, but for "the depth of his reporting into Polish affairs." On the day Punch Sulzberger decided to appoint Rosenthal as managing editor, Reston, without informing the publisher or Rosenthal, telephoned Anthony Lewis, the bureau chief in London, and offered him the position of assistant managing editor. Reached at the opera during an intermission, Tony unhesitatingly accepted the job as deputy, which meant he would become second in command of the News Department. He agreed to come to New York at once. Reston had acted unaware that Rosenthal already had decided to appoint me as his deputy. Selecting me had not been easy for Rosenthal. It meant bypassing his closest friend, Arthur Gelb, the very talented metropolitan editor, who very much wanted the job and later complained in his memoir *City Room* that he had felt betrayed.

Reminiscing years later in an interview about the affair with John Stacks, Reston's biographer, Rosenthal said: "I passed over Arthur Gelb, a very close friend, because we were both emotional and excitable. I chose Topping. There were things I was very good at, and things, I wasn't good at. Topping was very good. You didn't fuck around with Topping. He did not invite arguments. There was a quality of organization that he had. I thought we would be a very good team."

When Reston summoned Rosenthal to his office to congratulate him on his appointment as managing editor, the meeting was amicable until Rosenthal told him he had selected me as his deputy. Reston, very upset, disclosed he had offered the job to Tony Lewis. Rosenthal registered his opposition with no shortages of expletives, and when he left Reston's office, he felt his pending appointment as managing editor was very much in doubt. To mediate, Sulzberger summoned a meeting at which Reston accused Rosenthal of "wanting to do everything himself." Still raging, Rosenthal did not budge. The publisher, buffeted between his two senior news executives, made no decision. But when Lewis turned up in the office the following day, Punch told him: "Abe has decided he wants Top, and if he wants Top, he will have him." In compensation Lewis was offered, and accepted, a position as a columnist on the Op-Ed page, a job he was eminently suited for and one in which he achieved great distinction.

I had all of this in mind as I looked at Reston flipping the pages of the dictionary. Eager to make peace, I braced myself and went up to him. He glanced at me and said: "The power thing is over," and went back to turning the pages. I retreated to my desk. As he made plain, the shuffling in the hierarchy had been a "power thing" for Reston. Lewis had worked in the Washington Bureau and was one of a group there dubbed "Scotty's boys." Appointment of Lewis as assistant managing editor would have given Reston greater influence in the News Department and positioned Lewis as a possible successor to Rosenthal as managing editor. At the end of July, Sulzberger announced formally that Rosenthal was named managing editor succeeding Clifton Daniel, who became associate editor, and I was named assistant managing editor. Reston, unwilling to forgo writing his column and uncomfortable working in New York as a hands-on executive, elected to return to Washington as a vice president.

In the two decades I served as an editor at the *Times,* perhaps my most enjoyable years were spent on the Foreign Desk, working with correspondents and deeply involved daily with international news. One of the most challenging requirements of the job was selecting and preparing reporters to cover the wars in Indochina. I would brief them, deeply concerned about their safety, and tell them of my own field experience if it seemed useful. In the end what counted most, of course, was not my advice but their intelligence, discretion, courage, and luck.

Gloria Emerson was among the superb reporters that I was privileged to send to Vietnam. Emerson turned to me repeatedly seeking a Vietnam assignment. There was hesitancy among some of the executives about sending a woman to cover the war and particularly Emerson, who was regarded as quite emotional and fragile although she had done well in covering the Northern Ireland violence and the Nigerian civil war. I managed to clear the way for her, and she was sent to Vietnam in 1970 by Jim Greenfield, my successor as foreign editor. She performed brilliantly for two years, providing a profoundly human aspect to our Vietnam report that conveyed more poignantly the cruelty and hopelessness of the war. When she sent me her book *Winners and Losers,* a personal copy in which she had scribbled some second thoughts, she wrote on the flyleaf: "For Seymour Topping, the best Foreign Editor of them all, who started me on the long road, and who has my gratitude and respect." I treasured that note as a signature to my years as foreign editor.

Working as assistant managing editor to the talented, innovative Abe Rosenthal was a most fulfilling experience particularly in our creation of the four-section paper. But it also had its onerous turns. Several months after taking on the job of being his deputy I suffered one of my more unhappy journalistic experiences. In 1970 I contacted Edgar Snow by phone in China and asked him to do an article for the *Times*. He was traveling with Huang Hua and had been interviewing Chinese leaders. On October 1 he had been at the side of Mao Zedong on the rostrum of the Tiananmen Gate during the celebration of the twenty-first anniversary of the founding of the People's Republic of China. It was Mao's way of recognizing the American who had done more than anyone else beginning in the 1930s to bring the Chinese Communist movement to world attention. I was delighted to be in touch with Snow. As I have mentioned earlier, I had read Snow's *Red Star over China* while a senior in high school, just after it was published in 1938, and his epic adventures heightened my resolve to become a correspondent in China. In 1939 I followed Snow's career path by entering the University of Missouri to study journalism. After my telephone contact with Snow, I met his wife, Lois Wheeler Snow, in December when she was passing through New York, and I reiterated to her my interest in an article. Before leaving China for the United States to visit her daughter, who was a freshman at Antioch College, Lois had stood beside Mao and her husband on the Tiananmen Gate rostrum viewing the festivities. Edgar Snow submitted an article to us in February after his trip to China from his home in Geneva. He had made his family home in Switzerland, fleeing the umbrage directed by conservative critics against many China specialists in the press, the State Department, and academia during the McCarthy period and the Cold War.

The article Snow sent us was very lengthy and based largely on a series of interviews with Premier Zhou Enlai. Jim Greenfield, who had replaced me as foreign editor, and Rosenthal joined me in reviewing the piece. Rosenthal found the article overly long and propagandistic in some of its aspects. Strongly anti-Communist since his tour as a correspondent in Poland, Rosenthal was uneasy about giving too much space to an article by a journalist known to be very sympathetic to the Chinese Communists. He insisted on drastic cuts. Snow was resistant to making any cuts and asserted that none be made without his prior approval. He had assured Zhou Enlai that no cuts would be made in his answers to questions. I was eager to go forward with publication. Although the article was, in fact, lengthier than what was usually deemed acceptable in the *Times* format, it contained unique insights into the thinking of the Chinese leadership and clearly indicated that there was an open door to exchanges with the Nixon administration for an improvement in relations. At the time we were not aware that the article reflected the attitude of Mao Zedong, which had been conveyed to Snow in off-the-record remarks. The Snow article thus contained one of the first signals that Peking was ready to do business with the Nixon administration. Unable to elicit Snow's agreement to his proposed cuts, Rosenthal summarily rejected the article.

It fell to me unhappily to telephone Snow that night, rousing him from sleep to tell him that the *Times* would not publish his article. Despite my regrets proffered in anguished terms, Snow was furious. His fury extended later to instructing his agent to do no further business with the *Times*. Lois withdrew an Op-Ed piece about to be published ruminating about Peking street scenes. In the end, the affair proved costly in competitive journalistic terms to the *Times*. The *New Republic* published the Snow article starting in March in a five-part series. But it was to *Life* magazine that Snow gave his great China scoops. He turned to *Life* because the popular magazine would afford him the broad audience denied to him by the *Times*. Since the death in 1967 of publisher Henry Luce, a leading member of the China Lobby, *Life* had become a more freewheeling publication. In April, *Life* published a lengthy Snow article which commanded wide attention quoting Mao as stating that he would be happy to talk with Nixon "either as a tourist or as President" and that "the problems between China and the U.S.A. would have to be solved with Nixon." Snow felt free at that point to reveal details of his off-the-record interview with Mao because prospects had ripened for dialogue between Peking and Washington. Zhou Enlai had made an opening gambit by inviting an American ping-pong team to China. Speculation about the Snow article, whose substance some American officials had questioned, ended on July 16 when Nixon announced that Kissinger had returned from a secret visit to Peking and that he had accepted an invitation for a presidential visit to China. Overnight, Snow and his book *Red Star over China* became extremely hot properties. On July 30, *Life* published another Snow article headlined "What China Wants from Nixon's Visit." The portrait of a smiling Zhou Enlai on the cover of the magazine was a photograph taken by Audrey during her father's conversation with Zhou Enlai in May in the Great Hall of the People.

In December, Snow entered a hospital in Switzerland to undergo an operation for cancer. Zhou Enlai sent a team of doctors and nurses to Snow's home in Geneva hoping he would agree to return to China for treatment. The Chinese medical group was led by George Hatem, his old friend from

Yenan days. Hatem and Huang Hua, then the permanent representative of China to the United Nations, went together to Snow's bedside. Pleasantly surprised, Snow exclaimed: "Well, we three bandits." "Bandits" was the propaganda epithet used by Chiang Kai-shek during the Civil War in describing Mao's Eighth Route Army. Snow slipped into a coma not long after the visit and died in the early morning of February 15, less than three days before President Nixon enplaned for Peking.

In my book *Journey between Two Chinas,* published in the year of his death, I said of Snow: "Like so many of his colleagues in the field, I am bereaved by the death this year of Edgar Snow, and I salute his pioneering research and his reporting, which have been of so much value to us." Among my many great regrets at his passing: I never had a chance to thank him for what he had done for a kid from the Bronx.

33

THE PENTAGON PAPERS

Early in March 1971, unexpectedly and under the most extraordinary circumstances, we became privy at the *Times* to the secret history of the conduct of the Vietnam War by the administrations of presidents Truman, Eisenhower, Kennedy, and Johnson. The history, which became known as the Pentagon Papers, contained such stunning revelations as the fact that President Johnson went ahead with the expansion of the bombing of North Vietnam in 1965 despite the judgment of the government's intelligence community that it would not, as he intended, impel Hanoi to cease its support of the Vietcong insurgency in the South. Contained also was the estimate made a few months later that the bombing was militarily ineffective. The Pentagon Papers came into our possession through the ingenuity of Neil Sheehan, an investigative reporter in our Washington Bureau. They were made available to him secretly by Daniel Ellsberg, a political analyst employed by the Rand Corporation, a research firm which did work for the government on sensitive projects.

The Papers comprised a forty-seven-volume history of the United States' involvement in Indochina and Southeast Asia generally from World War II to May 1968, when peace negotiations with the North Vietnamese opened in Paris and President Johnson announced his intention not to seek another term as president. The study had been commissioned by Robert McNamara in June 1967 when he was secretary of defense, on the assumption that its findings would provide useful guidelines for future policy making. The project, designated the Vietnam Study Task Force, employing thirty-six historians and analysts, was headed by Leslie Gelb, a former Senate aide who later left government service to become a Washington reporter at the *Times,* then a columnist, and eventually president of the Council on Foreign Relations. Ellsberg, a summa cum laude graduate of Harvard, had been employed by Gelb as one of his analysts and had been given access to two copies of the existing fifteen which were held in the Rand office in Santa Monica, California. A former marine officer and once employed in Vietnam by the Defense Department, Ellsberg had been a hawkish supporter of the war. But

then observing the evolution of the war in Vietnam and Cambodia and reading through the Pentagon Papers, he had become disaffected and committed to doing what he could to bring the wars to an end. In making contact
with Sheehan, whom he had met in Vietnam, Ellsberg was seeking means
of making public forty-three volumes of the Pentagon Papers, although they
were still classified "'top secret," hoping that the disclosures would spur the
Congress and the public to resolve the Vietnam War. He was withholding
four volumes which related to the peace talks in Paris so as not to prejudice
the negotiations. Ellsberg copied the Papers with Anthony J. Russo, a close
friend, who was also employed at the Rand site and, like Ellsberg, passionately committed to seeking an end to the Vietnam War. Prior to contact-
ing Sheehan, Ellsberg had attempted unsuccessfully to interest members of
Congress, including Senator William Fulbright, chairman of the Foreign
Relations Committee, and Senator George McGovern. He found them unwilling to handle the files because of their highly classified nature. He had
been warned by lawyers that leaking the classified Papers might land him
in jail.

The Papers revealed details of how the Truman administration had aided
the French in perpetuating their colonial controls while ignoring Ho Chi
Minh's repeated appeals for cooperation in realizing the independence of
Vietnam, the origins of the gradual descent by the United States militarily
into the Indochina quagmire, and accounts of how covert sabotage operations had been carried out against North Vietnam by the Kennedy and Johnson administrations. Most significantly they documented how the Congress
and the public had been deceived through the withholding or distortion of
information about the conduct of the war.

Neil Sheehan brought us, without revealing his source, photocopied dupes
of what Ellsberg had carried piecemeal in his briefcase over months out of
the Rand offices. Over a weekend at an apartment in Boston where he had
stored the Papers Ellsberg permitted Sheehan to read the documents with
the understanding that he would only make notes. He was not yet prepared
to turn over the documents because Sheehan could not give him assurance
that the *Times* would publish the Papers in considerable detail prior to their
inspection by senior editors. Aware that some of the documents were already circulating in some circles, and determined not to be beaten out on the
story, Sheehan ignored Ellsberg's stipulation and went in search of a copying machine. Alerted earlier by Sheehan to his possession of the Papers, we
wired him the $1,500 needed to keep a copy shop open all weekend to dupli-
cate them. Sheehan and his wife, Susan, then drove with the Papers piled in

their car to Washington. From New York, we dispatched Gerald Gold, one of our most skilled copy editors, to Washington to join Sheehan in delving through 3,000 pages in narrative of studies made by Gelb's group and 4,000 pages of appended documents. Sheehan, Gold, and Max Frankel, the Washington bureau chief, then brought the Papers, with their notes, to New York to be scrutinized by A. M. Rosenthal, the managing editor, myself, and the foreign editor, James L. Greenfield.

Greenfield, a former assistant secretary of state for public affairs under Dean Rusk, with experience in processing government documents, was put in charge of the team preparing the Papers for publication, which was designated in-house the Vietnam Archive. Writers, editors, and researchers were assigned to work with Greenfield under the most secure arrangements. Our first task was to establish the authenticity of the documents, although we had the fullest confidence in Sheehan's reliability as an investigative reporter. I knew Sheehan well personally, and his wife, Susan, a writer for the *New Yorker* magazine, first having met Neil in Saigon in 1963 when he was working as a reporter for the United Press. Born in Holyoke, Massachusetts, the son of a dairy farmer, a cum laude graduate of Harvard, he was then twenty-seven years old, a tireless and dedicated reporter. Impressed with his talents, energy, and courage in covering Vietnam, I was instrumental in bringing him to the *Times* in 1964.

Greenfield soon told Rosenthal and me that checking discreetly with authoritative sources and studying the documents had convinced him of their authenticity. Internal transmission markings on the documents were scrubbed out to ensure that, if stolen, they not be used by hostile agents to break the codes. The "top secret" stamps had been removed earlier, presumably by Ellsberg. The operation then went into high gear, competitively spurred by information that some of the material had been seen by others, specifically a group which intended to publish some of the material in book form. We also learned that the *Washington Post* was tracking the Papers.

It was apparent that many weeks would be required to select and correlate contents of the documents so they could be published coherently. On April 22, the operation was expanded with additional staffers and moved into two suites in the New York Hilton, with guards posted at the doors to maintain security. The writers in addition to Sheehan were Fox Butterfield, E. W. Kenworthy, and Hedrick Smith. The editors included Gold, Allan Siegal, and Samuel Abt.

On April 29, Rosenthal, Greenfield, and I were called by Harding F. Bancroft, a lawyer, who was an executive vice president of the paper, to a meeting in the boardroom of the *Times* on the fourteenth floor, where Arthur O. Sulzberger, the publisher, and other executives had their offices. James Reston came up from Washington for the meeting. The subject was the Pentagon Papers. When Rosenthal and I entered the boardroom, we were disturbed by the number of people present, knowing that the more people aware of our possession of the Papers, the greater the chance of a leak. If the government learned of our project, it might move to seize the Papers or halt publication through a court injunction.

We were surprised to see Louis M. Loeb, a partner of Lord, Day & Lord, corporate counsel to the *Times* for twenty-three years, and two of his legal associates. Others present were Arthur Sulzberger, the publisher, Ivan Veit, another executive vice president who supervised our book-publishing enterprise, James C. Goodale, the general counsel of the paper, and Sydney Gruson, then assistant to the publisher.

As the News Department did on all stories that might bring legal repercussions, Rosenthal had informed Goodale about our plans to publish the Papers. Goodale, as was the normal practice in cases where court litigation was a possibility, had consulted with Lord, Day & Lord. With the publisher at the head of the table, the editors, Reston, Rosenthal, Greenfield, and I, sat facing the lawyers. It was the obligation of Loeb and his associates to point out possible legal pitfalls, and they did so scrupulously and emphatically. But it seemed to us, the editors, they did so without sensitivity to the broader questions of the public interest and the journalistic responsibilities of the *Times*. The lawyers read extracts from the federal secrecy codes pertinent to the dissemination of classified information which stipulated penalties for violations of up to imprisonment for ten years—whereupon Reston remarked wryly, with the concurrence of all the editors, that he would be delighted to go to jail on this one. If the *Times* did not publish, he said he would be glad to do so in the *Vineyard Gazette,* a weekly newspaper he owned on Martha's Vineyard, a resort island off the Massachusetts coast. The editors contended that the secrecy codes were not applicable since the documents were historical in nature, did not affect the national defense, and the press had repeatedly published, without penalty, classified material of a similar nature in the public interest. Max Frankel would later submit from Washington a detailed affidavit documenting that this was the case. I also advanced my contention that the publication of the Papers was vital to the national debate that was in progress on a question that transcended the Vietnam War. What was revealed in the Papers would help the Congress and the public determine whether new safeguards were needed against secret arbitrary action by the Executive Branch.

The meeting ended with the publisher ruling that we would go forward with the preparation of the Papers for publication, but he withheld his final decision as to whether to publish pending a final exhaustive review of all the factors involved. It was plain watching the forty-five-year-old publisher at the table as he looked side to side that the burden of making a ruling was weighing extremely heavily on him. It was falling to him to decide what ultimately was in the public interest, evaluate the warnings of his legal consultants that the *Times* and its executives might face criminal prosecution, and gauge how the reputation of the paper would be affected. The project would cost, at a time of economic recession, millions of dollars in staff commitments, many additional pages of newsprint for the Papers, and large legal fees when the controversy inevitably would go into the courts.

For these reasons, Rosenthal and I were deeply troubled as we left the boardroom and walked down the corridor to the elevators. "Our jobs may also be on the line here," I said. Abe looked at me, his brow creased, and he nodded. We knew that if the *Times* did not publish the Papers, our positions at the paper might become untenable. Apart from the obligation to our readers, it was dubious that we could retain the loyalty and respect of the staff if we failed to print the Papers. In keeping with the tradition of the paper and his family, the publisher, known to all as Punch, had always stood by the editors, regardless of risk or cost. I believed, as did Rosenthal, that he would do so again. But there was no certainty.

In early May, as I was working with our writers and editors preparing for publication a series of summary articles based on the revelations in the Pentagon Papers, I was abruptly diverted. A cable arrived from Audrey: "Zhou Enlai says you can come to China." Audrey had been traveling in China for seventeen days with her father, Chester Ronning, her sister, Sylvia, and a Canadian television team. They were doing a documentary on Ronning's return to his birthplace, Fancheng, Hubei Province, three hundred miles up the Han River from Hankou. Ronning grew up in the town where his Lutheran missionary parents had founded a church and established the first middle school in China for both boys and girls. Audrey's grandmother, Hannah Ronning, a tall, slim woman with piercing blue eyes and long chestnut hair drawn into a bun, mother of seven children, had been a spirited, dedicated missionary. When she died at the age of thirty-six, both Christian and non-Christian Chinese thronged to her funeral, remembering her as a teacher and the woman who had tended many infant girls abandoned on village byways. The documentary television crew had filmed the Ronnings at her graveside in the church courtyard and also scenes of Chester chatting with his Chinese boyhood friends. When Audrey's grandfather, Halvor, opened the middle school in 1894, only one youngster turned up on the first day. When Audrey visited the school for a second time in 2008, she was cheered in the school yard by four thousand students waving welcoming banners.

On May Day, before they left for Fancheng, Zhou Enlai had welcomed Ronning and Audrey to the Great Hall of the People on Tiananmen Square in Peking. The premier received Ronning at a private side entrance. Welcoming him as "my old friend" and grasping his hand, he said: "I never shall forget what you did for me at the Geneva Conference [1954]." In the Jiangsu Room, one of the twenty-eight reception rooms of the Great Hall, Zhou offered tea and Central Flowery Kingdom cigarettes to his guests and laughingly chided Ronning for retiring from the Canadian diplomatic service. When Ronning protested that he had retired at seventy-one, although the compulsory age was sixty-five, the seventy-three-year-old premier quipped: "Well, you and I are exceptions to the rule. Take me now? Why should I retire?" A set of Audrey's photographs of Zhou Enlai as he conversed with Ronning were published on the front page of the *Times*. One of them, published as the cover of *Life* magazine in connection with an article by Edgar Snow, was subsequently issued by the Chinese government as an official photo.

When the Ronning party returned from their visit to Fancheng, Zhou gave a banquet in the Great Hall for Ronning. The ambassador used the occasion to ask whether visas could be granted to James Reston and me. I had asked Ronning if he would put forward both names, giving the Chinese the option of granting admission to a prestigious columnist or myself, well known to them from Civil War days, who could serve both as a reporter and as an executive who could negotiate the opening of a news bureau in Peking. The premier said he would assent to both visa applications and told Audrey she could message the news to me.

On May 13, I was seated on the speaker's platform in the Windsor Ballroom of the Commodore Hotel, having been corralled into lecturing about China to the New York Rotary Club. Still waiting impatiently to receive my visa, I was brooding: Shall I delight them with tales of my wife's adventures in China, or should I read from my yellowed clippings of two decades ago?

Suddenly I was summoned from the platform to take a telephone message. I was to call the Chinese Embassy in Ottawa. Visas had been approved for Reston and me. I flew to Ottawa that night. When Yao Yanliu, the embassy cultural attaché, handed me my visa the next morning, I asked if I could cross into China from Hong Kong on May 20 and join Audrey on the following day, her birthday. Yao left the timing in doubt. Back in New York, I went at once to see Rosenthal in his office. In his warm, effusive manner, Abe was enthusiastic about my return to China. It was an important reporting opportunity, since the *Times* had no correspondent in China. He knew how eager I was, having broken the story in 1966 in the *Times* of the onset of the Cultural Revolution, to cover the next phase of the vast upheaval. He also knew how I yearned to join Audrey in touring the land where we met and were engaged. But both of us were troubled about the timing of my departure just as we were completing preparation for publication of the Pentagon Papers. At the Hilton hotel, our reporters and editors were tirelessly studying the Papers, gripped by mounting excitement as they delved into the startling revelations, and had begun readying analytical articles for publication. The target date for publication of the first article was June 14. Yet there many imponderables: Sulzberger had yet to give us license to publish. Would the courts uphold our First Amendment rights to publish if the Nixon administration moved to block publication on security grounds? And what would be the reaction to the articles by the public, which was already locked in debate about how the country should cope with the Vietnam morass? We felt that the public had a right to know the contents of the Papers, but we were not bent on publishing with the intent of galvanizing the antiwar movement. In fact, Rosenthal was personally supportive of the war, although he never allowed his sentiments to influence our news coverage. When Sheehan and I were reminiscing years later about those weeks of agonizing uncertainty, he told me that he remembered most vividly the day Rosenthal appeared unexpectedly in their hotel work suite. Assembling the writers and editors, he told them to have faith that, despite the warnings of lawyers and the hesitations of business executives wary of the risks and costs, the Papers would be published. "He inspired us," Sheehan said. In truth, Rosenthal was not certain then that the management of the paper would accede to our plan. In the next days, as a caution he began reviewing his personal financial affairs to determine how he might support his family if he felt compelled to leave the paper.

Despite our qualms, Rosenthal and I agreed that I should leave for China immediately, to be followed in July by Reston, and that I would return on

June 10, four days before we intended to publish the Papers. We planned to communicate by cable or telephone if Rosenthal had urgent need of my presence at his side using as a confirming code the designation "Lloyd," the middle name of our foreign editor, James L. Greenfield. We locked hands and embraced in farewell, knowing that there would be trying days ahead. As I was going out the door, Rosenthal shouted: "Have fun! I'll cable you when we're ready to go to press."

34

MAOIST PURGE OF THE PARTY AND GOVERNMENT

I landed in Hong Kong on May 18, 1971, preoccupied with a spate of concerns: worry about leaving Abe Rosenthal to cope with the burdens of publishing the Pentagon Papers; how to cover the tumultuous events in Peking coming in cold on the story after an absence of two decades from the mainland; and my longing to be with Audrey. Early the next day, an official of the China Travel Service telephoned me at the Mandarin Hotel, to say that I was awaited across the border in Guangzhou. After two days in Guangzhou reporting on the devastation the city had suffered at the hands of the rampaging Red Guards, I was put smartly on a plane for Hangzhou unaware of what was a Communist plot to put me, as ordered by Premier Zhou Enlai, into the arms of my wife on her May 21 birthday. The plane wheeled over the East China Sea and then skimmed over Hangzhou Bay to the garden city on the shore of the ethereal West Lake. Audrey was waiting beside the airport runway, told only an hour or so earlier that I would be arriving. Dressed in a red gingham shirt and blue jeans, draped in cameras, she was vivacious and beautiful as ever. We drove from the airport along the shore of West Lake, on whose waters were gliding gondola-like pleasure boats, to the elegant Hangzhou Hotel. Rising beyond the hotel were the green terraced hills of the tea-raising communes. In secluded sections of the lake's nine-mile-long wooded shore there were nestled walled vacation retreats of Mao and other Chinese leaders.

Audrey had come to Hangzhou from Wuhan in Central China, where she and her father witnessed the use of acupuncture anesthesia in major surgery. Through an observation dome in the Wuhan hospital they watched a surgeon remove a tumor from the throat of a fully conscious fifty-four-year-old woman. Twenty minutes before, an acupuncturist had inserted two flexible needles into each wrist and whirled them until the patient reported numbness in the throat. Seconds after the last suture was tied, the patient sat up, ate some orange slices, put on her robe, thanked the operating team, and walked out waving her "Little Red Book" of Mao's sayings, no doubt as suggested by party officials. After testing the technique of acupuncture anes-

336

thesia in thousands of operations, mainly in remote areas where the usual apparatus and drugs were not available, Chinese doctors decided to demonstrate it to Westerners. Audrey, who had observed the technique in Wuhan and later saw it performed in Shanghai in open-heart surgery, was the first Western journalist to witness the procedures. Her reports stirred debate in the United States about the efficacy of acupuncture. Acupuncture came into wide usage later in many countries outside of China for a variety of treatments including use as a pain killer, but not for anesthesia in surgery. Chinese doctors did continue to employ it in surgery in later years when they felt it was preferable to the use of drugs or where operations had to be conducted at localities lacking modern anesthesia apparatus, Dr. Elizabeth A. Frost, an international expert on anesthesiology, told me.

In Hangzhou Audrey and I visited the West Lake People's Commune. In June 1966, when the Cultural Revolution was just beginning to spill into the provincial cities, Audrey recalled seeing portraits of Liu Shaoqi hung beside those of Mao. Now, the portraits of Liu were gone. Outside a nursery where rosy-cheeked tots of three and four sang songs in praise of Chairman Mao, there were wall posters denouncing the "traitor Liu Shaoqi."

Ronning was returning to Canada, and we said good-bye before going on to Shanghai en route to Peking. We flew to the capital on a day when the "yellow wind" had brought the dust, as it does each spring, from the Great North China Plain. The city was enfolded in a haze that lent a mystic quality to the imperial palaces and temples. But I soon found, alas, that beyond those monuments little remained of the imperial capital I had known. In 1947, I left a gem of a walled city in which camel caravans and donkey carts plodded along narrow cobbled alleyways lined with garden villas. Now, there was an endless stream of cars, buses, and army trucks flanked by countless bicyclists on the boulevards. The walls were almost entirely gone, and the city radiated out from Tiananmen, the Gate of Heavenly Peace, onto a paved square of ninety-eight acres. The expanse was marked with tiny squares each numbered so that the people summoned to demonstrate fealty to the Communist leaders standing on the rostrum of the vermillion gate would know their assigned places. Preserved on the west was Xinhuamen Gate, flanked by stone lions, the entrance to Zhongnanhai, the secluded Central South Lake Park. There, in a wood of cedars and pines where once the Ming emperors dwelt, stood the pavilions now occupied by Mao, Lin Biao, Zhou Enlai, and other leaders. No mention was made in the Chinese press of where the new emperors resided, nor were photographs published revealing their living styles.

On the west side of Tiananmen Square stood the modern Great Hall of the People, where Zhou Enlai was presiding over what seemed to be a thaw in the Cultural Revolution. In the Great Banquet Hall he was receiving a steady influx of foreign delegations. Among the first to be invited had been an American ping-pong team for what was less of a sporting event and more of a subtly contrived political gesture serving as a stage setting for the forthcoming visit by President Nixon. People encountered on the bustling streets and shops appeared to be enjoying their most relaxed spring since 1966, when the capital was first swept by the tumult of the Cultural Revolution. But this surface calm was deceptive. The raw wounds inflicted during the Cultural Revolution were not yet healed. Zhou Enlai was having difficulty managing the affairs of the country in the aftermath of the massive purge of government and party officials which had disrupted normal life. Mao was in failing health, possibly the early symptoms of Parkinson's disease, and maneuvering had already begun within the party as to who might succeed him in the seat of power.

Audrey and her father had been in Peking on May Day when Mao made his first public appearance of the year. Hundreds of thousands massed in Tiananmen Square for the festivities, but Mao, accompanied by Lin Biao, spent only a few minutes on the rostrum greeting the crowds. Ronning was seated on the balcony beside Zhou Enlai, who introduced him to Mao. Ronning said afterward that Mao offered him a very limp handshake and he appeared in his manner to be somewhat confused. He was accompanied by two attendants who apparently were nurses. After leaving the rostrum, Mao sat at a table with Prince Sihanouk, chatted for a few minutes, glanced up at the evening fireworks, and left. Lin Biao, also on the rostrum, seemed frail as well. We heard rumors that Lin Biao, known to be tubercular, had undergone an operation to have a lung removed.

The capital was bedecked with Maoist portraits and emblems, but less so than in the previous year. The cult adulation had been a useful means of rousing the masses, especially the youth in the early days of the Cultural Revolution. But now the extremist cult worship had been reined in by Mao as he sought to bring the riotous Red Guards under control. There were warnings in the press about those who bowed before Mao but in reality "waved the red flag to oppose the red flag."

Audrey and I camped at the Xin Jiao, a plain six-story hotel near the old foreign Legation Quarter. Built in the Soviet style, it had a Western restaurant on the top floor and a Chinese restaurant in the lobby. There was a large sign at the entrance to the Chinese restaurant, which, in the Chairman's words, said: "The east wind is prevailing over the west wind." This seemed a fair commentary on the hotel food. On the street opposite to the hotel, mounds of earth were being removed, remains of the last section of the great south wall of the imperial capital that was being torn down to make way for the subway which doubled as an air raid shelter against the possibility of a Soviet missile strike. In the countryside we were shown huge storage bins filled with grain for emergency distribution in the aftermath of a possible Soviet attack. Our days were filled with calls on government and party officials, some of them old acquaintances, and visits to nearby communes, factories, and universities. Our notebooks became filled with the shocking details of what the city had endured during the Cultural Revolution and accounts of those leaders who had fallen in the massive purges.

As we made the rounds, I asked to see Foreign Minister Chen Yi. At his dinner during the Laos Conference in 1961, he had invited me to call upon him. I was told by ministry officials that the foreign minister was no longer active. From others, I learned that in May 1967 when ultra-leftist Red Guards were storming out of control through the streets of Peking, they had attacked the Foreign Ministry, stripped its files, and seized Chen Yi, condemning him as a "rightist." Zhou Enlai rushed to the Foreign Ministry and rescued him from Red Guards who were questioning and beating him. The seventy-three-year-old warrior who had led his armies across the Yangtze to occupy Nanking and Shanghai and later readied his Third Field Army for an invasion of Taiwan before Truman interposed the Seventh Fleet, never recovered from his ordeal. Upon his death from cancer on January 6, 1972, Zhou Enlai delivered the funeral eulogy before an urn containing his ashes at the Babaoshan ("Eight Treasure") cemetery for revolutionary martyrs. Mao rose from a sickbed to attend the funeral shod in slippers and wearing a silk robe over pajamas under a coat. The exposure to the brutal cold worsened his already poor health. It was Mao's last public appearance before his death in September 1976. Mao's appearance at Chen's bier was a gesture that symbolically gave Zhou Enlai license to rehabilitate other comrades purged as insufficiently loyal to Maoist dogma. "Old Cadres," Zhou declared, "are the property of the party. We cannot treat them like enemies and we can't struggle endlessly against them."

Chen Yi was not the only hero of the Long March and the Civil War to become a victim of the Cultural Revolution. In 1966, General Peng Dehuai paid the price of his expressed opposition to Mao's policies—the Great Leap

Forward and formation of the agricultural communes—at the Central Committee meeting at Mount Lu in 1959. Peng was replaced by Lin Biao as defense minister and put under house arrest. In December 1966, Red Guards broke into Peng's house in Chengdu, capital of Sichuan Province, at 4 A.M. Accused of opposing Mao and advocating a "bourgeois line," Peng was repeatedly beaten by the Red Guards, severely injured, and later paraded bound before mass demonstrations. No quarter was given, although Peng had served as deputy commander in chief of the People's Liberation Army (PLA) in the war against Japan, defeated Chiang Kai-shek's forces in western China during the Civil War, and commanded Chinese troops in the Korean War. In 1978, four years after his death, Peng Dehuai was politically rehabilitated by Deng Xiaoping and honored for his battlefield achievements. Marshal He Long, who fought beside Peng during the Civil War in the northwest in command of the Second Front Army, was also purged in 1966 by Mao, who charged him with attempting to usurp military power. He died in disgrace in 1969. Liu Bocheng, the famed "One-Eyed Dragon" of the Civil War, was blind by 1966 and spared in the purges. In 1971, Zhou Enlai restored Zhu De, whom I had met in Yenan when he was commander in chief of the Red Army, to his position as chairman of the Standing Committee of the National People's Congress, the rubberstamp parliament. He had been purged from that post in 1966.

Mao's nationwide purge beginning in 1966 of officials in government and the party who were seen as linked to Liu Shaoqi and Deng Xiaoping spilled over in a second stage into the leftist camp itself in a savage internecine struggle over policy and power. The line of the Cultural Revolution had oscillated left and right as Mao pursued a zigzag course. Those oscillations inspired at times armed struggle among the rival coalitions of Red Guards and revolutionary workers and cadres. At the onset of the Cultural Revolution, Mao had leaned hard to the side of the leftists or radicals. He told the Red Guards: "It is right to rebel against reactionaries" and not be afraid of disorder, encouraging them to paralyze the entrenched bureaucracy. He also instructed the army to support the "broad masses of the left." The army, obeying Mao's injunction, had stood aside as the Red Guards took over municipalities and assaulted opposition groups. However, in early 1967, the army grew uneasy about the excesses and moved in to protect vital installations. Mao's wife, Jiang Qing, intervened on behalf of the Red Guards. She persuaded Mao to issue a directive ordering the army to refrain from interfering with Red Guard activities. But the next month, Mao and Zhou

Enlai saw a serious threat to their power developing. Thousands of ultra-left-ist Red Guards took to the streets in Peking and attacked the Foreign Minis-try. Only the intervention of more moderate Red Guards averted destruction of the Foreign Ministry. Placards appeared on the streets denouncing Zhou as a "rightist." Over the next few months the ultra-leftists ruled the streets as the army looked on, growingly restive. Under pressure of the Peking radicals, intimidated army commanders allowed Red Guards to break into depots to seize guns and trucks, which they used in their factional strife. In August, hundreds of thousands of ultra-leftist Red Guards again surged through Pe-king. They burned down the British Embassy and attacked the Indonesian and Burmese embassies. An attempt was made to seize the files of the Cen-tral Committee. For two days Zhou Enlai was isolated by Red Guard mobs in the Great Hall of the People, subjected to questioning by radicals who ac-cused him of being a "right-wing deviationist."

Alarmed, Mao made his tour of the provinces, seeking to rein in the dis-order, and then yielded to the army's demands for restoration of order. Lin Biao's troops moved into the capital and after severe fighting managed to disarm and disperse the Red Guards. A purge began then of radicals who dominated the Central Cultural Revolution Group on the charge that they and others who were said to be members of an ultra-leftist "May 16 Faction" had tried to seize power, leaving Mao as only a figurehead. When I arrived in Peking, only four of the original eighteen members of the Central Cul-tural Revolution Group, the body that Mao had empowered to lead the Cul-tural Revolution, had not been purged. Jiang Qing's Gang of Four had sur-vived the purge. But with the decline of the radicals, Mao's wife had slipped from fourth to fifth in her standing in the party's Politburo. She now was ranked behind Mao, Lin Biao, Zhou Enlai, and Huang Yongsheng, a pro-tégé of Lin Biao, chief of the army's General Staff. Army officers were given the key posts in new Revolutionary Committees which took administrative control of the provinces. The army, under the leadership of Lin Biao, was in the ascendancy. But Jiang Qing had not given up her bid for power, and un-expected events later in 1971 gave her the opportunity.

From Peking I reported one of the more dramatic episodes in the de-cline of the radicals. I learned that Yao Dengshan, a high-ranking ultra-left-ist who headed the revolutionary group which had seized control of the For-eign Ministry in the summer of 1967, had been condemned to death. He had been taken before four thousand people in an indoor stadium where he was denounced and confessed to plotting to do injury to Zhou Enlai and holding

Chen Yi prisoner. He was also charged with responsibility for burning down the British Embassy. As a gesture of revenge, Zhou Enlai arranged for Chen Yi, who was still suffering the disabilities of his manhandling by the Red Guards, to attend the mass trial. Zhou personally apologized to John Denson, the British chargé d'affaires, and offered to pay the costs of replacing his burned-down embassy.

At midnight I filed a story to the *Times* about the Yao trial. At 3 A.M., my hotel phone rang. It was Ji Mingzhong of the Information Department of the Foreign Ministry, asking if he could drop by to see me. Ji was responsible for dealing with foreign correspondents; there were three permanently stationed in the country representing the *Toronto Globe and Mail,* Agence France-Presse, and DPA, the West German news agency. I waited at the hotel entrance for Ji. He soon arrived in a chauffeured Mercedes and ushered me back into the hotel lobby, where he ordered tea. He was a fine-featured man who had served as a diplomat in London and spoke flawless Oxford-accented English. Ji began: "Mr. Topping, just by chance, the clerk at the telegraph office who took your dispatch about Yao also attended the meeting you described. He noticed several errors"—Ji cleared his throat apologetically—"and he telephoned me." It seemed that Yao had been sentenced to a long prison term, not to death, as I had written. When I suggested that we go to the telegraph office to correct the dispatch, Ji welcomed my proposal as a fine idea, his manner suggesting that it had not occurred to him. We proceeded to the telegraph office, where I corrected my dispatch. Then back to the hotel, chatting about the weather, and with another graceful wave of his hand Ji was gone. We never discussed the matter again in our subsequent contacts. Correspondents were not always treated so gently. On August 18, 1967, Anthony Grey of Reuters was seized by ultra-leftist Red Guards and kept in a small room in his house in solitary confinement for twenty-six months in retaliation for the arrests of leftist Chinese by British authorities during their rioting in Hong Kong.

The Cultural Revolution was not yet over in 1971 as far as internal party struggle was concerned, but the enormous human cost up to that year was already very evident. There had been hundreds of thousands of casualties in the factional battles among Red Guards and other revolutionary groups. Other hundreds of thousands died or were maimed as consequence of persecution, torture, and other physical maltreatment. Millions of young Red Guards, once shock troops of the Cultural Revolution, were uprooted from their homes, lost their educational opportunities, and became the lasting de-

bris of the Cultural Revolution. The Red Guards—the "revolutionary successors" ranging in ages from twelve to the early twenties, mostly middle-school
and college students—had joined with a spirit blended of revolutionary dedication, romanticism, and adulation of Mao. Millions abandoned their class-
rooms. When the schools began to reopen in 1968, there were not enough
places for them. Confronted by millions of idle youths, rambunctious and
demonstrating for jobs or return to school, the Revolutionary Committees
began shipping hundreds of thousands of unhappy youths to the rural areas.
Some returned to schools, factories, and government jobs, but most were
compelled to remain in the rural areas and integrate with the peasantry in
the communes. They became a lost generation.

Our friend Huang Hua and his wife, He Liliang, were among the many
who suffered the excesses of the Cultural Revolution. In 1966, Zhou Enlai
appointed Huang as ambassador to Egypt, the key post in the Middle East.
Protected by Zhou, he was the only ambassador not recalled during the
early years of the Cultural Revolution for "reeducation." Recalled home in
late 1970, he and his wife were sent to one of the hundreds of May Seventh
Schools in rural areas to which officials and intellectuals were sent to do
manual labor supposedly to be reeducated by the peasants. The schools took
their name from Mao's May 7, 1966, directive in which he said: "Going down
to do manual labor gives vast numbers of cadres an excellent opportunity to
study again." Huang Hua worked in a machine shop and also as a peasant in
the rice and *gaoliang* fields separated from his wife, who did manual labor at
another location. After six months Zhou managed to bring Huang Hua back
to Peking. Zhou appointed him ambassador to Canada and then told him to
disappear and make arrangements for the secret arrival of Henry Kissinger,
in preparation for the visit of President Nixon. Huang Hua was at the Peking
Airport to welcome Kissinger on July 7. In September, I met Huang Hua at
his embassy in Ottawa. When I asked him about his days in the May Seventh School, loyal to the leadership of his country, he spoke proudly of the
experience of "reintegrating with the masses." He told me he felt that he had
learned a lot about peasant life.

In October 2006, when Audrey and I were guests of Huang Hua and his
wife at their vacation retreat in Hangzhou, we discussed the Cultural Revolution once again. He Liliang told us for the first time of her tragic family experience. "In 1966 I returned to Peking from Cairo. I was pregnant at
the time. I learned that my father, who was seventy-three and a professor at
the People's University and head of the philosophy department, had been

arrested by the Red Guards. He was living in the basement of one of the university buildings. The Red Guards refused to let him have his medicine pills for his high blood pressure. The city was then in total anarchy. My father was beaten around the head and suffered a brain injury. The Red Guards sent him to a hospital where I saw him. He died there."

Audrey asked Huang Hua: "Did you see any positive results coming out of the Cultural Revolution?" He replied: "Definitely not. The whole thing was a tragic mistake."

35

ZHOU ENLAI AND THE FUTURE OF TAIWAN

I nervously paced the floor of our Peking hotel room concerned about the absence of any word from Abe Rosenthal as to the status of our Pentagon Papers project. It was June 11, 1971, three days before the date we had set for publication of the Papers, and there had been only one message from him. As Audrey's and my China dispatches began appearing in the *Times,* Rosenthal cabled: "Audrey on Friday and Seymour on Saturday. But what's holding up copy from Joanna." Joanna was our four-year-old daughter. Rosenthal's silence persuaded me that publication of the Papers must have been stymied. I decided to return to New York.

Audrey was sitting on a sofa frowning as she watching my antics. I sighed and said to her, "Come, please." Then, to her puzzlement, I led her up to the roof of the Xin Jiao Hotel, where there would be no chance that we would be overheard, and as we sat in the hot sun leaning against a revetment wall, I related to her for the first time details of the Pentagon Papers project. I said it was hard for me to conceive that the publisher would balk at publication, but the pressures on him to desist were enormous and probably had increased since I left New York. I told Audrey I intended to leave straight away for New York, and if I found on arrival that a decision had been taken not to print the Papers, I might resign. Audrey approved of my plans without hesitation. We decided that she would go on to Yan'an, as she had planned to photograph Mao Zedong's old wartime haunts, and that we would meet in New York.

On the morning of June 13, as I was packing, a Chinese porter brought a telegram from Rosenthal. We had gone to press with the Papers. I sat for a long time on our hotel bed, face in my hands, silently giving thanks. Punch had decided to publish despite all the risks. Rosenthal, backed by Reston and others, had stood like a rock throughout. He had insisted, as he and I had agreed to print not only the articles written by *Times* staffers based on the Papers but also the pertinent texts. The first installment was published that morning, six pages of news stories and documents. Publishing the texts of

the classified documents had made the *Times* more vulnerable to government prosecution.

It was Sunday, and in the evening Audrey called from Yan'an over a
creaky telephone line and shouted "Great" when I told her the news. I told
her I still intended to return to New York. Tied up with the Pentagon Papers, Rosenthal would need me back at my job of running the news operation. On Tuesday morning I went to the Information Department of the Foreign Ministry to say good-bye. I was received by Ji Mingzhong, the official
who had escorted me to the cable office to correct my dispatch on the trial
of Yao Dengshan, and Ji's superior, Ma Yuzhen, an urbane but very tough
diplomat. I explained that my presence was required in New York because of
the repercussions anticipated from publication of the Papers. Although the
Chinese media had not, and would not, make mention of the Papers, senior
Chinese officials were cognizant of the Papers controversy from *Reference
News,* a compendium of monitored foreign news agency reports distributed
to specified offices by the Chinese on a need-to-know basis.

Then Ji casually expressed surprise that I would not be going to Nanjing.
His eyebrows arched, and he made no reply when I noted that this was the
first time that I had been told, despite numerous requests, that I would be
permitted to visit Nanjing. Obviously, for some reason, the Foreign Ministry did not want me to leave the country, and a Nanjing visit was now being
offered as an inducement to delay my departure. I agreed to stay on for several days. I was eager return to Nanjing with Audrey, the city where we had
courted, but there was also the other compelling reason. On our arrival in
Peking, I had asked to see Premier Zhou Enlai. Now my hopes were aroused
by the games the Information Department was playing with me. No American correspondent, other than Edgar Snow, had interviewed Zhou Enlai
since 1949.

When I returned to our hotel, there was a message from Rosenthal:
"Please keep in mind I would like you to return as soon as feasible stop Everything well under control stop Enormous reaction to Sheehan Project but
our fan is in good working order Regards."

I knew it was as close to a summons home as Rosenthal would send me.
I read the reference to the fan as meaning that the *Times* was fighting off attacks as a consequence of its publication of the Papers. I ran out of the hotel,
jumped into a taxi, and returned to the Foreign Ministry, catching Ji and Ma
before they left for lunch, and told them I must leave the next day. That night,
in a private dining room of the Peking Hotel, the Information Department
gave a farewell dinner for me at which I completed negotiations for the fu-

ture entry of *Times* correspondents into China. I then cabled Rosenthal to "keep fan running," and the next morning at 6:30 A.M., I boarded a plane bound for Guangzhou en route to New York.

Not long in the air, my Chinese jet airliner was diverted to Changsha in Hunan Province. I was told there was engine trouble. We landed at an air force base in the midst of a training exercise for new Chinese fighter planes of the Russian MIG model. Hours later, we were transferred to another plane, which took us to Guangzhou. I was on the tarmac of the Guangzhou airfield, trudging wearily to the terminal, when I was separated from the other passengers and led into a small waiting room. As I sat sipping tea, I was introduced to a Mr. Yang of the Foreign Affairs Section of the Guangzhou Revolutionary Committee. Without preliminaries he said: "Premier Zhou Enlai would like to see you. Will you return to Peking?" I looked at him dazed, nodded and asked: "When?"

"The plane leaves at 5 o'clock," Mr. Yang said. It was then 4:25 P.M. When I insisted that I must telephone the *Times* office in Hong Kong to report the postponement of my departure, I was driven at high speed to a hotel to make my call and then back to the airport. Never mind that the plane was delayed and disgruntled passengers were waiting on the tarmac. A China Travel agent led me to a counter to buy a return ticket to Peking. I grumbled only when asked to pay once again the excess baggage charge.

At the Peking airport I was greeted by Mr. Ji, and as I was going through the entry formalities, he asked me casually: "What would you like to do over the next several days? " I looked at him in stunned disbelief. In my Walter Mitty comedy reveries aboard the plane, I imagined myself whisked from the airfield into the presence of Zhou Enlai for that exclusive interview during which he would impart some great headline-making news. Now, reality intruded, and I understood that I had been summoned to await the pleasure of the premier. Back at the Xin Jiao Hotel, my aspirations were dealt another blow. I encountered William Attwood, publisher of the Long Island newspaper *Newsday,* and his wife, Sim. They had been the guests of Cambodia's Prince Sihanouk at his Peking residence. Attwood and I took the measure of each other and decided that candor would serve us best. I told my story, and he disclosed that he was promised an audience with a responsible official if he delayed his departure. Yet more. Bob Keatley of the *Wall Street Journal,* who had been exploring Yan'an with his wife, Ann, was in a high state of excitement, with visions of his own exclusive interview with Zhou Enlai dancing in his head. He too had been persuaded to rush back to Peking. The Chinese provided a special plane for the Keatleys and persuaded Audrey to accompany them. She had been photographing the old Mao cave in Yan'an when it was suggested to her coyly by Yu Zhangjing, the interpreter assigned to us by the Foreign Ministry, that she telephone me in Peking, notwithstanding her assumption that I was in New York. By the next day, the Keatleys, Attwoods, and Toppings had been shepherded into the Xin Jiao Hotel and asked to stand by. We were told not to stray, since the summons from Zhou Enlai, who often worked through the night until 5 A.M., might come at any hour. We waited three days.

As I waited, I wrote and cabled on June 19 the first article of a major four-part series based on the five-week tour of China from Manchuria to the southern provinces which we had just completed. It was front-paged on June 25. I would have been disconcerted if I had known that the lead of the paper that day was a story under a four-column headline which said: "Times Asks Supreme Court to End Restraints on Its Vietnam Series." I was unaware that publication of the Papers had stalled.

In my summary series for the *Times* I introduced the first article with these lead paragraphs:

PEKING, June 19—The doctrines of the Cultural Revolution have been translated into new Communist dogma. Under Mao Zedong that dogma has propelled China into a continuing revolution that is producing a new society, and a new "Maoist man."

Relative stability, prosperity and a surface tranquility have been restored with the end of the convulsive mass conflicts and great purge generated by the Cultural Revolution, which began in 1966 as a power struggle between Chairman Mao and Liu Shaoqi, then head of state and since deposed amid charges that he had deviated from revolutionary principles. Mao believes that he has interrupted an evolution that was turning China into a society on the Soviet model characterized by a privileged bureaucracy and tendencies toward the rebirth of capitalism in industry and agriculture.

The gigantic Maoist thought remolding program has profound implications not only for the 800 million Chinese but also for the world. It is producing a highly disciplined, ideologically militant population that is taught that Mr. Mao is the sole heir of Marx and Lenin and the interpreter and defender of their doctrine and that each Chinese must be committed to fostering a world Communist society.

Even so, underlying tensions persist in the party hierarchy and at the grass roots as the ideological struggle to resolve what Mr. Mao describes as "contradictions among ourselves" goes forward. "We have won a great victory." the leader says, echoed by his designated successor, Vice-Chairman Lin Biao. "But the defeated class still struggles. These people are still around and this class still exists. Therefore, we cannot speak of final victory, not even for decades."

While I was at work three days later on my series, which was running front page in the *Times*, Ji phoned to say that the Toppings in company with the Keatleys and the Attwoods would dine with Zhou Enlai in the Great Hall of the People at 6:15 P.M. As our motorcade sped through Tiananmen Square to the Great Hall of the People, we were not were aware that Henry Kissinger would be arriving secretly in Peking eighteen days hence. Nor were we yet aware that our interview was intended by Zhou Enlai as a stage setter for the visit of President Nixon.

The Chinese were awaiting Kissinger with some uncertainty as how to contend with him. At the conclusion of the dinner which Zhou gave for Ronning earlier in May in the Great Hall of the People, the premier asked my father-in-law to remain for a private talk. Seated in another reception room, the premier told Ronning of the impending visit of Henry Kissinger. "Can we trust Kissinger?" the premier asked. A critic of American policy in Vietnam, Ronning could only bring himself to reply: "All Chinese contacts with Americans are useful." It was obvious that Zhou was looking to the meeting with Kissinger with the intention of reaching an understanding with Nixon that would serve as a counterweight in the sharpening dispute with Moscow. During the dinner Zhou had spoken of the possibility of war with the Soviet Union and said that the Chinese as a precaution were building air raid shelters nationwide. He said the work on the shelters began in the aftermath of a deadly clash in Manchuria on March 2, 1969, over the border demarcation on Zhenbao ("Treasure") Island in the Ussuri River. Zhou unhesitatingly invited Audrey to report his remarks about the confrontation with the Soviet Union.

Ronning did not share with Audrey or me the information given to him by Zhou in confidence about the Kissinger visit. In the days immediately preceding our dinner with Zhou Enlai, Chinese officials had casually questioned us about Kissinger, asking about his background, his personality, and influence. We had become so inured to Chinese curiosity about American leaders that it did not occur to us that the visit of a presidential envoy was imminent. There was no reason to assume that was in the offing. There had been no slacking in the Chinese press of attacks on the United States, especially on the central issue of Taiwan. The Seventh Fleet was still patrolling the Taiwan Straits. There were American troops on the island, their bases being used for support of the war in Vietnam.

The Chinese maneuvers which brought Kissinger to Peking were put into play as early as November 1968 when Zhou Enlai proposed a meeting in Warsaw with delegates of the incoming Nixon administration. The forum was to be the private ambassadorial talks which had begun in 1955 on settlement of outstanding issues between the two countries and had continued for 134 fruitless meetings, first in Geneva and then in Warsaw. The Zhou Enlai gambit was undertaken for a complex of reasons. The turbulent phase of the Cultural Revolution in which Zhou Enlai had been personally threatened was coming to an end, and he could safely turn his attention to foreign affairs. Peking was eager to extricate itself from the isolation into which it had blundered as a consequence of the militant revolutionary policies it had pursued abroad during 1964–65. Relations with the Soviet Union were rapidly deteriorating, and there was a deep concern that the Russians might do a repeat on the Chinese of the Moscow-led Warsaw Pact invasion of Czechoslovakia in 1968 in reaction to Peking's ideological quarrels with Moscow and the border disputes. The Chinese also had been intrigued by an article under the title "Asia After Vietnam" in the October 1967 issue of *Foreign Affairs* under Nixon's byline which stated that "taking the long view, we simply cannot afford to leave China forever outside of the family of nations, there to nurture its fantasies, cherish its hates and threaten its neighbors."

The initial Chinese probe of the Nixon Administration's intentions foundered on February 18, 1969 two days before an exploratory meeting was to take place. Peking cancelled the meeting after lodging a complaint, charging that a Chinese diplomat, Liao Heshu, had been incited to defect by the Central Intelligence Agency. It was more likely that the Liao affair was used as a pretext for delaying the discussion until after the CCP'S Ninth Party Congress, which was summoned into session on April 1, 1969 to legitimize the shifts in power and policies stemming from the Cultural Revolution. Peking agreed the following year to resumption of the Warsaw talks for compelling reasons. The military confrontation with the Soviet Union continued to sharpen in 1969 in the aftermath of the border clashes in Central Asia and Manchuria. In February, Nixon offered to send a senior American official to Peking to discuss means of bettering relations. Then, on May 19, 1969, twenty-four hours before delegates were to meet in Warsaw, Peking once more canceled the session citing "the increasingly grave situation created by the United States government, which brazenly sent troops to invade Cambodia and expanded the war in Indochina." The disruption was part of the price paid by the Nixon administration for mounting the military strike into Cambodia designed to root out North Vietnamese bases. However, in a few weeks time, while lending support to the ousted Cambodian regime of Prince Sihanouk, the Chinese let it be known that *they* would resume contacts at a suitable time. In the next months, Nixon sent a series of secret messages to Peking in which he persuaded the Chinese it was his intention to withdraw from Vietnam and that he was committed to normalizing relations with Peking.

This is where matters stood in the realms of high diplomacy when the six American innocents entered the Great Hall of the People. Surrounded by a cluster of officials, Zhou Enlai, erect and smiling, awaited us at the end of a thickly carpeted hallway. The premier wore a well-tailored gray tunic with a Mao emblem inscribed "Serve the People" above the left breast pocket, matching trousers, and brown sandals over black socks. His right arm, slightly stiff from an old injury, was held bent at his side. He was grayer and thinner than when I last saw him, but the bushy eyebrows were still bold and black. His finely boned features radiated an incandescent personality. My last view of him had been in July 1954 at the conclusion of the Geneva Conference when he went to the airport to say good-bye to Soviet foreign minister Molotov. He was impassive and unsmiling when he bid farewell to the burley Russian bound back to Moscow. At the conference Zhou had been the most dramatic figure, striding about wearing a long, narrow black coat and broad-brimmed black hat. At the Great Hall of the People, the premier led us into the Fujian Room, where we were to dine, notebooks on our laps. The brown and cream furnishings of the spacious room were dominated by a huge painting of a group of Chinese, their red banners fluttering, atop a Gansu mountain peak overlooking a cloud-shrouded valley. We were guided past an exquisite lacquer screen to a round table set with blue and white porcelain, silver knives and forks, ivory chopsticks, and an assortment of glasses for Chinese wine, beer, and the 120-proof *maotai*. Among the six officials accompanying the premier at the table were two interpreters, Ji Jiaozhu, a former Harvard student, and the American-born Nancy Tang. The two served as interpreters for both Zhou Enlai and Mao Zedong. Zhou revealed some understanding of English during the dinner conversation by reacting to our remarks before they were translated, and in several instances he corrected the interpreters in Chinese.

As we walked into the room, Zhou said to Audrey: "The last time you were here we had dinner with your father, Chester Ronning." Then to me, smiling: "At that time she made use of the opportunity to note some words of opinion and wrote a story about it. It goes to show the prowess of a correspondent's wife." At the table he apologized for recalling me from Guangzhou, noting that I was hurrying home because of the Pentagon Papers. He compared publication of the Papers to the release by the State Department in 1949 of the White Paper on China, which reviewed U.S. involvement in the Chinese Civil War in the period 1944–49. "They published the White Paper on China to defend themselves, but it was great shock to the world," the premier commented. When I said the *Times* had published the Papers despite the opposition of the government because we felt it was in the interest of the United States, Zhou commended the *Times* and raised his glass in a toast to the withdrawal of American troops from Vietnam.

"Can you all drink *maotai*?" Zhou asked as he did a *ganbei*, or bottoms-up, with the small glass. "Oh, yes," I replied. "We believe when trade develops this will be one of your most successful exports." "Well, we probably won't be able to supply so much *maotai*," Zhou said laughing, "because it is produced only in a certain locality." He recalled that it was the Red Army during the Long March which found the Chishui River in Guizhou Province and discovered its waters were ideal for making the clear sorghum liquor. "This liquor won't go to your head," Zhou assured his dubious audience, "although you can light it with a match."

The premier's demeanor became cold and deliberate when inevitably we came to the central topic of the evening, Taiwan—the issue that had separated China and the United States for two decades—and he was asked if China intended to unite the island with the mainland by negotiation or force. At the farewell dinner given to me by the Information Department, I had contended—without getting a reply—that the American people would never be persuaded to favor Peking's takeover of the island until they knew what the fate of the Taiwanese would be. There had been talk, I told them, in the United States of a bloodbath if the Communists occupied the island. Zhou now undertook to answer my question. In effect, he elaborated for the first time for publication what was to be the government's long-term policy. Taiwan was to be united with the mainland by a policy of peaceful attraction. Although the Chinese government has never stated categorically that force would never be used, the policy as described by Zhou that night remains in effect.

Zhou began by saying that it was difficult to answer a question about the future of Taiwan if "one puts a time limit on it." He elaborated: "In the first place, Taiwan is Chinese. Historically, it has been a province of China for a long time. Because of the Sino-Japanese War of 1894, Taiwan was occupied following the Treaty of Shimonoseki in 1895. But in 1945, at the conclusion of the Second World War, in accordance with the Potsdam and Cairo declarations, Taiwan was returned to the embrace of its motherland and once again became a province of China. Topping and Ronning were in Nanjing for our entry there. They saw the new replace the old in April 1949." Zhou continued: "In January 1950, President Truman acknowledged these facts in a statement. Truman recalled that Taiwan had already been returned to China, that it was an internal Chinese affair, and that the United States had no territorial ambitions in regard to Taiwan. Truman said further the question between the mainland and Taiwan could be solved by the Chinese people themselves. Thus we can say that the position of the American government toward the new China was defined before the whole world. Then suddenly, in June 1950, the position was changed, and the Seventh Fleet was dispatched to the Taiwan Straits."

Zhou was referring to the statement made by President Truman on June 27, two days after the North Korean invasion of the South. Altering the U.S. position, which previously had been unequivocally that Taiwan belonged to China, the president stated: "The determination of the future status of Formosa [Taiwan] must await the restoration of security in the Pacific, a peace settlement with Japan, or consideration by the United Nations." The Seventh Fleet took up position in the Taiwan Straits as Chen Yi was preparing his Third Army in the South China ports for an invasion of the island.

The premier asserted: "At that time, China had nothing to do with the Korean War. It was interference in China's internal affairs." (During the Korean War, Chinese troops did not cross the border into North Korea to engage advancing American troops until October 25, 1950.)

> Now we demand that all American forces be withdrawn from Taiwan and the Taiwan Straits, that the United States respect the sovereign independence and territorial integrity of the People's Republic of China and there be no interference in our internal affairs . . . As to how Taiwan will be returned to China and how it will be liberated that is our internal affair. Mr. Topping knows that when I was about to leave Nanking [in 1946], they asked if we would come back. I said we surely would. Since then we

have returned to Nanjing. We will also return to Taiwan. It will not be all that difficult . If Taiwan returns to the motherland, the people will be making a contribution, so the motherland, far from exacting revenge on them, should reward them, and we will reward them.

In an obvious gesture to officials of the Chiang Kai-shek government on Taiwan, Zhou said:

You may know that we gave the last emperor of China, Pu Yi, his freedom in Peking as a free citizen. Unfortunately, he died three years ago, but his wife and younger brother, who is married to a Japanese, are still in Peking. Then there are the high-ranking officers of Chiang Kai-shek's army who were captured during the Civil War. They are now in Peking and looked after well. So we can say, returning to the motherland, Taiwan will receive benefits, and not be harmed, and relations between the United States will be bettered. If American forces were withdrawn from Taiwan, and the Taiwan Straits, it would be glorious. This action would be acclaimed and friendship would result. Under these circumstances, the world would change.

At the conclusion of the dinner, the premier walked with us to the side door by which we had entered the Great Hall of the People and warmly bade us goodnight. Before the dinner, Ma Zhuzhen of the Information Department told me privately that at the end of the evening I would be handed the premier's answers to a list of sixteen questions, many of which related to Taiwan, which I had submitted three weeks earlier appended to my request for an interview. As we waited on the steps of the Great Hall, I asked Ma for the written replies to my questionnaire, and he told me that he would contact me later in the evening. Near midnight as I was writing my dispatch, Ma telephoned: "The premier in his replies at dinner went much further than expected, and we see no point in giving you the written answers to your questions." He also told me that what Zhou had said at dinner about Taiwan was to be considered to be of the greatest importance. Another surprise awaited me. We had agreed before dinner to allow Ma to check direct quotes against the Chinese transcript prepared by the Chinese secretary at the table. About 1 A.M. I went to the Foreign Ministry with my dispatch, only to be told that the copy would not be cleared until the next afternoon. Presumably Zhou wanted to see the quotes himself. All the dispatches were cleared the next day without any changes.

In Peking, the news that we had a "friendly conversation" with the premier was published in a six-line item at the bottom of the front page of *People's Daily,* the official Chinese Communist newspaper. It was in the same format and space that was later assigned to the visit of Henry Kissinger.

––––––––––––

The following morning Audrey and I boarded a plane for Guangzhou and the next day walked across the railway bridge at Lo Wu to a car that took us to Hong Kong en route to New York. Zhou Enlai was still very much in my mind. His features, since the advent of ping-pong diplomacy, had become the visage of China for many Americans. I found him to be the only one among the top leaders who had the stature, talent, and experience to negotiate an understanding with the United States after two decades of separation and hostility. The Shanghai Communiqué which Zhou did sign with President Nixon on February 18, 1972, was in keeping with the conditions he had outlined in our interview, specifically withdrawal of American troops from Taiwan and recognition that "there is but one China and that Taiwan is a part of China." Implicitly, Zhou committed Peking to a policy of peaceful attraction of Taiwan. Yet when we met with Zhou in the Great Hall of the People, he was not wielding ultimate power in Peking, nor did he pretend to. Even at the time, as Kissinger embarked by a devious route for Peking from Pakistan, Zhou Enlai was being confronted with an internal crisis that might diminish his power.

Up until 1965, Zhou walked behind Liu Shaoqi, the head of state and heir apparent to Mao Zedong. When Liu was toppled, although Zhou had been in the forefront of the Cultural Revolution, he bowed to Mao's designation of Lin Biao as his "closest comrade-in-arms and successor" and stood by dutifully as this commitment was written into the new party constitution at the Ninth Congress in April 1969. Thereafter, on ceremonial occasions, Zhou Enlai walked two or three steps behind Lin Biao.

Lin Biao preferred seclusion, like Mao, emerging with him only on important public occasions. I had glimpsed Lin during the welcoming ceremonies in Peking for President Ceaușescu of Romania. He was a thin, frail-looking man, sixty-four years old, largely bald, which is unusual for a Chinese, with heavy black eyebrows and dark beard showing through pale skin. He wore a baggy army uniform as did his wife, Ye Qun, whom we saw at a banquet for the Romanian leader. Mao and Lin, closely associated since the Long March in the 1930s, were alike in many ways. They blended peasant earthiness with the mystic qualities of a guerrilla leader, ascetic revolutionary, and ideologue with a world outlook, although they spoke no foreign language and had not traveled abroad except to the Soviet Union. Lin went to the USSR in late 1938 or early 1939, remaining three years for treatment of a battle wound and chronic tuberculosis. Given his age, only fourteen years junior to Mao, who was seventy-seven, and in poor health, some Chinese in Peking privately expressed doubt about the wisdom of relying on Lin Biao for the succession.

Although Lin was dubbed Mao's "closest comrade-in-arms," the Chairman entrusted daily management of the country to Zhou Enlai. Mao, the visionary, the ideologue, and the strategist, worked comfortably with Zhou, the pragmatist, the administrator, the tactician. While loyal to Mao during the Cultural Revolution, Zhou exercised a moderating influence in defiance of Jiang Qing's extremism. He was instrumental in rescuing many of the old guard who had served China well, such as Chen Yi, from the purges inspired by Jiang Qing's radicals. When the Red Guards were carrying on their destructive rampages in keeping with Lin Biao's injunction to eliminate the "Four Olds," Zhou Enlai safeguarded many of China's treasured archaeological sites, imperial temples, and palaces.

In June, as we were leaving China, many in Peking were waiting to see whether Lin Biao and his military supporters, many of whom had served in his Fourth Field Army during the Civil War, would continue to tolerate a leadership constellation in which, although anointed as successor, Lin did not head the party or the government. An event was impending that would test the cohesion of the leadership. On New Year's Day the Peking press had proclaimed 1971 as the important year in which "we are going to greet the Fourth National People's Congress."

In name, the NPC is China's highest organ of state authority, but, in fact, it is a rubberstamp parliament controlled by the Communist Party. The importance of the Congress, which was to take place in the fall, the first since the Cultural Revolution, was that it would provide the platform for proclamation of the crucial decisions taken secretly by the party's Central Committee. A new state constitution was to be approved to replace the 1954 constitution, denounced during the Cultural Revolution as a "bourgeois document." The NPC had the authority to elect a new head of state to replace the purged Liu Shaoqi, and it was on this question that conflict within the ruling hierarchy was likely to erupt.

If he were to replace Liu Shaoqi, Lin Biao would head the government and be the superior of Zhou Enlai. This would not only subordinate Zhou, but it would also put Lin Biao in charge of two of the three pillars of power in China, the government and the army, which he already controlled as defense minister. Once before, Mao had in effect yielded two pillars of power—control over the apparatus of both the party and the government—to a potential rival leader, Liu Shaoqi, and his collaborator, Deng Xiaoping. Liu was then instrumental in pushing Mao aside prior to the Cultural Revolution. It was uncertain that Mao would be willing to once more risk assigning so much power to another by giving Lin Biao control of both the government and the army.

In June, when I spoke to the diplomats who read the political tea leaves in Peking, I found they could only speculate as to the ambitions of Lin Biao and his comrades from the old Fourth Field Army. It was Jiang Qing and the other Maoists who saw ominous signs. Systematically, the army had expanded its administrative power in the provinces, forcing aside Jiang Qing's radicals, and was now in effective control of the party apparatus on the local level. In Peking, at the center of power, the military was also strongly entrenched. Huang Yongsheng, the chief of the General Staff, was ranked fourth after Mao, Lin Biao, and Zhou Enlai in the Politburo. He had edged past Jiang Qing, Mao's wife, with whom he had quarreled during the Cultural Revolution when she had insisted on giving the radical Red Guards free rein. It was Lin Biao who had appointed Huang, his long-standing protégé, as chief of the General Staff.

The lines seemed drawn for a showdown between the Maoists and the military when the National People's Congress convened. I would be in New York when the drama unfolded, knowing that the future of China would turn on the outcome.

36

BATTLE OF THE PENTAGON PAPERS

I arrived in New York on the eve of a ruling by the U.S. Supreme Court on June 25 as to whether publication of the Pentagon Papers could go forward. Rosenthal had kept me informed in China about the unfolding legal battle. In a cable on June 18 prior to our departure from Peking, he said: "We all miss you but know it for wonderful purpose. Reaction around the world continues enormously strong behind the paper and the series and court case now universally recognized as landmark in journalism and law. Fondly."

Three installments of the Pentagon Papers had been published—on June 13, 14, and 15—before Judge Murray I. Gurfein of the U.S. Federal District Court issued a temporary restraining order on June 15. The first installment had been published on the top half of the front page, leading into six full pages inside of analytical articles and extracts from the Papers themselves. On the evening of June 14, John Mitchell, the attorney general, had wired the publisher asking the *Times* to refrain from further publication of the Papers and to return the documents to the Department of Defense. Punch had flown to Europe that morning but by telephone from London authorized Rosenthal to proceed with our publication schedule. The publisher returned to New York forty-eight hours later to announce his determination to fight the case through the courts. In his absence, Harding Bancroft telephoned Robert C. Maridan, the assistant attorney general in charge of the Internal Security Division. "We refuse to halt publication voluntarily," Bancroft told him. Lord, Day & Lord, whose lawyers had argued so strongly against publication, was not disposed to fight the case in court. The excuse was a conflict of interest. When Herbert Brownell, senior partner at Lord, Day & Lord, had been attorney general during the Eisenhower administration, he had drafted the Executive Order establishing the categories of government information that would be classified. James Goodale recalls that Brownell also received a telephone call from Attorney General Mitchell suggesting that it would not be good for the Republican Party if he became involved in the case.

Overnight, Bancroft and Goodale, as chief counsel for the *Times,* sought out Professor Alexander M. Bickel of the Yale Law School and Floyd Abrams as an assisting attorney in the case. They agreed to represent the *Times* in court the next morning. Abrams would go on from the case to become the country's leading First Amendment lawyer.

The Supreme Court had agreed on June 25 to review decisions by the lower courts. Judge Gurfein of the New York court had in the first instance issued the temporary restraining order while he reviewed an appeal by the government for an injunction to block publication. But he then denied the government's appeal for an extension of his temporary restraining order. In doing so, in what was a landmark guideline for the judiciary, he stated: "A cantankerous press, an obstinate press, a ubiquitous press must be suffered by those in authority in order to preserve the even greater values of freedom of expression and the right of the people to know."

To overturn Judge Gurfein's ruling, the government went to the Court of Appeals.

At the *Times*, while this struggle was in progress in the courts, we had become progressively uneasy about losing our competitive edge on the story. Eager to promote the widest possible circulation of the Papers, Ellsberg had made available portions to the *Washington Post* and subsequently to other newspapers including the *Christian Science Monitor* and the *Chicago Sun-Times*. Competitively, the *Washington Post* had earlier been reduced to the competitive journalistic humiliation of simply rewriting and quoting the first installments published in the *Times*. Then, on a telephone tip as to the source of the Papers, Ben Bagdikian, the national editor, flew to Boston on June 16, met with Ellsberg, and returned with more than four thousand pages of classified Pentagon documents in a cardboard box.

Before being enjoined by the Federal District Court early on June 19, the *Post* went to press with its first article on the night of June 18. The *Post* published in defiance of government warnings after Katherine Graham, the publisher, told Ben Bradlee, the executive editor: "Okay, I say let's go. Let's publish."

The Supreme Court agreed to intervene after the Court of Appeals in New York ruled in favor of the government. There was joy on June 30 at the *Times* when the Supreme Court decided in favor of the newspapers by a 6–3 vote, allowing our publication of the remaining four installments. The Supreme Court decision was a resounding First Amendment victory for the press. Justice Hugo Black commented that the *Times* and the *Washington Post* should be commended "for serving the purpose that the Founding Fathers saw so clearly." But it was not an absolute ruling in the sense that there might never be a legal exercise of prior restraint. The Court might so act if it was shown, as Judge Potter Stewart held, that there was likely "direct, immediate, and irreparable damage to our nation or its people." This formulation would later become a critical ruling when many government prosecutors sought to compel reporters to reveal their sources in reporting on controversial national security issues. The Stewart reservation was not seen as applicable to the publication of the Pentagon Papers. In an Op-Ed article written for the *Washington Post* in 1989, Erwin N. Griswald, who as solicitor general argued the case for the government, said: "I have never seen any trace of a threat to the national security from the publication" or "even seen it suggested that there was such an actual threat." He termed the case against the *Times* and the *Post* a "mirage."

In his book *Speaking Freely*, Floyd Abrams quotes Charles Nesson, a Harvard Law School professor, in an assessment common to most historians of the period, as concluding that publication of the Pentagon Papers "lent credibility to and finally crystallized the growing consensus that the Vietnam War was wrong and legitimized the radical critique of the war." A postscript was added years later by Cyrus Vance during his Senate confirmation hearings as secretary of state in the Carter administration. Vance, who served under McNamara as a deputy secretary of defense, noted that the impact on public opinion had been such that the publication of the Pentagon Papers shortened the American War in Vietnam.

The 1972 Pulitzer Prize for Public Service went to the *Times* for its publication of the Pentagon Papers. While the *Times* was widely viewed as deserving of the prize, the award process itself was fraught with controversy and became a factor in the revision of the Pulitzer Prize process. The procedure at the time of the Pentagon Pagers award required a recommendation by a jury to an Advisory Board, which in turn recommended awards for final decision to Columbia University's Board of Trustees. In the instance of the Pentagon Papers the jury for Public Service recommended that a joint award be made to the *Times* and to Neil Sheehan, stating: "It is fortuitous that the Pulitzer Prizes can recognize the accomplishments of both the newspaper and of a persistent, courageous reporter, and thus affirm to the American people that the press continues its devotion to the right to know, a basic bulwark in our democratic society." The Advisory Board, made up mainly of editors and academics, split and set aside the bid by Ben Bradlee for equal citations to the *Times* and the *Post* and also the jury recommendation that a joint award go to Sheehan, which the board put aside as "a complicating factor." Unanimously, the board then referred its award to the Board of Trustees with a simple citation which said: "The *New York Times* for the publication of the Pentagon Papers." The twenty-two-member Trustee Board voted down the recommendation, largely because many members had held that awards should not be given for "illegal acts." The dissenting members put the Pentagon Papers story into that category because they contended that Ellsberg's copying of the classified Pentagon Papers and his passing of the document to the *Times* constituted an illegal act. Columbia's president, William J. McGill, persuaded the Trustee Board to reconsider, and it finally gave qualified approval to the award to the *Times*. In 1975, as a consequence of the internal dispute over the Pentagon Papers award and similar controversies, the Trustee Board decided to delegate its responsibilities to the Advisory Board (later renamed the Pulitzer Prize Board), which then became a completely independent entity with its own endowment. The president of the university, by virtue of his office, continued as a voting member of the Pulitzer Prize Board to represent the interests of the university.

Like many members of the staff of the *Times*, I was bitterly disappointed by the decision of the board to put aside the recommendation that a joint award be made to Neil Sheehan. As in the case of Harrison Salisbury's venture into North Vietnam, there was failure to recognize the critical importance of enterprise by the individual reporter.

It should be noted that members of the nineteen-member Pulitzer Prize Board in general serve for no more than nine years, and this rotation results in changes of attitudes and policies, something I can testify to out of personal experience. When I retired in 1987 as managing editor of the *Times* as required at the age of sixty-five, I was appointed director of Editorial Development for the thirty-two regional newspapers of the company. When I retired from that post in 1992, I was appointed administrator of the Pulitzer Prizes by the Pulitzer Prize Board and served in that capacity until 2002. During those years, I can testify that the board in its private deliberations placed great emphasis on making awards for individual enterprise and achievement.

———————————

Publication of the Pentagon Papers was less of a rewarding experience for Daniel Ellsberg than for us at the *Times,* although eventually he would become something of a folk hero in the antiwar movement. On June 28, only two days before the Supreme Court set aside government injunctions on publication of the Papers, accused of theft, conspiracy, and espionage, Ellsberg surrendered to the U.S. Attorney's Office in Boston, knowing that if he was convicted he might spend the rest of his life in prison. He had been on the run, dodging the FBI, for sixteen days. Employing the FBI, President Nixon had moved strongly against Ellsberg on the urging of Henry Kissinger. In his memoir *The White House Years,* Kissinger wrote he reacted so strongly against the publication of the Pentagon Papers because he thought it might disrupt his forthcoming trip to Peking for negotiations to set up the Nixon visit. "Peking might conclude our government was too unsteady, too harassed, and too insecure to be a useful partner," Kissinger wrote. "The massive hemorrhage of state secrets was bound to raise doubts about the reliability of our political system." In fact, Kissinger contradicted what Premier Zhou Enlai told me when I met him with other journalists even as the premier was awaiting Kissinger's arrival in Peking. Zhou said that publication by the *Times* of the Papers was "not only in the interests of the United States, but of the whole world." He also perceived quite accurately that publication would help end the Vietnam War.

Ellsberg went to trial together with his collaborator, Anthony Russo, in the spring of 1973 in the Federal District Court on twelve felony counts posing the possibility that he could be sentenced to 115 years in prison if convicted on all charges. Chester Ronning, then retired from the Canadian foreign service, testified at the trial in March as a witness for the defense. He was summoned because government documents pertaining to his two missions to Hanoi to arrange peace negotiations had been published in the Pentagon Papers. Asked by Leonard Boudin, a defense attorney, if the leak of information by the government prior to his second visit to Hanoi in 1966 was one of the "principal factors" leading to the failure of his mission, Ronning replied: "It was not the principal factor, but it was a factor. The principal factor was the United States proposal to Hanoi." Ronning was referring to American insistence that Hanoi terminate aid to its Vietcong allies in the South as a precondition for ending the bombing of North Vietnam. He testified that the publication of the Pentagon Papers in 1971 disclosing details of his mission had no effect on his mission because his contacts with Hanoi had ended. Describing Ronning's appearance at the trial, correspondent Martin Arnold reported in the *New York Times:* "He was perhaps the most assured and relaxed witness to appear so far."

The Ellsberg case was thrown out of court on May 11, 1973, when the presiding judge dismissed the charges on grounds of government misconduct after learning that agents employed by the White House, known as the "Plumbers," had in September 1971 broken into the office of Dr. Lewis Fielding, Ellsberg's psychiatrist, seeking information about his mental state. The burglary of Dr. Fielding's office eventually would be shown to have a bearing on the Watergate scandal and the resignation of Richard Nixon from the presidency.

In the Watergate affair, on June 17, 1972, five men were arrested by police as they sought to break into offices of the Democratic National Committee Headquarters in the Watergate apartment complex in Washington, D.C., for the purpose of securing a wiretap. All of the burglars, known among themselves as the "Plumbers," were connected directly or indirectly with the Committee to Reelect the President (CREEP). Among those indicted was E. Howard Hunt, who was involved in the Fielding break in and the planner of the subsequent Watergate break-in. The Nixon administration's assumption that presidential executive power superseded conventional legal codes, implicit in the Fielding break-in, was what encouraged the similar burglary at the Watergate. That burglary led to the damning investigations, notably by the *Washington Post*, which led to the conviction of those responsible for the Watergate break-in and in the end compelled the resignation of Richard Nixon from the presidency on August 9, 1974. The Watergate link to the Ellsberg case was revealed in detail by Egil Krogh, a practicing lawyer, who was deputy counsel to President Nixon, in an Op-Ed article published in the *New York Times* on June 30, 2007. Krogh wrote:

> The Watergate break-in, described by Ron Ziegler, then the White House press secretary, as a "third-rate burglary," passes its 35th anniversary this month. The common public perception is that Watergate was the principal cause of President Nixon's downfall. In fact, the seminal cause was a first-rate criminal conspiracy and break-in almost ten months earlier that led inexorably to Watergate and its subsequent cover-up. In early August 1971, I attended a secret meeting in Room 16, a hideaway office in the basement of the Old Executive Office Building, across the street from the White House. Huddled around the table were G. Gordon Liddy, a former FBI agent; E. Howard Hunt, a former CIA agent; and David R. Young Jr., a member of the National Security Council staff. Two months earlier, the *New York Times* had published the classified Pentagon Papers, which had been provided by Daniel Ellsberg. President Nixon had told me that he viewed the leak as a matter of critical importance to national security. He ordered me and the others, a group that would come to be called the "Plumbers," to find out how the leak had happened and to keep it from happening again. Mr. Hunt urged us to carry out a "covert operation" to get a "mother lode" of information about Mr. Ellsberg's mental state,

to discredit him, by breaking into the office of his psychiatrist, Dr. Lewis Fielding. Mr. Liddy told us that the FBI had frequently carried out such covert operations—euphemism for burglaries—in national security operations, that he had even done some himself. I listened intently. At no time did I or anyone else ever question whether the operation was necessary, legal or moral. Convinced that we were responding legitimately to a national security crisis, we focused instead on the operational details— who would do what, when and where. Mr. Young and I sent a memo to John Ehrlichman, assistant to the President, recommending that "a covert operation be undertaken to examine all of the medical files still held by Ellsberg's psychiatrist." Mr. Ehrlichman approved the plan, noting in longhand on the memo, "if done under your assurance that it is not traceable." On Sept. 3, 1971, the burglars broke into Dr. Fielding's Beverly Hills office to photograph the files, but found nothing related to Mr. Ellsberg.

In May 1973 Krogh submitted an affidavit to the presiding judge at the Ellsberg trial in which he confessed to his role and the involvement of Hunt and Liddy in the Fielding break-in. He then resigned as undersecretary of transportation. Krogh pleaded guilty in November 1973 to criminal conspiracy in depriving Dr. Fielding of his civil rights, specifically his constitutional right to be free from an unwarranted search. Krogh, who was not involved in the Watergate break-in, was sentenced to two to six years in prison, of which he served four and a half months. Krogh's May 1973 affidavit and confession served to end Daniel Ellsberg's two-year nightmare of fear that he might spend the rest of his life in prison.

37
THE TRIAL

I was in the newsroom of the *Times* on September 21, 1971, three months after leaving Peking, when Jim Greenfield, our foreign editor, pointed out to me a Reuters dispatch from the Chinese capital. The October 1 National Day parade, which had been held every year since the founding of the People's Republic, had been canceled. All civil and military flights had been suspended without explanation from September 13 to 15. Cancellation of the parade meant there would be no lineup of the Politburo on the Tiananmen reviewing stand, the order of which would reveal any reshuffle of the leadership. Speculation all over the world centered on the health of Mao Zedong, intensified by a French Radio report that he was ill or dead.

One hour before the *Times* was to go to press with a front-page story reporting the speculation, I got through by telephone to the Information Department of the Foreign Ministry in Peking. Ji Mingzhong, my friendly overseer in Peking, who answered, was startled out of his customary imperturbability by the call, since there were no regular telephone connections between New York and Peking. When I asked him to confirm or deny the reports concerning Mao, there was a long silence before Ma Yuzhen, his superior, came on the line and said: "We usually do not answer questions on the telephone, but this is an exceptional case. The pernicious rumors about Chairman Mao Zedong are untrue. He is in very good health." The *Times* carried Ma's statement in the first edition, but we still did not know the nature of the crisis in China, and rumors continued to abound as to the health, whereabouts, and status of both Mao and Lin Biao, his designated successor. Lin Biao had earlier disappeared from public view, as did his four top generals: Huang Yongsheng, chief of the General Staff; Wu Faxian, the air force commander; Li Zuopeng, the navy political commissar; and Qiu Huizuo, chief of logistics for the armed forces.

The mystery deepened on September 30 when Tass, the Soviet press agency, announced that a Chinese Communist jet had violated the air space over the People's Republic of Mongolia on the night of September 12–13 and crashed in the mountains. Nine badly burned bodies were found in the wreckage of the plane, which had been bound for the Soviet Union. It would be almost a year before mention was made again in the Chinese press of Lin Biao's name and then only in conjunction with his denunciation and the revelation that he, his wife, Ye Qun, and his son, Lin Liguo, were aboard the crashed aircraft.

All of the circumstances preceding their flight on the night of September 12–13 have not yet, as late as the year 2009, been officially disclosed. The Chinese leadership has not been willing to reveal every detail. What has been gleaned from Chinese government archives is the official allegation that Lin Biao's son, an air force officer, having become convinced that the Maoists were planning the downfall of his father, gathered other officers into a group, which called itself the "Joint Fleet," with the intention of assassinating Mao Zedong. Lin Liguo was also said to have planned to kidnap Lin Biao's four senior generals and take them together with his parents to Guangzhou, where a rival regime would be set up to challenge the Maoists. When the plot was uncovered, Lin Liguo was said to have persuaded his parents, who were staying at Beidaihe, a coastal vacation resort not far from Peking, to flee with him and other conspirators to the Soviet Union. The Lin family boarded a Trident jet at an airport near Beidaihe. Aware of their flight, Zhou Enlai was said to have asked Mao if he should have the plane shot down. Mao is reputed to have shrugged off the suggestion with the comment: "Rain has to fall, girls have to marry, these things are immutable, let them go." The Trident jet commandeered hastily by Lin Liguo apparently did not have sufficient fuel and crashed in the Mongolian mountains.

It remains a mystery as to whether Lin Biao himself was involved in his son's alleged plot. Lin's four top generals, who disappeared after the plane crash, apparently were not involved. Nevertheless, they were dismissed by Mao on September 24 as members of what he characterized as a treacherous faction.

In November, the Chinese press emphasized that the armed forces were under "the direct leadership and command of Chairman Mao." Once again the slogan was revived: "The party commands the gun and the gun must never be allowed to command the party." The death of Lin Biao, whatever the circumstances preceding it, provided the Maoists with the rationale for diminishing the army's power in the provinces and control of the Defense Ministry by Lin's Fourth Field Army faction. To replace Lin Biao as defense minister, Mao appointed a trusted old stalwart, Marshal Ye Jianying, whom I knew well when he was chief of staff of the People's Liberation Army and head of the Communist branch of Executive Headquarters in Peking. There lingers the possibility that the story about an assassination plot directed against Mao may have been simply concocted. Lin Biao may have been targeted for a purge to eliminate the possibility of a challenge by him and his Fourth Field Army loyalists to Mao's authority. Lin may have fled in the Trident jet with his family in anticipation of a Maoist attempt to arrest him. I believe this to be a distinct possibility, and it remains a matter of very private speculation among some Chinese historians.

At the Tenth Party Congress held in Peking August 24–28, 1973, Lin Biao was formally denounced and expelled from the party. There was no acknowledgment of his historic victories in the war with Japan or that he was the most effective field commander during the Civil War. Earlier, just after the death of Lin Biao in 1971, the two top generals who fought in tandem with him in the defeat of Chiang Kai-shek's forces joined in the sweeping denunciations, obviously to please Mao. The famed "One-Eyed Dragon," Liu Bocheng, by then totally blind, declared: "In all the decades I knew him, he never spoke the truth." Chen Yi spoke of Lin's "sinister conduct, double dealing, cultivation of sworn followers, and persistent scheming," although he did concede: "I don't want to deny that previously he did some useful things, under the leadership of the Chairman and the Party center." Prior to the congress, the Central Committee distributed a confidential circular memo to key personnel of the party, government, and army all around the country laying out the accusations against Lin Biao. The memo came as a shock to many and for some put into question the stability of the leadership and the logic of the Cultural Revolution.

Zhou Enlai, who delivered the principal indictment of Lin Biao at the congress as well as the Politburo's Political Report, emerged as number two to Mao, but not necessarily his successor. With Mao's prior agreement, Zhou brought Deng Xiaoping back from his exile in Jiangxi Province and appointed him as a vice premier.

Ronning, Audrey, and our daughter Susan were present on October 14 when Deng made his first public appearance as the reinstated deputy to Zhou Enlai. The three were on a visit to Inner Mongolia when Zhou Enlai summoned Ronning to the Peking Railway Station for a reception in honor of Pierre Trudeau, the Canadian prime minister. Trudeau was leaving on a tour of provincial cities of China. Deng Xiaoping was in Zhou Enlai's entourage for the occasion as well as Li Xiannian, a member of the Politburo. Describing the meeting, Audrey said:

> We were back, arriving by train, from a cold two-week tour of Inner Mongolia and dad was wearing a coat lined with goat hair. We were met at the railway station by Zhou Enlai and escorted into a guest room where

Li Xiannian and Deng Xiaoping were waiting. Zhou introduced Deng, a short, pale man of austere demeanor, as his great friend and colleague. We then were invited to take off our coats and pose for pictures. When dad took off his coat, we saw that the white goat hair of the coat's lining had come off on his dark Sun Yat-sen tunic. "Oh!" said Zhou, "You can't meet your prime minister looking like that." Then Zhou and Deng began brushing off the hair. This was the moment, of course, for Trudeau to walk in and embrace his fellow Canadian. When they parted, Trudeau and the Chinese were covered with goat hair. Everyone laughed so loudly that the security people standing outside the door were alarmed and dashed in. When Deng laughed, he looked very different than when we first entered the room. He had become more relaxed, as if this incident had broken the ice.

At the reception, Zhou told dad privately that Deng was the man to watch. He said he had just reinstated him as a vice premier and he was preparing him to be his successor.

The previous month at a dinner in Peking for Iphigene Sulzberger, mother of the *New York Times* publisher Arthur Ochs Sulzberger, who was being escorted by Ronning and Audrey on a tour of China, Zhou indicated that he had a health problem. He had, in fact, been diagnosed on May 18, 1972, as suffering from bladder cancer. Despite his deteriorating health, Zhou accompanied Trudeau to the ancient city of Luoyang to visit the Buddhist caves at Longmen Temple. Ronning, who had another commitment, was not able to accept Zhou's invitation to accompany them.

At the Peking Railway Station, Zhou Enlai left the train vestibule to embrace Audrey on the station platform in farewell, saying: "I will never forget what you have done for China." He had just looked over her new book on China, *Dawn Wakes in the East*. It was the last meeting for Audrey and her father with Zhou Enlai. Their next attempted contact with him was an intensely painful and mysterious one.

———————————

In September 1975, Ronning was again in China, accompanied by Audrey; our daughter Lesley, a film editor; Richard Westlein, a nephew who worked as a television cameraman; and his mother, Meme, Audrey's sister. The group was planning to do a documentary on the Yangtze River. During the trip Audrey filed to the *New York Times* the first news story on the spectacular archaeological unearthing, forty miles east of the ancient capital of Xi'an, of more than six thousand life-size terra-cotta sculptures of warriors with their horses, guardians of the tomb of the first emperor of China, Xin Shi Huangdi, founder of the Qin dynasty (221–207 B.C.), which unified China. Audrey's articles and photos on the find became cover stories in the *National Geographic* and *Horizon* magazines.

On arrival in Peking on September 29, Ronning asked to see his old friend Zhou Enlai, who had been hospitalized. Zhou had undergone surgery for his cancer on September 20 for the fourth time. The previous year, with Mao's concurrence, he had turned over management of government affairs to Deng Xiaoping. Zhou remained peripherally involved, holding con ferences at times at his bedside. Ronning was told by the Foreign Ministry that the premier would see him when he returned from his tour of China, which was to take two months. On an intermittent stopover in Peking during the tour, Ronning was given a similar reply when he once more asked to see Zhou. Ronning began to suspect that something sinister was involved. On November 9, the Ronning party returned to the Chinese capital. They checked into the Peking Hotel, where Ronning received a message from the Foreign Ministry stating that the premier was too sick to see him. It was conveyed to him by Zhu Qiusheng, a diplomat of the Foreign Ministry, who was an old friend and had traveled in China with the Ronnings.

"Later, that same evening," as Audrey related the incident to me,

> Zhu returned to our room in the hotel and in a hushed voice told us that Zhou wanted Chester and me to come urgently to see him in the hospital. Zhu handed dad a penciled note from Zhou written in Chinese on a small scrap of paper. I didn't know exactly what it said, except dad was asked to come to the hospital to see him. Zhu nervously asked dad to destroy the note, which he did immediately. Zhu said that Zhou was in a nearby hospital. We didn't understand the urgency, but we grabbed our coats and hurried out the door with Zhu. In the lobby two men in blue Mao suits, whose demeanors were those of security agents, accosted us and told us to return to our room. They said that the premier was too sick to see us. Dad protested, but Zhu said it was better that we go back to our room and that we could go in the morning. Zhu, a frail man, looked pale and shaken. The next morning, without waiting for Zhu, we set out again but we were stopped at the hotel entrance by two armed army guards who said firmly that no one could leave the hotel because there had been an accident in the street. We went back to our room, but then,

Zhu returned and whispered: "Come, we can go now." We hurried down but were again turned back in the lobby by the security agents. We didn't want to get Zhu into trouble, so we turned back once again. But after Zhu left, we decided to try again. We got to the main entrance of the hotel, but we were stopped again by the armed guards. Dad argued with them in Chinese, saying we just wanted to go for a walk and then losing his patience shouted at them: "Out of our way!" At that, one of the guards pointed his bayoneted rifle at dad and ordered us back to our room. We had no choice. We never heard from Zhou Enlai again.

The incident occurred at a moment when the Politburo was mired in an ideological struggle whose outcome could determine who would rule China after Mao. The Chairman was ill, suffering from a number of critical health problems, Parkinson's disease among them. The struggle as to who would succeed him was very much in play. Deng Xiaoping, who had been returned to power as vice premier by Zhou Enlai, was under attack by Jiang Qing's Gang of Four. As pretext, they were citing criticism which Mao had leveled against Deng that had stemmed from a debate as to how the Politburo should evaluate the Cultural Revolution, which was nearing its end. Mao was pressuring the Politburo to assess the Cultural Revolution in a formal resolution as 70 percent successful and 30 percent as a failure. Deng Xiaoping, an early victim of the Cultural Revolution, was balking at adopting any such resolution. The Gang of Four was mounting a campaign on university campuses accusing Deng of seeking in opposition to Mao to discredit the Cultural Revolution. By implication, they were also denouncing his mentor, Zhou Enlai. A Politburo meeting was to take place on November 20 to resolve the issue, but in the interim, Jiang Qing's Gang of Four with the sanction of the sickly Mao was reigning as the dominant political force in Peking. Mao was also being urged by the Gang of Four to replace Zhou as premier with one of its members, Zhang Chunqiao.

At the time of the hotel incident on November 10, Ronning and Audrey were very aware of these political tensions and the aggressive role of Jiang Qing, although they did not have specific knowledge of what was transpiring within the Politburo. But it seemed to them that being barred from seeing Zhou Enlai was part of a plot by Jiang Qing's Gang of Four to isolate their political adversary, Zhou Enlai. This view was shared by Huang Hua, one of the premier's closest associates and friend over many years, and his wife, He Liliang, who told us that they too had been barred from entering the hospital to see Zhou. The Ronnings speculated that Zhou Enlai was trying to get a message out through his friends, likely one expressing support for his ally, Deng Xiaoping. A month earlier, on September 7, Zhou had received a delegation of Communist officials from Romania in the hospital. At that meeting he had voiced his support of Deng Xiaoping and expressed his conviction that Deng, to whom he had already turned over his official duties, would continue to carry out the policies he had set forth. It was entirely likely that Zhou wanted to meet with his trusted friend Chester Ronning and Audrey, the journalist, so as to have them reveal his support of Deng to the world. There was no indication that the Romanians, possibly not wishing to meddle in internal Chinese Communist Party affairs, had told others of Zhou's endorsement of Deng. Huang Hua and the Ronnings also anxiously wondered whether Zhou Enlai was being given the medicines and the other necessary medical care he needed to survive.

Two months later, at dawn on January 9, the Peking Radio announced that Zhou Enlai had "died of cancer at 09:57 hours on January 8, 1976, in Peking, at the age of seventy-eight." China was plunged into mourning, and unprecedented homage was paid to him both within the country and abroad for his role in the Chinese revolution and conduct of international affairs. At the Congregational Church in Scarsdale, New York, Chester Ronning, at the request of the congregation, delivered a eulogy in tribute to his old friend.

I too was personally saddened by the death of Zhou Enlai. I felt that he had served the Chinese people extremely well as a statesman and government leader. True, he had been involved or simply remained silent when Mao committed some of his worst abuses as party chief, but it had been a matter of survival not only for himself but for the nation so that he could carry on effectively and serve to moderate Maoist policies where possible, which he did at great risk. In Peking, I would years later view an inscription on a bronze plaque in front of the Yonghegong Tibetan Buddhist Temple, which said in part: "The Temple survived ten turbulent years of the Cultural Revolution thanks to Premier Zhou Enlai." His action in preserving the largest lamasery in Peking, built in 1964, was typical of what Zhou Enlai did to safeguard the Chinese heritage.

On January 15, at the memorial service for Zhou Enlai, which was not attended by Mao, Deng Xiaoping delivered the eulogy. Deng had already been effectively stripped of power by Mao's criticism of him at Jiang Qing's urging, and it was his last public appearance for a year. As late as May 1976, the Chinese press was still denouncing him "for crimes of trying to subvert the dictatorship of the proletariat and restore capitalism." Several days after the Zhou funeral, the Politburo appointed Hua Guofeng, one of its members, as acting premier. He was a compromise choice acceptable to all the factions.

But even in death Zhou Enlai continued to exercise profound influence on events shaping the future of the country. On March 19, during the Qingming Festival, when traditionally Chinese sweep the graves of their ancestors, a wreath honoring Zhou Enlai was laid by the Cow Lane Primary School on the Monument to the Revolutionary Martyrs in the center of Tiananmen Square. When word spread that wreaths in tribute to Zhou Enlai were being placed at the monument, it inspired numerous marches to the square, embracing people from every sort of institution as well as ordinary folk who wished to render tribute. Almost 2 million people were said to have passed through the square on April 4 in organized demonstrations or simply to view the hundreds of wreaths, inscribed manifestos, and poems stacked around the monument in dedication to Zhou Enlai and his principles. For some, hailing Zhou Enlai was by implication support for Deng Xiaoping. There was also an outpouring of condemnation by ordinary folk of Jiang Qing and her Gang of Four. In placards and poems the Gang of Four was denounced for bringing about the savagery and disruption of the Cultural Revolution. Jiang Qing was accused of ambition to become the ruling queen of China.

Alarmed by the uncontrolled mass demonstrations, the like of which had not been seen in the capital since the founding of the People's Republic in 1949, with Mao's approval, Hua Guofeng acted to restore order. In the early morning hours of April 5, Peking garrison troops cleansed the square of wreaths and posters. This served only to induce protest demonstrations by thousands of people before the Great Hall of the People. In the evening, thousands of troops and police stormed through the square once again to clear it of the last stubborn demonstrators. Deng Xiaoping, who did not visit the square, was spirited away with his wife to a small villa in Peking, where for the next three months they were in effect under house arrest. But this second purge was not lasting and ended with the death of Mao on September 9, 1976.

Two days after the death of Mao, Hua Guofeng became alarmed when the Gang of Four made a number of moves within the party bureaucracy that indicated its members were positioning themselves for an outright seizure of power. Drawing on a study of Chinese archives, Professors Roderick MacFarquhar and Michael Schoenhals described in their book *Mao's Last*

Revolution what transpired in the next weeks. Working secretly with Wang Dongxing, a senior member of the Politburo and a key security official influential in party affairs, and Marshal Ye Jianying, now the secretary-general of the Central Military Affairs Commission, Hua Guofeng readied a countercoup. On October 6, Hua summoned a Politburo meeting to take place in Huairen Hall in Zhongnanhai, the secluded enclave behind the walls of the Forbidden City where the offices of State Council, the party's Central Committee, and the residences of the leadership were located. Three members of the Gang of Four, Wang Hongwen, Zhang Chunqiao, and Yao Wenyuan, as they arrived for the meeting, were in turn seized by guards. Jiang Qing was also arrested in her Zhongnanhai residence. All were charged with plotting a coup to seize power.

With Jiang Qing's arrest, the catastrophe of the Cultural Revolution had come to its end. The Gang of Four, accused of attempting to subvert the state in plots against Zhou Enlai and Deng Xiaoping, and the torturous persecution of Liu Shaoqi, were put on trial on November 26, 1980, before thirty-five judges and six hundred selected spectators arrayed in the Ceremonial Hall of the Public Security compound on Peking's Street of Righteousness. It was more of a show trial than a legal proceeding, since the process and the subsequent conviction and sentencing were likely dictated not by the judges but secretly by the Politburo. At the conclusion of the trial, which lasted until January 1981, Jiang Qing and Zhang Chunqiao were sentenced to death with two-year reprieves. The sentences were commuted to life imprisonment in 1983. Wang Hongwen and Yao Wenyuan, who had written the article denouncing Wu Han's play *Hai Rui Dismissed from Office,* the opening gun in the Cultural Revolution, also received lengthy prison sentences.

Jiang Qing never confessed or repented, insisting that all she did was on the command of Mao. "I was Chairman Mao's dog. Whoever he asked me to bite, I bit," she was quoted as saying at the trial. While confined in Qincheng Prison, notorious for its cruel maltreatment of inmates during the Cultural Revolution, she was diagnosed sometime during the mid-1980s with throat cancer. She declined an operation. Her next years were divided thereafter between detention in prison and house arrest in the Public Security Hospital. She was in the hospital on May 14, 1991, when she committed suicide by hanging herself in her bathroom. When her death at the age of seventy-one was announced briefly in the Chinese media, I thought of that evening in Yenan forty-five years earlier when I saw her chatting and laughing gaily sitting beside Liu Shaoqi in the front row of the Peking Opera House, then only housewife to Mao Zedong.

Chinese scholars are still documenting the full cost in terms of human suffering of the Cultural Revolution. Extrapolating from Chinese archives, the
scholars Yang Su and Andrew G. Walter, in their March 2003 article published in the *China Quarterly,* "The Cultural Revolution in the Countryside:
Scope, Timing and Human Impact," estimated that in rural areas alone 36
million people experienced some form of persecution between 1966 and 1971.
Of that total, between 750,000 and 1.5 million were killed and about the same
number injured. The persecutions were perpetrated by a variety of political
and military groups and organizations in the name of purging those said
to be opponents of Mao Zedong Thought, counterrevolutionaries, class enemies such as "capitalist-roaders," or those accused of some relationship with
Chiang Kai-shek's Kuomintang. The study's figures do not include the hundreds of thousands of dead and maimed in urban areas where, in addition
to those swept up in the purges, factional struggles among the Red Guards
and worker organizations took a deadly toll.

The horror also extended to Tibet. On a visit there in 1979, Audrey and
I found the Chinese assisting the Tibetans in repairing the destruction
wreaked during the Cultural Revolution on the Jokhang Temple, the Potala
Palace, and the Drepung Monastery. In 1966, as in the rest of China, Tibet
had been engulfed suddenly by the ideological frenzy of the Cultural Revolution. Hundreds, perhaps thousands were killed or wounded in the fighting in Lhasa and other towns among rival Red Guards made up largely of
young Chinese sent down to Tibet. The Red Guards sacked the monasteries
and also vandalized and closed the Buddhist temples. When we arrived in
Lhasa, we learned that only 10 of the 2,464 monasteries in Tibet remained
intact and the number of monks had declined to 2,000 from 120,000 in 1959,
the year in which the Chinese crushed a Tibetan uprising for independence
and the Dalai Lama fled to exile in Dharmsala, India.

Our first effort in October 1979 to travel to Tibet was frustrated. We were
turned back at the border by Chinese guards. But the effort proved very rewarding in another, most unusual way.

We had planned to go to Tibet on the Old Silk Road entering China from
Pakistan. Shortly after arriving in Islamabad, the capital of Pakistan, we interviewed Prime Minister Zia-ul Haq, the military dictator of the country.

Then, with his sanction and with an escort of Pakistani soldiers and army engineers, we set out for China on the newly opened Himalayan Karakoram Highway, the first foreign journalists permitted to travel the length of the road. For two years we had sought Pakistani and Chinese permission to view this engineering marvel. It took twenty years for Pakistani and Chinese engineers to construct the Karakoram Highway through remote parts of Pakistani-controlled Kashmir to the Khunjerab Pass, where the highway enters China's Xinjiang Uygur Autonomous Region. The engineers cut through mountains—which Audrey and I circled in a helicopter—that are among the highest in the world. They are topped by glaciers exceeded in size only by those in the polar regions. While circling K-2, the highest, Audrey lost one of her cameras to the wind as she leaned out of the helicopter door, held only by a seat belt, to photograph the mountain. I pulled her back into the craft.

In building the paved road, the engineers suffered glacial mudflows, avalanches, and seismic convulsions which, we were told, cost one Pakistani or Chinese life for each mile of the 500-mile length of the highway. The highway, now a truck route for trade, was more important at the time for another, more compelling reason. It was built to support the passage of heavy tanks. Strategically, it gave the Chinese an overland link to friendly Pakistan as they confronted massed Russian divisions on their Xinjiang border.

On the highway, we traveled by car, jeep, and helicopter, at times circumventing rockslides, to the Khunjerab Pass on the China border. From 15,100 feet we looked into China. Beneath us lay the winding road to Kashgar, the great caravan oasis on the Old Silk Road which we had hoped to reach that day. The Pakistanis served us tea and sugar lumps so that we could better stand the altitude but then told us regretfully that for some reason the Chinese had closed the border road temporarily. We returned to Islamabad and flew to Peking. Our account and photos of the journey on the Karakoram Highway became a cover story in the *New York Times Magazine*.

Upon arrival by air in Peking from Islamabad, we were invited to the Great Hall of the People for a talk with Li Xiannian, whom Audrey had met at the Peking Railway Station with Deng Xiaoping in 1973. At the time of our meeting he was a member of the Politburo and a vice premier and later would serve as state president, the head of government, from 1983 to 1988. We had just visited Memorial Hall in Tiananmen Square, where we viewed the mummified body of Mao Zedong. We had filed past a white marble statue of a seated Mao and into a cavernous, dimly lit chamber where, in a crystal sarcophagus, the Great Helmsman lay embalmed, dressed in a gray tunic, partially draped in a flag. The Chinese walking by the bier, four abreast, gazed upon the Great Helmsman with gaping curiosity. But as we watched, there were no tears for Mao—no manifestations of the adulation which we had witnessed in past years.

At the Great Hall of the People, I asked Li Xiannian how Mao and his writings would be viewed by the Chinese in generations to come. "We do not believe Mao Zedong Thought implies a cult of personality," Li said. "His writings represent the collective wisdom and experience of many Chinese leaders. The words of every leader, including Chairman Mao, must be tested through social practices. What the Chairman said during the Cultural Revolution might not be applicable today. Communist leaders are not fortune-tellers. The test of social practice is the only criterion of truth. The people now know that Chairman Mao made errors in his work. But they also understand his role in the Chinese Revolution and the next generations will remember him as a great leader and teacher."

After our talk with Li, we then set out on a 5,000-mile journey which on this second effort took us to Tibet, through the Sichuan heartland and back to Shanghai from Lhasa. Interviewing senior officials, workers, and peasants, we found that the new folk hero was Zhou Enlai, revered as the leader who had struggled within the party enclaves against Jiang Qing, mitigating the worst abuses of the Cultural Revolution. At an exhibition of paintings in Shanghai, we found an array of canvases depicting Zhou Enlai as a student and as a visionary, as the man who had brought Deng Xiaoping out of political limbo. There was only a single portrait of Mao, as a teacher instructing a young soldier. And in a nearby alcove, the positioning of two paintings on opposite walls offered an implied rebuke of the Chairman: one canvas showed Mao's first wife, Yang Kaihui, seated in a cell with bloodied forehead before her execution by Chiang Kai-shek's troops in 1930; the other depicted a street artist cartooning Jiang Qing as a dowager empress while spectators jeered.

At the time of our talk with Li, Deng Xiaoping had already become the country's "paramount leader," although Hua Guofeng perfunctorily held the titles of party chairman and premier. Deng was already at work settling old scores. In the next year, Liu Shaoqi and other comrades purged in the Cultural Revolution would be politically rehabilitated. In May, Liu was honored at a state funeral at which his ashes were presented to his widow. The memory of the denunciation of Liu and his wife by their eldest daughter resonated for me in 2003 when Audrey and I dined in the luxurious house in Peking owned by the couple's younger daughter, Liu Ding, whose fortunes had flourished in the market economy introduced by Deng Xiaoping under his slogan "To Be Rich Is Glorious." She was president of the Asia Link Group, consultants in corporate finance, after having graduated from Boston University and the Harvard Business School.

Mao's portrait adorns the Tiananmen Gate, and for most Chinese he remains more than anything else the heroic revolutionary who founded the People's Republic. Traveling through China in 2008, I found that it had become cliché among many Chinese when asked about Mao to rate him as 60 percent heroic and 40 percent destructive. After Mao's death, his heir, Deng Xiaoping, evaluated him as "seven parts good, three parts bad." As for the bad, the tyrannical regime Mao established after the Civil War, marked by massive political purges, the economic blunders of his Great Leap Forward, and the upheaval of the Cultural Revolution, cost the lives of many millions of his compatriots. But as a revolutionary, military strategist, and visionary, he earned the respect of his compatriots. He secured the borders of China and laid down the foundation for the eventual emergence of a new, powerful nation. He defeated Chiang Kai-shek in the Civil War against enormous odds and unified the mainland. He wiped out the humiliating colonial concessions wrested from China by an array of foreign powers such as the extraterritorial enclaves at Shanghai, Tianjin, Qingdao, and Hankou. President Truman blocked him from retrieving Taiwan by interposing the Seventh Fleet in the Taiwan Strait. But President Nixon was compelled by Zhou Enlai in their joint Shanghai Communiqué to accept that "there is but one China and that Taiwan is part of China." Reasserting China's historic claim to Tibet in 1950, Mao reincorporated it in 1951 as an autonomous region. The designation was more bureaucratic than real, however, since as late as 2008 the exiled Dalai Lama was still struggling to bring about greater autonomy for his people from domination by Peking's Han administrators. In the Korean War, although his troops suffered enormous casualties, Mao succeeded in driving MacArthur's forces back across the thirty-eighth parallel and thus repositioned North Korea as a buffer state. Mao also rebuffed Russian penetration of both Manchuria and Xinjiang Province in Central Asia. In 1955 he regained Soviet-occupied Dalian and Lüshun in the northeast. Mao provided the weaponry and the safe haven for training, together with Chinese advisers, that enabled the Vietnamese Communists to defeat the French and subsequently the United States with its South Vietnamese allies. His support of Hanoi, apart from the ideological, was motivated by the need he saw of securing his southern border through the elimination of American bases in Southeast Asia. Mao thus banished his fear which he often voiced since the 1960s of hostile encirclement and dismemberment by a coterie of hostile powers. The hostile coalition, more phantom than real, of which he warned comprised the United States, poised in military bases in Southeast Asia, Japan in alignment with the United States, the Soviet Union, and India. He interpreted the Treaty of Peace, Friendship and Cooperation, signed by the Soviet Union and India in 1971, as a military alliance aimed at China. In furtherance of Mao's goal of bringing about a unified China, his heir, Deng Xiaoping, negotiated the arrangements for the return of the leased British colony of Hong Kong in 1997 and of Macau by Portugal in 1999. Deng pledged that Peking would tolerate Hong Kong's capitalist economy for fifty years in keeping with a political philosophy of "one country–two systems" which he envisioned as a potential framework for reuniting Taiwan with the mainland.

In sum, as a consequence of Mao's consolidation of China's strategic position, coupled with the global expansion of economic influence stemming from Deng Xiaoping's policies, the foundation was laid for a bid by China to supplant the United States as the leading power in East Asia.

Deng Xiaoping is rendered tribute by most Chinese, who recognize that his economic policies raised the living standards of millions of Chinese and elevated China to a leading position in the world. But as in the case of Mao, there are reservations about Deng's domestic legacy, both economic and political. While igniting an explosion of urban development and wealth, he did not substantially reduce the huge income gap between the middle-class affluent of the cities and the peasants. It was not until 2008 that President Hu Jintao, alarmed by peasant discontent, the flight of millions of impoverished farmers to the cities, and shrinking agricultural development, introduced a rural reform policy that allowed farmers to lease or transfer land-use rights, a step that should significantly raise lagging peasant incomes. A target date of 2020 was set to bring about a doubling of the disposable income of the 750 million peasants.

Deng's free market has evolved into a form of authoritarian capitalism under strict government control. While there has been a remarkable expansion of free enterprise in some sections of the economy, key industries remain state owned. About three-fourths of the some fifteen hundred domestic companies listed in 2009 on the Chinese stock exchange were state owned. Corrupt practices by some local officials managing properties pose a continuing problem. Nevertheless, through the earnings of its export industries and foreign investments China has become the largest holder of U.S. Treasury securities, about $212 trillion in official reserves in September 2009.

In their relentless drive to reinforce the Chinese economy and maintain living standards, Chinese leaders stress the need to maintain societal stability. This has been made an excuse for the lack of progress toward major political reforms and suppression of any dissidence that might challenge or dilute the authority of the Communist Party hierarchy. To maintain that discipline, the media and the Internet are censored by a Propaganda Department.

There is a chapter in Chinese history which the Communist Party does everything it can to hide. In 1989, as the country's paramount leader, Deng Xiaoping compelled Zhao Ziyang to resign from the post of general secretary of the party. As both premier and then party chief, Zhao had inspired the first moves toward a free market economy but also urged the Politburo to begin to consider the possibilities of transition to a more democratic society. When students in the spring of 1989 demonstrated in Tiananmen Square en masse for democratic reforms, Zhao went to the square to consult with them and urged moderation and calm. At a meeting of the party leadership before going to Tiananmen, Zhao withstood demands by hard-liners that troops be used to crush the student demonstrations. Deng Xiaoping brushed him aside and ordered tanks and troops into Peking, resulting in clashes during which hundreds of the demonstrating students and their supporters were killed. When Zhao protested, he was ousted as general secretary of the party and placed under house arrest. His name was expunged from all public mention. But Zhao Ziyang, whose death in 2005 was noted in a party obituary by a single line, is not forgotten by those Chinese who hope for an atoning statement by the party leadership confessing that the Tiananmen repression was a mistake and greater progress toward a more democratic society.

Rising generations of Chinese are likely to learn of the Zhao Ziyang saga as a consequence of a most unexpected development. In May 2009, a Zhao memoir of his travails, *Prisoner of the State: The Secret Journal of Premier Zhao Ziyang,* surfaced in Hong Kong. The book is based on transcriptions made by Zhao on thirty musical tape cassettes relating his experiences in the Tiananmen episode and his policies prior to his ouster from the Politburo. The tapes were transcribed during his imprisonment and smuggled out to Hong Kong by friends. The book was banned on the mainland, but details have become known there through Chinese bloggers on the Internet who have learned how to evade the censors.

Zhao's legacy will interest China's youth, but it will not stir them to demonstrations such as those in Tiananmen Square in 1989, when students were protesting both lack of democracy and adverse economic conditions. In the fall of 2008, when I traveled through China lecturing at several universities, I found no inclination among the students to become involved in political action. They were primarily interested in jobs and enhancement of lifestyle. Like others of the middle class, they deplore censorship and corruption among some officials but seem content to await fulfillment of government promises of greater democracy through consensus and respect for human rights within the existing political framework.

38
FALL OF INDOCHINA
AMERICA IN RETREAT

The wars which consumed Vietnam, Cambodia, and Laos for thirty years ended during April 1975 in Communist victories and the eviction of the U.S. presence from all Indochina. North Vietnamese troops seized Vietnam, while the Khmer Rouge took over in Cambodia and the Pathet Lao triumphed in Laos. The American withdrawal was total: embassies, military and economic aid missions, the Central Intelligence Agency, and the few units of marine embassy guards, which were remnants of what once had been a force of more than a half million American soldiers.

Saigon fell to the North Vietnamese on April 30, 1975, in the final phase of a war that was fought first and lost by France, then by the United States and its South Vietnamese allies. It followed the breakdown of the cease-fire concluded in Paris on January 17, 1973, by Henry Kissinger and Le Duc Tho, the envoy of the Democratic Republic of Vietnam. Sporadic fighting erupted between South Vietnamese and North Vietnamese troops along the agreed line of demarcation between the two forces. In December 1974 the North Vietnamese launched a major attack along the Cambodian border north of Saigon, and when after a pause they resumed their advance in March 1975, the South Vietnamese retreated in disarray. The South Vietnamese appeals for intervention by American B-52 bombers went unanswered. President Nixon had already resigned, and the withdrawal of American troops under his policy of Vietnamization, the turnover of ground operations to the South Vietnamese, was nearly complete. On April 20, after a hard-fought ten-day battle, the North Vietnamese captured Xuan Loc, twenty-six miles from downtown Saigon, and a week later encircled the city.

In New York, as the North Vietnamese closed on Saigon, we debated: Should we order our correspondents to leave so as to ensure their safety or allow them to remain to cover the fall of the capital?

In Phnom Penh, the decision as to whether to remain for the Khmer Rouge occupation was left to Sydney Schanberg, and he chose to stay on. Our Saigon correspondents were not allowed a choice. In the *Times* newsroom, we watched television images of marine Chinook helicopters evacuating

Americans from the U.S. Embassy compound. Unnerved by what happened to Schanberg, publisher Arthur Ochs Sulzberger intervened and ordered our Vietnam correspondents to leave Saigon. We waited apprehensively to learn whether they would be among the 978 Americans being loaded into marine helicopters on the embassy roof to be taken to ships of the Seventh Fleet and other vessels standing by in the South China Sea.

Viewing the television images, I was appalled by the sight of thousands of Vietnamese, many of whom had been employed in the U.S. war effort, clawing at the gates of the embassy compound, hoping to get aboard the evacuation helicopters. Graham Martin, the American ambassador, had managed to evacuate about 1,100 Vietnamese before orders came from Henry Kissinger, President Gerald Ford's secretary of state, to break off the evacuation of the Vietnamese by the marine helicopters, so that priority would be given to Americans. At 5 A.M. on April 30, at the insistence of the president that he leave, the ambassador mounted a ladder to a helicopter, clutching the embassy's American flag, reluctantly abandoning several hundred Vietnamese in the compound and thousands of others at the gates.

In the afternoon of April 29, the two *New York Times* correspondents remaining in Saigon, Malcolm Browne and Fox Butterfield, heeding the order of the publisher, donned backpacks in the *Times* office and boarded a U.S. Army bus heading for an evacuation center at Ton Son Nhut Airport. Americans throughout Saigon were boarding buses even before the American radio station began playing Bing Crosby's "I'm Dreaming of a White Christmas," the agreed signal for departure. The North Vietnamese were shelling the city as the Americans headed for the airport.

Earlier, Browne had contrived to get those members of the *Times*' Vietnamese staff who chose to leave and their families aboard the CIA's leased Air America planes which were shuttling to Guam. President Nguyen Van Thieu had forbidden any Vietnamese emigration, but Browne and David Greenway of the *Washington Post* covertly loaded their Vietnamese employees and families into office cars and smuggled them past the guards at the Ton Son Nhut Airport. Browne's Vietnamese wife, Le Lieu, a photographer, together with her two brothers and their children, left on April 28 on Air Vietnam's last commercial flight.

Browne had unexpectedly taken charge of the Saigon Bureau on March 20. On that day, inexplicably, and without notifying his colleagues, James Markham, the bureau chief, had decamped with his family to Hong Kong. (Markham later distinguished himself at posts in Europe and the Middle East, but in 1989 he committed suicide in Paris, where he had been serving as the *Times* bureau chief.) Fortunately, Browne was not a newcomer to Vietnam. He came to the *Times* in 1968 from the Associated Press after sharing the Pulitzer Prize with David Halberstam for their coverage of the downfall of the Diem regime. In 1972 he was expelled from Vietnam in retaliation for his articles exposing corruption in President Nguyen Van Thieu's government. Browne had muscled his way back into Saigon to reinforce the bureau only a few days before Markham left.

At Ton Son Nhut, Browne and Butterfield found that the runways had been shelled and were unusable for fixed-wing aircraft. The helicopter evacuation was in its last stage, with most of the 393 Americans and 4,000 Vietnamese to be lifted out already gone. Browne and Butterfield waited for four hours in a bunker before one of the marine choppers, which were landing at two-minute intervals, lifted them out. The helicopters were tracked by North Vietnamese antiaircraft, but their commanders, apparently on orders, refrained from firing at the craft. The chopper carrying the *Times* men landed on the *Mobile,* a U.S. Navy supply ship standing off the coast, in the center of a chaotic scene. There was not enough deck space on the evacuation ships to accommodate all the incoming helicopters. Crews were dumping South Vietnamese helicopters overboard rather than let any return to shore into the possession of the North Vietnamese. The sea was strewn with burning sampans and other boats set aflame as their refugee occupants boarded ships.

Browne filed his last Vietnam dispatch from the *Mobile*'s radio. No better epitaph to the fall of Saigon could have been written than the lead of his story. The dispatch, which brought tears to my eyes, said: "Like a failed marriage, the Vietnamese-American relationship of the last generation has ended in a mixture of hatred and suspicion, coupled with a strong remnant of tenderness and compassion on both sides. The tens of thousands aboard the huge evacuation armada sailing away from Vietnam have told endless stories of heroism, loyalty and love in the last hours. But for millions of Vietnamese and not a few Americans, the dominant memory will be sorrow and betrayal and guilt."

Days before the fall of the city, the cry of betrayal was sounded by President Thieu. As the North Vietnamese closed in on Saigon, Thieu appealed for further American military aid, but President Ford was unable to make good on Nixon's promises of additional support. The Congress balked at Ford's request for $722 million in aid. On April 21, appearing on Saigon television to announce his resignation, President Thieu said: "The United States has not respected its promises. It is unfair. It is inhuman. It is not trustworthy. It is irresponsible." He made no reference to the fifty-eight thousand American soldiers who had died in support of a succession of failed Saigon regimes, confining himself solely to a last call for more aid and resumption of bombing by B-52s in support of retreating South Vietnamese troops. Thieu's image recalled for me the parade of South Vietnamese leaders I had known, beginning with Bao Dai in 1950, who had been unable, despite massive American support, to rally their people against an enemy who promised their troops little more than freedom from foreign invaders. When the Paris cease-fire accord collapsed in 1973, Thieu commanded an army of about a million troops armed with American weapons and supported by an unopposed air force. What was lacking was competent, incorruptible leadership which could inspire and marshal the South Vietnamese armed forces. The U.S. Senate in early April called for the replacement of Thieu by better leadership, but the collapse of the South Vietnamese government came more swiftly than anyone in Washington, including the CIA, had anticipated.

The issue of betrayal was also raised in Laos, as it was in Phnom Penh, by Lon Nol in 1970 when he was told that American ground troops would be withdrawn from Cambodia, leaving his slender forces to face the more powerful Khmer Rouge and North Vietnamese. In Laos, following dissolution of the Royal Lao Government, headed by the neutralist prime minister, Souvanna Phouma, the United States terminated its aid programs and in effect abandoned its most loyal allies, the Hmong hill people. The CIA had employed the Hmong to battle the Pathet Lao and disrupt Communist traffic from North Vietnam through Laos down the Ho Chi Minh Trail and through Cambodia into South Vietnam. Following withdrawal of the American missions from Vientiane, the Hmong chief, General Vang Pao, fled with more than ten thousand of his people to the town of Long Cheng. They assembled there, as Sucheng Chan recounted in his book *Hmong Means Free,* believing the CIA would airlift them to safe havens. In recruiting the Hmong, the CIA had assured Vang Pao that the United States would safeguard his people. However, only a single C-130 transport was sent to the Long Cheng assembly area by the American military command in the Philippines. Vang Pao and several hundred of his people escaped, but many thousands of others at Long Cheng and elsewhere in the country were left behind to face the retribution of the Pathet Lao.

In Saigon, before noon on April 30, 1975, the North Vietnamese Army (NVA) 203rd Armored Regiment broke into Saigon, and one of its tanks, flying the flag of the National Liberation Front, crashed through the front gate of the Presidential Palace. The National Liberation Front (NLF) flag was flown by the North Vietnamese to posture the Vietcong, their allies in the

South, as the victors. That afternoon Duong Van Minh, who had been president of South Vietnam for only three days, surrendered in a radio broadcast. The North Vietnamese triumph brought forth media comment about the military genius of General Vo Nguyen Giap. There was reason enough to be in awe of Giap's victory against great odds and the inspirational leadership of his mentor, Ho Chi Minh, who had died in 1969. Little mention, if any, was made of Mao Zedong's role. There was symbolism in that the North Vietnamese tank that crashed through the gate of the Independence Palace was a Soviet-designed T-54, handed over to the North Vietnamese by the Chinese. It was a symbol in steel of Mao's indispensable contribution to Giap's victory.

With their occupation of Saigon, as in the cities of Cambodia and Laos, the Communists began almost at once rounding up hundreds of thousands of people who had served or befriended the Americans. Le Duan, the hardcore Marxist successor to Ho Chi Minh, instituted a purge which eventually would consign about 400,000 South Vietnamese to harsh reeducation camps. The crackdown targeted South Vietnamese soldiers and officials, Western-influenced intellectuals, students, businesspeople, and others suspected of being ideologically opposed to the regime. More than a million Vietnamese, including a half million of Chinese origin, would flee the country during the years 1975 to 1989.

Some Western and Eastern European reporters, photographers, and media technicians stayed on in Saigon for the Communist occupation. But Westerners were not permitted to remain long enough to witness the purges. In Cambodia, all AP correspondents were recalled before the Khmer Rouge entered Phnom Penh, but in Saigon three AP men—Peter Arnett, George Asper, and Matt Franjola—were given clearance by Wes Gallagher, president of the AP, to remain for the entry of the Communists. "From our point of view it was worth the risk," Gallagher said. Western correspondents were permitted by the North Vietnamese briefly to file reports but then were ordered to shut down their transmitters. After a twenty-five-day hiatus, eighty-three of those who stayed on, including the AP reporters, left on an Ilyushin transport painted with Hanoi's yellow-starred flag. It took them to Vientiane and connections home. They were permitted to carry out their files and film.

The fall of Saigon was the last act in the coverage of the Indochina wars by American correspondents that began when I arrived in Saigon in February 1950. In America's Vietnam War, correspondents did not suffer military censorship of their dispatches like I did during the French Indochina conflict. But there were similar problems for correspondents in both wars in terms of instances of official denial of information and distorted press releases. American correspondents learned early on in the Vietnam War that they could not always rely or trust the information imparted to them in the briefings by American and Vietnamese officials in Saigon. The daily press briefings staged by the Military Assistance Command Vietnam (MACV) were dubbed by cynics among the correspondents as the "Five O'Clock Follies." Correspondents found nothing more damaging to the credibility of the briefing officers than the dubious "body count" statistics, the number of Communist soldiers said to have been killed, which were cited. The "body count" was put forward as proof that General Westmoreland's "War of Attrition" was being conducted successfully.

In January 1968, when I visited the Saigon Bureau for the last time, then as foreign editor, I found that some correspondents were skipping the briefings, which they termed useless. The "Follies" were terminated, after an eight-year run, in February 1973. The AP Saigon Bureau chief, Richard Pyle, who covered the war for five years, then publicly characterized the Follies as "the longest-playing tragicomedy in Southeast Asia's theater of the absurd." But later he told me: "Whatever their failings, limitations and drawbacks, they provided the only opportunity to get United States and Vietnamese officials, military and diplomatic, on the record, and to confront and challenge them in real time with contradictory information."

The correspondents learned early on that they would have to go into the field if they were to get the straight facts. Making up for the vagaries of the "Follies" briefings, the military did provide transport to take correspondents just about anywhere they wanted to go. Horst Faas, the AP photographer who won two Pulitzer Prizes for his work, commented that he was grateful to the American military for making it easy to get around but noted the drawback: "It was easy to get killed." According to AP records of casualties among the correspondents of the fifteen countries who covered the war from 1965 to 1975, the toll was thirty-three killed or missing and presumed dead in Vietnam, four in Laos, and thirty-four in Cambodia. The list included twenty Americans.

Many American military officers left Vietnam blaming the news media for undermining the war effort by fueling the antiwar movement in the United States with critical reporting. After the war, when I lectured at West

Point, I heard cadets voicing that same opinion. I saw no basis for the allegation, and army historians in later years did not give the complaint much weight. The Pentagon was impelled by its Vietnam experience to institute a number of training programs for officers designed to improve relations with the media and facilitate coverage of military operations. Stung by the heated disputes with the press during the Iraq Gulf War in 1991, the Pentagon experimented in the second Iraq War with the "embedding" of correspondents in front-line units. Restrictions were imposed on the correspondents where unit commanders deemed there were security risks either by their presence or in the transmission of dispatches during combat situations. There was a virtual embargo on the transmission of photographs of the bodies of soldiers killed in action. But embedding gave many correspondents a valuable close-up of what the troops faced.

The American correspondents whom I observed as a reporter in the field or worked with as an editor served the public extraordinarily well, courageous and faithful in their reporting. It was certainly true of the Saigon Bureau chiefs of the *Times*, including such correspondents as Charles Mohr; A. J. Langguth, later author of the prizewinning book *Our Vietnam;* Peter Grose, later a distinguished biographer of Allen Dulles, the director of the Central Intelligence Agency; Johnny Apple, later a brilliant chief Washington correspondent; Gene Roberts, later national editor and managing editor; Craig Whitney, later an assistant managing editor; and Malcolm Browne. Not the least among the many outstanding correspondents was Tom Johnson, our only black reporter, who told the story of the commitment of black servicemen better than anyone else. There was no lack of excellent news coverage and analysis by the press corps as a whole. Television images brought home graphically, at times better than print, the horrendous nature of the war. Together with the shocking accounts of the sufferings of the Indochinese peoples, the correspondents portrayed passionately the heroism and self sacrifice of American troops in combat.

Many Vietnamese see parallels between their war with the United States and the struggle in Iraq. This was apparent when Audrey and I returned to Vietnam in 2005, revisiting Hanoi, Saigon (now Ho Chi Minh City), and the battlegrounds I knew. For almost four decades I had shied away from revisiting Vietnam. When I left the country in 1966, I said in bitterness I would never return. Revisiting would resurrect too many painful memories of the suffering and the dead—and the anguish of knowing that the Vietnam War could have been averted. But I was moved to return out of the desire to learn how the Vietnamese people were faring and also somewhat curious as to how they were viewing the invasion of Iraq in the context of their experience.

We arrived in Hanoi as the Vietnamese were marking the thirtieth anniversary of the end of the war with the United States. We were immediately seized upon by newspapers and television, eager for our recollections of the Vietnam War. The Vietnamese look back on 1945 as a time when war with the United States might have been averted. I had just published a historic novel, *Fatal Crossroads: A Novel of Vietnam 1945,* whose plot recalls the unanswered appeals of Ho Chi Minh to President Truman for cooperation in bringing about Vietnamese independence. It also recalls the support given to Ho's guerrillas in operations against the Japanese by agents of the American Office of Strategic Services (OSS).

I found criticism of the United States muted as the Vietnamese marked the anniversary of their victory. The government was seeking to divert the people from brooding about the past to the promise of a rewarding future. But the memorials to be seen in virtually every hamlet inevitably revived memories. Americans were grieving for more than 58,000 service people killed in the Vietnam War, and the search was going on for the remains of some 1,500 still missing. The Vietnamese grieve for nearly 4 million civilian and military dead. Some 300,000 of their soldiers are still missing and mourned spiritually by their families as souls wandering endlessly, since they have not, in keeping with ancestral religious custom, been accorded traditional burial rites.

Vu Xuan Hong, a prominent member of the National Assembly, spent considerable time with us in Hanoi extolling the development of closer relations with the United States. Since the death of Le Duan in 1986, Communist strictures had been gradually relaxed, and the country moved to a largely free market economy. America has become Vietnam's leading export market. Tacitly, the government is cultivating the United States as a counterweight to China, its historical adversary. Vu cited his government's cooperation with the United States in counterterrorism. U.S. Navy ships were calling at Vietnamese ports. American nongovernmental organizations were at work in the country removing the many unexploded bombs and in other aid projects. Hundreds of thousands of American tourists were being warmly welcomed annually. But when asked about the invasion of Iraq three years earlier, Vu darkened and had this to say: "The Vietnamese people are very negative about the invasion. We are a small country and we know the consequences of war—what it is like to be bombed. We are against a big power invading a small country. The Iraqi people should solve their own problems. They have their own culture and religion, and their own dreams. Perhaps democracy or maybe they will continue to fight among themselves. The Americans better heed the resistance. Sooner or later they will have to withdraw."

EPILOGUE

LESSONS OF THE ASIAN WARS

Those who do not learn from history are doomed to repeat it.
—George Santayana, philosopher and poet

From 1946 to 1975, the United States suffered in Asia some of its worst political, diplomatic, and military reverses. Those defeats stemmed in great part from policy missteps by the American presidents who were in office during the Chinese Civil War, the French Indochina War, the Korean War, and the American military interventions in Vietnam, Cambodia, and Laos. I cite some of the most costly mistakes in this epilogue, persuaded that there are lessons to be derived which can be useful in coping with other confrontations such as those involving Iraq, Afghanistan, North Korea, and Cuba. I review also the mixed history of how the press covered government decision making during those three decades to underline how profoundly the performance of the news media affects national security.

THE WHITE HOUSE AND NATIONAL SECURITY

RELUCTANCE TO TALK TO ADVERSARIES

For ideological and domestic political reasons, President Harry Truman balked at direct talks with his foreign adversaries. Scorning Ho Chi Minh as simply a Communist rather than a nationalist revolutionary, he ignored eight bids by Ho in late 1945 and early 1946 for friendship and cooperation if only the United States would help in freeing Vietnam of French colonialism. If Ho's offer had been accepted, America's Vietnam War might have been averted. Truman also failed to take advantage of proffered opportunities to open direct exploratory contacts with Mao Zedong. Rebuffed, Mao intervened militarily in the Korean War and provided the border sanctuary in South China and the arms which enabled the Indochinese Communists to triumph. Mao was motivated in these policies by a conviction that the United

States intended to undermine his regime. If there had been high-level talks, Mao might have been dissuaded from his obsessive fear. When President Nixon eventually engaged in conciliatory talks with Mao and Zhou Enlai during his 1972 visit to China, the United States was already committed to withdrawal of its troops from war in Vietnam. China thus gained what Mao had sought for more than two decades of strife: recognition and elimination of what he perceived to be the threat to the security of his regime from American bases in Southeast Asia.

Acting for the Eisenhower administration, the secretary of state, John Foster Dulles, refused during the 1954 Geneva Conference on Indochina and Korea to talk or otherwise engage directly with the Chinese delegation, headed by Premier Zhou Enlai. At a crucial turning point in the conference negotiations on Indochina, as I have detailed earlier, the Chinese out of frustration turned to me as a channel for conveying a pivotal message to the American delegation. After the collapse at the Geneva Conference of talks on Korea, Dulles rejected a proposal by Premier Zhou Enlai that there be a continuation of discussions in another forum in search of a settlement of the strife on the peninsula. Thereafter, the stalemate in Korea hardened, compelling the indefinite stationing of some twenty-nine thousand American troops, comprising ground, air, and naval divisions, in South Korea behind the Demilitarized Zone as a trip-wire defense force against any incursion by the powerful North Korean army.

Comparable to the reluctance of the White House to enter into exploratory talks with the Maoist regime was the hesitancy of the George W. Bush administration to enter into high-level talks with the governments of Iran and Syria during the war in Iraq. Both of those governments, branded terrorist regimes by the Bush administration, provided the Iraqi insurgents with indispensable sanctuaries and cross-border supply of arms. As in Indochina, bombing and covert ground actions were not effective in sealing Iraq's porous borders with Syria and Iran. It was left to the incoming Barack Obama administration to explore the alternative of high-level talks. In Afghanistan, the Obama administration reached out to less radical tribal factions of the Taliban seeking peace settlements.

DEPENDABLE ALLIES

The most vital lesson to be derived by Barack Obama from President John F. Kennedy's experience was the finding that no American counter-insurgency program could fully succeed unless the United States was allied with a native government, highly efficient, incorruptible, and capable of attracting popular homegrown support. Kennedy went to the extent of approving the violent coup unseating President Ngo Dinh Diem because he believed that a suitable replacement had to be found for the flawed Diem regime. In the final phase of the Vietnam War, Congress held to that standard in denying further military aid to the Thieu government.

The horrors that befell individuals allied with the United States in Indochina after the withdrawal of American troops speaks to the obligation to include in any exit strategy for Iraq or Afghanistan contingency plans to safeguard those supporters left behind. Such plans could range from their evacuation or, alternatively, the protective presence of a residual American force during the extended transition, to arrangements with successor or adversary powers, or ultimately if necessary, reintervention with international sanction.

RELIANCE ON BOMBING

From the administration of President Lyndon Johnson to that of Richard Nixon, the United States relied heavily in Indochina on bombing as a means of gaining decisive military advantages that would bend the Communist foes to Washington's political will. These massive bombing campaigns failed to achieve their goals. Worse, they often were counterproductive in that by inflicting civilian casualties and other collateral damage they incited powerful native anti-American sentiment and resistance. In Cambodia, many thousands of peasants threw their support to the Communist Khmer Rouge out of resentment of the devastating American bombing. This was a major contributing factor to the military victory of the Khmer Rouge, headed by the genocidal maniac Pol Pot, over the American-supported Lon Nol government.

As late as 2008, American military strategists were still failing to take account of the lessons of Indochina in the use of air power. In the fight against the Taliban in Afghanistan, civilian casualties resulting from American air strikes evoked repeated protests by the allied Afghan government. Finally, concerned about losing the support of the Afghan people, the secretary of defense, Robert M. Gates, visited Afghanistan late in the year and promised "we will do everything in our power to find new and better ways" to take aim at the "common enemies." But the bombing by drones and manned combat aircraft continued into 2009, inflicting civilian casualties and evoking even more vehement protests by the Afghan allies.

STRATEGIC MISCONCEPTIONS

The United States' interventions in Indochina beg comparison with its invasion of Iraq in 2003. In both episodes the United States intervened militarily not on the express invitation of a majority of the native peoples but for what was perceived to be American strategic interests. In the deployment of troops in both Indochina and Iraq little account was taken of the historical nationalist resistance common to the populations of those countries to any foreign intervention. In Indochina this nationalist resistance was a major factor in the defeat of both France and the United States. In Iraq, the American invasion, ostensibly launched to defeat the unpopular Saddam Hussein regime, encountered insurgent attacks rather than the cheering crowds as forecast by the Central Intelligence Agency. Foreign invaders whatever their purpose were anathema.

In both Vietnam and Iraq the original rationale for intervention was discarded and another substituted.

In 1950 the Truman administration made its initial commitment to the French in their war against Ho Chi Minh as a trade-off for President Charles de Gaulle's cooperation in the confrontation with Stalin in Europe. Subsequently, as the United States became deeply mired in Vietnam, the so-called domino theory—which held that the fall of Indochina would lead to Communist domination of all Southeast Asia and diminish U.S. influence in the world—was put forward as the rationale for intervention. The domino theory was dismissed as invalid in 1967 by Richard Helms, director of the CIA, in a secret assessment submitted to President Johnson. Robert McNamara in his memoir, *In Retrospect,* published in 1995, recalling the Helms assessment, stated that he too had belatedly concluded that the domino theory, initially enunciated by President Eisenhower and subscribed to by his three successors, was wrong and that the United States "could have withdrawn from South Vietnam without any permanent damage to U.S. or Western security." No dominos fell in Southeast Asia following the Communist conquest of Indochina. If anything, the triumphant Vietnamese became more isolated.

In Iraq there was a comparable flip by the Bush administration in justifying intervention. Spreading democracy throughout the Middle East became the rationale for pursuing the war in Iraq after it was shown that there were no weapons of mass destruction in Saddam Hussein's armory. What transpired in Southeast Asia also put into question President George W. Bush's theory that establishing an effective democratic government in Iraq would lead to regime change in other Middle East countries ruled by authoritarian regimes. The Indochina experience demonstrated that independent nations tend to evolve in terms of their own culture, history, and internal problems rather than from the ideological influence of neighboring states.

THE NEWS MEDIA AND NATIONAL SECURITY

Observing the evolution of American foreign policy over the past half century, as a reporter and editor, I hold that the press has no more vital obligation to public service than providing penetrating and comprehensive coverage of national security issues. It is the responsibility of the press to lay out for citizen voters what are the policies of the government in coping with commitments abroad and any threats to national security such as terrorism. No less critical is the concomitant responsibility of the press to report on whether officials are telling the truth about the character and viability of their policies. The performance of the news media since the end of World War II in fulfilling those obligations in the coverage of national security policy making has been most uneven.

In 1950, the American people lacked the information that would have enabled them to grasp what might be the consequences of President Truman's decision to become involved on the side of the French in Indochina. I must make the point once again that were no American correspondents stationed in Saigon covering the French Indochina War before my arrival in February 1950. Truman established diplomatic relations with the Bao Dai satellite government and made his commitment to support the French military campaign against Ho Chi Minh's forces, announced only a few days after I reached Saigon, without the American people being aware of what their nation was getting into. It is reasonable to speculate that if there had been comprehensive reporting by American correspondents prior to 1950 on the nature of the nationalist revolution in Indochina, an informed American public might have resisted being led step by step into the Indochina morass.

During the Lyndon Johnson administration, in the first six months of 1964, the American military mounted clandestine attacks on North Vietnam. None were reported in the press. If the news media had investigated and revealed these actions taken without the sanction of Congress, the subsequent turn in American policy toward engaging in a widening war might have been forestalled. During the period of the clandestine raids, the administration was preparing a congressional resolution tantamount to a declaration of war. On August 4, the Pentagon announced that North Vietnamese PT boats had made the second of two torpedo attacks on U.S. Navy destroyers in the Gulf of Tonkin. That evening President Lyndon Johnson went on national television to announce that in retaliation he had ordered air strikes against North Vietnam. Like the news media generally, the *New York Times* accepted without question the Pentagon report of an attack and commented editorially that Johnson had presented the "somber facts" to the American people. On August 7, Congress, responding to the urging of the Johnson administration, approved a Gulf of Tonkin Resolution authorizing military action against North Vietnam. Not long after Congress acted, the public learned through leaked statements by navy officers that the North Vietnamese "torpedo attack" exploited by the administration to spur Congress into passing the Gulf of Tonkin Resolution never happened. American destroyers had been shooting in the dark at what one navy pilot on reconnaissance described as phantom targets, not at North Vietnamese torpedo boats. Congress and the public had been misled. Attacks on North Vietnam continued.

The *New York Times* served the country well in 1971 by publishing the Pentagon Papers. The Papers disclosed covert military operations by secret presidential fiat and other executive actions taken without the approval of Congress. If the breaches of executive license documented in the Papers had been published by the press in "real time," Congress and the public might have been sufficiently aroused to demand rethinking of the commitments which led the United States into the Indochina quagmire.

The belated disclosure by the press of the Gulf of Tonkin deception can be compared to the lapses of the press in 2002 when the Bush administration was putting forward its case for regime change in Iraq preparatory to the invasion. On August 26, Vice President Dick Cheney stated that there was no doubt that Saddam Hussein had weapons of mass destruction and was preparing to use them against the United States. As proof, President Bush told the United Nations General Assembly on September 12 that Iraq had made several attempts to buy aluminum tubes used to enrich uranium for use in building nuclear weapons. The tubes story, given prominent play in the *New York Times* and other media, became a key factor in the administration's case for war. Few news organizations seriously questioned the tubes story or other prewar intelligence reports put forward by the Bush administration as justification for war. The Knight Ridder newspapers were a notable exception due to the investigative work carried out by their reporters Jonathan Landay and Warren Strobel. Not until late 2003 and early 2004, after the Iraq war was in full progress, did the press generally begin to challenge convincingly the questionable prewar intelligence paraded by the White House, particularly that from such Iraqi defectors as the notorious Ahmed Chalabi. Headlines blossomed then, such as the one in the *Washington Post*, "Iraq's Arsenal Was Only on Paper," or in the *Wall Street Journal*, "Pressure Rises for Probe of Pre-War Intelligence." The tubes story collapsed as research revealed that the aluminum tubes cited were not designed for use in the manufacture of nuclear weapons. Also discounted but belatedly were reports circulated by the White House holding that Saddam Hussein was closely allied with the Al-Qaeda terrorists.

There was valuable work done by national security reporters. Growingly distrustful of the Bush administration, having been misled, they began to examine government policies more closely. In 2004, Seymour Hersh of the *New Yorker* magazine revealed the harsh interrogations of Iraqi inmates by American soldiers at the Abu Ghraib prison, and an exposé by Dana Priest of the *Washington Post* uncovered the CIA's operation of an overseas network of prisons in which terrorist suspects were subjected to torture. James Risen and Eric Lichtblau of the *New York Times* revealed in 2005 that in the wake of the 9/11 terrorist attacks the National Security Agency had instituted without court warrant secret eavesdropping of domestic-to-international communications.

Reporters covering national security affairs were handicapped during the Bush administration by a blitz of subpoenas served by federal prosecutors who were investigating government leaks and also by the imposition of measures restricting Freedom of Information access to official records such as those at the presidential libraries. The Reporters Committee for the Freedom of the Press in a study conducted in 2007 found a fivefold increase since 2001 in subpoenas issued by prosecutors seeking the identity of confidential sources.

At a time of great need, press coverage of national security affairs began to shrink perceptibly, beginning in about 2002. Suffering from a precipitous decline in income resulting from the migration of advertising and consumers to the Internet, newspapers, television networks, and newsmagazines were compelled to cut newsroom budgets. The ax fell heavily on their Washington and foreign bureaus, many of which were cut back in size, consolidated with other news outlets, or eliminated entirely. Cutbacks of staff coverage accelerated with the onset of the economic recession of 2008–9. Newspapers, which provided the core of critical investigative and national security coverage, suffered severely. Only a few news organizations, notably the *New York Times,* the *Wall Street Journal,* the *Washington Post,* and the Associated Press, although also hard hit, managed to sustain to any substantial degree their Washington and foreign bureau operations. Rebuilding of the Washington and foreign staffs waited on economic recovery, which in turn related to how the media would adjust to the evolving digital world.

As late as the year 2009, newspapers had not yet found a means of earning income from presentation of their news coverage and advertising on the Web sufficient to compensate for the loss of advertising from their print editions. The *New York Times* was no exception, although its Web site in 2009 had 20 million unique users, as compared with about a million subscribers to print editions. Because of their economic straits and changes in consumer habits, all newspapers felt compelled to move from emphasis on print to diverse presentations on their Web sites of news content, such as blog commentaries. In 2009, there were two benchmark changes in American journalism—which in prior years I would have found it hard to contemplate—that reflected this intensifying trend. The hallowed American Society of Newspaper Editors, which I headed as president in 1992–93, changed its name to the American Society of News Editors, thus opening admission to editors who had forsaken print entirely for Web sites. The other event: the Pulitzer Prize Board, on which I served as administrator of the prizes from 1993 to 2002, opened up its fourteen news categories to entries made up entirely of online content.

Looking to the future, I believe that newspapers will adjust to their digital-era challenges if they retain the courage and quality of journalism that made such news organizations as the *New York Times,* the *Washington Post,* and the Associated Press worldwide the most respected and quoted of news outlets. These standards must be adhered to whether the industry continues to go digital with limited output of print editions or goes solely digital on the Web. The rising generations must be persuaded that the integrity and viability of their society, particularly as they relate to national security and safeguarding of constitutional democracy, require a "Fourth Estate," to borrow Thomas Carlyle's nineteenth-century writ, able to monitor and report with competence and independence on the performance of the Executive, Legislative, and Judicial branches of government. From the Harry Truman to the George W. Bush administrations, the record of flawed government handling of national security issues testifies to the absolute need for a press capable of fulfilling its "Fourth Estate" functions.

A NOTE ON CHINESE LANGUAGE ROMANIZATION

In the period covered in this memoir, roughly from the end of World War II to about 2005, three different systems of transcription of Chinese characters were used in published works and by foreigners residing in China. The oldest is Wade-Giles, developed in the mid-nineteenth century by a British scholar and a British diplomat, which was used in all books about China in English up until 1979 and which has been employed by the Republic of China for decades. The second is the Chinese Postal Map romanization system for place-names, which came into use in the late Qing dynasty (1644–1911) and was retained after the fall of the dynasty during the republican era on the mainland (1912–49). While based on Wade-Giles for postal purposes, it differs in a number of respects, including slightly different spellings that incorporate local Chinese dialects (e.g., Peking, Nanking) and also popular pre-existing European names for places in China (e.g., Canton). The third and current system used on mainland China since the Communist takeover in October 1949 is the Hanyu Pinyin system, which is the official romanization of the People's Republic of China and, since 1979, the most popular system employed in published works on China, including newspapers.

In this book, Wade-Giles and/or the Chinese Postal Map romanization systems are used for all references to Chinese terms and place-names prior to October 1949, while references after that date are, with a few exceptions, in Pinyin. Wade-Giles is also used throughout for all references to republican political and military leaders, while in the case of Communist officials (e.g., Mao Zedong) their names, for purposes of clarity, are rendered in Pinyin both before and after 1949. Below in their order of appearance in the text are major place-names and other Chinese terms in both their pre- and post-1949 rendering.

Pre-1949	Post-1949
Yenan	Yan'an
Nanking	Nanjing
Chungking	Chongqing

Pre-1949	Post-1949
Shensi	Shaanxi
Tat'ung	Datong
Shansi	Shanxi
Kalgan (derived from Mongolian)	Zhangjiakou
mou-t'ai	maotai
Shantung	Shandong
Kansu	Gansu
Ninghsia	Ningxia
Dairen	Dalian
Mukden (derived from Manchu)	Shenyang
Ch'angch'un	Changchun
Manchouli	Manzhouli
Liaotung	Liaodong
yang-ko	yangge
Chinchow	Jinzhou
Kiangsu	Jiangsu
Kuling	Guling
Hankow	Hankou
Hsuchow	Xuzhou
Hwaipei	Huaibei
Tsinan	Xinan
Anhwei	Anhui
Tientsin	Tianjin
Pukow	Pukou
Hopei	Hebei
Tsingtao	Qingdao
Chekiang	Zhejiang
Fukien	Fujian
Sinkiang	Xinjiang
Hangchow	Hangzhou
Kwangsi	Guangxi
Kwangtung	Guangdong
T'aiyuan	Taiyuan
Hupei	Hubei
Ch'angsha	Changsha
Ch'engtu	Chengdu
Szechwan	Sichuan
Hoihow	Haikou
Canton	Guangzhou

"Peking" is the name of China's capital according to the Chinese Postal Map romanization and is used throughout the text for both pre- and post-1949 periods, as are "Peking University" and "Tsinghua University," the official English renderings of these two institution names.

The Note on Chinese Language Romanization is used by courtesy of Professor Lawrence Sullivan, Adelphi University.

BIBLIOGRAPHY

This book is based on my personal experiences, research, lectures, and my news dispatches, magazine articles, and relevant correspondence from the years 1946 to 2009. This includes reporting from 1946 to 1947 for the International News Service from China and Japan; the years 1947 to 1959 for the Associated Press from China, Indochina, London, Geneva, and Berlin; and the years 1960 to 1985 for the *New York Times* from the Soviet Union, Geneva, Hong Kong, Indochina, Indonesia, China, and Mongolia. I am indebted in particular to the AP and the *Times* for providing me with clipping and carbon files as well as correspondence to supplement my own extensive notes and records, which date back to 1946. In my archival research at the AP, the staff of President Thomas Curley, notably Richard Pyle, Valerie Komor, Charles Zoeller, Susan James, and Sam Markham, provided invaluable guidance. In the *Times* archives, my valued guides were Frederick Brunello, corporate records manager, and Alan Siegal, an assistant managing editor in the News Department. I am also indebted to William Stingone, curator of manuscripts at the New York Public Library, who made available its collection of *Times* documents. My appreciation also extends to my daughter Lesley Topping, who assisted me in the research. I have drawn reminiscences, notably on China, Indochina, and the Geneva Conferences, from my historical memoir, *Journey between Two Chinas* (Harper & Row, 1972). In his recent *Memoirs,* Huang Hua, the former foreign minister of the People's Republic of China, described *Journey* as "among the 25 books which anyone studying the China question in Western countries must read." *Journey between Two Chinas* also includes my experiences in reporting the French Indochina War. I have also made use of impressions and interviews obtained during numerous visits to East Asia over the past thirty years extending to 2008, usually in connection with university lecture tours, most frequently at Tsinghua University in Peking, and research for this book.

The books listed in this bibliography include those cited in my text, others which I have consulted, and a number that I offer simply as useful references for the reader. I have also listed source articles and other materials which I deem of special interest.

PROLOGUE

"Leyte: The Return to the Philippines." In *U.S. Army in World War II,* HyperWar Foundation, 1980, www.ibiblio.org/hyperwar/index.html.

CHINA

Barnett, A. Doak. *Communist China: The Early Years, 1949–55.* New York: F. A. Praeger, 1966.

Barrett, General David D. *Dixie Mission: The United States Army Observer Group in Yenan, 1944.* Berkeley: University of California Press, 1970.

Birns, Jack. *Assignment Shanghai: Photographs on the Eve of Revolution.* Photographs by Jack Birns. Edited by Carolyn Wakeman and Ken Light. Berkeley: University of California Press, 2003.

Chang, Iris. *The Rape of Nanking: The Forgotten Holocaust of World War II.* New York: Basic Books, 1997.

Chassin, Lionel Max. *The Conquest of China: A History of the Civil War, 1945–1949.* Cambridge, MA: Harvard University Press, 1965.

Clubb, O. Edmund. *Twentieth Century China.* New York: Columbia University Press, 1972.

———. Oral History Interview, Truman Library, June 16, 1974.

Davies, John Paton, Jr. *Dragon by the Tail: American, British, Japanese, and Russian Encounters with China and One Another.* New York: W. W. Norton & Co., 1972.

Donovan, Robert J. *Tumultuous Years: The Presidency of Harry S. Truman, 1949–1953.* New York: W. W. Norton & Co., 1984.

———. *Conflict and Crisis: The Presidency of Harry S. Truman, 1945–1948.* Columbia: University of Missouri Press, 1996.

Durdin, Tillman, James Reston, and Seymour Topping. *Report from Red China.* With photographs and additional articles by Audrey Ronning Topping. Chicago: Quadrangle Books, 1971.

Fairbank, John King. *The United States and China.* Cambridge, MA: Harvard University Press, 1971.

———. *Chinabound: A Fifty Year Memoir.* New York: HarperCollins, 1982.

Gao Wenqian. *Zhou Enlai: The Last Perfect Revolutionary.* Translated by Peter Rand and Lawrence Sullivan. New York: Public Affairs, 2007.

Griffith, Samuel B., II. *The Chinese People's Liberation Army.* London: Weidenfeld & Nicolson, 1968.

Guillermaz, Jacques. *A History of the Chinese Communist Party.* New York: Random House, 1968.

Hamilton, John Maxwell. *Edgar Snow: A Biography.* Bloomington: Indiana University Press, 1988.

Hooton, E. R. *The Greatest Tumult: The Chinese Civil War, 1936–49.* London: Brassey's, 1991.

Huang Hua. *The Album.* Hong Kong: Commercial Press, 2003.

———. *Memoirs.* Beijing: China Language Press, 2008.

Kahn, E. J. *The China Hands: American Foreign Service Officers and What Befell Them.* New York: Viking Books, 1975.

Kissinger, Henry A. *Years of Upheaval.* Boston: Little Brown & Co., 1982.

Ledovsky, Andrei. "Marshall's Mission in the Context of U.S.S.R.-China Relations." George C. Marshall Foundation, 1998, www.marshallfoundation.org.

Liu, F. F. *Military History of Modern China, 1924–1949.* Princeton, NJ: Princeton University Press, 1956.

Liu, Peter. *Mirror: A Loss of Innocence in Mao's China.* Xlibris.com, 2001.

MacFarquhar, Roderick, and Michael Schoenhals. *Mao's Last Revolution.* Cambridge, MA: Harvard University Press, 2006.

Mao Zedong. "On Protracted War." May 1938. In *Selected Works of Mao Tse-tung* [*Zedong*], 2:113–94. Beijing: Foreign Language Press, 1963.

———. "Talk with the American Correspondent Anna Louise Strong." August 1946. In *Selected Works of Mao Tse-tung* [*Zedong*], 4:97–102. Beijing: Foreign Language Press, 1963.

———. "The Concept of Operations for the Huai-Hai Campaign." October 11, 1948. In *Selected Works of Mao Tse-tung* [*Zedong*], 4:279–282. Beijing: Foreign Language Press, 1963.

Marks, Col. Donald M. "The Ussuri River Incident as a Factor in Chinese Foreign Policy." *Air University Review* 22, no. 5 (July–August 1971): 53–63.

Medvedev, Roy. *Khrushchev.* Garden City, NY: Anchor Press, 1983.

Melby, John F. *The Mandate of Heaven.* Toronto: University of Toronto Press, 1968.

O'Donovan, Patrick. *For Fear of Weeping.* London: MacGibbon & Kee, 1950.

Pan, Philip. *Out of Mao's Shadow.* New York: Simon & Schuster, 2008.

Pickler, Lt. Col. Gordon K. "The USAAF in China, 1946–47." *Air University Review* 24, no. 1 (May–June 1973): 69–74.

Powers, Thomas. *The Man Who Kept the Secrets: Richard Helms and the CIA.* New York: Knopf, 1979.

Rittenberg, Sidney, and Amanda Bennett. *The Man Who Stayed Behind.* New York: Simon & Schuster, 1993.

Roderick, John. *Covering China: The Story of an American Reporter from Revolutionary Days to the Deng Era.* Chicago: Imprint Publications, 1983.

Ronning, Chester. *A Memoir of China in Revolution.* New York: Pantheon, 1974.

Selden, Mark. *The Yenan Way in Revolutionary China.* Cambridge, MA: Harvard University Press, 1971.

Snow, Lois Wheeler. *Edgar Snow's China*. New York: Random House, 1981.

Solomon, Richard H. *Mao's Revolution and the Chinese Political Culture*. Berkeley: University of California Press, 1971.

Strong, Anna Louise. *The Chinese Conquer China*. Garden City, NY: Doubleday, 1949.

Tai Sung An. *The Lin Piao [Biao] Affair*. Lexington, MA: Lexington Books, 1974.

Terrill, Ross. *Madame Mao: The White Boned Demon*. Stanford, CA: Stanford University Press, 1999.

Topping, Audrey. *Dawn Wakes in the East*. New York: Harper & Row, 1973.

———. *The Splendors of Tibet*. New York: Sino Publishing, 1980.

Truman, Harry S. *Memoirs by Harry S. Truman: 1945, Year of Decisions*. Saybrook, CT: Konecky & Konecky, 1955.

Tuchman, Barbara. *Stillwell and the American Experience in China, 1911–45*. New York: Macmillan, 1970.

———. "If Mao Had Come to Washington: An Essay in Alternatives." *Foreign Affairs*, October 1972.

U.S. Department of State. *United States Relations with China, with Special Reference to the Period 1944–1949* (aka White Paper on China). Washington, DC: Department of State, 1949.

———. *Foreign Relations of the United States*. Vols. 1946–49, "The Far East: China." Washington, DC: Department of State, 1974.

White, Theodore H. *In Search of History*. New York: Harper & Row, 1978.

Zi Zhongyun. *No Exit: The Origin and Evolution of U.S. Policy toward China, 1945–1950*. Norwalk, CT: EastBridge Books, 2003.

KOREAN WAR

Brown, Brig. Gen. John S., ed. "The Korean War, The Chinese Intervention." Brochure. Washington, DC: U.S. Army Center of Military History, n.d.

Chen Jian. *China's Road to the Korean War*. New York: Columbia University Press, 1994.

"The Chinese Offensive, 25 November 1950–25 January 1951." Washington, DC: U.S. Naval Historical Center, August 10, 2000.

DiNicolo, Gina, U.S. Marine Corps (Ret.). "The Chosin Reservoir." In *The Korean War*, vol. 56, no. 11. Fifth Anniversary of the Korean War Commemoration Committee, 2000.

Goncharov, Sergei N., John W. Lewis, and Xue Litai. *Uncertain Partners: Stalin, Mao, and the Korean War*. Stanford, CA: Stanford University Press, 1993.

Manchester, William. *American Caesar: Douglas MacArthur, 1880–1964*. New York: Random House, 1978.

Roe, Maj. Patrick C., U.S. Marine Corps (Ret.). "Destruction of the 31st Infantry: A Tragedy of the Chosin Campaign." At patroe@rockisland.com, n.d.

"Statement of Policy by the National Security Council on United States Objectives and Courses of Action with Respect to Southeast Asia." June 25 1952. In *The Pentagon Papers: The Defense Department History of the United States Decision-making on Vietnam,* Senator Gravel ed., 1:385–90. Boston: Beacon Press, 1971.

Stueck, William. *Rethinking the Korean War.* Princeton, NJ: Princeton University Press, 2002.

Talbot, Strobe, and Edward Crankshaw. *Khrushchev Remembers.* Boston: Little, Brown & Co., 1970.

Thornton, Richard C. *Odd Man Out: Truman, Stalin, Mao, and the Origins of the Korean War.* Washington, DC: Brassey's, 2000.

Whiting, Allen S. *China Crosses the Yalu.* Stanford, CA: Stanford University Press, 1960.

INDOCHINA

Arnett, Peter. *Live from the Battlefield.* New York: Simon & Schuster, 1994.

Bird, Kai. *The Color of Truth: McGeorge Bundy and William Bundy: Brothers in Arms.* New York: Simon & Schuster, 1998.

Birns, Jack. *Assignment: Shanghai: Photographs on the Eve of Revolution.* Berkeley: University of California Press, 2003.

Bodard, Lucien. *The Quicksand War: Prelude to Vietnam.* Boston: Little, Brown & Co., 1967.

Browne, Malcolm. *Muddy Boots and Red Socks: A Reporter's Life.* New York: Random House, 1993.

Burchett, Wilfred G. *Vietnam North: A First-Hand Report.* New York: International Publishers, 1966.

———. *My War with the CIA: The Memoirs of Prince Norodom Sihanouk.* New York: Pantheon, 1972.

Duiker, William J. *Ho Chi Minh: A Life.* New York: Hyperion, 2000.

Emerson, Gloria. *Winners and Losers.* New York: Random House, 1977.

Fall, Barnard B. *The Two Viet-Nams: A Political and Military Analysis.* New York: Praeger, 1963.

Halberstam, David. *The Best and the Brightest.* New York: Random House, 1969.

Kiernan, Ben. *The Pol Pot Regime.* New Haven, CT: Yale University Press, 2002.

Kraslow, David, and Stuart H. Loory. *The Secret Search for Peace in Vietnam.* New York: Random House, 1968.

Lamb, David. *Vietnam Now.* New York: Public Affairs, 2002.

Langguth, A. J. *Our Vietnam: The War, 1954–1975.* New York: Simon & Schuster, 2000.

Levant, Victor. *Quiet Complicity: Canadian Involvement in the Vietnam War.* Toronto: Between The Lines, 1986.

Marr, David G. *Vietnam 1945: The Quest for Power.* Berkeley: University of California Press, 1995.

McNamara, Robert S. *In Retrospect: The Tragedy and Lessons of Vietnam.* New York: Times Books, 1995.

McNamara, Robert S., et al. *Argument without End: In Search of Answers to the Vietnam Tragedy.* New York: Public Affairs, 1999.

Mydans, Carl. *More Than Meets the Eye.* New York: Harper & Brothers, 1959.

Owen, Taylor, and Ben Kiernan. "Bombs over Cambodia: New Light on U.S. Air War." *Third World Traveler,* May 12, 2007.

Patti, Archimedes L. A. *Why Viet Nam?* Berkeley: University of California Press, 1980.

Pyle, Richard, and Horst Faas. *Lost over Laos: A True Story of Tragedy, Mystery, and Friendship.* Boston: Da Capo Press, 2003.

Qiang Zhai. *China and the Vietnam Wars, 1950–1975.* Chapel Hill: University of North Carolina Press, 2000.

Schanberg, Sydney H. *The Death and Life of Dith Pran.* New York: Penguin, 1980.

Schulzinger, Robert D. *A Time for War: The United States and Vietnam, 1941–1975.* Oxford: Oxford University Press, 1997.

Shaplen, Robert. *The Lost Revolution.* New York: Harper & Row, 1966.

Shawcross, William. *Sideshow: Kissinger, Nixon, and the Destruction of Cambodia.* New York: Cooper Square Press, 1979.

Sheehan, Neil. *A Bright Shining Lie: John Paul Vann and America in Vietnam.* New York: Random House, 1988.

Sherry, Norman. *The Life of Graham Greene.* Vol. 2, *1939–1955.* New York: Viking Books, 1995.

Smith, R. Harris. *OSS: The Secret History of America's First Central Intelligence Agency.* Berkeley: University of California Press, 1972.

Sucheng Chan. *Hmong Means Free.* Philadelphia: Temple University Press, 1994.

Taylor, Charles. *Snow Job: Canada, the United States, and Vietnam (1954 to 1973).* Toronto: Anansi, 1974.

Tonnesson, Stein. *The Vietnamese Revolution of 1945: Roosevelt, Ho Chi Minh and de Gaulle in a World at War.* Thousand Oaks, CA: Sage Publications, 1991.

Turner, Robert F. *Vietnamese Communism: Its Origins and Development.* Stanford, CA: Hoover Institution Publications, 1975.

INDONESIA

Brackman, Arnold C. *The Communist Collapse in Indonesia.* New York: W. W. Norton & Co., 1969.

Hughes, John. *Indonesian Upheaval.* New York: McKay, 1967.

THE PENTAGON PAPERS

Abrams, Floyd. *Speaking Freely: Trials of the First Amendment.* New York: Viking, 2005.

New York Times Staff. *The Pentagon Papers: The Secret History of the Vietnam War.* Chicago: Quadrangle Books, 1971).

The Pentagon Papers: The Defense Department History of the United States Decision-making on Vietnam. Vols. 1–4. Senator Gravel ed. Boston: Beacon Press, 1971.

Prados, John, and Margaret Pratt Porter, eds. *Inside the Pentagon Papers.* Lawrence: University Press of Kansas, 2004.

FOREIGN EDITOR

Bassow, Whitman. *The Moscow Correspondents: Reporting on Russia from the Revolution to Glasnost.* New York: Paragon House,1989.

Catledge, Turner. *My Life and The Times.* New York: Harper & Row, 1971.

Frankel, Max. *High Noon in the Cold War: Kennedy, Khrushchev and the Cuban Missile Crisis.* New York: Ballantine Books, 2004.

Gelb, Arthur. *City Room.* New York: G. B. Putnam, 2003.

Reston, James. *Deadline: A Memoir.* New York: Random House, 1991.

Risen, James. *State of War: The Secret History of the C.I.A. and the Bush Administration.* New York: Free Press, 2006.

Salisbury, Harrison E. *Behind the Lines—Hanoi.* New York: Harper & Row, 1967.

———. *Without Fear or Favor: An Uncompromising Look at The New York Times.* New York: Times Books, 1980.

Sanger, David E. *The Inheritance: The World Obama Confronts and the Challenges to American Power.* New York, Crown, 2009.

Shepard, Richard. *The Paper's Papers: A Reporter's Journeys through the Archives of The New York Times.* New York: Times Books, 1996.

Stacks, John F. *Scotty, James B. Reston and the Rise and the Fall of American Journalism.* Boston: Little, Brown & Co., 2002.

Talese, Gay. *The Kingdom and the Power.* New York: World Publishing Co., 1966.

Trift, Susan, and Alex Jones. *The Trust: The Private and Powerful Family behind The New York Times.* Boston: Little, Brown & Co., 1999.

Tuchman, Barbara. *The March of Folly: From Troy to Vietnam.* New York: Knopf, 1984.

INDEX

Page numbers in italics refer to photographs. "ST" refers to Seymour Topping.

371; and Sihanouk, 268; and Sino-Soviet split, 201, 203; Snow's interviews with, 325–26, 346; and social events in Great Hall of the People, 269, 301, 326, 333, 338, 341, 349, 351–55; ST's interview with, 311, 332–34, 347–48, 351–54; ST's view of, 371; and Stuart, 97–99; on Taiwan, 352–55; and U.S. Army Observer Group, 23; and U.S.

recognition of Communist China, 96; and Vietnam War, 189, 232, 268
Zhou Sufei, 16
Zhu De, 15–17, 44, 66, 83, *following p. 110*, 179, 340
Zhu Qiusheng, 369–70
Ziegler, Ron, 363
Zorthian, Barry, 227–28